Resilience in Education

Marold Wosnitza • Francisco Peixoto
Susan Beltman • Caroline F. Mansfield
Editors

Resilience in Education

Concepts, Contexts and Connections

Springer

Editors
Marold Wosnitza
Institute of Education
RWTH Aachen University
Aachen, Germany

School of Education
Murdoch University
Perth, WA, Australia

Susan Beltman
School of Education
Curtin University
Perth, WA, Australia

Francisco Peixoto
ISPA-Instituto Universitário/CIE – ISPA
Lisbon, Portugal

Caroline F. Mansfield
School of Education
Murdoch University
Perth, WA, Australia

ISBN 978-3-319-76689-8 ISBN 978-3-319-76690-4 (eBook)
https://doi.org/10.1007/978-3-319-76690-4

Library of Congress Control Number: 2018939552

Printed on acid-free paper

This Springer imprint is published by the registered company Springer International Publishing AG part of Springer Nature.
The registered company address is: Gewerbestrasse 11, 6330 Cham, Switzerland

Contents

About the Authors

Giusy Beddia (University of Pavia, Italy)
Giusy Beddia is a licensed psychologist and ABA (applied behavioural analysis) therapist. She is an expert in learning disabilities. She has been involved in a number of educational projects related to resilience and school readiness at national and international level working with the Department of Brain and Behavioural Science at the University of Pavia (Italy). Presently, she is working in a private health care center that provides psychological treatments for children and young adults with autism.

Susan Beltman (Curtin University, Australia)
Susan Beltman is an Associate Professor in the School of Education at Curtin University in Western Australia. Her current research interests involve using qualitative methods (including drawings) to examine mentoring, as well as teacher resilience and identity. She was a team member for an ALTC-funded project Keeping Cool: Embedding Resiliency in the Initial Teacher Education Curriculum, and a project team member for two other resilience projects: a European Union Lifelong Learning Programme project called ENTREE (ENhancing Teacher REsilience in Europe), and an OLT project BRiTE (Building Resilience in Teacher Education). Susan is President of WAIER (Western Australian Institute for Educational Research).

Cynthia Renner (Breuer) (RWTH Aachen University, Germany)
After having studied in the teacher training programme at RWTH Aachen University, Cynthia Renner now is a teacher trainee for English Biology and bilingual education. She has written her Diploma thesis on the topic of teacher resilience and was developing materials for the European Union Lifelong Learning Programme project called ENTREE (ENhancing Teacher REsilience in Europe). During her studies, she has specialised herself on promoting orality of students during foreign language courses taking part in the Speak Up! project (a cooperation between RWTH Aachen University and local schools).

Tania Broadley (Queensland University of Technology, Australia)
Tania Broadley is an Assistant Dean (Teaching and Learning) and a Professor in the Faculty of Education at Queensland University of Technology. She is Adjunct Associate Professor at Curtin University. Tania provides strategic leadership and is responsible for the quality of design and implementation of initial teacher education, undergraduate and postgraduate courses. Tania previously worked for the Deputy Vice Chancellor (Academic) at Curtin to establish an Institute of academic development and enhance student learning through innovative teaching and technology. Tania continues to conduct research into Teacher Education, which follows on from her background as Lecturer in Educational Technology. Tania is project team member on the Office for Learning and Teaching project BRITE (Building Resilience in Teacher Education).

Vanessa Camilleri (University of Malta, Malta)
Dr Vanessa Camilleri is an academic at the Department of Artificial Intelligence, Faculty of ICT, University of Malta. Her expertise is in the area of Human Computer Interactions, with a specialisation in Virtual Worlds and Serious Games. Her areas of interest include Virtual Reality applications for developing emotional intelligence values. Her previous experience in the area of education and pedagogy, as well as educational technologies and use of games for learning, has contributed to her overall academic profile. Her main publications are in the areas of online learning and the use of innovative and emerging technologies for learning. More recently, she has started working on developing virtual reality experiences for teaching and learning purposes related to various aspects of emotional intelligence. Vanessa was team member in the European Union Lifelong Learning Programme project called ENTREE (ENhancing Teacher REsilience in Europe).

José Castro Silva (ISPA-Instituto Universitário/CIE – ISPA, Portugal)
José Castro Silva, PhD in Educational Sciences, specialisation in Organisational Leadership is an Assistant Professor at ISPA-Instituto Universitário. He lectures in Educational Psychology, Educational Sciences, and Learning and Motivation, and also has experience with teacher training programmes focused on special education needs and teacher professional development. His current research interests include teacher professional development and well-being, school organisational climate, culture, and health, and information and communication technology in education. He is a team member of the Centre for Educational Research – CIE-ISPA, and project team member of European-funded projects – ENTREE (ENhancing Teacher REsilience in Europe), ERAMUS+ HOPE's (Happiness, Optimism, and Ethos in Schools), and ERAMUS+ SUnStAR (Supporting UNiversity STudents At Risk of dropping out).

Valeria Cavioni (University of Milano-Bicocca, Milan, Italy)
Valeria Cavioni (PhD) is a licensed psychologist, psychotherapist, and postdoctoral researcher at the Department of Human Sciences for Education at the University of Milano-Bicocca, Milan, Italy. Her main areas of research include the implementation and assessment of school-based mental health and school readiness

programmes. She has been involved in various national and international projects at the University of Pavia, the National Institute for the Educational Evaluation of Instruction and Training (INVALSI), the Institute for Research and Innovation for the Italian Schools (INDIRE), the Centre for Resilience and Socio-Emotional Health (University of Malta), and local Mental Health Services. She has published numerous papers and books, including the co-author of *Social and Emotional Education in Primary School: Integrating Theory and Research into Practice*.

Carmel Cefai (University of Malta, Malta)
Professor Carmel Cefai, Phd (Lond), FBPS, is the Director of the Centre for Resilience and Socio-Emotional Health at the University of Malta. He is Joint Honourary Chair of the European Network for Social and Emotional Competence and joint founding editor of the *International Journal of Emotional Education*. His research interests are focused on how to create healthy spaces which promote the resilience, well-being, and psychological well-being of children and young people, particularly those at risk. He has led various research projects in mental health in schools, risk and resilience in children and young people, children's well-being, and the development of a resilience curriculum for early years and primary schools in Europe (*RESCUR Surfing the Waves: A Resilience Curriculum for Early Years and Primary Schools* published in 7 languages).

Leanne Crosswell (Queensland University of Technology, Australia)
Leanne Crosswell (Dr) is a Senior Lecturer in Education at QUT. Her research interests span early career teachers (with a focus on transition to teaching, resilience, and well-being), career change teachers, and mentoring as a dialogic practice. She particularly enjoys working with school communities to develop mentoring programmes, practices, and tools for feedback and evaluation.

Ralph Delzepich (RWTH Aachen University, Germany)
Ralph Delzepich is a Research Associate at the Institute for Education at RWTH Aachen University, Germany. His current research interests include online (self) assessment, online learning, and resilience. Ralph worked on several European Union projects in these areas, including the Lifelong Learning Programme project called ENTREE (ENhancing Teacher REsilience in Europe) and the Erasmus+ project PrevDrop (Detecting and Preventing Drop out from Higher Education or Supporting Students to Switch successfully to VET) and currently working on the development of self-reflection and learning tools for students in national and international contexts.

Liesel Ebersöhn (University of Pretoria, South Africa)
Liesel Ebersöhn is Director of the Centre for the Study of Resilience and Full Professor in the Department of Educational Psychology, Faculty of Education, University of Pretoria. Liesel is known for educational psychology studies on resilience in schools in challenged settings – specifically for an indigenous psychology theory, relationship-resourced resilience, that describes flocking as a collectivist pathway to counter chronic risk. She is Secretary General of the World Education Research Association, is invited often to read keynote papers (i.e., Plenary at the

2016 Global Development Network Conference, Lima, Peru), has been visiting professor (Yale University, Edith Cowan University), and has received research awards (including the Women in Science Awardee, 2012, Department of Science and Technology).

Vera Faust (RWTH Aachen University, Germany)
Vera Faust currently is a Research Fellow at the Center for Teacher Education at RWTH Aachen University, Germany, after having worked at the RWTH Institute for Education. Her research interests include social movements, resilience, and gender. Vera was on the coordination team for the European Union Lifelong Learning Programme project ENTREE (ENhancing Teacher REsilience in Europe). She is also editorial staff of the socioscientific journal *Forschungsjournal Soziale Bewegungen* on participation, protest, and democracy.

Maria Assunção Flores (University of Minho, Portugal)
Maria Assunção Flores is an Associate Professor with qualification at the University of Minho, Portugal. She received her PhD at the University of Nottingham, UK. She was visiting scholar at the University of Cambridge, UK, in 2008/2009 and at the University of Glasgow in 2016/2017. Her research interests include teacher professionalism and identity, teacher education and professional development, teacher appraisal, and higher education. She has published extensively on these topics both nationally and internationally. She was the Chair of the Board of Directors of the International Council on Education for Teaching (ICET) between 2011 and 2015, and she is currently the Chair of the International Study Association on Teachers and Teaching (ISATT). She is also executive director of the journal *Teachers and Teaching: Theory and Practice* and co-editor of the *European Journal of Teacher Education*.

Katya Galea (University of Malta, Malta)
Katya Galea is a registered Educational Psychologist with a Master's degree in Educational Psychology obtained in 2014 from the University of Malta. She currently works as a practitioner within the Secretariat for Catholic Education carrying out psycho-educational assessments, interventions, and consultations. She also runs her own private practice in Malta. Ms Galea collaborated with the Centre for Resilience and Socio-Emotional Health at the University of Malta on the Lifelong Learning Programme Comenius Project RESCUR- Developing a Resilience Curriculum for Primary Schools in Europe. Through the project, she was a team member in training schools to deliver the RESCUR Surfing the Waves Curriculum. Ms Galea has experience in assisting schools who need support with developing their resilience as a school community and has given training and continuous professional development sessions to school staff on school and teacher resilience, particularly in relation to challenging behaviour.

Andrew Gibson (Sydney University of Technology, Australia)
Andrew Gibson (Dr) is a Research Fellow in Writing Analytics at the Connected Intelligence Centre, University of Technology Sydney (UTS). His primary research focus is on Reflective Writing Analytics (RWA) for psychosocial meaning.

Originally a secondary school music teacher, he now works across both educational and computational domains, combining an understanding of pedagogy with software development experience to design and develop software that supports teaching and learning with text.

Qing Gu (University of Nottingham, United Kingdom)
Qing Gu (Dr) is a Professor of Education in the School of Education of the University of Nottingham. She is Chair of the British Association for International and Comparative Education. Her research interests include teacher development, school leadership, and school improvement. She has led a range of international and national government and research council funded projects. She is currently leading three UK Education Endowment Foundation funded projects on promoting and embedding evidence-based practices in schools in England. She has published internationally and nationally. Some of these books have been translated in Chinese, Japanese, and Spanish. She is editor of *The Work and Lives of Teachers in China* (Routledge, 2014), and co-editor of *The Routledge International Handbook of Education and Development* (2015) and *Handbook of Education in China* (Edward Elgar Books, 2017).

Gavin Hazel (Everymind and University of Newcastle, Australia)
Gavin Hazel's work focuses on the development, implementation, and evaluation of evidence-informed resources, practices, and professional education. Gavin is an experienced education and capability development professional, specialising in the area of child and youth mental health, well-being, and resilience. Gavin has worked as a lecturer in teacher education, a research academic, a senior research scientist, and a mental health projects manager. He holds a conjoint appointment with the School of Medicine and Public Health at the University of Newcastle. Gavin leads a multidisciplinary team who work on building the capacity of professionals through practical programmes, resources, and polices to support children and families.

Kerstin Helker (RWTH Aachen University, Germany)
Kerstin Helker (Dr) currently is a Postdoctoral Research Fellow and Lecturer at the Institute of Education at RWTH Aachen University, Germany. After completing her dissertation on the interplay of students', parents', and teachers' judgments of responsibility in the school context and how these are related to student motivation and school outcomes, Kerstin worked as interim professor for didactics and school theory at the University of Bonn, Germany. Her research interests lie in the field of motivation and emotion, focusing on university teachers and peer mentors as well as schools. One project across different German universities and schools focuses on how deschooling programmes affect students' motivation, responsibility, and resilience.

Mylène Leroux (Université du Québec en Outaouais, Canada)
Mylène Leroux is a Professor in the Département des sciences de l'éducation at Université du Québec en Outaouais in Canada. She is also an Associate Researcher at the Centre de recherche interuniversitaire sur la formation et la profession enseignante (CRIFPE). Her current research interests include teacher resilience,

well-being and reflection, teacher induction, professional development, practical training, as well as differentiated instruction and classroom observation.

Lucas Lohbeck (RWTH Aachen University, Germany)
Lucas Lohbeck (Dr) is a Senior Lecturer and Researcher at the Institute of Education at RWTH Aachen University, Germany. Furthermore, he works as a teacher at a vocational school where he is responsible for organising the practical training of the trainee teachers. His current research interest includes the development of the teacher education system as well as stress and strain of teachers and teacher resilience.

Tilda Loots (University of Pretoria, South Africa)
Tilda Loots is a part-time lecturer in the Department of Educational Psychology, University of Pretoria, and recently completed her postdoctoral research fellowship. Her current research focuses on asset-based psychosocial support, school-community partnerships, and resilience in dealing with stressors. Tilda is also a registered educational psychologist in private practice, utilising an eclectic approach to therapeutic intervention.

Caroline F. Mansfield (Murdoch University, Australia)
Dr Caroline Mansfield is an Associate Professor in Education and Associate Dean of Research in the School of Education, Murdoch University, Western Australia. Her research focuses on teachers and students, with an emphasis on motivation, well-being, and resilience. Caroline has led two large projects about teacher resilience – Keeping Cool: Embedding resilience in initial teacher education curriculum, and BRiTE: Building Resilience in Teacher Education. In 2016, she was awarded a National Teaching Fellowship (Staying BRiTE: Promoting resilience in higher education) to lead a team of colleagues across Australia to embed resilience in teacher education programmes and build a national and international network of interested researchers and practitioners.

Helen McGrath (RMIT University & Deakin University, Australia)
Helen McGrath, PhD, is a leading psychologist and university educator with expertise in mental health, social skills, relationships, student resilience, positive psychology/education, and effective teaching and learning. She is an Adjunct Professor in both the School of Education at RMIT University and the School of Education at Deakin University. She has been a Psychologist in part-time private practice for many years. She has received the Vice Chancellor's Award for Excellence in Community Service for her contributions to Deakin's partnership with governments, the media, the teaching profession, and the wider community. She has been a member of the National Centre Against Bullying (NCAB) since its inception.

Mark Morgan (Dublin City University, Ireland)
Mark Morgan has just finished a three-year term as co-director of Growing up in Ireland (the National Longitudinal Study of Children) at the Children's Research Centre, Trinity College. Previously he was Cregan Professor of Education and Psychology at St. Patrick's College and Head of the Education Department. Having

qualified as a teacher in St. Patrick's college, he was a teaching Principal following which he was a lecturer in the college. He is the author of over 80 scholarly publications amongst which are a number that focus on teachers' motivation, stress, and resilience. In 2010, he was awarded the President's Prize for research by Dublin City University.

Chad Morrison (Tabor University, Australia)
Chad Morrison (Dr) is the Academic Director of Professional Experience in the Faculty of Education. His research interests include the preparation of pre-service teachers (with a specific interest in Professional Experience programmes) and early career teachers and teaching. These research fields incorporate a range of interrelated topics including the development, well-being, and identity work of teachers; their teaching contexts; and the structural, cultural, and political factors that shape this work and the outcomes associated with it.

Toni Noble PhD (Australian Catholic University, Australia)
Toni Noble is an Adjunct Professor in the Institute for Positive Psychology at Australian Catholic University. Her areas of expertise and research include student resilience and well-being, social and emotional learning, student engagement in learning, positive school communities, and positive psychology/education. She has been awarded an Australian Government (Carrick) citation for her outstanding contributions to university teaching in education and psychology. She is co-author (with Helen McGrath) of the award-winning Bounce Back Wellbeing and Resilience programme as well as many other teacher resource books plus numerous chapters and journal articles on student well-being and resilience.

Margaret O'Donnell (Dublin City University, Ireland)
Dr Margaret O'Donnell is a Lecturer in the Institute of Education, Dublin City University. She has wide experience in the field of special education, teacher education, curriculum studies, assessment, and educational policy and practice. The area of teacher education has long been a topic of interest and study. Her doctorate studies examined teacher efficacy – the extent to which teachers believe they were adequately prepared with the knowledge, skills, and competencies to work in inclusive classroom in mainstream schools. In addition, she has wide research experience, both at a personal and national level, gleaned through her own studies and through her involvement in major national commissioned research projects. She was a leading researcher who contributed to the ENTREE research project, which examined teacher resilience across five European jurisdictions.

Francisco Peixoto (ISPA-Instituto Universitário/CIE – ISPA, Portugal)
Francisco Peixoto is Vice-Rector and Professor at ISPA – Instituto Universitário, the oldest Psychology school in Portugal. His current research interests include identity construction in general, and particularly in teachers, as well as teachers' resilience. He was member and leader of project teams funded by the Portuguese National Science and Technology Foundation and is a project team member of the funded project by the European Union Lifelong Learning Programme project called ENTREE (ENhancing Teacher REsilience in Europe). He published several papers

in national and international journals, authored book chapters, and presented his research at national and international conferences.

Joana Pipa (ISPA-Instituto Universitário/CIE – ISPA, Portugal)
Joana Pipa holds a Master Degree in Educational Psychology from ISPA – Instituto Universitário. Her current research interests include the affective components in teaching and learning, namely: self-concept, self-esteem, motivation, emotions in education, school engagement, and peer relationships. She worked as a research assistant in the funded project by the European Commission's Lifelong Learning Programme "ENTREE – Enhancing Teacher Resilience in Europe." Currently, she is a PhD candidate at CIE – ISPA, ISPA – Instituto Universitário, Lisbon. Her project relates to the effects of grade retention on the affective components in learning.

Mary Ryan (Macquarie University, Australia)
Mary Ryan (Dr) is a Professor and Head, Department of Educational Studies at Macquarie University in Sydney. Prior to this position, she was the Assistant Dean (Research) in the Faculty of Education at Queensland University of Technology, Brisbane. Her research is interested in discourses of literacy, learning, youth culture, and teachers' work. She applies theories of reflexivity, socio-spatiality, and criticality to the "texts" produced in classrooms, schools, higher education institutions, and social media.

Jennifer Schwarze (RWTH Aachen University, Germany)
Jennifer Schwarze is a Research Fellow and Lecturer at the Institute of Educational Science at RWTH Aachen University. Her current research interests include resilience, especially apprentice and teacher resilience, and teacher motivation. She has been a member of the coordinating team of the Lifelong Learning Programme project ENTREE – ENhancing Teacher REsilience in Europe.

Mara Lupicia Spagnolo (University of Pavia, Italy)
Mara Lupica Spagnolo is a licensed psychologist and psychotherapist. She collaborated with the Department of Brain and Behavioural Science at the University of Pavia (Italy) working in the fields of educational and clinical psychology in national and international projects. She is a licensed expert of learning disabilities and school difficulties. Her main areas of interest focus on the design and implementation of educational programmes to promote social and emotional skills, school readiness, and resilience. She also provides training courses for medical staff and teachers.

Hendrieke Stiller (RWTH Aachen University, Germany)
Hendrieke Stiller holds a master's degree in Linguistics and Communication Studies and in Education and Knowledge Management from the RWTH Aachen University, Germany. In her master's thesis, she focuses on the topic University Teachers' Resilience at German and Australian Universities. Since 2016, she has worked as an educator for blind and visually impaired adults at Berufsförderungswerk Düren (BFW). Additionally, she works as an honorary examiner for the Chamber of Industry and Commerce (IHK), Aachen.

Linda C. Theron (Universtiy of Pretoria, South Africa)
Linda Theron, D.Ed., is a full professor in the Department of Educational Psychology, Faculty of Education, University of Pretoria; an associate of the Centre for the Study of Resilience, University of Pretoria; and an extraordinary professor in Optentia Research Focus Area, North-West University, South Africa. Her research and publications focus on the resilience processes of South African young people challenged by chronic adversity and account for how sociocultural contexts shape resilience (see www.Lindatheron.org.). She is lead editor of *Youth Resilience and Culture: Complexities and Commonalities* (Springer, 2015). She is also an associate journal editor of *Child Abuse & Neglect* (Elsevier).

Noelene Weatherby-Fell (University of Wollongong, Australia)
Noelene Weatherby-Fell is a Senior Lecturer in Education at the University of Wollongong, NSW. As Head of Students (Education) and Faculty Director of Academic Programmes, Noelene provides leadership in supporting students in their academic progress and well-being, and in curriculum and pedagogy. Noelene is committed to preparing classroom and school-ready teachers, and her research interests include preservice teacher preparation, leadership and professional learning in schools, and pastoral care of students and teachers. Noelene has presented and written about her work nationally and internationally with the Response Ability Project (HIMH), is a project team member on the OLT project BRiTE (Building Resilience in Teacher Education), and continues to work with colleagues across the higher education sector with the Staying BRiTE Project.

Jill Willis (Queensland University of Technology, Australia)
Jill Willis (Dr) is a Senior Lecturer in Education at QUT. She has always been interested in the transformative power of learning, and how social collaboration and innovative structures can support learner agency. Her research interests include classroom assessment practices, digital feedback loops, learner agency, leadership of change, and collaborative qualitative research methodologies. She is currently investigating how changes to Queensland Senior Assessment and the Australian Curriculum can enhance student experiences of learning in schools.

Marold Wosnitza (RWTH Aachen University, Germany & Murdoch University, Australia)
Dr. Marold Wosnitza is a Professor of Education at RWTH Aachen University and Adjunct Professor at Murdoch University in Perth (Australia). His research interests include teacher motivation and emotions and resilience. He is head of several national and international research projects including a Lifelong Learning Programme funded project: ENTREE (Enhancing Teacher Resilience in Europe). Marold Wosnitza has published numerous journal articles, books, and book chapters and presented his research at national and international conferences. He is currently faculty dean research and is heading three different research groups.

Maria Assunta Zanetti (University of Pavia, Italy)
Maria Assunta Zanetti (PhD) is an Associate Professor at the Department of Brain and Behavioural Sciences at University of Pavia (Italy) and Director of the Italian

Laboratory of Research and Intervention for the Development of Talent, Potential and Giftedness. She teaches Psychology of Language Development and Educational Psychology and she collaborates with the Italian Ministry of Education (MIUR) and other local Institutions promoting mental health. She is currently leading several national and international projects to promote well-being in schools. Her main research interests include socio-emotional development, youth risk behaviours, language development, bullying and cyberbullying, vocational guidance, decision-making processes, and early achievement and gifted children development.

Part I
Introduction

Chapter 1
Resilience in Education: An Introduction

Susan Beltman and Caroline F. Mansfield

Abstract This volume has arisen from burgeoning international interest in the field of resilience in a variety of educational contexts. It gathers together current thinking, research and practice from international scholars. Over the past 10 years in particular, researchers have focused not only on resilience in significant adversity but also on how students and educators overcome everyday challenges to learn and thrive. The increasing interest in resilience in educational contexts has, in part, stemmed from an increased societal attention to issues of wellbeing and mental health and to broader concerns about issues such as teacher quality and retention in some countries. As a result, both individual researchers and research groups have emerged, making significant contributions to understanding resilience in educational contexts through theory development and empirical studies.

The catalyst for this volume was the European Union-funded project Enhancing Teacher Resilience in Europe (ENTREE) which responded to international concerns about teacher resilience and the 'need to safeguard and promote teachers' wellbeing' (http://entree-project.eu/en/). It aimed to support pre-service and practising teachers' capacity for resilience through the development of face-to-face training and online modules. Project members comprised researchers and practitioners from Germany, Ireland, Portugal, Malta and the Czech Republic, as well as third-country partners from Australia.

S. Beltman (✉)
School of Education, Curtin University, Perth, WA, Australia
e-mail: s.beltman@curtin.edu.au

C. F. Mansfield
School of Education, Murdoch University, Perth, WA, Australia
e-mail: caroline.mansfield@murdoch.edu.au

M. Wosnitza et al. (eds.), *Resilience in Education*,
https://doi.org/10.1007/978-3-319-76690-4_1

This volume showcases the international body of work related to the ENTREE project and, in addition, includes invited contributors from Europe, Australia, South Africa, Canada and the United Kingdom, thus providing a picture of resilience from around the globe. The authors share their conceptualisations of resilience, their empirical research and interventions developed to support resilience in a variety of educational settings. The volume has five parts: Part 1, 'Introduction'; Part 2, 'Conceptualising resilience'; Part 3, 'Researching resilience in educational contexts'; Part 4, 'Connecting to practice'; and Part 5, 'Conclusion'.

Conceptualising Resilience

The ENTREE project was guided by a comprehensive definition of resilience developed from research associated with previous Australian projects (e.g. Beltman et al. 2011; Mansfield et al. 2016a, b) and a comprehensive annotated bibliography on teacher resilience (https://www.brite.edu.au/annotated-bibliography-of-teacher-resilience). Although the ENTREE project was concerned specifically with resilience for pre-service and in-service teachers, the definition is applicable to other settings as it incorporates the complexity and dynamic nature of resilience:

> In the ENTREE project, teacher resilience refers to the process of, capacity for, or outcome of positive adaptation and ongoing professional commitment and growth in the face of challenging circumstances. Resilience is shaped by individual, situational and broader contextual characteristics that interrelate in dynamic ways to provide risk (challenging) or protective (supportive) factors. Individuals, drawing on personal, professional and social resources, not only "bounce back" but are able to thrive professionally and personally, experiencing job satisfaction, positive self-beliefs, personal wellbeing and an ongoing commitment to the profession. (Wosnitza et al. 2014, p. 2)

The construct of resilience has been explored in different disciplines over time with similarities emerging in the way it has been conceptualised (e.g. Gu and Day 2013). There is agreement that resilience is a 'complex, dynamic and multi-dimensional phenomenon' (Mansfield et al. 2012, p. 364) or a 'composite construct' (Gu and Li 2013, p. 292). Individuals, their contexts and the process whereby they overcome challenges over time are all part of the complexity. Different theoretical lenses provide a focus on different aspects of this complexity. Some approaches prioritise the role of the individual, and Pretsch et al. (2012), for example, write about a 'resilient personality' and 'resilience as a personal resource' (p. 323). Where the resilience process is the focus, the researcher 'centres not on key attributes of the teacher or resources in the environment, but on strategies teachers employ' (Castro et al. 2010, p. 623). A more ecological or contextual focus 'directs our attention away from the "here-and-now" specifics of individual teachers' lives and contextualises their experiences within broader social, cultural, and political arenas' (Johnson et al. 2014, p. 533). When viewed as a collective construct, resilience is seen as 'the culmination of collective and collaborative endeavours' (Gu and Li 2013, p. 300).

Other writers have emphasised resilience as an outcome, incorporating aspects such as commitment, enjoyment, enthusiasm and passion (Day and Gu 2014). In all the chapters in this volume, the authors present the conceptualisation of resilience or specific lens that has guided their work.

The chapters in Part 2 focus more specifically on the theoretical viewpoint adopted, arguing for a particular conceptualisation and presenting illustrative research findings. Gu (Chap. 2) argues that a social ecological perspective on teacher resilience is required to best understand the ‘contemporary landscape of teaching’ in which teachers both influence and are influenced by their professional worlds. Drawing on a range of international research, she concludes with four propositions ‘about teacher resilience and its implications for sustaining teacher quality in the complex and changing contexts in which teachers work and live’. Schwarze (Chap. 3) presents a comprehensive generic model of resilience that incorporates appraisal theory, internal and external resources, strategies and resilience outcomes. She then applies this model to apprentices in the German vocational education setting, presenting some illustrative data. In Chap. 4, Mansfield, Ebersöhn, Beltman and Loots adopt a systems approach to understand teacher resilience in South Africa and Australia. This cross-national study uses data from teachers in these countries to examine risks and resources for resilience at the personal level as well as the micro-, mesa-, exo- and macro-levels of context. In the final chapter of this section (Chap. 5), Peixoto, Wosnitza, Pipa, Morgan and Cefai also adopt a multilevel model of teacher resilience – the model guiding the ENTREE project. In this case, the model directed the collection of quantitative data from pre-service teachers across four countries: Germany, Malta, Ireland and Portugal.

Researching Resilience in Educational Contexts

Chapters in this volume illustrate the expansion of resilience research to a wider range of national contexts and specific educational settings. An earlier review (Beltman et al. 2011) reported that few studies on teacher resilience included pre-service teachers, and most studies were conducted in the USA. Part 3 of the volume illustrates how this scope has broadened and concentrates on studies of resilience in a range of educational settings in Germany, Canada, Australia, Malta, Portugal and South Africa. Whilst each context has its particular cultural, social and economic characteristics, there are some synergies in terms of the challenges educators experience and the ways in which they respond to challenges. With participants including practising teachers, pre-service teachers and university teachers, the chapters provide insights into the critical role that contexts play in supporting or challenging resilience for educators at various levels.

Research methodologies used to examine resilience have included quantitative, qualitative and mixed methods. Previous studies have included quantitative measures of factors such as emotion regulation and self-efficacy (Ee and Chang 2010), wellbeing and mindfulness (Jennings et al. 2011) and quality of working life (Leroux and Théorêt 2014). Qualitative data have been generated from open-ended survey comments (Mansfield et al. 2012) and from comprehensive longitudinal case studies comprising focus groups, interviews, observations and visual methods (Ebersöhn 2012). A common issue across methodologies is 'the conflation of resilient characteristics of teachers and the environmental supports' (Yonezawa et al. 2011, p. 915), making it difficult to take into account the many relevant variables. The group of chapters in this section includes cross-sectional and longitudinal studies using a range of methodologies. Surveys are used to gather data about participants' resilience, motivation, psychological health and work experience. Interviews are used to provide more nuanced understandings about the interplay between person and contexts over time, and a digital tool is used in an innovative approach to gathering data.

The following brief overviews of each chapter in Part 3 indicate the variety of contexts and methodologies. Lohbeck (Chap. 6) presents a questionnaire study of German pre-service teachers (293 at the beginning of their degree; 126 transitioning to practice) which focuses on the interplay of motivation to teach and resilience of pre-service teachers. This study highlights the relationship between intrinsic motivation and resilience. In Chap. 7, Leroux reports a longitudinal, mixed-method study of early career Canadian teachers' resilience. Risk and protective factors during the first 2 years of induction are explored, using a survey of teachers' work experience and psychological health to identify indicators of psychological distress or positive adaptation and using semi-structured interviews to provide more nuanced understandings of positive adaptation and the developmental process of resilience during early career years.

Crosswell, Willis, Morrison, Gibson and Ryan (Chap. 8) present a longitudinal qualitative study of three Australian early career teachers working in rural settings. Using an innovative digital tool as the main method of data collection, plotlines of resilience over time are described. Use of the digital tool provided the impetus for regular reflections, and the data generated show the fluctuations of resilience over time. Galea (Chap. 9) focuses on how secondary school teachers in Malta respond to challenging behaviour in a boys' school. Using 'narrative exploration of teacher stories through in-depth interviews', this chapter highlights the individual and contextual factors that have helped strengthen their resilience. In Chap. 10, Flores draws on a large-scale study from Portugal and explores sources of teacher motivation and resilience in challenging school contexts using surveys, focus groups and interviews. The importance of relationships is emphasised, particularly with regard to their role in supporting teachers.

Moving away from school teachers, Helker, Mansfield, Wosnitza and Stiller (Chap. 11) present a mixed-method study that investigates the resilience of university teachers in Australia and Germany. Survey and interview data show the range of challenges in university teaching including maintaining a productive balance between research and teaching responsibilities. Although some challenges are consistent across contexts, different promotional structures and employment practices influence how these are managed. The authors present a model of university teacher resilience. The research by Theron in the final chapter in this section (Chap. 12) is located in the school context but focuses on how teachers support the resilience of their students. As part of a large-scale phenomenological study and 'using the lens of Ungar's social ecology of resilience theory', this chapter addresses the question of how secondary school teachers in rural disadvantaged contexts in South Africa inform the resilience of their students. Resilience-supporting teacher actions and apathies are explored.

Connecting to Practice

The five chapters in the Part 4 of this volume focus on how conceptual understandings and research findings related to resilience can be applied in educational settings. It has been argued that classrooms, schools and teachers should all play a role in enhancing the resilience of a whole school community through broad general principles and practices (e.g. Cefai 2004, 2007; Cefai and Cavioni 2014). Teacher educators can assist in preparing classroom teachers for the future (e.g. Gardner 2011; Mansfield et al. 2016a, b). In addition to general principles, specific interventions have been developed in different countries to enhance resilience and wellbeing in school children and their families (Kennedy et al. 2015), in higher education students (Ryan et al. 2014) and in practising teachers (Jennings et al. 2011). The chapters in this part of the volume continue this call to connect what we know about connecting resilience to practice.

Two Australian-based works begin the section. In Chap. 13, Hazel argues that resilience is a 'bridging concept that links together the cognitive, emotional, social and physiological domains of wellbeing' and that teacher educators have a key role in preparing future teachers to enhance the resilience of their pupils. The Australian ResponseAbility project is used to illustrate the proposed strategies. Beltman, Mansfield, Wosnitza, Weatherby-Fell and Broadley (Chap. 14) share the findings of a study examining the impact of using the BRiTE online modules. In this study Australian teacher education students completed the modules before their final school placement and pre- and post-test data provide some indication that the modules helped pre-service teachers develop their capacity for resilience.

Chapter 15 is linked to the ENTREE project, and a team of researchers and practitioners (Castro Silva, Pipa, Renner and O'Donnell) from Portugal, Germany and Ireland provide an overview of the face-to-face training that was part of this project. The training modules' conceptual underpinning and practical implementation are presented. Also linked to the ENTREE project, in Chap. 16, Wosnitza, Delzepich, Schwarze, O'Donnell, Faust and Camilleri (from Germany, Ireland and Malta) explain the TRSR (Teacher Resilience Self-Reflection Tool). The chapter outlines this web-based instrument which is based on the project's theoretical framework of teacher resilience.

The final two chapters in Part 4 are related to specific programmes developed for use in schools. Noble and McGrath (Chap. 17) write about the contemporary challenges leading to the need for 'educational policy and school practices' that can 'help children and young people develop greater resilience'. They report on research conducted over many years regarding a whole-school programme to develop resilience that they developed in Australia. Finally, in Chap. 18, a team from Italy (Cavioni, Zanetti, Beddia and Lupica Spagnolo) reports on the development of a school curriculum to promote resilience in schools in Europe. The underpinning conceptual framework of RESCUR and findings from a pilot implementation are presented.

In conclusion, it is the intention of the chapters in this volume to illustrate a current picture of resilience understanding, research and practice. Conceptualisations aim to incorporate the complexity of individuals and systems. The work presented illustrates multiple national contexts and educational settings, each with their own unique challenges and resources. Using a variety of methods, the chapters illustrate the breadth of research being conducted and its implications for practice, with specific interventions included.

References

Beltman, S., Mansfield, C. F., & Price, A. (2011). Thriving not just surviving: A review of research on teacher resilience. *Educational Research Review, 6*, 185–207. https://doi.org/10.1016/j.edurev.2011.09.001.

Castro, A. J., Kelly, J., & Shih, M. (2010). Resilience strategies for new teachers in high-needs areas. *Teaching and Teacher Education, 26*(3), 622–629. https://doi.org/10.1016/j.tate.2009.09.010.

Cefai, C. (2004). Pupil resilience in the classroom: A teacher's framework. *Emotional and Behavioural Difficulties, 9*(3), 149–170.

Cefai, C. (2007). Resilience for all: A study of classrooms as protective contexts. *Emotional and Behavioural Difficulties, 12*(2), 119–134.

Cefai, C., & Cavioni, V. (2014). From neurasthenia to eudaimonia: Teachers' well-being and resilience. In C. Cefai & V. Cavioni (Eds.), *Social and emotional education in primary school: Integrating theory and research into practice* (pp. 133–148). New York: Springer.

Day, C., & Gu, Q. (2014). *Resilient teachers, resilient schools*. New York: Routledge.

Ebersöhn, L. (2012). Adding 'Flock' to 'Fight and Flight': A honeycomb of resilience where supply of relationships meets demand for support. *Journal of Psychology in Africa, 22*(1), 29–42.

Ee, J., & Chang, A. (2010). How resilient are our graduate trainee teachers in Singapore? *The Asia-Pacific Education Researcher, 19*(2), 321–331.

Gardner, S. (2011). Stress among prospective teachers: A review of the literature. *Australian Journal of Teacher Education, 36*(1), 18–28. https://doi.org/10.14221/ajte.2010v35n8.2.

Gu, Q., & Day, C. (2013). Challenges to teacher resilience: Conditions count. *British Educational Research Journal, 39*(1), 22–44. https://doi.org/10.1080/01411926.2011.623152.

Gu, Q., & Li, Q. (2013). Sustaining resilience in times of change: Stories from Chinese teachers. *Asia-Pacific Journal of Teacher Education, 41*(3), 288–303. https://doi.org/10.1080/1359866X.2013.809056.

Jennings, P. A., Snowberg, K. E., Coccia, M. A., & Greenberg, M. T. (2011). Improving classroom learning environments by Cultivating Awareness and Resilience in Education (CARE): Results of two pilot studies. *The Journal of classroom interaction, 46*(1), 37–48.

Johnson, B., Down, B., Le Cornu, R., Peters, J., Sullivan, A., Pearce, J., & Hunter, J. (2014). Promoting early career teacher resilience: A framework for understanding and acting. *Teachers and Teaching: Theory and Practice, 20*(5), 530–546. https://doi.org/10.1080/13540602.2014.937957.

Kennedy, P., Rooney, R., Kane, R., Hassan, S., & Nesa, M. (2015). The enhanced Aussie optimism positive thinking skills program: The relationship between internalizing symptoms and family functioning in children aged 9–11 years old. *Frontiers in Psychology, 6*, 504.

Leroux, M., & Théorêt, M. (2014). Intriguing empirical relations between teachers' resilience and reflection on practice. *Reflective Practice: International and Multidisciplinary Perspectives*. https://doi.org/10.1080/14623943.2014.900009.

Mansfield, C. F., Beltman, S., Price, A., & McConney, A. (2012). "Don't sweat the small stuff": Understanding teacher resilience at the chalkface. *Teaching and Teacher Education, 28*, 357–367. https://doi.org/10.1016/j.tate.2011.11.001.

Mansfield, C. F., Beltman, S., Broadley, T., & Weatherby-Fell, N. (2016a). Building resilience in teacher education: An evidenced informed framework. *Teaching and Teacher Education, 54*, 77–87. https://doi.org/10.1016/j.tate.2015.11.016.

Mansfield, C. F., Beltman, S., Weatherby-Fell, N., & Broadley, T. (2016b). Classroom ready?: Building resilience in teacher education. In R. Brandenburg, S. McDonough, J. Burke, & S. White (Eds.), *Teacher education: Innovation, interventions and impact* (pp. 211–229). Singapore: Springer.

Pretsch, J., Flunger, B., & Schmitt, M. (2012). Resilience predicts well-being in teachers, but not in non-teaching employees. *Social Psychology of Education, 15*(3), 321–336. https://doi.org/10.1007/s11218-012-9180-8.

Ryan, M. L., Shochet, I. M., & Stallman, H. M. (2014). Universal online interventions might engage psychologically distressed university students who are unlikely to seek formal help. *Advances in Mental Health, 9*(1), 73–83. https://doi.org/10.5172/jamh.9.1.73.

Wosnitza, M., O'Donnell, M., Morgan, M., Mansfield, C. F., Beltman, S., et al. (2014). *Teachers resilience in Europe. A theoretical framework*. Aachen: ENTREE. Retrieved from http://entree-project.eu/wp-content/uploads/2014/11/ENTREE1-new-v2_EN-1.pdf.

Yonezawa, S., Jones, M., & Singer, N. R. (2011). Teacher resilience in urban schools. *Urban Education, 46*(5), 913–931. https://doi.org/10.1177/0042085911400341.

Part II
Conceptualising Resilience

Chapter 2
(Re)conceptualising Teacher Resilience: A Social-Ecological Approach to Understanding Teachers' Professional Worlds

Qing Gu

Abstract This chapter builds upon but extends current understanding of resilience in teachers by exploring the nature of teacher resilience from a social-ecological perspective. The social-ecological understanding of resilience as an environment-centred, process-oriented latent concept enables us to place teachers in their complex worlds of work and analyse the ways in which their capacity to teach to their best *influences* and *is influenced* by their professional worlds. It argues that at a time when the contemporary landscape of teaching has become increasingly complex and diverse and when teachers' professional worlds are populated with successive and persisting government policy reforms which have increased their external accountabilities, work complexity and emotional workload, understanding why and how many teachers are able to manage the complexity challenge, sustain their capacity to be resilient and continue to work for improvement is an important quality retention issue.

Although a considerable body of research has looked into teacher resilience over the last decade, compared to resilience research on children and young people, empirical and conceptual work on resilience in adults, and teachers in particular, is still in its infancy. Drawing upon resilience research across disciplines and empirical evidence on the work and lives of teachers internationally, this chapter contributes to understandings of the meaning and importance of resilience in teachers' work from a social-ecological perspective.

The chapter begins with a review of the wider policy and reform contexts for teachers and teaching. The purpose is to establish at the outset that at a time when teachers' professional worlds are populated with successive and persisting govern-

Q. Gu (✉)
University of Nottingham, Nottingham, UK
e-mail: Qing.Gu@nottingham.ac.uk

M. Wosnitza et al. (eds.), *Resilience in Education*,
https://doi.org/10.1007/978-3-319-76690-4_2

ment policy reforms which have increased their external accountabilities, work complexity and emotional workload, understanding why and how many teachers are able to manage the complexity challenge, sustain their capacity to be resilient and continue to teach to their best is a relevant and important quality retention issue.

Following a synthesis of the research literature on what we already know about teacher resilience, this chapter focusses on exploring the conceptual and methodological relevance of using the social and ecological lens of human development to make sense of what teacher resilience is. The process-oriented and person x environment model of resilience reinforces the view that teacher resilience is a latent concept which is neither innate nor stable. Teachers' capacity to be resilient fluctuates as a result of the influence of personal conditions, school leadership and the relational and organisational conditions in which they work. Amongst these, relational trust in the work contexts is found to have a profound influence on teacher resilience.

Whilst acknowledging the significance of social and physical ecologies in shaping resilient qualities in both children and teachers, the chapter also points to two important differences. First, in contrast to the conceptualisation of resilience in children which presupposes the presence of significant adversity, resilience in teachers needs to be perceived as being closely allied to their everyday capacity to sustain their educational purposes and successfully manage the unavoidable uncertainties inherent in their world of work. Related to this is a second observation that the roles values play in childhood and in teachers' professional lives are profoundly different. One has to understand the integral role of teachers' vocational values and purposes in influencing what they do and why they do it in their everyday classrooms in order to understand what resilience in teachers really is:

> Over the years, the evidence from our work with outstanding teachers and outstanding schools in changing social, cultural and political landscapes of education nationally and internationally has led us to believe that, regardless of age, experience or gender or school context, teachers and schools can change the worlds of their students and that many of them do! They are not simply survivors but committed and competent professionals and organisations that are proud of being at the centre of a profession which is charged with making a difference to the learning, lives and achievement of all children and young people. (Day and Gu 2014, p. 140)

This chapter concludes with four propositions about teacher resilience. Taken together, they emphasise the importance of exploring teachers' inner and external professional worlds to understand why many are still committed and passionate about making a difference and continue to do so – despite the unpredictable nature of their every school day and the many physical, emotional and intellectual challenges that are associated with this. Drawing upon research evidence from teacher and school improvement, they also emphasise that the improvement in the quality of teachers and teaching must be understood within the social, cultural and organisational environments of the school – which are designed, nurtured and shaped by the educational architect who lives in the principal's office.

Teachers in a Complex World

Teachers' work is carried out in an era of testing times where the policy focus in many countries has shifted from provision and process to outcomes (OECD 2012). The OECD's Programme for International Student Assessment (PISA), in particular, is having an unprecedented influence on national policies for improvement and standards across many nation states. The rapidly growing international interest in 'surpassing Shanghai' and outperforming the world's leading systems (Tucker 2011) has contributed to the intensification of national and international emphases upon standards, performativity and external accountability. In the latest *Global Education Monitoring Report*, UNESCO (2016) stated:

> Education systems have traditionally measured whether children go to school rather than whether learners benefit from their schooling experience, let alone what happens inside schools and classrooms. The focus has gradually shifted over the past 15 years, however, with the rapid increase in the use of national, regional and international learning assessments. (UNESCO 2016, p. 193)

For many schools in many countries, this means that their educational values and practices, particularly in relation to the progress and achievement of their students, are now under increased public scrutiny. Whether the use of high-stake test scores is achieving (or can achieve) the desired improvement in the *quality* and *relevance* of teaching, learning and educational performance continues to remain an open question in policy, education and academic debate (Anagnostopoulos et al. 2013; Berliner et al. 2014; Burns and Köster 2016; UNESCO 2016).

At the same time, widespread movement of population, especially sharp increase in permanent migration flows in many countries, has seen the makeup of the local communities which schools serve become more diversified (OECD 2010, 2016a). Coupled with this change in student populations are the additional language and academic support that schools are expected to provide for the children of immigrants (OECD 2016a) and the broader, more explicitly articulated social and societal responsibilities that they are also expected to have in supporting school communities, other schools and other public services (Gu et al. 2016; OECD 2008).

Moreover, in many countries the decentralisation of funding, resources and quality control functions to local authorities and schools has resulted in increasingly diversified and complex education systems. A profound change has been the relationship between the central, regional and local levels which moves away from top-down hierarchies to 'a division of labour and more mutual independence and self-regulation' (Burns and Köster 2016, p. 18). In England, for example, the national policy drive towards a school-led self-improving system has seen rapid emergence of teaching school alliances and multi-academy trusts across the country which are expected to take the place of local authorities by taking up the responsibility for school improvement within their localities (Gu et al. 2016; Hargreaves 2014). The challenge, however, in England and in many other countries, is that autonomy and accountability are not always intelligently combined. Increased local autonomy continues to be monitored by centralised high-stake accountability that is regulated through standardised, measurable performance indicators (Baker and LeTendre 2005; Ball 2000, 2003; Burns and Köster 2016; OECD 2008, 2010). The rush to create autonomised schools and systems is often running ahead of the reform of the architects of the accountability system. Reflecting on the paradoxes of two generations of centralised accountability systems in the United States, Mintrop and Sunderman (2013) argue that:

> it is imperative to recognise that instructional excellence probably cannot emanate from the perch of the centre or the primacy of administration; it must be an internal striving of actively participating professional workers who are sensitive to articulated community needs. (Mintrop and Sunderman 2013, p. 39)

Put simply, it is not necessarily the school performance accountability but the commitment and quality of the teaching workforce that matters most to the learning and achievement of pupils. However, to teach to one's best over time in such a complex world is not easy. It requires teachers and their schools to be forward-thinking, outward-looking, optimistic, hopeful and, above all, resilient.

Teacher Resilience: What We Already Know

Over the past 20 years, a considerable body of research has established that resilience is a relative, multidimensional and developmental construct (e.g. Howard et al. 1999; Luthar et al. 2000; Rutter 1990). Although there are differences in how it is defined by scholars from multiple disciplines (e.g. psychology, trauma studies, social work and biology), there are also shared core considerations across the disciplines which suggest that resilience presupposes the presence of threat to the status quo and is thus a positive response to conditions of significant adversity (e.g. Gordon et al. 2000; Masten et al. 1999); that it is a dynamic process within a social system of interrelationships influenced by the interaction between the individual and the environment (Benard 1995; Garmezy and Rutter 1983; Luthar et al. 2000); and that it can be promoted, nurtured and enhanced (Cefai 2004).

However, advances in understandings about resilience are primarily built upon research on children. The empirical work on adults is still in its infancy. Emerging evidence reaffirms that resilience in adults, like that in children, is not associated with personal attributes only (Luthar and Brown 2007). Rather, it is 'a social construction' (Ungar 2004, p. 342) influenced by multidimensional factors that are unique to each context (Ungar 2004). In his work on cognitive-behaviour approach to resilience, Neenan (2009) adds that it is not a quality that is reserved for 'an extraordinary few'; rather, it can be learned and achieved by the 'ordinary many' (Neenan 2009, p. 7; see also 'ordinary magic' in Masten 2001). He advocated the concept of 'routine resilience' to emphasise that resilience comprises cognitive, behavioural and emotional responses to the vicissitudes of daily life. Through an 'active process of self-righting and growth' (O'Connell Higgins 1994, p. 1), it enables individuals to move forward towards their goals and pursue what is perceived to be important to them, 'however slowly or falteringly' (Neenan 2009, p. 17). He argues that 'attitude (meaning) is the heart of resilience' (Neenan 2009, p. 17).

Advancement in understandings of resilience in different disciplines provides important conceptual bases for the research work on resilience in teachers. I have discussed in our earlier publications (Gu and Day 2007, 2013; Gu and Li 2013; Gu 2014) that teacher resilience bears three distinctive characteristics. First, it is *context specific* in that teachers' resilient qualities are best understood by taking in not only 'the more proximal individual school or classroom context' but also 'the broader professional work context' (Beltman et al. 2011, p. 190; see also Mansfield et al. 2012). In recent years, Bruce Johnson and his colleagues in South and Western Australia have conducted extensive research into early career teacher resilience (Johnson and Down 2013; Johnson et al. 2016). Their work identified five conditions or influences on early career teachers – relationships, school culture, teacher identity, teachers' work, and policies and practices. This work is a reminder of the key role in nurturing and shaping teachers' resilience of school leaders in promoting supportive school cultures and providing strong and consistent support for all teachers' emotional and practical selves but especially those in their early years whose professional sense of self and whose capacities to be resilient may not yet be fully formed. There is abundant evidence in the educational literature which shows that in-school management support for their learning and development, leadership trust, and positive feedback from parents and pupils are key positive influences on teachers' motivation and resilience (e.g. Brunetti 2006; Castro et al. 2010; Day et al. 2007; Huberman 1993; Leithwood et al. 2006; Meister and Ahrens 2011; Webb et al. 2004). Empirical evidence on how successful principals mediate the negative influences of macro-level policy contexts and meso-level external school intake contexts and, through this, create a positive school culture which nurtures teachers' capacity for learning and development is also strong and evident (Day and Leithwood 2007; Gu et al. 2008; Gu and Johansson 2013; Leithwood et al. 2006, 2010; Robinson et al. 2009; Sammons et al. 2011).

Second, teacher resilience is, also, *role specific* in that it is closely associated with the strength and conviction of teachers' vocational commitment and it is indeed this inner calling to teach and commitment to serve which distinguishes teaching from many other jobs and occupations (Hansen 1995). In his research on teachers working in inner-city high schools in the United States, Brunetti (2006) defined teacher resilience as 'a quality that enables teachers to maintain their commitment to teaching and teaching practices despite challenging conditions and recurring setbacks' (Brunetti 2006, p. 813). Over time research has also consistently found that teachers' self-efficacy beliefs as to whether they have the capacity to effectively help children learn and achieve are one of the most important factors influencing teachers' resilient qualities (Hong 2012; Kitching et al. 2009; Morgan et al. 2010). In this sense, resilient teachers are not survivors in the profession because they 'do more than merely get through difficult emotional experiences, hanging on to inner equilibrium by a thread' (O'Connell Higgins 1994, p. 1; see also Gu and Li 2013). Rather, they display capacity for growth and fulfilment in pursuit of personally and professionally meaningful goals which, as research on teachers and teaching tells us, 'joins self and subject and students in the fabric of life' and connects their 'intellect and emotion and spirit' in their hearts (Palmer 2007, p. 11).

Third, we have learned from teachers in our research that being a resilient teacher means more than 'bouncing back' quickly and efficiently from difficulties. In addition to the routine pressures and unavoidable uncertainties which feature many teachers' everyday work and lives, and thus the need for *everyday resilience* (Day and Gu 2014), they also face challenges that are specific to their professional life phases. Empirical evidence from Gu and Li's (2013) study of 568 primary and secondary school teachers in Beijing, for example, shows that although the scenarios that challenge them in each milestone of their professional and personal lives may be different in nature, the intensity of the physical, emotional and intellectual energy required to manage them can be very similar. Given this, we have argued that teachers' ability to be resilient 'is not primarily associated with the capacity to "bounce back" or recover from highly traumatic experiences and events but, rather, the capacity to maintain equilibrium and a sense of commitment and agency in the everyday worlds in which teachers teach' (Gu and Day 2013, p. 26).

Teacher Resilience As a Social-Ecological Concept

Over the last 20 years, there has been strong and consistent evidence from educational research which suggests that the social and intellectual organisation of the school, and by extension, schools' connections with local communities, society and the policy structure – when characterised with supportive and trusting relationships between different stakeholders – foster teachers' collective capacity, commitment, resilience and effectiveness (Bryk and Schneider 2002; Day and Gu 2010, 2014; Sammons et al. 2007; Tschannen-Morgan and Barr 2004). However, with the exception of some scholars who have argued for the relevance of adopting a theoretical and practical ecological framework to research resilience in childhood and adulthood (e.g. Howard et al. 1999) and early career teachers especially (e.g. Johnson et al. 2016), few research papers have used the social and ecological lens to explore how the multiple environments in which teachers work and live influence, and are influenced by, their capacity to be resilient over the course of their professional lives. This may be because, at least in part, a social-ecological interpretation of resilience has only begun to ground its theoretical thoughts in the new advances of scientific research over the last 20 years; and above all, the research community has, as yet, predominantly focussed on the resilience of children rather than adults. In his seminal work on the social ecology of resilience, Ungar (2008) defines it as: 'In the context of exposure to significant adversity, resilience is both the capacity of individuals to navigate their way to the psychological, social, cultural, and physical resources that sustain their well-being, and their capacity individually and collectively to negotiate for these resources to be provided and experienced in culturally meaningful ways' (Ungar 2008, p. 225). As the remainder of the chapter will show, the conceptual and methodological relevance and strengths of using the social-ecological approach to researching teachers' resilience are at least threefold.

First, an *environment-centred approach* reinforces the importance of emphasising the impact of multilevel contexts on the growth and development of teachers over the course of their professional lives, especially in terms of their capacity to maintain a sense of commitment and agency in the everyday worlds in which they teach. The theoretical underpinning of the social ecology of resilience emerged from Bronfenbrenner's (1979) ground-breaking work on human development which is, in essence, concerned with the interconnectedness and interactions between multilevel systems and the ways they shape the course of human development throughout the life span. In contrast to the decontextualised approach to constructing the reality of child development, Bronfenbrenner defined human development as 'the person's evolving conception of the ecological environment, and his relation to it, as well as the person's growing capacity to discover, sustain, or later its properties' (Bronfenbrenner 1979, p. 9). Applying Bronfenbrenner's theory to research on resilience in children, Ungar and his colleagues argue that 'it is children's interactions with multiple reciprocating systems, and the quality of those systems that account for most children's developmental success under negative stress (their resilience)' (Ungar et al. 2013, p. 349).

The same argument applies to the research on teacher resilience. As the growing literature on teacher resilience show, the quality of the intellectual, social and organisational conditions in which teachers work and the people with whom they work has significant impacts, positively or negatively, on their capacity to be committed, resilient and effective (Beltman 2015; Day and Hong 2016; Gu 2014; Gu and Day 2007, 2013; Johnson et al. 2016). However, this is by no means a surprising finding. The wider research literature on teachers and teaching has been consistently reporting how the contexts of schools shape *why* and *how* many teachers continue to commit their time, energy and passion to a profession which can make them 'feel a sense of invisibility and powerlessness' (Nieto 2015, p. 252; see also Gu and Johansson 2013; Johnson 2004; OECD 2016b; UNESCO 2015). The research literature on teacher supply and retention, for example, suggests that for diverse and complex socio-economic and political reasons, a context-sensitive, differentiated approach is needed to understand variations in issues relating to teacher supply and retention nationally and internationally. In many developing countries, a lack of resources and financial incentive packages to attract qualified personnel into teaching has meant that quantity, rather than quality, continues to be a primary concern in their efforts to provide basic education (UNESCO 2011, 2016). This has meant that, unfortunately, children in countries needing teachers the most tend to be taught by the least qualified personnel (UNESCO 2006).

In contrast, in the developed world, such as the United States, the United Kingdom and many European countries, shortage of teacher supply tends to be a particularly pressing problem for core subject areas such as maths, modern foreign languages and science (European Commission 2012) and for schools serving socio-economically deprived communities (Boyd et al. 2008; Guarino et al. 2006; Ingersoll 2001; Nieto 2015). Moreover, there are also troubling indicators which suggest that teacher quality is especially lower in schools which serve high-need communities (Boyd et al. 2008; Goldhaber and Hansen 2009; Loeb et al. 2005) where most children, who are already disadvantaged in accessing or benefiting from rich capital and social capital in their early years, are then denied access to quality teachers and quality education to which they are entitled when entering the formal school system.

Second, this social-ecological model of person x environment interaction (Ungar et al. 2013) enables us to place teachers in their complex worlds of work and analyse the ways in which their capacity to teach to their best *influences* and *is influenced* by their professional worlds. In our earlier work on teacher resilience, we explored its relational nature by drawing upon findings from our research on the work and lives of 300 teachers in 100 schools in England (Day and Gu 2010). It shows that resilience in teachers is a 'relational dynamic' (Jordan 2012) which resides in individual teachers' *agency* and *capacity* in maintaining collegial and emotional connection or forming reconnection with the children and adults in their context of work (Gu 2014). Such healthy connections function as resources which support personal growth and transformation as well as social change in their work environment (Jordan 2004). Thus, a particular strength of this conceptual lens is that it does not treat the social and relational contexts of work as a 'given' asset or protective factor (Jordan 1992). Rather, it emphasises the connection between the individual and the environment. However, although the concept of relational resilience has enabled us to probe deep into the emotional and relational nature of teachers' work and lives and the roles that multilayered relationships play in supporting the development of their professional identity, efficacy and resilience (Day and Gu 2010, 2014; Gu 2014), the focus on the reciprocal interaction between the capacity of the individual and the quality of *multiple reciprocating systems* offers a more nuanced and powerful conceptual lens to understand why many teachers are able to sustain their commitment, resilience and effectiveness in a place called school:

> To reach out positively and supportively to 27 youngsters for five hours or so each day in an elementary school classroom is demanding and exhausting. To respond similarly to four to six successive classes of 25 or more students each day at the secondary level may be impossible. (Goodlad 2004, p. 112)

Earlier in this chapter, I insisted that teacher resilience is role specific. Bronfenbrenner (1979) defines a role as 'a set of activities and relations expected of a person occupying a particular position in society, and of others in relation to that person' (Bronfenbrenner 1979, p. 85). For teachers, if their role expectations were primarily defined by prescribed standards, methods and techniques, then these expectations would have missed a simple but fundamental truth about 'a good teacher':

> Good teachers possess a capacity for connectedness. They are able to weave a complex web of connections among themselves, their subjects and their students so that students can learn to weave a world for themselves. … The connections made by good teachers are held not in their methods but in their hearts – meaning heart in its ancient sense, as the place where intellect and emotion and spirit and will converge in the human self. (Palmer 2007, p. 11)

The voice of the *heart* flows from the identity and integrity of the inward teacher (Palmer 2007) and speaks out why many teachers in many countries regard teaching as 'a lifestyle' (Day and Gu 2014) and 'a way to live in the world' (Nieto 2015, p. 1). In other words, what keeps many teachers going in a new era of accountability and standardisation has to be something that is greater than *just a job*. Hansen (1995) argues that it is the call to teach that helps teachers to find inner motivation and strength to achieve personal autonomy and personal significance. In a similar vein, Nias (1999) has long argued that it is teachers' 'missionary zeal' and 'moral values' that enable them to be 'vocationally and professionally "committed" over the course of their lives in teaching' (Nias 1999, p. 225).

Understanding the role of moral values and vocation in influencing what many teachers do and why they do it in their schools and classrooms is key to understand the dynamic and complex nature of the interaction between the teacher and their context of work. In his analysis of the social ecologies and their contribution to children's development and resilience, Ungar (2012) argues that 'to understand resilience we must explore the context in which the individual experiences adversity, making resilience first a quality of the broader social and physical ecology, and second a quality of the individual' (Ungar 2012, p. 27). This is because, as Ungar and his colleague (Ungar et al. 2013) later explained in their excellent annual research review, 'Children are not usually born resilient: they are made resilient through the many different interactions with their social and physical ecologies. These aspects of their environment depend on social policy and structures to make resources available' (Ungar et al. 2013, p. 360).

Although the literature has established that teachers are not born resilient either and that policy structures and work conditions also have profound influences on the strengths of their resilience, what makes teachers distinctively different from children is that what they do in schools and classrooms is driven by deep-seated moral values: 'Many of us became teachers for reasons of the heart, animated by a passion for some subject and for helping people learn' (Palmer 2007, p. 17). Such values and vocational zeal are found to be associated with a strong sense of professional goals and purposes, persistence, professional aspirations, achievement and motivation (Gu and Day 2007) – the essential qualities that Benard (1995) has observed in resilience. More importantly, study after study has reinforced that when individual teachers' moral values and purpose have been harnessed to become the hub of a school's culture or, in other words, a shared sense of mission, then schools are more likely to succeed in terms of energising collaboration, learning and achievement: 'Like a butterfly, a school must be nurtured by its inner energy in order to thrive' (Deal and Peterson 2009, p. 180). This reinforces the observation that teachers' actions, commitment and beliefs also influence, individually and collectively, the social and organisational culture and contexts in which they work and live. Buchanan (2015) found in her research on teacher identity and agency that the discourse of education policy and structures do not completely redefine teachers' self-concepts: 'Teachers are more complex and multifaceted than that' because individual teachers bring with them "a unique mix of personal and professional experiences and commitments"' (Buchanan 2015, p. 700):

> Teachers therefore confront the policies and professional discourses they encounter not as tabulae rasae, but rather actively use their own pre-existing identities to interpret, learn from, evaluate, and appropriate the new conditions of their work in schools and classrooms. In this process, their identities are reformed and remade – and professional agency is carved out. (Buchanan 2015, p. 700)

Thus, although teachers' capacity to be resilient, committed and effective in what they do can be fostered or faltered in the intellectual, social and emotional connections that they make in the everyday worlds in which they teach, in contrast to child resilience which presupposes the presence of adversity, they require 'everyday resilience' to teach to their best in 'a place called school' (Goodlad 2004). Also, in contrast to resilience in children which recognises that environmental factors account for more of the positive developmental outcomes than individual characteristics (e.g. DuMont et al. 2012; Lerner 2005; Ungar et al. 2013; Wyman 2003) and which emphasises 'the nature of the child's social and physical ecology first, interactional processes between the environment and the individual child second, and child-specific propensities toward positive development third' (Ungar 2011, p. 6), the relationship between the quality of the broader social and physical ecology and the capacity of the teacher in resilience-building processes are not sequential or conditional but reciprocal and of *equal* importance. This is because unlike children whose own individual resources (e.g. optimism) are believed to be 'only as good as the capacity of his or her social and physical ecologies that facilitate their expression and application to developmental tasks' (Ungar 2011, p. 6), teachers act in response to their individually held moral values, vocational commitment and professional integrity, as well as in relation to their perceived 'collective image of the teaching occupation' (Soder 2004, p. 11):

> Would-be teachers know the negative aspects of teaching. They know that teaching will not make them rich. They know that teaching will not give them high status in the community. But that is not why they turn to or are called by teaching. In talking with teachers and would-be teachers over the years, I remain convinced that most people go into teaching for solid, morally defensible reasons. They sense that to be a teacher is, well, to be a teacher, and teaching has its own moral grounding, its own demands, its own rewards. … Teachers and would-be teachers had a strong sense that they were indeed moral and political agents, morally responsible to and for those they chose to teach. (Soder 2004, p. 15)

Third, the social-ecological understanding of resilience as a *process-oriented* latent concept closely aligns with the learning and developmental nature of teachers' career. It has now been widely accepted that the capacity of individuals to be resilient is nurtured, learned and acquired. Over time such capacity unfolds progressively in a developing individual (Schoon 2012) as they learn to navigate and negotiate their way to the psychological, social, cultural and physical resources that sustain their well-being (Ungar et al. 2013). In essence, this process of navigation and negotiation is *developmental* and *socially facilitated* (Ungar 2011) and takes place in the interaction between the individual and the environment:

> Over the life course, human development takes place throughout life through processes of progressively more complex reciprocal interaction between an active evolving biopsychological human organism and the persons, objects, and symbols in its immediate external

> environment. To be effective, the interaction must occur on a fairly regular basis over extended periods of time. Such enduring forms of interaction in the immediate environment are referred to as proximal processes. (Bronfenbrenner 2001, p. 6965)

Building on Bronfenbrenner's and the other scholars' (e.g. Lerner 1996; Sameroff 2010) study of human development, Schoon (2012) argues that a developmental-contextual perspective is essential in understanding the processes underlying effective functioning in the face of adversity and, subsequently, the dynamic and multifaceted nature of resilience in a changing context.

Such a process-oriented, developmental-contextual perspective is also essential in understanding how and why many teachers remain committed in the profession. It is no secret that to teach and to teach well over time is sheer hard work. In his rich and engaging analysis of what good teaching is, Ayers (2010) explains succinctly why such sheer hard work for many teachers is 'a lifetime affair':

> Becoming a wonderful teacher, or a great or awesome teacher, is a lifetime affair. This is because good teaching is forever pursuing better teaching; it is always dynamic and in motion, always growing, learning, developing, searching for a better way. Teaching is never finished, never still, never easily summed up. "Wonderful Teacher" might be inscribed on someone's lifetime achievement award, printed on a retirement party banner, or etched on a tombstone, but it is never right for a working teacher. (Ayers 2010, p. 160)

In other words, a sustained pursuit of continuing professional learning and development is what makes good teachers and great teaching. This is a career-long moral commitment and 'a sustainable investment for professional capital' (Hargreaves and Fullan 2012, p. 186). In her study of American high school teachers, Nieto (2003) described teaching as an intellectual endeavour which involves love, anger and depression and hope and possibility and concluded that to retain teachers' commitment in the profession, schools need to become places where teachers find community of learning and engage in intellectual work. Almost a decade later, our resilience research with more than 500 teachers in Beijing (China) also showed that it was both the *intellectual* and *emotional fulfilment* that had kept most of the teachers in our research committed, optimistic and resilient in the profession (Gu and Li 2013):

> … teachers' job fulfilment is a satisfying state of mind which they attribute to the reward they derive from their students' success and also, the ways in which their capacities have developed to enable them to bring about such success. Moreover, students' appreciation of their effort connects their hearts and soul with the very people whom they care about and care for and adds an indispensable emotional dimension to their feelings of being fulfilled. (Gu and Li 2013, p. 295)

Thus, to understand why some teachers are resilient irrespective of the complexity of their professional worlds, one has to understand that 'expecting teachers to work hard is not, in itself, a problem' (Dunford 2016, p. 129). Problems arise when teachers struggle to see the *meaning* of their hard work and/or struggle with their capacities to make a difference. Providing social, cultural and organisational conditions that enable teachers, individually and collectively, to be engaged in 'a personal path towards greater professional integrity and human growth' (Hargreaves 2003,

p. 48) is crucial. It is within the processes of continuing professional learning and development that teachers improve their capacities to support pupils' learning and ultimately fulfil their professional needs to 'build character, maturity and other virtues in themselves and others, making their schools into moral communities' (Hargreaves 2003, p. 48).

From a social-ecological perspective, it is important to note that these processes in which teachers learn, develop and enact their capacity to teach and teach well over time are embedded in the multiple contexts of their everyday professional lives – which are inherently featured with uncertain and unpredictable circumstances and scenarios. Such circumstances present a constant intellectual and emotional challenge to those who strive to learn and to teach to their best. For many teachers who have managed to sustain their commitment and motivation in the profession, the ability to weather the often unpredictable 'storm' of school and classroom life (Patterson and Kelleher 2005) is not an option but a necessity. Given this, we have argued in our earlier work (Gu and Day 2013) that resilience in teachers is the capacity to manage the unavoidable uncertainties inherent in the realities of teaching. It is driven by teachers' educational purposes and moral values. Although it 'arises in interaction between individual and the practices they inhabit' (Edwards 2011), it is also influenced by their biographies and the social, cultural, organisational and policy conditions of their work and lives.

Four Propositions: Sustaining Resilience and Quality in Teachers' Complex Worlds

Taken together, I conclude this chapter with four propositions about teacher resilience and its implications for sustaining teacher quality in the complex and changing contexts in which teachers work and live. These propositions build on but extend our recent work on resilience in teachers and schools (Day and Gu 2014). They are grounded in the social-ecological understanding of resilience as an environment-centred, process-oriented dynamic latent concept and highlight how the interactions between teachers' inner professional and moral values and their worlds of work influence, positively or negatively, their commitment and effectiveness over the course of their professional lives.

Proposition One Resilience is closely associated with teachers' sense of identity, commitment and moral purpose and the extent to which their workplace contexts are able to support them to enact their moral values and commitment. Schools and school leadership matter in creating and sustaining optimal organisational conditions that develop teachers and nurture their capacities to teach to their best.

The truism about teaching is that it is a difficult and 'enormously complex activity' (Olsen 2008). Most teachers enter teaching because they want to make a difference, and many of them do not leave teaching. Nieto (2003) observes that 'Teachers who keep going in spite of everything know that teaching is more than a job' (Nieto 2003, p. 128). Over the years, our work with many committed school leaders and teachers also reaffirms our belief that it is the commitment to serve and the joy of being able to make a difference to the lives and achievement of children and young people that have kept them in the profession. We hear pupils of these leaders and teachers say to us 'Our teachers are not here for the money. They are here because they care about us'.

Resilient schools are places where teachers and students are aspired to their own learning and development and where a clear sense of moral purpose is shared, valued and embedded in the daily lives of the school. Resilience without moral purpose, without a willingness to be self-reflective and learn, and without collegial and leadership support in order to change and improve collectively and collaboratively is not enough. For many teachers, then, teaching still essentially represents a commitment to human development:

> Knowing things and knowing how to communicate them, creating the conditions for learning to occur, being on your perceptual toes, scanning the room for opportunity – all of these aid in the growth of other human beings. Such a goal, this commitment to human development, places the teacher's work squarely in the ethical and moral domain. (Rose 2010, p. 168)

For many hard-working teachers and leaders, this is perhaps the most powerful testimony of their vocation of teaching. It is also, perhaps, their most powerful emotional reward. Consistent with this, there is strong evidence from research which shows that bonuses and incentive pay do not affect teacher motivation or quality (Gamoran 2012; Kelley 1999; Yuan et al. 2013) because 'teachers view the receipt of a bonus as an acknowledgement of their hard work rather than an incentive to work harder' (Marsh et al. 2011, cited in Yuan et al. 2013, p. 17). A sense of moral purpose and pride in being a teacher provides many committed teachers with the inner drive, strength and optimism to help every child learn, grow and achieve. Resilient teachers, then, do not have to be extraordinary heroes. They can be, and often are, teachers who are striving to make a difference in their classroom on every ordinary school day.

The quality of school leadership matters in creating, developing and broadening intellectual, social and emotional capital within and beyond the school gate and in providing optimal relational and organisational conditions that support teachers to make a difference. Supportive organisational communities do not happen by chance. They require good leadership. Knoop (2007) argues that 'Considering the present pace of sociocultural change, it is difficult to imagine a time in history when good leadership was more important than it is today, and when the lack of it was more dangerous' (p. 223).

Building resilience in an organisational setting places a great deal of importance on the effectiveness of the organisational context, structure and system and on how the system functions as a whole to create a supportive environment for individuals' professional learning and development, to build a trusting relationship amongst its staff, and to foster a collective sense of efficacy and resilience and, through this, to sustain its continuous improvement. However, to date this concept has been developed largely outside education. Hamel and Välikangas (2003), writing in the context of business, describe a truly resilient organisation as a workplace that is filled with excitement and argue that strategic renewal, i.e. 'creative reconstruction', 'must be the natural consequence of an organisation's innate resilience' (Hamel and Välikangas 2003, p. 2).

When reviewing the relationship between power, accountability and teacher quality, Ingersoll (2011) found that 'In plain terms, poorly run schools can make otherwise excellent teachers not so excellent' (Ingersoll 2011, p. 98). By extension, we can argue that poorly led schools can diminish rather than enrich the capacities of teachers to grow and sustain their commitment and resilience. Some teachers in our research on teachers' work and lives (Day and Gu 2014) would probably have had a nervous breakdown and a prolonged dip in their perceived effectiveness if the senior leadership team and the principal, in particular, had not offered them the very kind of professional and personal support that they needed to boost their confidence and sense of efficacy.

Understanding the nature of the schools' internal and external contexts, how they are mediated by school leadership, especially the leadership of the principal, and, through this, how the interplay between contexts may influence, positively or negatively, the fabric of every ordinary school day, is key to a deep understanding of the secrets of their teachers' and pupils' success (or lack of success) over time.

Proposition Two Teacher resilience-building processes are relational.

Teachers build and develop their sense of resilience within and through a web of trusting relationships in schools. This relational model of resilience places the capacity for mutual empowerment and growth and the importance of mutual support at the heart of the resilience-building process (Jordan 2004) and thus has enabled us to understand teacher resilience in a situated, contextual way.

Teachers' professional worlds are made up of 'a web of communal relationships' (Palmer 2007, p. 97). Three sets of relationships are at the centre of teachers' professional work and lives, teacher-student relations, teacher-teacher relations and teacher-leader relations, and each of these has a distinctive role to play in building and sustaining their sense of resilience over time. Trusting relationships between teachers and students, for example, are the heartbeat of teachers' vocational commitment. Relational trust between these two parties signals a mutual confidence in each other's endeavour to teach to their best and to learn to their best. It functions as a primary source of teachers' long-term job fulfilment – through which they feel that their hard work is rewarded and valued by the very people whose academic and individual welfare first drew them into teaching.

Collegial connections with colleagues also provide a necessary intellectual and emotional condition for collective and collaborative learning and development. Exploring the resilience-building process from the lens of collegiality has enabled us to reaffirm our earlier observation that resilience is not a quality that is reserved for the select few 'heroic' teachers. Rather, building resilience in teachers must be both an individual and social process within school communities which are driven by a shared sense of moral purpose and in which building mutually supportive and 'growth-fostering relationships' (Jordan 2006) is a shared goal:

> Social support has also been viewed as vital to resilience; it has been defined as emotional concern, instrumental aid, information, and appraisal. Most social support studies have emphasized one-way support, getting love, getting help. A relational perspective points to the importance of engaging in a relationship that contributes to all people in the relationship. The power of social support is more about mutuality than about getting for the self. (Jordan 2006, p. 83)

Finally, relational trust between teachers and school leaders is essential in developing resilient teachers and building resilient schools. As Fullan (2003) has noted, relational trust 'reduces the sense of vulnerability when staff take on new tasks' and also 'creates a moral resource for school improvement' which affects teacher motivation, commitment and retention (Fullan 2003, p. 42). Our research on the impact of successful school leadership on pupil outcomes (Day et al. 2011) found that such relational trust is built through the layered and cumulative application of a variety of strategic actions. The growth of organisational trust is driven by actions at all levels, but all strategic actions rely on cooperation from other members of the organisation. Communication, modelling actions, coaching and mentoring, developing staff, sharing the vision, explaining values and beliefs, making visible and viable pedagogical and curriculum decisions, appropriately restructuring organisational structures and cultures, and redesigning roles and functions all contribute to the moral, intellectual and social health and improvement capacities of schools.

> Only when participants demonstrate their commitment to engage in such work and see others doing the same can a genuine professional community grounded in relational trust emerge. Principals must take the lead and extend themselves by reaching out to others. On occasion, the principal may be called on to demonstrate trust in colleagues who may not fully reciprocate, at least initially. But they must also be prepared to use coercive power to reform a dysfunctional school community around professional norms. Interestingly, such authority may rarely need to be invoked thereafter once these new norms are firmly established. (Fullan 2003, p. 64)

Proposition Three Resilience in teachers is essential, but it is not the only condition for them to be effective.

We know that what teachers do in the classroom has the single, greatest effect on the quality of students' learning (Hattie 2009). We also know from our work that pupils of teachers who are committed and resilient are more likely to attain results at or above the level expected (Day et al. 2008; Gu 2014). This is because, at least in part, resilience describes 'what arises in a dynamic or dialectic between person and practices that reflects the evidence that the person is acting on and reshaping challenging circumstances in their lives so that they can propel themselves forward' (Edwards 2010, p. 118).

However, it does not follow that every resilient teacher will be effective. Teachers need to be knowledgeable about their students' needs and the subject(s) they teach. They need to have the skills to draw upon combinations of classroom teaching and management skills and apply them appropriately and care deeply for the well-being and achievement of every student in their classrooms.

Proposition Four Building and sustaining the capacity for resilience is more than an individual responsibility.

Over the years, we have worked with teachers who, despite their hard work, commitment, moral purpose and dedication to the education of their students, struggle to improve outcomes. Those teachers who excel and whose students excel with them do not just do so on their own. Whilst it is clearly the responsibility of each teacher to teach to their best, it is the responsibility of each individual school, school district and national government to ensure that they are able to do so through high-quality leadership and the provision of physical and other resources. Policymakers, teacher educators, school principals and other key stakeholders in the multiple-level education system need to design the means to build and sustain teachers' capacities to be resilient. A central task for all concerned with enhancing quality and standards in schools is, therefore, not only to have a better understanding of what influences teachers' resilience over the course of a career but also the means by which the resilience necessary for these to be sustained may be nurtured in the contexts in which they work. Promoting and cultivating healthy individual and collective learning and achievement cultures in schools is essential to how they feel about themselves as professionals. The extent to which they are able to find continuing professional and personal fulfilment through their work, and, through these, sustain their commitment to teach to their best over time, will depend to a large extent upon the opportunities they have to grow, sustain and renew their capacities to be resilient.

Conclusions

This chapter builds upon but extends current understanding of resilience in teachers by exploring the nature of teacher resilience from a social-ecological perspective. An important strength of this perspective is that it 'defines resilience as a quality of both individuals and their environments' (Ungar et al. 2013, p. 361) and thus enables us to conduct a nuanced analysis of the ways in which the policy, organisational, relational and personal contexts in which teachers work and live influence and, are influenced by, their values and capacity to teach to their best over time. It also provides a way of thinking about teacher learning and development over time as a journey towards greater intellectual and emotional growth and fulfilment – the responsibility for which is individual as well as organisational and political.

The implication for teachers' quality retention is at least twofold. First, the focus on individual quality points to the importance of *attracting* individuals with the right calibre to the teaching profession – who are passionate and committed lifelong learners, who stay in teaching to share their passion for learning with children and young people and, importantly, who know how to inspire to them learn and grow within and outside the everyday classroom. Second, the social-ecological understanding of resilience as an environment-centred, process-oriented latent concept emphasises the important role that policy, sociocultural, organisational, relational and intellectual environments play in *nurturing* and *retaining* teachers with the right calibre in the profession. Resilience-building process should be understood, at least in part, as a process of teachers seeking to understand the multisystemic contexts in which they work and live, and also, a process of constructing their professional identities and capacities in such contexts. Teachers' capacity to be resilient is not a given. Rather, it is contextual and can fluctuate. Teachers can be made resilient if their contexts of work provide optimal opportunities, resources and conditions that support their professional needs, sustain their well-being and a positive identity and, importantly, enable them to develop their capacities to teach to their best over time.

References

Anagnostopoulos, D., Rutledge, S., & Jacobsen, R. (Eds.). (2013). *The infrastructure of accountability: Data use and the transformation of American education.* Cambridge, MA: Harvard Education Press.

Ayers, W. (2010). *To teach: The journey of a teacher* (3rd ed.). New York: Teachers College Press.

Baker, D., & LeTendre, G. (2005). *National Differences, global similarities: World culture and the future of schooling.* Stanford: Stanford University Press.

Ball, S. (2000). Performativities and fabrications in the education economy: Towards the performative society. *Australian Educational Researcher, 17*(3), 1–24.

Ball, S. (2003). The teachers' soul and the terrors of performativity. *Journal of Education Policy, 18*(2), 215–228.

Beltman, S. (2015). Teacher professional resilience: Thriving not just surviving. In N. Weatherby-Fell (Ed.), *Learning to teach in the secondary school* (pp. 20–38). Melbourne: Cambridge University Press.

Beltman, S., Mansfield, C. F., & Price, A. (2011). Thriving not just surviving: A review of research on teacher resilience. *Educational Research Review, 6*, 185–207.

Benard, B. (1995). *Fostering resilience in children* (ERIC/EECE Digest, EDO-PS-99).

Berliner, D., Glass, G., & Associates. (2014). *50 myths and lies that threaten America's public schools: The real crisis in education.* New York: Teachers College Press.

Boyd, D., Grossman, P., Lankford, H., Loeb, S., & Wycoff, J. H. (2008). *Who leaves? Teacher attrition and student achievement* (NBER Working Paper No. W14022).

Bronfenbrenner, U. (1979). *The ecology of human development: Experiments by nature and design.* Cambridge, MA: Harvard University Press.

Bronfenbrenner, U. (2001). The bioecological theory of human development. In N. J. Smelser & P. B. Baltes (Eds.), *International Encyclopaedia of the social and behavioural sciences* (Vol. 10, pp. 6963–6970). New York: Elsevier.

Brunetti, G. (2006). Resilience under fire: Perspectives on the work of experienced, inner city high school teachers in the United States. *Teaching and Teacher Education, 22*, 812–825.

Bryk, A. S., & Schneider, B. L. (2002). *Trust in schools: A core resource for improvement.* New York: Russell Sage Foundation.

Buchanan, R. (2015). Teacher identity and agency in an era of accountability. *Teachers and Teaching: Theory and Practice, 21*(6), 700–719.

Burns, T., & Köster, F. (Eds.). (2016). *Governing education in a complex world.* Paris: OECD Publishing.

Castro, A. J., Kelly, J., & Shih, M. (2010). Resilience strategies for new teachers in high-needs areas. *Teaching and Teacher Education, 26*(3), 622–629.
Cefai, C. (2004). Pupil resilience in the classroom: A teacher's framework. *Emotional and Behavioural Difficulties, 9*(3), 149–170.
Day, C., & Gu, Q. (2010). *The new lives of teachers*. Abingdon: Routledge.
Day, C., & Gu, Q. (2014). *Resilient teachers, resilient schools: Building and sustaining quality in testing times*. Abingdon: Routledge.
Day, C., & Hong, J. (2016). Influences on the capacities for emotional resilience of teachers in schools serving disadvantaged urban communities: Challenges of living on the edge. *Teaching and Teacher Education, 59*, 115–125.
Day, C., & Leithwood, K. (Eds.). (2007). *Successful principal leadership in times of change: An international perspective*. Dordrecht: Springer.
Day, C., Sammons, P., Stobart, G., Kington, A., & Gu, Q. (2007). *Teachers matter: Connecting lives, work and effectiveness*. Maidenhead: Open University Press.
Day, C., Sammons, P., & Gu, Q. (2008). Combining qualitative and quantitative methodologies in research on teachers' lives, work, and effectiveness: From integration to synergy. *Educational Researcher, 37*(6), 330–342.
Day, C., Sammons, P., Leithwood, K., Hopkins, D., Gu, Q., Brown, E., & Ahtaridou, E. (2011). *School leadership and student outcomes: Building and sustaining success*. Maidenhead: Open University Press.
Deal, T. E., & Peterson, K. D. (2009). *Shaping school culture* (2nd ed.). San Francisco: Jossey-Bass.
DuMont, K. A., Ehrhard-Dietzel, S., & Kirkland, K. (2012). Averting child maltreatment: Individual, economic, social and community resources that promote resilient parenting. In M. Ungar (Ed.), *The social ecology of resilience: A handbook for theory and practice* (pp. 199–217). New York: Springer.
Dunford, J. (2016). *The school leadership journey*. London: John Catt Educational Ltd..
Edwards, A. (2010). *Being an expert professional practitioner: The relational turn in expertise*. Dordrecht: Springer.
Edwards, A. (2011). *Position statement on resilience*. Retrieved on July 3, 2016, from http://slideplayer.com/slide/4843373/
European Commission. (2012). *Key data on education in Europe 2012*. Brussels: Education, Audiovisual and Culture Executive Agency.
Fullan, M. (2003). *The moral imperatives of school leadership*. Thousand Oaks: Corwin Press.
Gamoran, A. (2012). Improving teacher quality. In S. Kelly (Ed.), *Assessing teacher quality: Understanding teacher effects on instruction and achievement* (pp. 201–214). New York: Teachers College Press.
Garmezy, N., & Rutter, M. (1983). *Stress, coping and development in children*. New York: McGraw-Hill.
Goldhaber, D., & Hansen, M. (2009). National board certification and teachers' career paths: Does NBPTS certification influence how long teachers remain in the profession and where they teach? *Education Finance and Policy, 4*(3), 229–262.
Goodlad, J. (2004). *A place called school*. New York: McGraw-Hill.
Gordon, K. A., Longo, M., & Trickett, M. (2000). *Fostering resilience in children*. The Ohio State University Bulletin 875–99. http://ohioline.osu.edu/b875
Gu, Q. (2014). The role of resilience in teachers' career long commitment and effectiveness. *Teachers and Teaching: Theory and Practice, 20*(5), 502–529.
Gu, Q., & Day, C. (2007). Teachers resilience: A necessary condition for effectiveness. *Teaching and Teacher Education, 23*, 1302–1316.
Gu, Q., & Day, C. (2013). Challenges to teacher resilience: Conditions count. *British Educational Research Journal, 39*(1), 22–44.
Gu, Q., & Johansson, O. (2013). Sustaining school performance: School contexts matter. *International Journal of Leadership in Education, 16*(3), 301–326.

Gu, Q., & Li, Q. (2013). Sustaining resilience in times of change: Stories from Chinese teachers. *Special Issue of Asia-Pacific Journal of Teacher Education, 41*(3), 288–303.

Gu, Q., Sammons, P., & Mehta, P. (2008). Leadership characteristics and practices in schools with different effectiveness and improvement profiles. *School Leadership & Management, 28*(1), 43–63.

Gu, Q., Rea, S., Smethem, L., Dunford, J., Varley, M., Sammons, P., Parish, N., Armstrong, P., & Powerll, L. (2016). *Teaching schools evaluation: Final report*. London: Department for Education.

Guarino, C. M., Santibanez, L., & Daley, G. A. (2006). Teacher recruitment and retention: A review of the recent empirical literature. *Review of Educational Research, 76*(2), 173–208.

Hamel, G., & Välikangas, L. (2003). The quest for resilience. *Harvard Business Review, 81*, 52.

Hansen, D. T. (1995). *The call to teach*. New York: Teachers College Press.

Hargreaves, A. (2003). *Teaching in the knowledge society*. New York: Teachers College Press.

Hargreaves, D. (2014). A self-improving school system and its potential for reducing inequality. *Oxford Review of Education, 40*(6), 696–714.

Hargreaves, A., & Fullan, M. (2012). *Professional capital: Transforming teaching in every school*. New York: Teachers College Press.

Hattie, J. A. C. (2009). *Visible learning: A synthesis of over 800 meta-analyses relating to achievement*. London: Routledge.

Hong, J. Y. (2012). Why do some beginning teachers leave the school, and others stay? Understanding teacher resilience through psychological lenses. *Teachers and Teaching: Theory and Practice, 18*(4), 417–440.

Howard, S., Dryden, J., & Johnson, B. (1999). Childhood resilience: Review and critique of literature. *Oxford Review of Education, 25*(3), 307–323.

Huberman, M. (1993). *The lives of teachers*. London: Cassell.

Ingersoll, R. M. (2001). Teacher turnover and teacher shortages: An organizational analysis. *American Educational Research Journal, 38*(3), 499–534.

Ingersoll, R. (2011). Power, accountability, and the teacher quality problem. In S. Kelly (Ed.), *Assessing teacher quality: Understanding teacher effects on instruction and achievement* (pp. 97–109). New York: Teachers College Press.

Johnson, S. M. (2004). *Finders and Keepers*. Cambridge, MA: Harvard Education Press.

Johnson, B., & Down, B. (2013). Critically re-conceptualising early career teacher resilience. *Discourse: Studies in the Cultural Politics of Education, 34*(5), 703–715.

Johnson, B., Down, B., Cornu, R., Peters, J., Sullivan, A., Pearce, J., & Hunter, J. (2016). *Promoting early career teacher resilience*. New York: Routledge.

Jordan, J. (1992) *Relational resilience*. Paper presented on April 1st, 1992 as part of the Stone Centre Colloquium Series.

Jordan, J. (2004). Relational resilience. In J. Jordan & M. Walker (Eds.), *The complexity of connection: Writings from the Stone Center's Jean Baker Miller Training Institute* (pp. 28–46). New York: Gildford Press.

Jordan, J. (2006). Relational resilience in girls. In S. Goldstein & R. B. Brooks (Eds.), *Handbook of resilience in children* (pp. 79–90). New York: Springer.

Jordan, J. (2012). Relational resilience in girls. In S. Goldstein & R. B. Brooks (Eds.), *Handbook of resilience in children* (2nd ed., pp. 73–86). New York: Springer.

Kelley, C. (1999). The motivational impact of school-based performance awards. *Journal of Personnel Evaluation in Education, 12*, 309–326.

Kitching, K., Morgan, M., & O'Leary, M. (2009). It's the little things: Exploring the importance of commonplace events for early-career teachers' motivation. *Teachers and Teaching: Theory and Practice, 15*(1), 43–58.

Knoop, H. H. (2007). Control and responsibility. In H. Gardener (Ed.), *Responsibility at work*. San Francisco: Jossey-Bass.

Leithwood, K., Day, C., Sammons, P., Harris, A., & Hopkins, D. (2006). *Seven strong claims about successful school leadership*. Nottingham: National College for School Leadership.

Leithwood, K., Harris, A., & Strauss, T. (2010). *Leading school turnaround*. San Francisco: Jossey-Bass.

Lerner, R. M. (1996). Relative plasticity, integration, temporality, and diversity in human development: A developmental contextual perspective about theory, process, and method. *Developmental Psychology, 32*(4), 781–786.

Lerner, R. M. (2005). Forward: Urie Bronfenbrenner: Career contributions of the consummate developmental scientist. In U. Bronfenbrenner (Ed.), *Making human beings human: Bioecological perspectives on human development* (pp. viii–xxvi). Thousand Oaks: Sage.

Loeb, S., Darling-Hammond, L., & Luczak, J. (2005). How teaching conditions predict teacher turnover in California schools. *Peabody Journal of Education, 80*(3), 44–70.

Luthar, S., & Brown, P. (2007). Maximizing resilience through diverse levels of inquiry: Prevailing paradigms, possibilities, and priorities for the future. *Development and Psychopathology, 19*, 931–955.

Luthar, S., Cicchetti, D., & Becker, B. (2000). The construct of resilience: A critical evaluation and guidelines for future work. *Child Development, 71*(3), 543–562.

Mansfield, C. F., Beltman, S., Price, A., & McConney, A. (2012). "Don't sweat the small stuff:" Understanding teacher resilience at the chalkface. *Teaching and Teacher Education, 28*, 357–367.

Marsh, J., Springer, M. G., McCaffrey, D. F., Yuan, K., Epstein, S., Koppich, J., Kalra, N., DiMartino, C., & Peng, A. (2011). *A big apple for educators: New York City's experiment with schoolwide performance bonuses*. Santa Monica: RAND. MG-1114-FPS.

Masten, A. S. (2001). Ordinary magic: Resilience processes in development. *American Psychologist, 56*(3), 227–238.

Masten, A. S., Hubbard, J. J., Gest, S. D., Tellegen, A., Garmezy, N., & Ramirez, M. (1999). Adaptation in the context of adversity: Pathways to resilience and maladaptation from childhood to late adolescence. *Development and Psychopathology, 11*, 143–169.

Meister, D. G., & Ahrens, P. (2011). Resisting plateauing: Four veteran teachers' stories. *Teaching and Teacher Education, 27*, 770–778.

Mintrop, H., & Sunderman, G. (2013). The paradoxes of data-driven school reform. In D. Anagnostopoulos, S. Rutledge, & R. Jacobsen (Eds.), *The infrastructure of accountability: Data use and the transformation of American education* (pp. 23–40). Cambridge, MA: Harvard Education Press.

Morgan, M., Ludlow, L., Kitching, K., O'Leary, M., & Clarke, A. (2010). What makes teachers tick? Sustaining events in new teachers' lives. *British Educational Research Journal, 36*(2), 191–208.

Neenan, M. (2009). *Developing resilience*. Hove: Routledge.

Nias, J. (1999). Teachers' moral purposes: Stress, vulnerability, and strength. In R. Vandenberghe & A. M. Huberman (Eds.), *Understanding and preventing teacher burnout: A sourcebook of international research and practice* (pp. 223–237). Cambridge: Cambridge University Press.

Nieto, S. (2003). *What keeps teachers going?* New York: Teachers College Press.

Nieto, S. (Ed.). (2015). *Why we teaching now*. New York: Teachers College Press.

O'Connell Higgins, G. (1994). *Resilient adults: Overcoming a cruel past*. San Francisco: Jossey-Bass.

OECD. (2008). *Improving school leadership*. Paris: OECD.

OECD. (2010). *Education today: The OECD perspective*. Paris: OECD.

OECD. (2012). *Education today*. Paris: OECD Publishing.

OECD. (2016a). *International migration outlook 2016*. Paris: OECD Publishing.

OECD. (2016b). *Education at a glance: OECD indicators*. Paris: OECD Publishing.

Palmer, P. J. (2007). *The courage to teach: Exploring the inner landscape of a teachers' life*. San Francisco: Jossey-Bass.

Patterson, J., & Kelleher, P. (2005). *Resilient school leaders: Strategies for turning adversity into achievement*. Alexandria: Association for Supervision and Curriculum Development.

Robinson, V., Hohepa, M., & Lloyd, C. (2009). *School leadership and student outcomes: Identifying what works and why*. New Zealand: Best Evidence Syntheses Iteration (BES), Ministry of Education. Available from http://educationcounts.govt.nz/goto/BES.

Rose, M. (2010). Afterward. In W. Ayers (Ed.), *To teach: The journey of a teacher* (pp. 167–169). New York: Teachers College Press.

Rutter, M. (1990). Psychosocial resilience and protective mechanisms. In J. Rolf, A. Masten, D. Cicchetti, K. Neuchterlein, & S. Weintraub (Eds.), *Risk and protective factors in the development of psychopathology*. New York: Cambridge University Press.

Sameroff, A. J. (2010). A unified theory of development: A dialectic integration of nature and nurture. *Child Development, 8*(1), 6–22.

Sammons, P., Day, C., Kington, A., Gu, Q., Stobart, G., & Smees, R. (2007). Exploring variations in teachers' work, lives and their effects on pupils: Key findings and implications from a longitudinal mixed-method study. *British Educational Research Journal, 33*(5), 681–701.

Sammons, P., Gu, Q., Day, C., & Ko, J. (2011). Exploring the impact of school leadership on pupil outcomes. *International Journal of Educational Management, 25*(1), 83–101.

Schoon, I. (2012). Temporal and contextual dimensions to individual positive development: A developmental-contextual systems model of resilience. In M. Ungar (Ed.), *The social ecology of resilience: A handbook of theory and practice* (pp. 143–156). Dordrecht: Springer.

Soder, R. (2004). When I get my own classroom. In J. Goodlad & T. McMannon (Eds.), *The teaching career* (pp. 1–18). New York: Teachers College Press.

Tschannen-Morgan, M., & Barr, M. (2004). Fostering student learning: The relationship of collective teacher efficacy and student achievement. *Leadership and Policy in Schools, 3*(3), 189–209.

Tucker, M. (2011). *Surpassing Shanghai*. Harvard: Harvard Educational Publishing Group.

UNESCO. (2006). *Teachers and educational quality: Monitoring global needs for 2015*. Paris: UNESCO.

UNESCO. (2011). *The global demand for primary teachers – 2011 update*. Paris: UNESCO.

UNESCO. (2015). *EFA global monitoring report: Education for all 2000–2015: Achievements and challenges*. Paris: UNESCO.

UNESCO. (2016). *Global education monitoring report: Education for people and planet: Creating sustainable futures for all*. Paris: UNESCO.

Ungar, M. (2004). A constructionist discourse on resilience: Multiple contexts, multiple realities among at-risk children and youth. *Youth & Society, 35*, 341–365.

Ungar, M. (2008). Resilience across cultures. *British Journal of Social Work, 38*, 218–235.

Ungar, M. (2011). The social ecology of resilience: Addressing contextual and cultural ambiguity of a nascent construct. *American Journal of Orthopsychiatry, 81*(1), 1–17.

Ungar, M. (2012). Social ecologies and their contribution to resilience. In M. Ungar (Ed.), *The social ecology of resilience: A handbook of theory and practice* (pp. 13–32). Dordrecht: Springer.

Ungar, M., Ghazinour, M., & Richter, J. (2013). Annual research review: What is resilience within the social ecology of human development? *Journal of Child Psychology and Psychiatry, 54*(4), 348–366.

Webb, R., Vulliamy, G., Hämäläinen, S., Sarja, A., Kimonen, E., & Nevalainen, R. (2004). Pressures, rewards and teacher retention: A comparative study of primary teaching in England and Finland. *Scandinavian Journal of Educational Research, 48*(2), 169–188.

Wyman, P. A. (2003). Emerging perspectives on context specificity of children's adaptation and resilience: Evidence from a decade of research with urban children in adversity. In S. S. Luthar (Ed.), *Resilience and vulnerability: Adaptation in the context of childhood adversities* (pp. 293–317). Cambridge, UK: Cambridge University Press.

Yuan, K., Le, V., McCaffrey, D., Marsh, J., Hamilton, L., Stecher, B., & Springer, M. (2013). Incentive pay programs do not affect teacher motivation or reported practices: Results from three randomized studies. *Educational Evaluation and Policy Analysis, 35*(1), 3–22.

Chapter 3
How Does Apprentice Resilience Work?

Jennifer Schwarze and Marold Wosnitza

Abstract Researchers in the field of educational sciences have realised the necessity to understand and enhance resilience in educational settings in order to improve the quality of life for all persons involved in educational processes and consequently improve learning processes. Various definitions and conceptualisations of resilience exist (e.g., on teachers or college students); however, despite evidence of alarming high dropout rates and occupational stress in some apprentice occupations, a dearth of research exists with regard to their resilience. This chapter aims to contribute to resilience research by first presenting, based on appraisal theory, a generic process model of resilience, which is influenced by internal and external resources. This process is embedded in a context model, as context and resilience processes are interrelated, further creating specific resilience processes. The generic model is applied to the German vocational education context using a specific case from research in a vocational setting.

Although it is problematic to identify exact dropout rates in vocational education (Althoff 2002; Beicht and Walden 2013), they can be estimated to be 16% for the dual vocational education system in Germany on the basis of the numbers on early contract dissolutions (Uhly 2014). These numbers are not as high as dropout rates in German universities with 28% (Heublein et al. 2014), but not less alarming, considering that dropping out of an apprenticeship might result in a "personal tragedy" (Frey et al. 2014, p. 131), that may impact on career opportunities in the future.

J. Schwarze (✉)
RWTH Aachen University, Aachen, Germany
e-mail: jennifer.schwarze@rwth-aachen.de

M. Wosnitza
Institute of Education, RWTH Aachen University, Aachen, Germany

School of Education, Murdoch University, Perth, WA, Australia
e-mail: marold.wosnitza@rwth-aachen.de

M. Wosnitza et al. (eds.), *Resilience in Education*,
https://doi.org/10.1007/978-3-319-76690-4_3

Moreover, a survey study with more than 18,000 German apprentices about their job conditions and satisfaction found that 30% of the participants were not satisfied with their apprenticeship and experienced increased stress levels due to various reasons (e.g., doing overtime or too high or too low demands in their apprenticeship (DGB-Bundesvorstand 2015)). Such dissatisfaction and perceived stress are reasons for early contract dissolutions and consequently might lead to dropping out of the apprenticeship altogether (Schöngen 2003).

One factor, amongst others, that has been found to enhance academic achievement, help to handle stress and dissatisfaction and prevent dropout in various educational settings, is resilience (e.g., Allan et al. 2013; Huang and Lin 2013; Mansfield et al. 2012). Specifically, in the vocational educational setting, Brahm and Euler (2013) emphasise the importance of resilience in the school-to-work transition process. In addition, an intervention study to enhance the resilience of adolescents, who were rejected for apprenticeships at the initial stage of application, points to the importance of motivational aspects, such as goal orientation and attributional style, during the application process (Oser et al. 2004).

But beside these limited insights, resilience research in vocational education is scarce, and there exists no general understanding or conceptualisation of resilience of apprentices. Thus, it seems necessary to further examine resilience in the vocational setting and to provide a model of resilience that can be adapted to the situation of apprentices and that is grounded in the literature. This chapter follows two assumptions: firstly, that the underlying principles of resilience are generic. Consequently, the presented model builds on a wide range of literature on resilience (including the literature of well-researched professions in the educational field like teacher resilience), without limiting it to the scarce literature on resilience in vocational educational settings. Secondly, whilst the underlying principles are generic, the context is specific, meaning that external conditions are different. Therefore, this chapter discusses and presents a generic process model of resilience, which then is specified and adapted to the vocational setting.

Generic Model of Resilience

Definitions and conceptualisations of resilience vary considerably, depending on the area of research and on the perspectives taken (Hanewald 2011; Windle 2010). The definition of resilience, which serves as a starting point for this conceptualisation, originates from the beginnings of resilience research. Masten et al. (1990) define resilience as "process of, capacity for or outcome of successful adaptation despite challenging or threatening circumstances" (p. 425). This definition includes four aspects, namely, antecedents, resilience as a process, capacities or personal resources and resilience as outcome. Although in this definition resilience is seen as either capacity for *or* outcome of successful adaptation, other authors (e.g., Mansfield et al. 2016) conceptualise resilience as both capacity for *and* outcome of successful adaption. Besides this more general perspective on resilience, more recent research tends to understand resilience as being situational, which means that the resilience process depends on the specific situation and whether it is perceived as stressful or not, and multidimensional, which means that various dimensions form and influence the process, such as motivational, emotional, professional and social aspects (Beltman et al. 2011; Bengel and Lyssenko 2012; Friborg et al. 2003; Luthar et al. 2000). Furthermore, researchers started to acknowledge the importance of contextual factors for resilience (e.g. Ungar 2011). In this conceptualisation of resilience, context is seen as the factor that differentiates resilience processes from one another and therefore is integrated in the model.

Following this line of argument, a generic model of resilience should comprise at least the following elements:

1. Antecedents
2. A process, depending on internal (capacities) and external resources
3. The positive or resilient outcome
4. Contextual aspects

In the model of resilience presented here, the second element of the model is conceptualised as an *appraisal process*, to address the subjectivity of stressful events or situations. Additionally, a *point of reference*, which is relative to the outcome, is introduced, addressing the question of what is a good, i.e. a positive or resilient, outcome.

In the following, such a generic model of resilience will be described in detail. A graphical representation of this model is presented in Fig. 3.1.

Antecedents of Resilience

Using Perrez et al. (2005) categorisation of stressors, o*ccurring events or antecedents* (Windle 2010) might range from micro-stressors, which are the daily hassles (Day and Gu 2007; Kitching et al. 2009) to major or traumatic life events, such as loss of significant others (Bonanno 2004) to chronic stressors or risk factors, which are either continuing conditions or situations or recurring events, such as parental psychopathology (Werner 1994) or chronic poverty (Ebersöhn 2014).

If such an event or situation occurs, individuals react or perceive them differently (Bengel and Lyssenko 2012; Lazarus and Folkman 1984). What is stressful for one individual may not necessarily be stressful for another.

The Appraisal Process

In order to explain differences in the *appraisal process*, Lazarus' and Folkman's appraisal theory (Lazarus and Folkman 1984) serves as a useful theoretical framework. According to Lazarus, cognitive appraisal is "the process of categorizing an

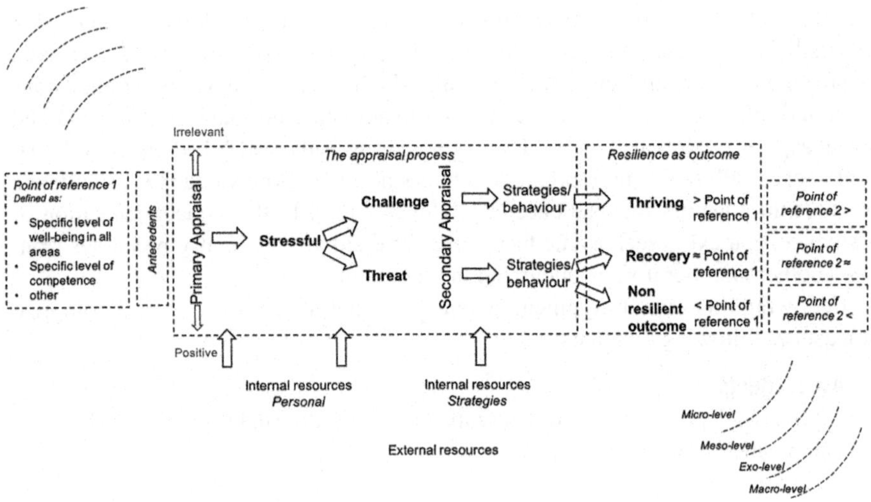

Fig. 3.1 Generic model of the resilience process in context
The resilience process is conceptualised on basis of Lazarus' (1984) appraisal theory and is influenced by internal and external resources. Each box symbolises one necessary element of the resilience process. The horizontal arrows display the development of resilience, whereas the vertical arrows represent the influence of internal and external resources on the process. The broken lines symbolise the interaction of the elements. The point of reference 2 might be above, equal or below the point of reference 1, depending on the outcome. The curves on the bottom right and upper left indicate the interrelation of the process with context

encounter, and its various facets, with respect to its significance for well-being" (Lazarus and Folkman 1984, p. 31). In a primary appraisal, the person identifies a situation or an encounter and its implications as either irrelevant with regard to her/his well-being or as benign-positive or stressful. Since the precondition for a resilience process is the existence of adversity, the appraisal of a situation or event as stressful is the necessary precondition (Ebersöhn 2014).

Depending on the primary appraisal of the event or situation as stressful or not, the individual will decide, in the phase of secondary appraisal, how to handle the situation, which strategies to adapt and which behaviour to display and in the last step, the individual reappraises the situation (Lazarus and Folkman 1984). A positive conscious or unconscious reappraisal precedes a resilient outcome.

Internal Resources

The focus on internal resources or resilient qualities forms part of the first wave of resilience research (Richardson 2002). Rutter (1990) states that resilience "describes the positive pole of the ubiquitous phenomenon of individual differences in people's responses to stress and adversity" (p. 181). These individual differences arise from differences in certain internal (and external – see below) protective factors or resources that help people when faced with stressful events to handle the situation in a resilient way.

With regard to the appraisal process, these internal resources consist, on the one hand, of personal resources and on the other hand of strategies used to handle the antecedent (Mansfield et al. 2016). Regarding the personal resources, resilience research gives evidence for the importance of positive emotions and motivational aspects, as well as personality traits (e.g., Bengel and Lyssenko 2012), which forms the first column of resources in this process. Although resilience is not conceptualised as a personal trait per se, studies have shown a correlation between personality (Costa and McCrae 1992) and resilience. Hjemdal (2007) and Campbell-Sills et al. (2006), for instance, found that neuroticism, extraversion and consciousness contribute significantly to the prediction of resilience, whereas neuroticism is inverse to resilience. Another trait associated with resilience is optimism. An optimistic person, in general, expects a good outcome, which also is associated with the use of adaptive coping strategies (Carver et al. 2010). Also, other studies give evidence of the importance of self-efficacy or, in case of teacher resilience, teacher efficacy, (e.g., Peixoto et al. 2018, Chap. 5, this volume; Tait 2008; Tschannen-Moran and Woolfolk Hoy 2001). Further factors associated with resilience are amongst others: an internal locus of control and a positive self-concept (Skodol 2010). For a review of protective factors in adolescent resilience, see Olsson et al. (2003), and for teacher resilience, see Mansfield et al. (2016).

The second column of the internal resources consists of coping strategies, which are adaptive strategies and behaviour used to regain equilibrium after stressful occurrences (Perrez et al. 2005). Both constructs, resilience and coping, are related (Campbell-Sills et al. 2006). In this chapter, coping is understood as a sub-construct of resilience (e.g., Connor and Davidson 2003), i.e. coping is one factor amongst others.

External Resources and Context

Context plays an ambivalent role in the conceptualisation of resilience. On the one hand, context might provide external resources; on the other hand, context might contribute to creating adverse situations or events and therefore influences the process.

As a framework for the context of resilience and the interplay between the individual and contextual aspects, an adaptation of Bronfenbrenner's (1979) ecological context model is used, as is also proposed and used by, e.g. Gu (2018, Chap. 2, this volume), Mansfield et al. (2012), Mansfield et al. (2018, Chap. 4, this volume), Peixoto et al. (2018, Chap. 5, this volume), Schoon (2006) and Ungar (2011). The process of resilience explained above is located on the micro-level of the ecological context model and interacts with meso-, exo- and macro-systems. Schoon (2006) outlines in her context model (p. 25) – from proximal to distal effect – individual, family, neighbourhoods, institutions and sociohistorical and cultural context as influencing spheres of individual adjustment. As for the external resources, the most important ones are located more proximal to the individual on the meso-level, namely, supportive networks. Werner (2000) names teachers as role models or mentors as protective factor and stresses the important role of friends and supportive family members.

Evidence for the importance of external resources can also be found in the well-researched area of teacher resilience. Examples from these areas are the importance of supportive relationships in the working context as an important external resource for (pre-service) teachers (Ebersöhn 2012; Le Cornu 2009). Papatraianou and Le Cornu (2014) stress the importance not only of professional relationships but especially personal relationships as a resource that enhances pre-service teachers' resilience. For an overview on external resources, see Mansfield et al. (2016).

The Positive or Resilient Outcome and Reference Point

Regarding the *outcome*, the questions that rise and are also discussed in the literature are firstly, "What is a positive or resilient outcome?" and, secondly, "In comparison to what measure?" (Masten 2001; Windle 2010). In recognition of these questions, the model introduces a *reference point*, which is the subjective point of well-being and competence relevant to the situation at a specific point in time before the occurrence of the antecedent. The outcome is conceptualised as being relative to the reference point, whereas an outcome that is either higher than the reference point or relatively equal to the reference point is a resilient outcome. If well-being or competence is subjectively lower as the reference point, the outcome is considered to be a non-resilient outcome.

A potentially stressful situation or event – the antecedent – could be perceived as threat or challenge. The difference between threat and challenge is that "challenge appraisals focus on the potential for gain or growth inherent in the encounter" (Lazarus and Folkman 1984, p. 33). This growth or thriving is described in resilience research as a possible outcome of being or behaving resilient (Beltman et al. 2011) or in the logic of the model as an outcome in which the level of well-being and competence relevant for the experienced situation or event is higher than the reference point. Since a threat does not include the positive perspective of challenge, the outcome of an event appraised as threat is conceptualised as recovery or "bouncing back", which means the returning to a positive level of well-being after a temporary decline (Masten and O'Dougherty Wright 2010). In the logic of the model, recovery means that the level of well-being and competence relevant for the experienced situation in the outcome is relatively equal to the reference point and is therefore considered as a positive outcome of the resilience process.

This outcome in turn can serve to further influence a future point of reference and future resilience processes. This also means that, e.g. in the case of thriving, the future point of reference, like the outcome, might be higher than the initial point of reference.

Conceptualising Apprentice Resilience

The German Dual Vocational System and Context

As discussed above, the basic assumption is that the generic model is adaptable to any context, setting or target group. Because of its particular context and the need to further investigate resilience in vocational education, the generic model is adapted to German vocational settings, in which apprentices learn their occupation in the dual vocational education system, i.e. the individual learns in two learning places, namely, vocational school and the workplace. Specifically, an apprenticeship[1] trainee spends 3–4 days a week at the workplace, where she/he gains practical knowledge and skills and the rest of the time she/he spends in vocational schools, where she/he gains theoretical knowledge related to her/his work. Both contents are matched by the curriculum by Berufsbildungsgesetz (BBiG) (2005). The dual vocational education system is, using the model explained above, found on the macro-level (see Fig. 3.2), along with economy and culture as major aspects. In some other vocational careers which are mainly based in the finance sector and administrative occupations, apprentices attend university instead of vocational schools and, after completion of their training, receive a bachelor's degree. However, in both approaches, learning takes place in two learning places, namely, one for practical knowledge and one for theoretical background, as can be seen in Fig. 3.2 on the meso-level. The particularity of the dual vocational educational system lies in the fact that the individual is part of two contexts, school and workplace, within the broader apprenticeship context.

The impact of context is twofold. On the one hand, it may form antecedents of resilience, and by shaping these, contextual aspects create a specific apprentice resilience process. Specific antecedents, such as low payment or a high workload due to the two learning places, workplace and school (e.g. over hours at work and exams in school in 1 week), are located on the macro-level. On the other hand, context might also provide potential external resources. The interrelations of individual and contextual factors create specific individual external resources, e.g. supportive colleague, superiors and/or classmates and teachers. Such resources are located on the meso-level of the used model. Internal resources, located in the individual and hence on the micro-level, might also be influenced by more distal contextual factors, like having an economically stable family background.

A personal area, with friends and family as influential aspects on the meso-level and their networks on the exo-level, is also included in the contextual model, as these are relevant for the resilience process (see below, External Resources). The context of vocational education in Germany and the most influential factors

[1] In Germany, trainees absolve an apprenticeship in branches such as construction or plumbing, which holds true for other international contexts as well, but also for sales, nursing, administrative positions, etc. The words *trainee* and *apprentice* are used synonymously in this chapter.

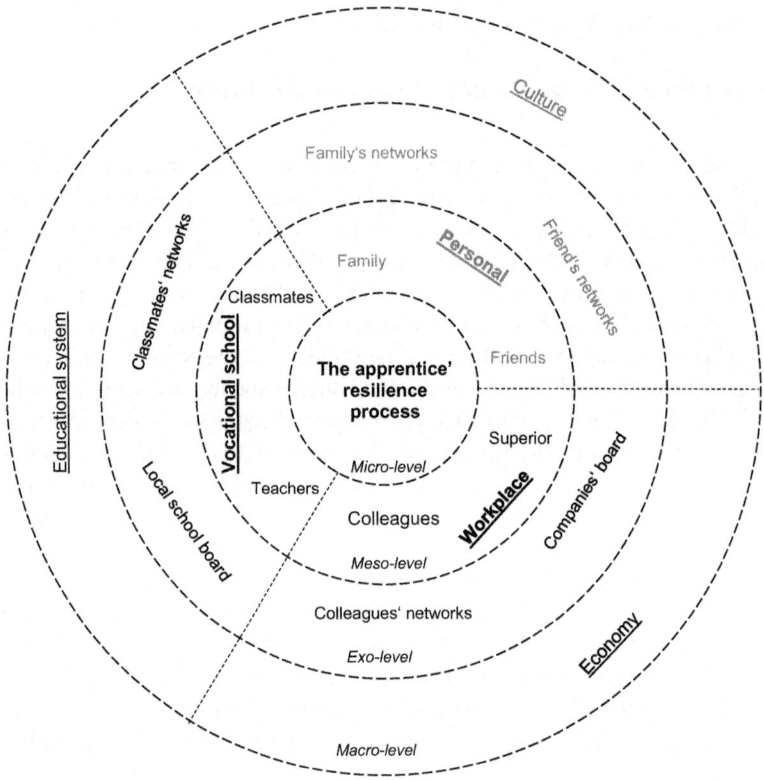

Fig. 3.2 Context model of apprentice resilience
The figure displays the contextual aspects of the resilience process (for details see Fig. 3.1) of an apprentice. Vocational school and workplace, forming the dual system, are the settings that specifically shape apprentice resilience. The personal setting is included in grey, as it influences resilience processes in general, but is not specific to the apprenticeship. Levels and settings interact and are interrelated, indicated by the broken lines. Examples of influencing factors on each level are given (Adapted from Mansfield et al. 2014)

regarding the apprenticeship, using the afore-presented ecological framework model as a basis, are displayed in Fig. 3.2.

Data from one interview, which was conducted in the course of an interview study on challenges they face in their apprenticeships with 24 German apprentices (41.7% female; 58.3% male; age, M, 21.8; SD, 2.9) from various branches, are used as an example to illustrate the whole resilience process in the apprenticeship context. This interview is chosen as an example, because the interviewee wanted to leave the apprenticeship at one point but in the end stayed. This illustrates the main question of resilience in educational settings: what makes people stay despite perceived adversity? The interviewee is a male, is 18 years old and is in his first year of an apprenticeship as specialist of warehouse logistics.

Antecedents of Apprentice Resilience

In the generic conceptualisation of resilience, the antecedents range from trauma to daily hassles. As this chapter focuses on resilience of apprentices, the antecedents are defined as the daily events or the micro-stressors (Perrez et al. 2005) in the two learning places that are perceived as stressful. An apprentice might additionally be exposed to other risk factors, e.g. the loss of a loved one. This antecedent would cause another resilience process that might run parallel to the resilience process in the apprenticeship context and would also influence it. However, it would not be specific to the apprenticeship context.

The resilience process of the interviewee, chosen to illustrate the adaptation of the generic model to the apprenticeship contexts, begins with the antecedent of repeatedly being bossed around by a co-worker, which is located on the meso-level of the contextual model. The specific aspect of the apprenticeship context is the implicit hierarchical structure, as "in the end, I'm just the apprentice". He describes the problematic event as follows: […] A colleague, we don't get along too well […] he is a normal worker and bosses me around […] and once for example, I was working on the forklift truck and talking briefly to a colleague, he said "please come here" and then I said "one moment, please, I'll be right there" and then he suddenly screamed "when I say you come here now, you must come here instantly" #5.[2]

This occurs "more often. Well, very, very often. Nearly every day" #5. This problem, namely, the repeated feeling of not being respected and being bossed around, is a typical example of micro-stressors, as defined by Bengel and Lyssenko (2012) and which turns here into a situation. The antecedent here is not a singular event, where the apprentice is bossed around, but the situation of constantly being disrespected by one colleague.

This problem, the apprentice has to face in his daily working life and which threatens the apprentices' well-being or competence, is in accordance with findings in the literature on stress and dropout of apprentices and is considered to be typical antecedents of the apprentice resilience processes (e.g., Beicht and Walden 2013; DGB 2015; Schöngen 2003).

Apprentice Appraisal Process

Internal Resources

As outlined in the generic model, whether there are resilience processes or not depends on the cognitive appraisal of the event or situation as stressful, which in turn depends on the available resources. The research on resilience in the broader area of vocational education stresses the importance of motivational and affective aspects, such as self-efficacy, goal orientation and a positive attributional style (Oser

[2] The interviews were conducted in German. Translations of the quotes are provided by the authors.

et al. 2004). Motivational aspects were also named by the interviewee #5: "I've just chosen this [apprenticeship] [...] *It's fun there*. You know each other and as I said, it's a good atmosphere and *it's not that hard*, the apprenticeship". Also, when asked if he was confident to finish the apprenticeship successfully, he answered: "Yes, I think so. I hope so, too, but yes, I think it's not that hard. I could do it. Certainly. I hope so". These statements show that he is motivated and chose the apprenticeship, and there is an indication of self-efficacy.

When faced with the colleague, who would boss him around repeatedly, he appraised it as stressful "I was really annoyed because of him" and also thought about quitting "Yes, because of him, as well [...] and I thought 'Never mind, I just quit' you know". Furthermore, he stated to have a headache because of the colleague: "Headaches, a bit. It just really annoyed me. And I really got upset about him".

In the secondary appraisal, he chose different ways to deal with it. In the first instance, he chose to be calm: "I was quiet. I didn't say anything. I only said 'yes, ok'". He reappraised the situation, which had not improved, that is, he felt not being respected. When the same problem occurred again, he again appraised it as stressful and as threat, because the previously tried strategy has failed, but he chose another coping strategy to regain his well-being: "At some point I got louder a bit, and said: it's ok. Listen, I can do it, and I will do it, but say it normally. Calm down and don't scream. I don't scream at you neither [...] since then, it's better". #5 The reappraisal of the situation therefore is positive. So, the interviewee used emotion-focussed coping strategies (staying calm) and a problem-focussed coping strategy, namely, confronting the colleague. Problem-focussed strategies are those which actively engage with the problem in order to solve it, such as help-seeking and other problem-solving strategies (Werner 1993, 2000), whereas emotion-focussed strategies are used to manage the corresponding emotions, for example, by maintaining a healthy work-life balance, expressing negative emotions, turning to religion (Bengel and Lyssenko 2012) or acceptance of the situation or event (Carver et al. 2010).

In the literature, Oser et al. (2004) stress the importance of enhancing coping strategies, and Brahm and Euler (2013) include conflict management strategies in their intervention study with youths in the school-to-work transition, which, as the example shows, is also of importance *in the course of* the apprenticeship.

External Resources

As stated above, context is twofold. The resilience process is shaped by the interrelation of context and individual. This interrelation creates external resources, such as supportive networks, at the workplace and school as well as in the individual's private life. The apprentice named a "good atmosphere" and to get along well with colleagues and classmates a few times as an important external resource at work and in the classroom: "I think, we [the classmates] get along well, yeah, since the first day. We talked and laughed". Furthermore, the support of the family was highlighted: "Sometimes, I get upset about it at home. Then I say: I don't want to go there anymore and my parents say for example 'never mind, don't allow him to get yourself down' [...] and my girlfriend says the same". Additionally, he got support from a superior, referring to the colleague: "He said: 'he's a bit older and...you know, he's overworked. Don't listen to him'...yes, since then..." #5.

This is in accordance with results in the literature on male apprentices in construction during their school-to-work transition, where du Plessis et al. (2012) stress the importance of social networks and relationships as supportive resources both personally and in the workplace.

The Resilient Outcome and Reference Point

Regarding the outcome, the example cited shows a resilient outcome, as he regained his enjoyment of the apprenticeship. The former stressful situation is not stressful anymore: "It's fun [working with a colleague and friend] and it motivates me. And now I think: 'yeah, let him talk'" and "Now it's better" #5. In this case, the criteria for a resilient outcome in the point of reference are the level of enjoyment of the apprenticeship before the occurrence of the event, and the same state of well-being has been restored as evidenced by the absence of headaches. In the logic of the model, this outcome is regarded as recovery. For a schematic representation of the process using the example of apprentice #5, see Fig. 3.3.

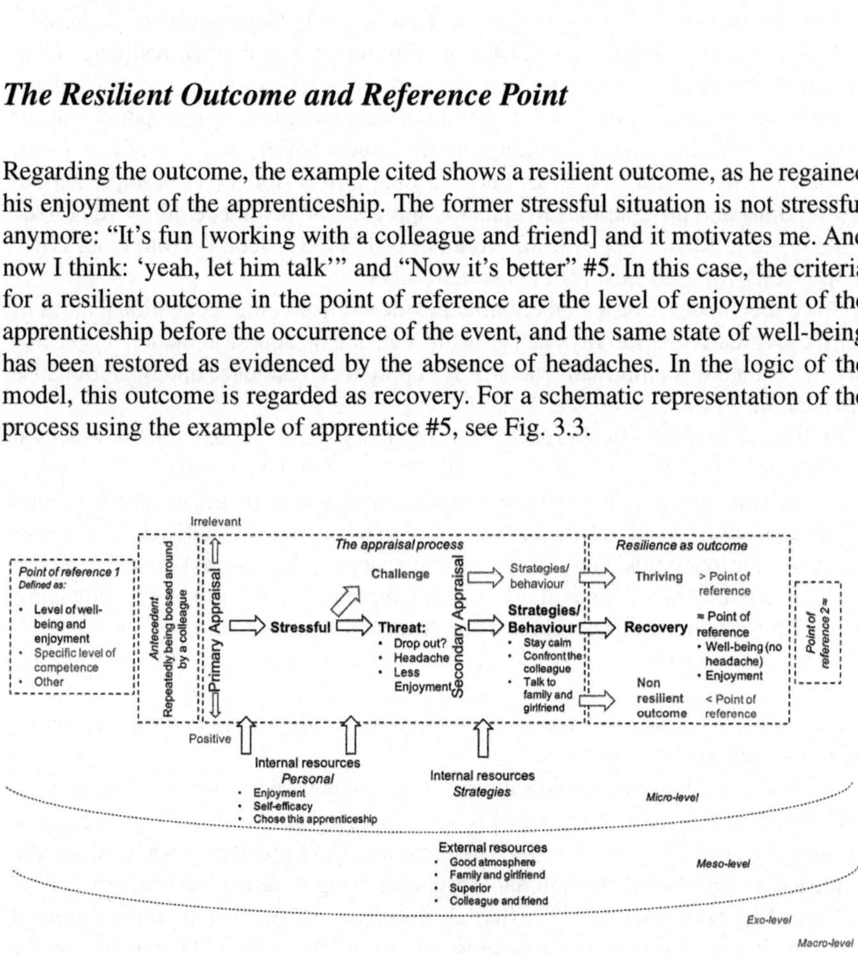

Fig. 3.3 Exemplary resilience process of one interviewed apprentice
The figure is a schematic representation of the interviewee's resilience process. Theoretically possible other ways are displayed in grey. The broken curves indicate the context levels (see Fig. 3.2)

Discussion

In addressing the question "what is apprentice resilience?", this chapter presented a generic model of resilience and then applied it to vocational settings. By doing so, the authors considered the necessity to include a starting point, which is defined by subjective elements, such as well-being and competence and conceptualised the actual resilience process as an appraisal process of occurrences in the vocational setting. This appraisal process is shaped by internal and external resources. The outcome of these processes is also seen as part of the resilience model and ranges from growing or thriving to a non-resilient outcome, relative to the starting point.

The aim of this conceptualisation is to present a holistic model of apprentice resilience, showing that contextual factors differentiate apprentice resilience from resilience of others, for example, student or teacher resilience, as the antecedents are different. Moreover, this model provides a clear structure for the operationalisation of resilience in vocational settings. If all elements of the model could be operationalised, this would serve to find starting points for more comprehensive interventions and programmes to enhance apprentices' resilience, like BRiTE (see Beltman et al. 2018, Chap. 14, this volume) or ENTREE (see Peixoto et al. 2018, Chap. 5, this volume) exist for beginning teachers.

Since this model is based on empirical evidence from other educational areas of resilience research, especially teacher resilience, and on appraisal theory, it is necessary to validate this empirical evidence for apprentice resilience and operationalise the theoretical basis.

In order to empirically approach the complexity of this model, a mixed-method research design is necessary. Using qualitative, longitudinal methods, such as the structured documentation of working days or diaries of apprentices, takes account of the subjectivity of the resilience process, including the antecedents and the outcome. In addition to this method, a quantitative approach is needed to further examine especially the role of internal resources of apprentices. The use of questionnaires allowed for a more accurate assessment of psychological constructs such as self-efficacy, motivation or personality. For this purpose, existing resilience measurements, such as the Connor-Davidson Resilience Scale (Connor and Davidson 2003) or the ENTREE instrument (Peixoto et al. 2018, Chap. 5, this volume), might be used in an adapted version.

With regard to the operationalisation of motivational aspects as part of the internal resources, it will be necessary to choose a theoretical framework, e.g. goal theory or attribution theory. Mansfield et al. (2016) found in their literature review on teacher resilience 35 studies on motivational aspects, all using different frameworks.

Regarding both internal and external resources, although it is a more general question, it would moreover be interesting to further explore the relation of the available resources. Are these resources additive, that is, the more the better, or are some resources qualitatively more important than others? As outlined above, evidence exists that some internal resources, for example, self-efficacy, seem to be more important in order to explain resilience (Peixoto et al. 2018, Chap. 5, this volume), but this result needs to be replicated for vocational settings and the specific antecedents. Such qualitative differences would have implications for choosing an appropriate starting point for possible interventions.

Although the model includes contextual factors and the interrelations between different levels, it does focus only on one instant at a time and does not examine the interplay of various stressful events and the following resilience processes in other levels than the micro-level in the apprenticeship context. This means that it excludes cases in which a "potentially traumatic event" (Bonanno 2004, p. 20), for example, loss of a loved one, occurs at the same time as a stressful event at the workplace and how these events interact and influence each other.

Another limitation of the adaptation of the model is that the antecedents of the apprentice resilience process in this chapter focus solely on German data and therefore may not hold true for other countries. For future research, it would be interesting to examine how far antecedents vary in different cultural contexts, especially focussing on the events that were localised on the more distal levels of the context model in this chapter.

A resilient outcome is conceptualised to be a new starting point for future stressful events, but again the model only functions as a snapshot of a certain situation in the life of an apprentice. According to this model, the whole span of the apprenticeship would be depicted as a series of resilience processes, whereas, for example, Bonanno et al. (2015) stress the importance of the temporal aspect of resilience.

A question of a more general nature is, whether apprentice resilience is distinct from, for instance, resilience in phases of transition, like school-to-work transition or school to university transition or college student resilience. Although the antecedents are specific to vocational settings, equivalents in other settings, for example, university, do exist. Too high demands occur in apprenticeships, as well as in university studies. The question is whether the resilience process and the available resources are generic or how much they differ or are specific in nature. Since the resilience model is generic, it would be possible to adapt it to university contexts and to complete comparative studies.

But not only the interplay of the resources needs to be further clarified, also the nature of the resources itself (Rutter 1990). For instance, poverty is regarded as risk factor or antecedent of resilience. But it might be that living in poverty forms the goal to do well in the apprenticeship to improve living conditions. This goal, to overcome poverty, would consequently turn into an internal resource in the apprentice resilience process. This process character of resilience over the lifespan is stressed by researchers who take a developmental perspective on resilience (e.g. Masten and O'Dougherty Wright 2010). Longitudinal studies on how facing adversity and building resilience in, for example, childhood influences, resilience processes in the vocational education context would be highly interesting.

Although this paper focuses on resilience in vocational settings to facilitate further research in this area and, in a second step, enhance apprentices' resilience, the questions raised above are not only relevant to apprentice resilience but aim at the very nature of resilience. Since this model of resilience is generic, it might be used in various settings to further investigate those questions. Consequently, it enhances theory development on resilience.

References

Allan, J. F., McKenna, J., & Dominey, S. (2013). Degrees of resilience: Profiling psychological resilience and prospective academic achievement in university inductees. *British Journal of Guidance and Counselling, 42*(1), 9–25. https://doi.org/10.1080/03069885.2013.793784.

Althoff, H. (2002). Vertragslösungen und Ausbildungsabbruch – Berechnung der Lösungsraten in der betrieblichen Berufsausbildung. [Contract dissolutions and dropout – Calculation of diccolution rates in vocational training]. *Berufsbildung in Wissenschaft und Praxis, 31*(3), 52–54.

Beicht, U., & Walden, G. (2013) *Duale Berufsausbildung ohne Abschluss: Ursachen und weiterer bildungsbiografischer Verlauf. Analyse auf Basis der BIBB-Übergangsstudie 2011* [Dual vocational education without certificate: Reasons and educational biography] (Vol. 21, BIBB Report – Forschungs- und Arbeitsergebnisse aus dem Bundesinstitut für Berufsbildung). Bonn: Bundesinstitut für Berufsbildung (BIBB).

Beltman, S., Mansfield, C. F., & Price, A. (2011). Thriving not just surviving: A review of research on teacher resilience. *Educational Research Review, 6*, 185–207. https://doi.org/10.1016/j.edurev.2011.09.001.

Beltman, S., Mansfield, C. F., Wosnitza, M., Weatherby-Fell, N., & Broadley, T. (2018). Using online modules to build capacity for teacher resilience. In M. Wosnitza, F. Peixoto, S. Beltman, & C. F. Mansfield (Eds.), *Resilience in education: Concepts, contexts and connections* (pp. 237–253). New York: Springer.

Bengel, J., & Lyssenko, L. (2012). *Resilienz und psychologische Schutzfaktoren im Erwachsenenalter: Stand der Forschung zu psychologischen Schutzfaktoren von Gesundheit im Erwachsenenalter* [Resilience and psychological protective factors: Status of research on psychological protective factors of health in adulthood]. Köln: BZgA.

Berufsbildungsgesetz (BBiG) [Law on vocational education]. (2005).

Bonanno, G. A. (2004). Loss, trauma, and human resilience: Have we underestimated the human capacity to thrive after extremely aversive events? *American Psychologist, 59*(1), 20–28. https://doi.org/10.1037/0003-066X.59.1.20.

Bonanno, G. A., Romero, S. A., & Klein, S. I. (2015). The temporal elements of psychological resilience: An integrative framework for the study of individuals, families, and communities. *Psychological Inquiry, 26*(2), 139–169. https://doi.org/10.1080/1047840X.2015.992677.

Brahm, T., & Euler, D. (2013). Resilienzförderung als Beitrag zur Persönlichkeitsentwicklung im Übergang in Ausbildung und Beruf. [Resilience support as a further goal of vocational education in the transition system]. *bwp@ Berufs- und Wirtschaftspädagogik – Online, 24*, 1–17. Retrieved from http://www.bwpat.de/ausgabe24/brahm_euler_bwpat24.pdf.

Bronfenbrenner, U. (1979). *The ecology of human development: Experiments by nature and design*. Cambridge, MA: Harvard University Press.

Campbell-Sills, L., Cohan, S. L., & Stein, M. B. (2006). Relationship of resilience to personality, coping, and psychiatric symptoms in young adults. *Behaviour Research and Therapy, 44*(4), 585–599. https://doi.org/10.1016/j.brat.2005.05.001.

Carver, C. S., Scheier, M. F., & Segerstrom, S. C. (2010). Optimism. *Clinical Psychology Review, 30*(7), 879–889. https://doi.org/10.1016/j.cpr.2010.01.006.

Connor, K. M., & Davidson, J. R. (2003). Development of a new resilience scale: The Connor-Davidson Resilience Scale (CD-RISC). *Depression and Anxiety, 18*(2), 76–82. https://doi.org/10.1002/da.10113.

Costa, P., & McCrae, R. R. (1992). Normal personality assessment in clinical practice. The NEO personality inventory. *Psychological Assessment, 4*(1), 5–13. Retrieved from http://www.researchgate.net/profile/Paul_Costa3/publication/232463584_Normal_Personality_Assessment_in_Clinical_Practice_The_NEO_Personality_Inventory/links/550ed48d0cf2ac2905ad119a.pdf.

Day, C., & Gu, Q. (2007). Variations in the conditions for teachers' professional learning and development: Sustaining commitment and effectiveness over a career. *Oxford Review of Education, 33*(4), 423–443.

DGB-Bundesvorstand, Abteilung Jugend und Jugendpolitik. (2015). *Ausbildungsreport 2015.* [Report on apprenticeships] Retrieved from http://jugend.dgb.de/meldungen/ausbildung/++co++17b94d5c-5148-11e5-8415-525400808b5c.

du Plessis, K., Corney, T., Broadbent, R., & Papadopoulos, T. (2012). Socio-emotional support of apprentices during the school-to-work transition. *Education + Training, 54*(5), 344–354. https://doi.org/10.1108/00400911211244650.

Ebersöhn, L. (2012). Adding 'flock' to 'fight and flight': A honeycomb of resilience where supply of relationships meets demand for support. *Journal of Psychology in Africa, 22*(1), 29–42. https://doi.org/10.1080/14330237.2012.10874518.

Ebersöhn, L. (2014). Teacher resilience: Theorizing resilience and poverty. *Teachers and Teaching, 20*(5), 568–594. https://doi.org/10.1080/13540602.2014.937960.

Frey, A., Balzer, L., & Ruppert, J.-J. (2014). Transferable competences of young people with a high dropout risk in vocational training in Germany. *International Journal of Educational and Vocational Guidance, 14*, 119–134. https://doi.org/10.1007/s10775-013-9257-8.

Friborg, O., Hjemdal, O., & Rosenvinge, M. (2003). A new rating scale for adult resiliency: What are the central protective resources behind healthy adjustment? *International Journal of Methods in Psychiatric Research, 12*(2), 65–76. https://doi.org/10.1002/mpr.143.

Gu, Q. (2018). (Re)conceptualizing teacher resilience: A social ecological approach to understanding teachers' professional worlds. In M. Wosnitza, F. Peixoto, S. Beltman, & C. F. Mansfield (Eds.), *Resilience in education: Concepts, contexts and connections* (pp. 13–33). New York: Springer.

Hanewald, R. (2011). Reviewing the literature on "at-risk" and resilient children and young people. *Australian Journal of Teacher Education, 36*(2), 16–29. https://doi.org/10.14221/ajte.2011v36n2.2.

Heublein, U., Richter, J., Schmelzer, R., & Sommer, D. (2014). Die Entwicklung der Studienabbruchquoten an den deutschen Hochschulen: Statistische Berechnungen auf der Basis des Absolventenjahrganges 2012 [Development of dropout rates in German universities: Statistic calculations on basis of the year of 2012]. *Forum Hochschule, 4*. Retrieved from http://www.dzhw.eu/pdf/pub_fh/fh-201404.pdf

Hjemdal, O. (2007). Measuring protective factors: The development of two resilience scales in Norway. *Child and Adolescent Psychiatric Clinics of North America, 16*(2), 303–321. https://doi.org/10.1016/j.chc.2006.12.003.

Huang, Y.-C., & Lin, S.-H. (2013). Development of the inventory of college students' resilience and evaluating the measurement invariance. *British Journal of Guidance and Counselling, 41*(5), 471–486. https://doi.org/10.1080/03069885.2012.749973.

Kitching, K., Morgan, M., & O'Leary, M. (2009). It's the little things: Exploring the importance of commonplace events for early-career teachers' motivation. *Teachers and Teaching: Theory and Practice, 15*(1), 43–58.

Lazarus, R. S., & Folkman, S. (1984). *Stress, appraisal, and coping*. New York: Springer Publishing Company LLC.

Le Cornu, R. (2009). Building resilience in pre-service teachers. *Teaching and Teacher Education, 25*(5), 717–723.

Luthar, S. S., Cicchetti, D., & Becker, B. (2000). The construct of resilience: A critical evaluation and guidelines for future work. *Child Development, 71*(3), 543–562.

Mansfield, C. F., Beltman, S., Price, A., & McConney, A. (2012). "Don't sweat the small stuff": Understanding teacher resilience at the chalkface. *Teaching and Teacher Education, 28*(3), 357–367. https://doi.org/10.1016/j.tate.2011.11.001.

Mansfield, C. F., Beltman, S., & Price, A. (2014). 'I'm coming back again!' The resilience process of early career teachers. *Teachers and Teaching, 20*(5), 547–567. https://doi.org/10.1080/13540602.2014.937958.

Mansfield, C. F., Beltman, S., Broadley, T., & Weatherby-Fell, N. (2016). Building resilience in teacher education: An evidenced informed framework. *Teaching and Teacher Education, 54*, 77–87. https://doi.org/10.1016/j.tate.2015.11.016.

Mansfield, C. F., Ebersöhn, L., Beltman, S., & Loots, T. (2018). Great Southern lands: Making space for teacher resilience in South Africa and Australia. In M. Wosnitza, F. Peixoto, S. Beltman, & C. F. Mansfield (Eds.), *Resilience in education: Concepts, contexts and connections* (pp. 53–71). New York: Springer.

Masten, A. S. (2001). Ordinary magic. Resilience processes in development. *American Psychologist, 56*, 227–238.

Masten, A. S., & O'Dougherty Wright, M. (2010). Resilience over the lifespan: Developmental perspectives on resistance, recovery, and transformation. In J. W. Reich, A. J. Zautra, & J. S. Hall (Eds.), *Handbook of adult resilience* (pp. 213–237). New York: Guilford Press.

Masten, A. S., Best, K. M., & Garmezy, N. (1990). Resilience and development: Contributions from the study of children who overcome adversity. *Development and Psychopathology, 2*(4), 425–444. https://doi.org/10.1017/S0954579400005812.

Olsson, C. A., Bond, L., Burns, J. M., Vella-Brodrick, D. A., & Sawyer, S. M. (2003). Adolescent resilience: A concept analysis. *Journal of Adolescence, 26*(1), 1–11. https://doi.org/10.1016/S0140-1971(02)00118-5.

Oser, F., Gamboni, E., Düggeli, A., & Masdonati, J. (2004). *Die Zeitbombe des "dummen" Schülers: Eine Interventionsstudie zur Erhöhung von Resilienz bei drohender oder erfahrener Erwerbslosigkeit* [Timebomb "stupid" student: An intervention study for enhancing resilience in face of potential or experienced unemployment]. Retrieved from http://edudoc.ch/record/3712/files/Oser.pdf

Papatraianou, L. H., & Le Cornu, R. (2014). Problematising the role of personal and professional relationships in early career teacher resilience. *Australian Journal of Teacher Education, 39*(1), 99–116. https://doi.org/10.14221/ajte.2014v39n1.7.

Peixoto, F., Wosnitza, M., Pipa, J., Morgan, M., & Cefai, C. (2018). A multidimensional view on pre-service teacher resilience in Germany, Ireland, Malta and Portugal. In M. Wosnitza, F. Peixoto, S. Beltman, & C. F. Mansfield (Eds.), *Resilience in education: Concepts, contexts and connections* (pp. 73–89). New York: Springer.

Perrez, M., Laireiter, A.-R., & Baumann, U. (2005). Psychologische Faktoren: Stress und Coping. [Psychological factors: Stress and coping]. In M. Perrez & U. Baumann (Eds.), *Lehrbuch Klinische Psychologie – Psychotherapie* (3rd ed., pp. 272–304). Bern: Verlag Hans Huber.

Richardson, G. E. (2002). The metatheory of resilience and resiliency. *Journal of Clinical Psychology, 58*(3), 307–321. https://doi.org/10.1002/jclp.10020.

Rutter, M. (1990). Psychosocial resilience and protective mechanisms. In J. Rof, A. S. Masten, D. Cicchetti, K. Nüchterlein, & S. Weintraub (Eds.), *Risk and protective factors in the development of psychopathology* (pp. 181–214). Cambridge, MA: Cambridge University Press.

Schöngen, K. (2003). Ausbildungsvertrag gelöst = Ausbildung abgebrochen? Ergebnisse einer Befragung. [Contract dissolution = dropout of the apprenticeship? Results from a survey]. *Informationen für die Beratungs- und Vermittlungsdienste der Bundesagentur für Arbeit (ibv), 25*, 5–19.

Schoon, I. (2006). *Risk and resilience. Adaptations in changing times*. Cambridge, MA: Cambridge University Press.

Skodol, A. E. (2010). The resilient personality. In J. W. Reich, A. J. Zautra, & J. S. Hall (Eds.), *Handbook of adult resilience*. New York: The Guildford Press.

Tait, M. (2008). Resilience as a contributor to novice teacher success, commitment, and retention. *Teacher Education Quarterly, 35*(4), 57–75. Retrieved from http://files.eric.ed.gov/fulltext/EJ838701.pdf.

Tschannen-Moran, M., & Woolfolk Hoy, A. (2001). Teacher efficacy: Capturing an elusive construct. *Teaching and Teacher Education, 17*, 783–805. Retrieved from http://mxtsch.people.wm.edu/Scholarship/TATE_TSECapturingAnElusiveConstruct.pdf.

Uhly, A. (2014). *Zu Problemen der Berechnung einer Abbruchquote für die duale Berufsausbildung: Alternative Kalkulationen auf Basis der Berufsbildungsstatistik der statistischen Ämter des Bundes und der Länder. Diskussionspapier* [On problems of calculating dropout rates for vocational education and training: Alternative calculations on basis of the

Vocational Education and Training statistics by the Federal Statistical Office and statistical offices of the states. Discussion paper]. Retrieved from http://www.bibb.de/dokumente/pdf/a21_dazubi_methodenpapier_abbruchquote_jan-2014.pdf
Ungar, M. (2011). The social ecology of resilience: Addressing contextual and cultural ambiguity of a nascent construct. *American Journal of Orthopsychiatry, 81*(1), 1–17. https://doi.org/10.1111/j.1939-0025.2010.01067.x.
Werner, E. E. (1993). Risk, resilience and recovery: Perspectives from the Kauai longitudinal study. *Development and Psychopathology, 5*, 503–515.
Werner, E. E. (1994). Overcoming the odds. *Developmental and Behavioral Pediatrics, 15*(2), 131–136.
Werner, E. E. (2000). Protective factors and individual resilience. In J. P. Shonkoff, S. J. Meisels, & E. F. Zigler (Eds.), *Handbook of early childhood intervention* (2nd ed., pp. 115–132). New York: Cambridge University Press. Retrieved from http://ebooks.cambridge.org/chapter.jsf?bid=CBO9780511529320&cid=CBO9780511529320A017. https://doi.org/10.1017/CBO9780511529320.008.
Windle, G. (2010). What is resilience? A review and concept analysis. *Reviews in Clinical Gerontology, 21*(02), 152–169. https://doi.org/10.1017/s0959259810000420.

Chapter 4
Great Southern Lands: Making Space for Teacher Resilience in South Africa and Australia

Caroline F. Mansfield, Liesel Ebersöhn, Susan Beltman, and Tilda Loots

Abstract Teacher resilience is an issue of international concern, yet few cross-national studies exist. This chapter examines teacher resilience in two postcolonial, economically disparate, Southern hemisphere contexts: South Africa and Australia. Data from studies in each country are examined to investigate the nature of risks and resources to support teacher resilience in each context. A conceptual model is developed to illustrate how the ecologies in these two countries differ with regard to the specific adversities teachers face, as well as protective resources available to teachers to buffer against such risk. Findings show that irrespective of context, certain teacher personal resources (optimism, perseverance, motivation) and adaptive coping strategies (relational support, problem-solving) remain similar across dissimilar contexts. In addition, whilst the broad origin of the risks was similar, how these were manifested differed in each context due to broader socio-economic conditions. Implications for further research, teacher preparation and professional development are discussed.

Teacher resilience has become recognised as an important international field of research as there has been increasing interest in what sustains teachers, enabling them to remain in the profession and thrive in their work, despite challenging conditions. In countries where there has been concern about teacher quality retention and effectiveness, research has highlighted the importance of personal and contextual resources teachers draw on to respond to risk. Many studies on teacher resilience

C. F. Mansfield (✉)
School of Education, Murdoch University, Perth, WA, Australia
e-mail: Caroline.Mansfield@murdoch.edu.au

L. Ebersöhn · T. Loots
University of Pretoria, Pretoria, South Africa
e-mail: Liesel.Ebersohn@up.ac.za

S. Beltman
School of Education, Curtin University, Perth, WA, Australia
e-mail: s.beltman@curtin.edu.au

M. Wosnitza et al. (eds.), *Resilience in Education*,
https://doi.org/10.1007/978-3-319-76690-4_4

originate in the global north (e.g., Brunetti 2006; Castro et al. 2010; Day and Gu 2007; Kitching et al. 2009; Tait 2008), yet few of these are comparative (Beltman et al. 2011). Some investigation of teacher resilience has its origins in the southern hemisphere (e.g., Ebersöhn 2012, 2014; Mansfield et al. 2012, 2014; Johnson et al. 2014), where studies are predominantly from Australia and South Africa. Currently there are no comparisons of teacher resilience in southern hemisphere countries, yet resilience has been identified internationally as an important factor in teacher retention, effectiveness and well-being.

The literature strongly argues that the contexts in which teachers work play a critical role in shaping teacher resilience, providing risks and resources to support or challenge resilience (Day and Gu 2014). From an ecological perspective, "context" refers to the multiple systems at the micro and macro levels (Bronfenbrenner 1979). Although South Africa and Australia are both postcolonial countries, geographically located in the southern hemisphere, the broader socio-economic contexts and educational systems in which South African and Australian teachers work are quite different. Interestingly though, teacher resilience research has burgeoned in each country.

Education systems are heavily influenced by political, social and economic factors. As an efficiency-driven, emerging economy (Shawab 2014), South African investment in public education in 2012 was 6.1% of GDP (compared with the OECD average of 4.8%) (OECD 2014). Investing in education can promote economic growth, increasing productivity and reducing social inequality. Historically however, the socio-political transformation in post-apartheid South Africa means that there are still many factors that challenge the education sector, such as inefficient government bureaucracy, corruption, inadequate supply of infrastructure and broader societal issues such as unemployment, poverty, crime and poor public health (Shawab 2014). Many schools, especially rural schools, experience difficulties such as lack of classrooms, poor access to services such as water and electricity, no landline telephones nor internet and minimal or non-existent libraries (Gardiner 2008). Approximately 62% of South Africa's public schools are situated in the poorest and most underdeveloped South African rural communities and include more than half of South Africa's children between the ages of 7 and 18 years. The challenges experienced in South African schools are often compounded by socio-economic factors such as unemployment, chronic poverty and HIV and have a direct influence on the quality of, and engagement with, education.

As Australia has an innovation-driven (Shawab 2014), developed economy, the education system has benefited from investment in infrastructure, teacher training, technology and resources. Although, in 2012, public expenditure on education in Australia was 4.6% of GDP, most schools have reliable infrastructure, internet and computer access, school libraries and access to support staff. Even so, rural-urban school divides exist. In Western Australia (where the Australian data were gathered), over 31% of students attend schools in non-metropolitan areas, and 8.2% of these are in remote locations (Department of Education, Western Australia 2012).

Rural communities experience greater health and socio-economic challenges, unemployment and lower household incomes (Commonwealth of Australia 2008). Student academic achievement is lower in rural and especially remote schools (Australian Curriculum, Assessment and Reporting Authority 2012), and schools experience difficulties attracting and retaining teachers (McKenzie et al. 2011). Teacher attrition is a concern in Australia with an estimated 25% of teachers leaving the profession in the first 5 years (Australian Government Productivity Commission 2012).

This chapter uses cross-national data on teacher resilience from South Africa and Australia to add a unique comparative and southern hemisphere contextual lens to the teacher resilience literature. The aim is to investigate the challenges (risks) teachers face and the resources they draw on to manage risks. How teacher resilience is experienced in each context is examined.

Theoretical Framework

Pooley and Cohen (2010) propose resilience to be "the potential to exhibit resourcefulness by using available internal and external resources in response to different contextual and developmental challenges" (p. 30). In this regard, teacher resilience has been understood as the process where teachers demonstrate capacity to interact dynamically over time with their context by using protective resources to respond adaptively to risk factors (Mansfield et al. 2016). Positive outcomes of resilience could include professional commitment, job satisfaction, sustained motivation and engagement.

To examine the teacher resilience process, accounting for personal and contextual risks and resources, systems approaches are beneficial. Describing an adaptive subsystems approach to understanding resilience processes, Masten (2014) argued that the resilience process involves "many systems *within* the individual as well as many systems *outside* the individual" (p. 170) and that "adaptive function of the individual is interdependent with many other systems at different levels of function that are continually interacting" (p. 170). In this regard the teacher resilience process involves the dynamic interplay between personal, relational, physical (school infrastructure) and broader country-specific health, welfare and education systems to address risks through maximising resources. As shown in Fig. 4.1 (based on Bronfenbrenner 1979), an ecological approach (Theron 2018, Chap. 12, this volume) to understanding teacher resilience involves exploring personal risks and resources, microsystem and mesosystem relationships, as well as elements in the exosystem and macrosystem. Furthermore the interaction between these systems over time is critical to the resilience process. This systems approach is used to examine the resilience process of teachers participating in studies in South Africa and Australia.

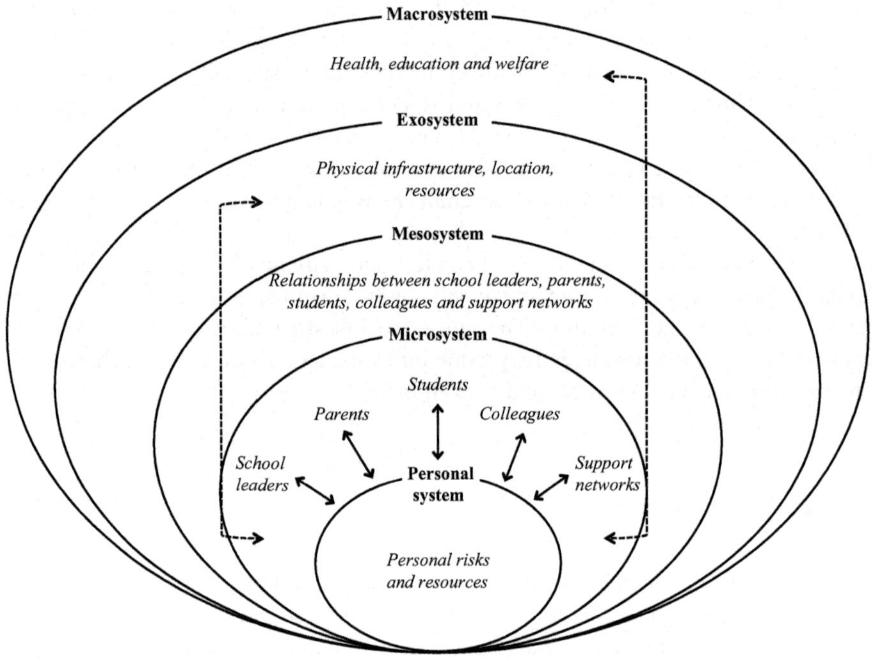

Fig. 4.1 A systems approach to understanding teacher resilience (Adaptation of Bronfenbrenner 1979)

Personal System

Within the personal system, risks and resources have been identified in the literature (see Beltman et al. 2011) including difficulty in asking for help, low levels of confidence or efficacy (Day 2008), conflicts between personal ideologies and current practices (Flores 2006) and family pressures (Olsen and Anderson 2007). Personal resources for teacher resilience include motivation and efficacy (Morgan 2011), optimism and social and emotional competence (Ee and Chang 2010), having a sense of moral purpose and vocation (Gu 2014; Gu and Day 2013), courage (Le Cornu 2013), hope and high expectations (Huisman et al. 2010) and having intrinsic value with regard to enjoying working as a teacher (Hong 2012). Individuals may also mobilise resources such as coping strategies to enable resilience (Sharplin et al. 2011).

Micro- and Mesosystems

Micro- and mesosystems comprise various groups of people such as students, school leaders and colleagues and the relationships between these and individual teachers. Teachers draw on resources at these levels to manage risks and help navigate through challenges. Classroom or school challenges include classroom management (Castro et al. 2010), meeting needs of disadvantaged students (Brunetti 2006), unsupportive leadership staff (Day 2008), lack of resources (Flores 2006), relationships (Castro et al. 2010) and scrutiny of peers, parents and the principal (Goddard and Foster 2001). The micro- and mesosystems may also provide extensive resources that support teacher resilience such as positive relationships with colleagues (Cameron and Lovett 2014), mentors (Huisman et al. 2010), school leaders (Peters and Pearce 2012) and students (Kitching et al. 2009). Having personal and professional support networks such as family support and social networks (Papatraianou and Le Cornu 2014) can also be an asset. In high-risk school settings, teachers used interpersonal pathways evidenced as group effectiveness skills (group communication, roles and responsibilities, positive group dynamics) to support resilience (Ebersöhn et al. 2015a).

Exo- and Macrosystems

Exosystems incorporate physical infrastructure, characteristics of a location and resources. Connected to this are the broader macrosystem factors such as policies related to health, education and welfare that would impact on teacher resilience through producing risks as well as available resources. Related risks for teachers include heavy workload and lack of time (Castro et al. 2010), difficult schools or classes (Flores 2006), externally imposed regulations (Day 2008), low salary and poor funding (Fantilli and McDougall 2009).

The Resilience Process

The different contextual or systemic levels of risks and resources interact with each other to shape resilience in what is known to be a complex, dynamic, process (Mansfield et al. 2014). The relationship between risks and resources and system levels has been examined in some studies (Kitching et al. 2009). Morgan et al. (2010) found that teachers can cope with negative experiences as long as they constantly experience positive episodes, such as strong relationships with students. Likewise, Ebersöhn et al. (2015b) highlighted that despite high risk and high need, teachers demonstrated strong intrinsic capacities and skills to assist them in overcoming negative contextual risks. It therefore seems that more distal systems could play a secondary role to that of personal resources in teacher resilience.

Masten and Wright (2010) argue for the conceptualisation of resilience to go beyond being an individual characteristic and rather to regard resilience as a dynamic process and interaction between an individual and an ever-changing context. Researchers are increasingly focusing more on exploring and understanding cultural and contextual specific factors and mechanisms that could assist at-risk populations not only survive but also thrive (Ungar 2012). Therefore, contributing to a social ecological understanding of resilience, it is necessary to study the tension between aspects of resilience that are shared and those that are distinctive to a specific cultural group or social context (Ungar 2012).

Method

The data set for this chapter were generated from studies examining teacher resilience in South Africa and Australia.

The South African Study

In this chapter, the South African study reports on data from a long-term (2003–2012) collaborative partnership project, STAR (Supportive Teachers Assets and Resilience), between teachers in high-risk schools with high levels of adversity and educational psychology scholars aligned with the *Centre for the Study of Resilience*, University of Pretoria (Ferreira and Ebersöhn 2012). The aim of STAR was to explore school-based resilience processes in high-risk, low-resource school settings, utilising the asset-based approach (Ebersöhn and Eloff 2006) as the theoretical lens and participatory reflection and action (PRA) (Chambers 2008) as a methodology to design the collaborative intervention. STAR focuses on existing resources, assets and strengths in every teacher, school and community, despite a shortage of resources may dominate the context.

STAR started in a pilot phase with ten teachers from a primary school in an urban informal settlement in a South African province (Eastern Cape), consisting of several interrelated studies (Ferreira and Ebersöhn 2012) which span from 2003 to 2005. In the second phase (2005–2007), the pilot project was replicated in two other South African provinces (two urban primary schools in Gauteng, as well as a rural secondary school in Mpumalanga). Dissemination research followed in 2007–2011, where teachers from the first two phases were trained as STAR facilitators who in turn trained teachers in six neighbouring schools (two schools in each of the three South African provinces) (Ferreira and Ebersöhn 2012).

In this chapter, we draw on data from the entire long-term South African study, which spans three South African provinces and includes 14 schools (10 primary and 4 high schools; 6 = rural and 8 = urban). Purposeful sampling was used to identify schools with high adversity, characterised by high risk, high need and resource constraints (low socio-economic status, high HIV infection rates, irregular infrastructure and limited services). School principals invited teachers "interested in addressing challenges in the school" to participate ($n = 87$, 73 female, 14 male).

Data were collected over time (between 1 and 10 years) through STAR intervention sessions (based on PRA principles) in the classrooms of the respective schools at 3-month intervals over a 1-year time frame. The assumption of the STAR intervention was to facilitate teachers' acquisition of asset-based competencies in order to provide school-based psychosocial support within their school-community contexts. Individual interviews and small group conversations (both before and after the STAR intervention) with all participating teachers at the same school discussing aspects of risk and resilience in school settings were audio recorded and transcribed.

Multiple researchers were involved in the data collection; however common interview schedules were maintained. Multiple coders analysed the South African transcriptions using Charmaz's (2005) constructivist grounded theory principles to identify risks and resources with regard to internal personal systems, micro- and mesosystems, exosystems as well as macrosystems.

The Australian Study

Data from 18 Australian teachers were gathered during two separate studies, the first with early career teachers (n = 13, 10 female, 3 male) (Mansfield et al. 2014) and second with experienced teachers (n = 5, 4 females, 1 male) (Harris 2014). In the first study, early career teachers (in their first or second year of teaching) were recruited via the university they attended for their teacher training. Having participated in earlier phases of a larger project regarding teacher resilience, they were invited to be interviewed. In the second study, experienced teachers working in challenging schools were recruited using purposeful sampling. Potential schools were identified through a funding programme aimed at improving educational outcomes for students from disadvantaged backgrounds (Department of Education, Western Australia 2013). Principals from four schools were asked to recommend teachers who they viewed as resilient, were successfully managing the challenges of their work and who had been teaching for a minimum of 5 years. Teachers volunteered to participate in a semi-structured interview.

In both studies participants were asked about the challenges they experienced, strategies they used to manage challenges and sustain commitment and their main sources of support. For this chapter, a secondary analysis of data from both studies was conducted. Interview transcripts were re-analysed through a deductive content analysis using a predetermined coding system (Fraenkel et al. 2012) from Fig. 4.1. Researchers in each country worked together to determine the risks and resources according to the various system levels. This in turn enabled cross-country analysis to identify common and unique risks and resources.

Table 4.1 describes the sample of schools and teachers. In summary, the majority of participants in both countries comprised female, urban primary school teachers, although the South African sample was approximately five times larger than the Australian cohort.

Table 4.1 Overall number of schools and participants for type of school and country

Type of school	South African schools	South African teachers	Australian schools	Australian teachers
Urban primary	6	43	10	11
Urban secondary	2	10	3	3
Rural primary	4	12	3	3
Rural secondary	2	22	1	1
Subtotals (% of total)	14 (45%)	87 (83%)	17 (55%)	18 (17%)

Findings

The findings are presented according to *similar* and *unique*, *risks* and *resources* that shape teacher resilience, at the various system levels (Fig. 4.1) in each country. Within each section, key ideas as reported by teachers in South Africa and Australia are presented.

Personal System

At the personal system level, teachers described risks they experienced and resources they harnessed to manage risks.

Similar risks: At the internal personal system level, teachers in both South Africa and Australia reported feeling overwhelmed by multiple demands, roles and responsibilities: "We are overwhelmed at the school on daily basis … I want to see my learners …I want to change the way they are living in the community" (SA).

Unique risks: Six beginning teachers in Australia expressed the challenge of maintaining a work-life balance, for example: "it's just been so stressful that I haven't had time to get back into any of my hobbies". This concern was not evident in comments of more experienced Australian and South African teachers.

Similar resources: Teachers in both countries used similar personal resources when responding to challenges. They showed persistence, perseverance, motivation and determination: "We stay motivated" (SA) and we "just put one foot after the other" (AUS) and "choose not to get upset" (AUS). Optimism was prevalent amongst South African teachers: "I can do it irrespective of financial constraints" who also echoed pride and a sense of accomplishment regarding their achievements: "We know as teachers we are achieving".

Teachers in both countries used a variety of adaptive coping strategies (Folkman 2011). Problems were solved by working together and brainstorming: "we sat down and focused" (SA) and "look at the issue, resolve it or improve it" (AUS). The use of faith practices was another common coping strategy: "We are a support group, to pray" (SA). Being open about the role of faith was less common for Australian teachers although one indicated: "I'm a Christian so I have my faith.… that to me is a very sustaining thing". Another coping strategy was help seeking: "I know where to get assistance" (SA) and "you ask for help...'I'm drowning – hello – help!'" (AUS). Emotional management, staying "calm and focused" (SA) was mentioned: "I have to be very focused and play the ball not the person" (AUS).

Unique resources: One personal resource described by Australian teachers was exercise: "no matter what, I go for a run, to the beach, try and avoid thinking of school, burn up energy and calm my mind". They also described other purposeful strategies for managing stress and inducing positive affect, such as listening to music, eating chocolate or drinking tea.

Similar yet unique resources: Although teachers in both countries used reflection as a personal resource, how this was operationalised differed. In South Africa, teachers reflected more in groups: "We used to meet time and again, and share how far have we gone and what is it that we can do". In Australia reflection was more often a personal activity: "I always documented...it not only sustained me, gave me the opportunity to look at myself and see what I could do better".

Micro- and Mesosystems

At the micro- and mesosystem level, the data showed the source of risks and resources was often similar (students, parents, colleagues, school leaders and support networks), yet how these were manifested differed in each country.

Similar Yet Unique Risks

Students. Although teachers in both countries described challenges with students, in South Africa challenges emerged from broader welfare conditions and poverty: "We have many needy children and households, they don't get food at home each day". The implications of chronic health issues were noted: "Because of the high AIDS number in our community ... children are living alone in the house, they need to look after their siblings...they don't have time for schoolwork". For teachers in Australia, student challenges were more concerned with diverse needs, "catering for children who are significantly below the rest of the class" (AUS). Behaviour problems with specific children were also mentioned: "Being punched by students, having computers thrown at us, being threatened to be shot..." (AUS). Other concerns arose from some students' disadvantaged home backgrounds, which meant students may come to school without breakfast or food for the day.

Parents. Teachers in both countries experienced challenges related to parental involvement (or lack of) and communication: "The only time [parents] come to school is when there is a serious problem" (SA). In Australia, challenges included managing complaints from parents: "It's all sunshine and roses when they're happy but if they don't like something you're doing ... then batten down the hatches" (AUS).

Colleagues. Teacher continuity was a challenge experienced in both countries. Absenteeism and high staff turnover were issues: "it's either one teacher is absent or there is no teacher" (SA): "some can't handle the situation and physical and emotional strain" (AUS).

School leaders. Teachers noted pressure from school leaders regarding student achievement. Students deemed to be underperforming contributed to stress: "now the principal wants results" (SA). Some Australian teachers felt unsupported by their school leadership teams: " … not having any type of recognition… or here is the support that you need to do this".

Unique risks

A unique challenge expressed by Australian teachers was maintaining a social life with friends and keeping contact with their families: "the amount of time that teaching takes up means that my friends and my social life suffered quite a lot… I have friends that I haven't seen all year".

Similar Resources

Students. Despite many socio-economic challenges associated with students in South Africa, teachers reported positive relationships with students: "we have a good relationship with our learners" (SA). Positive relationships were sustaining: "if I'm away at a course and the next day they'll say you know 'I missed you so much where were you?' – that makes me feel really nice" (AUS).

Support networks. Teachers in both countries described interpersonal resources, particularly collaborative networking with colleagues: "It is better to work as a team … as a team we can support each other… then nothing is unachievable" (SA). An Australian teacher emphasised the value of "a supportive network of people around you".

Similar Yet Unique Resources

In both countries, teachers found that community involvement was a powerful relational resource. In South Africa collaborative partnerships with community organisations benefitted the school community: "We are working with different people, all those workshops were catered for by different [organisations]" (SA). One Australian teacher based at a remote school described intentional, proactive strategies to become part of the local community, such as coaching a soccer team and starting a band that played at the local hotel. Such differences may be the result of Australian teachers relocating and recognising the need to build new support networks.

Unique Resources

In Australia, teachers emphasised the important role families played as a relational resource. One beginning teacher described "an incredible amount of support from home". Experienced teachers also drew on their family for emotional and practical support: "My mum's a teacher so on the academic side of things and the teaching related issues I've got someone to bounce off".

Exosystem

When considering risks associated with the physical infrastructure system, there were again common broad themes of isolation and of resources, but these took a different form in each country.

Similar Yet Unique Risks

Challenges relating to working in remote or isolated areas were similar. For South African teachers travelling distances to work and being available after school hours was challenging: "Our main challenge as you see us here, we work here but we don't stay here" (SA). One single male Australian teacher, relocated to a remote community, experienced loneliness: "I'm bringing my dog up for the fourth term which is going to be very good".

Teachers in both countries reported challenges with resources to support teaching, although the quality of and quantity of these differed. South African teachers reported barriers unique to their school-community context such as a shortage of classrooms and lack of maintenance on buildings: "… there were three Grade 7 classes in a hall … when another teacher is speaking in one class, he disturbs the other teachers in other classes". One Australian teacher described going to second-hand bookshops to purchase books and resources.

Unique Risks

South African teachers reported widespread challenges related to infrastructure such as transportation to and from school, frequent power shortages, problematic water supply to schools and issues with sanitation: "…many of the houses have long drops". In Australia however, challenges were more localised. One teacher described the poor standard of teacher accommodation in a remote area: "I arrived and there was a stinking fridge full of dirty old rotten food, a toilet that was bunged up [blocked]".

Similar Resources

Teachers in both countries described their aim to make schools safe and supportive places for students and the community: "We are also aware of the fact that one's roles as educators is to make a difference in our communities" (SA). Similarly, physical and psychological safety was noted: "For a lot of kids this is their stability,… this is where it's safe, … they've got their space and they know the rules are consistent and they know how things are going to go". Safe and supportive schools acted as a resource for both students and teachers.

Unique Resources

South African teachers drew on physical resources to facilitate the establishment of vegetable gardens which connected community and school: "… it [vegetable garden] helps a lot with the community because now the parents are taking care of the school…". The harvest from vegetable gardens also supported needy families: "The orphans take the vegetables home, we share it amongst them and the people who are needy". Teachers also referred to educational resources, using underutilised buildings for classrooms: "We organised additional classrooms in the assembly hall" and donation of books for library.

Macrosystem

At the macrosystem (health, welfare and education) level, there were two common educational risks: curriculum pressures and student achievement. Disadvantage was a common broad theme but was very different in each context. There were no common resources at this perhaps more distal level, with teachers in each country accessing different kinds of resources to enable resilience.

Similar Risks

In both countries, teachers experienced pressure from external education bodies, particularly with implementing a changing curriculum (The Revised National Curriculum 2005; building on the vision of the South African Constitution and Curriculum 2005): "We are jumping around with the curriculum and you know if you check on the government, it is pressing buttons on the high school" (SA). High school teachers reported pressure from the Department of Education to improve Grade 12 results, taking up much of their time and attention and contributing additional stress. Unrealistic expectations of the curriculum and political discussions "about performance pay and pitting teachers against one another and NAPLAN

[*National Assessment Program – Literacy and Numeracy]* and whose fault are the bad NAPLAN results" (AUS) were a common theme.

Similar Yet Unique Risks

Although disadvantage was mentioned by teachers in both countries, what this actually entailed differed. Australia teachers described instances where families could not afford to buy school supplies, yet in South Africa poverty was more widespread and severe: "Our school is situated in the informal settlement, most families are so disadvantaged, most parents are not working, there is a lot of poverty and crime".

Unique Risks

The health risk associated with HIV/AIDS is a unique and growing challenge in South African schools. Teachers reported the influence of HIV/AIDS on children's academic performance and learning: "... she is having a child in her classroom who is infected. This child has been in and out of hospital". Consequently, individuals need to adopt different roles and/or take on additional responsibilities: "Grannies and grandfathers are left with the burden of raising the kids because the parents died of the AIDS pandemic" and "Children must take care of each other, because their parents died".

Unique Resources

There were no common resources at this system level. In South Africa, teachers referred to socio-economical health and welfare resources, in the form of social grants for parents: "We talked about the grant they qualified for, that can give her support so that she can buy medicine and all those things". South African teachers managed to establish networks with hospitals, clinics and hospices in their communities in order to enhance health support in their communities: "… there are school nurses that we are working with".

Australian teachers mentioned educational resources such as further university study, centres to assist teachers to manage children with autism and extreme behavioural difficulties, formal mentors for new teachers and professional development and networking opportunities: "I think you need a lot of PD [professional development] for strategies that you can use in the school for behaviour especially". A range of resources to support education were also available. Even with long waiting lists, Australian teachers could refer children to services such as speech and occupational therapy, and schools could apply for additional funding to support particular programmes: "We're lucky because our principal's really proactive … she puts applications in all the time to get funding for our school". Free counselling sessions for teachers and their families were also available.

Discussion

This chapter explored teacher resilience in two postcolonial, southern hemisphere contexts, investigating the commonalities and disparities in quality and quantity of risks and resources in each. Although there were differences in sample size and method of data collection, there are findings that are important for moving the field forward.

The key finding was that irrespective of context, the risks and resources in the personal system remain consistent. A common risk for teachers was feeling overwhelmed, and similar resources and adaptive coping strategies were used. Although there were some resources unique to each context (e.g. group vs individual reflection) and the Australian participants expressed concern about finding manageable work-life balance, the general quality and quantity of perceived risks and resources were similar. This finding suggests that internal protective resources, particularly of optimism (Forgeard and Seligman 2012), positive emotions and sense of achievement (Meister and Ahrens 2011), matter for teacher resilience. Although the particular resources teachers drew for support have been addressed in other literature in each country, cross-country comparisons have not been undertaken. The finding that personal system risks and protective resources share more similarities than differences highlights the important role of personal protective resources in the teacher resilience process, irrespective of context.

Moving to the external micro- and mesosystem level, the origin of risks encountered (students, parents, colleagues) was similar, yet the quality and quantity differed. For Australian teachers, managing student diversity was a risk, yet in South Africa student risk incorporated significant health and welfare needs. Teachers in South African emphasised the critical role of community partnerships to support the needs of students and their families, yet Australian teachers described support from family and friends. The fact that teachers in both contexts draw on some similar resources (collaboration with colleagues and local community) suggests that collaboration (Cameron and Lovett 2014) and networking (Papatraianou and Le Cornu 2014) matter as a protective resource (irrespective of context) to provide a safe and supportive school setting. The literature points to the importance of relationships (Gu 2014), but much describes the impact of positive and supportive relationships for individuals, particularly early career teachers (Le Cornu 2013). The South African data suggests relationships had a collective power to meaningfully support community cohesion which in turn buffered against systemic risk to support resilience processes of teachers and students. Collaboration was a key protective resource (Ebersöhn 2012).

Although there were some similar risks regarding physical infrastructure on a broad level (isolation, limited resources), perhaps not surprisingly, how the risks were manifested was unique in each context. Again, quality and quantity differed. Isolation in South African rural schools meant challenges with transport and limited school services; however in Australia, teachers described risks such as unsatisfactory accommodation, isolation and disconnect from regular support structures. The findings in this study show that across countries the origin of risk is similar, yet how the risk plays out differs in each context.

The findings support other studies in the teacher resilience literature arguing that context matters (Day and Gu 2014), yet this study has provided a more nuanced and comparative examination of context at multiple levels. What was particularly apparent was that there were more differences in context at the most distal external macrosystem level, where there was greater variation in country-specific health, welfare and education systems/policies. In Australia, professional staff outside schools have been shown to play a part in encouraging early career teachers (Le Cornu 2013), and school psychologists can provide various forms of support (Anderson et al. 2007; Beltman et al. 2015). In South Africa, chronic poverty was likely to be widespread and compounded by unemployment and prolonged health risks and resilience required drawing on available and unique cultural and social resources, such as community building, developing partnerships, mobilising unused resources and applying for social development grants. So although the origins of risks were similar, there were unique risks at the micro- and macrosystem levels which required mobilisation of unique resources to manage.

From a conceptual viewpoint, this study contributes to the teacher resilience literature by providing insights about how person-context interactions enable teachers to manage risk and harness resources to support resilience in two countries. These descriptive comparisons add depth to the teacher resilience literature and provide support for using Ungar's (2012) notion of resilience as transactional-ecological within the teacher resilience knowledge base. Although there were significant contextual differences, the resources teachers used bear similarity, particularly at the personal level. There was also interaction between the system levels. For example, there were similar micro-risks, yet at the macrosystem level, there was variability in how these risks were manifested. As noted by Masten (2014), the resilience process involves systems both within and outside the individual, and adaptive functioning "is interdependent with many other systems at different levels of function that are continually interacting" (p. 170).

The greater variation in risks and resources at the external macrosystem level also influences the process of teacher resilience in each context. In the South African context where the intensity and frequency of need were high, teachers needed to know how to network to identify and use resources for collective well-being (Theron 2018, Chap. 12, this volume). Conversely, in the Australian context, teachers needed to know how to access existing support services, build collaborative and collegial relationships, manage work-life balance and maintain their personal well-being.

Conclusion

This cross-country comparative study is unique in the teacher resilience field, and findings show some common risks and resources, despite differing contexts, that contribute to teacher resilience. Irrespective of context, certain teacher resources and adaptive coping strategies remained similar. Although teachers managed different challenges and mobilised different external resources, they appeared to use similar personal resources and coping strategies to address challenges. The extent to which contexts differ not only across countries but also between urban and rural school settings highlights the need for teacher candidates and in-service teachers to be cognisant of resilience promoting strategies to use available resources to manage risks. More cross-cultural studies are needed to explore variability or similarity in personal resources and challenges for teacher resilience and investigate patterns of adaptation in multiple contexts. Finally, the importance of resilience for positive teacher and student outcomes emphasises the need for teachers to develop awareness of the influence multiple systems have on resilience processes and how they can use this to maximise professional resilience throughout their careers.

References

Anderson, C., Klassen, R., & Georgiou, G. (2007). Inclusion in Australia: What teachers say they need and what school psychologists can offer. *School Psychology International, 28*(2), 131–147. https://doi.org/10.1177/0143034307078086.

Australian Curriculum, Assessment and Reporting Authority. (2012). *National assessment program—literacy and numeracy report*. Retrieved from http://www.nap.edu.au/verve/_resources/NAPLAN_2012_ National_Report.pdf.

Australian Government Productivity Commission. (2012). Schools workforce: Research report. http://www.pc.gov.au/__data/assets/pdf_file/0020/116651/schools-workforce.pdf. Retrieved from http://www.pc.gov.au/__data/assets/pdf_file/0020/116651/schools-workforce.pdf.

Beltman, S., Mansfield, C. F., & Price, A. (2011). Thriving not just surviving: A review of research on teacher resilience. *Educational Research Review, 6*(3), 185–207. https://doi.org/10.1016/j.edurev.2011.09.001.

Beltman, S., Mansfield, C. F., & Harris, A. (2015). Quietly sharing the load? The role of school psychologists in enabling teacher resilience. *School Psychology International, 37*(2), 172–188. https://doi.org/10.1177/0143034315615939.

Bronfenbrenner, U. (1979). *The ecology of human development: Experiments by nature and design*. Cambridge, MA: Harvard University Press.

Brunetti, G. J. (2006). Resilience under fire: Perspectives on the work of experienced, inner city high school teachers in the United States. *Teaching and Teacher Education, 22*(7), 812–825. https://doi.org/10.1016/j.tate.2006.04.027.

Cameron, M., & Lovett, S. (2014). Sustaining the commitment and realising the potential of highly promising teachers. *Teachers and Teaching: Theory and Practice 21*(2), 150–163. https://doi:10.1080/13540602.2014.928132.

Castro, A. J., Kelly, J., & Shih, M. (2010). Resilience strategies for new teachers in high-needs areas. *Teaching and Teacher Education, 26*(3), 622–629. https://doi.org/10.1016/j.tate.2009.09.010.

Chambers, R. (2008). *Revolutions in development enquiry*. London: Earthscan.

Charmaz, K. (2005). Grounded theory in the 21st century: Applications for advancing social justice studies. In N. K. Denzin & Y. S. Lincoln (Eds.), *The Sage handbook of qualitative research* (pp. 507–536). Thousand Oaks: Sage Publications.

Commonwealth of Australia. (2008). *Mental health in rural and remote communities*. Retrieved from http://www.responseability.org/home/fact-sheets-and-podcasts/groups-at-increased-risk-of-mental-ill-health.

Day, C. (2008). Committed for life? Variations in teachers' work, lives and effectiveness. *Journal of Educational Change, 9*(3), 243–260. https://doi.org/10.1007/s10833-007-9054-6.

Day, C., & Gu, Q. (2007). Variations in the conditions for teachers' professional learning and development: Sustaining commitment and effectiveness over a career. *Oxford Review of Education – Special Issue, 33*(4), 423–443. doi: 0.1080/03054980701450746.

Day, C., & Gu, Q. (2014). *Resilient teachers, resilient schools: Building and sustaining quality in testing times*. Oxon: Routledge.

Department of Education, Western Australia. (2012). *Annual report 2011–2012*. Retrieved from http://det.wa.edu.au/about/detcms/education/department- homepage/annual-report/department-of-education- annual-report-.en?oid=MultiPartArticle-id-13313350.

Department of Education, Western Australia. (2013). *Partnership schools*. Government of Western Australia. Retrieved from http://det.wa.edu.au/partnershipschools/detcms/navigation/low-ses-school-communities/participating-schools/.

Ebersöhn, L. (2012). Adding 'flock' to 'fight and flight': A honeycomb of resilience where supply of relationships meets demand for support. *Journal of Psychology in Africa, 27*(1), 29–42.

Ebersöhn, L. (2014). Teacher resilience: Theorizing resilience and poverty. *Teachers and Teaching, 20*(5), 568–594. https://doi.org/10.1080/13540602.2014.937960.

Ebersöhn, L., & Eloff, I. (2006). *Life skills and assets* (2nd ed.). Pretoria: Van Schaik.

Ebersöhn, L., Loots, T., Eloff, I., & Ferreira, R. (2015a). In-service teacher training to provide psychosocial support and care in high-risk and high-need schools: School-based intervention partnerships. *Journal of Education for Teaching, 41*(3), 267–284. https://doi.org/10.1080/02607476.2015.1044226.

Ebersöhn, L., Loots, T., Eloff, I., & Ferreira, R. (2015b). Taking note of obstacles research partners negotiate in long-term higher education community engagement partnerships. *Teaching and Teacher Education, 45*, 59–72. https://doi.org/10.1016/j.tate.2014.09.003.

Ee, J., & Chang, A. (2010). How resilient are our graduate trainee teachers in Singapore? *The Asia-Pacific Education Researcher, 19*(2), 321–331.

Fantilli, R. D., & McDougall, D. E. (2009). A study of novice teachers: Challenges and supports in the first years. *Teaching and Teacher Education, 25*, 814–825.

Ferreira, R., & Ebersöhn, L. (2012). *Partnering for resilience*. Pretoria: Van Schaik Publishers.

Flores, M. A. (2006). Being a novice teacher in two different settings: Struggles, continuities, and discontinuities. *Teachers College Record, 108*(10), 2021–2052.

Folkman, S. (2011). Stress, health and coping: An overview. In S. Folkman (Ed.), *The Oxford handbook of stress, health and coping* (pp. 3–11). New York: Oxford University Press.

Forgeard, M. J. C., & Seligman, M. E. P. (2012). Seeing the glass half full: A review of the causes and consequences of optimism. *Pratiques Psychologiques, 18*(0), 107–120. https://doi.org/10.1016/j.prps.2012.02.002.

Fraenkel, J. R., Wallen, N. E., & Hyun, H. H. (2012). *How to design and evaluate research in education*. Boston: McGraw-Hill.

Gardiner, M. (2008). Education in rural areas. In *Issues in educational policy number 4*. Johannesburg: Centre for Education Policy Development.

Goddard, J., & Foster, R. (2001). The experiences of neophyte teachers: A critical constructivist assessment. *Teaching and Teacher Education, 17*, 349–365.

Gu, Q. (2014). The role of relational resilience in teachers' career-long commitment and effectiveness. *Teachers and Teaching: Theory and Practice, 20*(5), 502–529. https://doi.org/10.1080/13540602.2014.937961.

Gu, Q., & Day, C. (2013). Challenges to teacher resilience: Conditions count. *British Educational Research Journal, 39*(1), 22–44. https://doi.org/10.1080/01411926.2011.623152.

Harris, A. (2014). *Teacher resilience in challenging primary schools located in low SES suburbs, (Bachelor of Education (Honours))*. Perth: Curtin University.

Hong, J. Y. (2012). Why do some beginning teachers leave the school, and others stay? Understanding teacher resilience through psychological lenses. *Teachers and Teaching: Theory and Practice, 18*(4), 417–440. https://doi.org/10.1080/13540602.2012.696044.

Huisman, S., Singer, N. R., & Catapano, S. (2010). Resiliency to success: Supporting novice urban teachers. *Teacher Development: An International Journal of Teachers' Professional Development, 14*(4), 483–499. https://doi.org/10.1080/13664530.2010.533490.

Johnson, B., Down, B., Le Cornu, R., Peters, J., Sullivan, A., Pearce, J., & Hunter, J. (2014). Promoting early career teacher resilience: A framework for understanding and acting. *Teachers and Teaching: Theory and Practice, 20*(5), 530–546. https://doi.org/10.1080/13540602.2014.937957.

Kitching, K., Morgan, M., & O'Leary, M. (2009). It's the little things: Exploring the importance of commonplace events for early-career teachers' motivation. *Teachers and Teaching: Theory and Practice, 15*(1), 43–58. https://doi.org/10.1080/13540600802661311.

Le Cornu, R. (2013). Building early career teacher resilience: The role of relationships. *Australian Journal of Teacher Education, 38*(4), 1–16. https://doi.org/10.14221/ajte.2013v38n4.4.

Mansfield, C. F., Beltman, S., Price, A., & McConney, A. (2012). "Don't sweat the small stuff:" Understanding teacher resilience at the chalkface. *Teaching and Teacher Education, 28*, 357–367. https://doi.org/10.1016/j.tate.2011.11.001.

Mansfield, C. F., Beltman, S., & Price, A. (2014). 'I'm coming back again!' The resilience process of early career teachers. *Teachers and Teaching, 20*(5), 547–567. https://doi.org/10.1080/13540602.2014.937958.

Mansfield, C. F., Beltman, S., Broadley, T., & Weatherby-Fell, N. (2016). Building resilience in teacher education: An evidenced informed framework. *Teaching and Teacher Education, 54*, 77–87. https://doi.org/10.1016/j.tate.2015.11.016.

Masten, A. S. (2014). *Ordinary magic: Resilience in development*. New York: The Guildford Press.

Masten, A. S., & Wright, M. O.'. D. (2010). Resilience over the lifespan: Developmental perspectives on resistance, recovery and transformation. In J. W. Reich, A. J. Zautra, & J. Stuart Hall (Eds.), *Handbook of adult resilience* (pp. 213–236). New York: The Guilford Press.

McKenzie, P., Rowley, G., Weldon, P., Murphy, M. (2011). *Staff in Australia's schools 2010: Main report on the survey*. Australian Government Department of Education, Employment and Workplace Relations (DEEWR).

Meister, D. G., & Ahrens, P. (2011). Resisting plateauing: Four veteran teachers' stories. *Teaching and Teacher Education, 27*(4), 770–778. https://doi.org/10.1016/j.tate.2011.01.002.

Morgan, M. (2011). Resilience and recurring adverse events: Testing an assets-based model of beginning teachers' experiences. *The Irish Journal of Psychology, 32*(3–4), 92–104. https://doi.org/10.1080/03033910.2011.613189.

Morgan, M., Ludlow, L., Kitching, K., O'Leary, M., & Clarke, A. (2010). What makes teachers tick? Sustaining events in new teachers' lives. *British Educational Research Journal, 36*(2), 191–208. https://doi.org/10.1080/01411920902780972.

OECD. (2014). *Education at a Glance 2014: OECD indicators.* OECD Publishing. https://doi.org/10.1787/eag-2014-en Retrieved from www.oecd.org/edu/Education-at-a-Glance-2014.pdf.

Olsen, B., & Anderson, L. (2007). Courses of action: A qualitative investigation into urban teacher retention and career development. *Urban Education, 42*(1), 5–29. https://doi.org/10.1177/0042085906293923.

Papatraianou, L. H., & Le Cornu, R. (2014). Problematising the role of personal and professional relationships in early career teacher resilience. *Australian Journal of Teacher Education, 39*(1), 100–116. https://doi.org/10.14221/ajte.2014v39n1.7.

Peters, J., & Pearce, J. (2012). Relationships and early career teacher resilience: A role for school principals. *Teachers and Teaching: Theory and Practice, 18*(2), 249–262. https://doi.org/10.1080/13540602.2012.632266.

Pooley, J. A., & Cohen, L. (2010). Resilience: A definition in context. *The Australian Community Psychologist, 22*(1), 30–37.

Sharplin, E., O'Neill, M., & Chapman, A. (2011). Coping strategies for adaptation to new teacher appointments: Intervention for retention. *Teaching and Teacher Education, 27*, 136–146. https://doi.org/10.1016/j.tate.2010.07.010.

Shawab, K. (Ed.). (2014). *The global competitiveness report 2015–2015. Full data edition.* Geneva: World Economic Forum.

Tait, M. (2008). Resilience as a contributor to novice teacher success, commitment, and retention. *Teacher Education Quarterly, 35*(4), 57–76.

Theron, L. C. (2018). Teacher championship of resilience: Lessons from the pathways to resilience study, South Africa. In M. Wosnitza, F. Peixoto, S. Beltman, & C. F. Mansfield (Eds.), *Resilience in education: Concepts, contexts and connections* (pp. 203–217). New York: Springer.

Ungar, M. (Ed.). (2012). *The social ecology of resilience: A handbook of theory and practice.* New York: Springer.

Chapter 5
A Multidimensional View on Pre-service Teacher Resilience in Germany, Ireland, Malta and Portugal

Francisco Peixoto, Marold Wosnitza, Joana Pipa, Mark Morgan, and Carmel Cefai

Abstract Teacher resilience is a key factor to understand how teachers effectively cope with the strains and stresses of their profession. In this chapter, we are presenting results from a survey study, in four different countries (Germany, Malta, Ireland and Portugal), on pre-service teacher resilience which was part of the project ENTREE (ENhancing Teacher REsilience in Europe). The main goals were to examine the relationships between a global dimension of resilience and its related dimensions and to test the communalities and differences in these relationships amongst the four different countries. Participants were 764 pre-service teachers from Germany, Ireland, Malta and Portugal who answered to a questionnaire including perceptions of individual (e.g. teacher efficacy, commitment, personal life, rumination) and social/contextual (e.g. school support, social context) factors, as well as a global evaluation of resilience. Results showed that self-efficacy appears as one of the key factors related to resilience. Furthermore, differences in the relationships between the variables were found according to each country, suggesting that resilience is influenced by the context in which teachers live and work.

F. Peixoto (✉) · J. Pipa
ISPA-Instituto Universitário/CIE – ISPA, Lisbon, Portugal
e-mail: fpeixoto@ispa.pt; jpipa@ispa.pt

M. Wosnitza
Institute of Education, RWTH Aachen University, Aachen, Germany

School of Education, Murdoch University, Perth, WA, Australia
e-mail: marold.wosnitza@rwth-aachen.de

M. Morgan
Dublin City University, Dublin, Ireland
e-mail: Mark.Morgan@spd.dcu.ie

C. Cefai
University of Malta, Msida, Malta
e-mail: carmel.cefai@um.edu.au

M. Wosnitza et al. (eds.), *Resilience in Education*,
https://doi.org/10.1007/978-3-319-76690-4_5

It is estimated that in many countries nearly half of the early career teachers leave their profession during the first 5 years of teaching (Ingersoll 2003; OECD 2005). The teaching profession has become more and more demanding: teachers experience a high level of pressure to improve standards and performance, a heavy workload, lack of support, inadequate professional preparation and challenging students. These lead to attrition, stress and burnout and are the main reasons for the decision to leave the profession at such an early stage of the career (Cefai and Cavioni 2014; Gu and Li 2013). But what keeps the other half teaching? What helps them not to burnout? What helps them to maintain their "courage to teach" (Gu and Li 2013), to thrive in their career, to ensure quality learning for all students and to contribute to the overall improvement of educational standards? These questions change the perspective in the discussion on teacher retention from those who leave to those who stay (Hong 2012) and move the focus from the more negative concept of teacher burnout to the concept of teacher resilience, where retention is associated with constructs like commitment, engagement and motivation. It focuses on those who continue to develop professionally and deliver high-quality teaching, regardless of their career stage (Day and Gu 2014; Mansfield et al. 2016). Teacher resilience research furthermore tries to find answers on how to help those who struggle by understanding those who not only survive but also thrive.

Teacher resilience emerged as an alternative approach to understand why some teachers remain in their profession, despite the everyday challenges they face. In the literature, it has often been described as a quality for sustaining teacher commitment (Brunetti 2006) or as a dynamic process, where teachers' personal characteristics interact over time with their contextual resources (Mansfield et al. 2012, 2016; Schwarze and Wosnitza 2017, Chap. 3, this volume). This process involves strategies to cope with adverse events (Castro et al. 2010), emotion regulation (Ee and Chang 2010; Tait 2008) and the crucial role that protective and risk factors exert in how individuals respond to adverse events (Cefai and Cavioni 2014; Mansfield et al. 2012).

More recently, resilience has been conceptualised as a multidimensional construct rather than a personal quality (Mansfield et al. 2012). Whilst the concept of resilience from a psychological perspective outlines resilience as a personal quality (Brunetti 2006), the notion of resilience which takes account of the social and cultural contexts of the individual's work (Mansfield et al. 2016) advances a perspective that views resilience as a relative, multidimensional and developmental construct or a dynamic process which encompasses positive adaptation within a given context of significant adversity. In this sense, teacher resilience is not only associated with the capacity to "bounce back" but, rather, is the capacity to maintain equilibrium, a sense of commitment and agency in everyday life and the capacity to manage the unavoidable uncertainties inherent in the realities of teaching (Gu and Day 2013; Schwarze and Wosnitza 2018, Chap. 3, this volume). In this light, Wosnitza et al. (2014) defined teacher resilience as follows:

> Teacher resilience refers to the process of, capacity for, and outcome of positive adaptation as well as on going professional commitment and growth in the face of challenging circumstances. Resilience is shaped by individual, situational and broader contextual characteristics that interrelate in dynamic ways to provide risk (challenging) or protective (supportive)

> factors. Individuals, drawing on personal, professional and social resources, not only "bounce back" but also are able to thrive professionally and personally, experience job satisfaction, positive self-beliefs, personal wellbeing and an on-going commitment to the profession. (p. 2)

In the light of this definition, they propose a heuristic model on teacher resilience, which is based amongst others on Mansfield et al. (2012), who interviewed both graduating and early career teachers and, as a result, proposed a framework that organises the multiple aspects of teacher resilience. A multidimensional model and dynamic perspective has emerged, emphasising the role of professional, motivational, emotional and social aspects of teacher resilience. Aspects of commitment, organisation, flexibility, reflection, time management and teaching skills are central to the professional dimension. The motivational dimension combines features of optimism, positivity and enthusiasm, persistence, confidence, self-efficacy, goal setting, "inner drive" (Hong 2012) and intrinsic motivation (Kitching et al. 2009). Emotions are another key factor of resilience and comprise aspects such as humour (Bobek 2002), emotional management, social and emotional competence (Ee and Chang 2010; Jennings and Greenberg 2009), coping strategies (Castro et al. 2010; Tschannen-Moran and Woolkfolk Hoy 2007) and enjoyment. Finally, the social dimension gathers aspects related to building support and trusting relationships (Cefai and Cavioni 2014), to interpersonal and communication skills, problem-solving and the capacity for seeking help when needed (Tait 2008).

Whilst this framework outlines possible dimensions of teacher resilience, it doesn't take into account the impact of external policy change which has become "a dominant feature in the changing landscape of school governance, curriculum and classrooms" resulting in the fact that "being a teacher and achieving success has become more complex, more highly cognitive and emotionally demanding" (Day and Gu 2014, p. 25). Accordingly, within the context of the project ENTREE[1] (ENhancing Teacher REsilience in Europe), a multilevel heuristic model of teacher resilience was proposed (Wosnitza et al. 2014). In this model, it is postulated that all individual behaviour – "resilient" or "non-resilient" – is a result of an interaction between experiences, skills, knowledge and beliefs and develops in interaction with the environment. This means that every teacher is entering the profession with specific beliefs, capacities, skills and a set of strategies that helps her/him to cope with stressful or challenging situations that may encounter as they adapt to a new context. It is furthermore assumed that teachers can learn how to respond in resilient ways and that resilience can be enhanced over time by specific support systems and environmental factors. Therefore, within this framework, teacher resilience is understood as a multifaceted phenomenon that results from the process of interaction between individual characteristics and contextual factors (see Fig. 5.1).

[1] This project has been funded with support from the European Commission (539590-LLP-1-2013-1-DE-COMENIUS-CMP). This publication [communication] reflects the views only of the author, and the Commission cannot be held responsible for any use which may be made of the information contained therein.

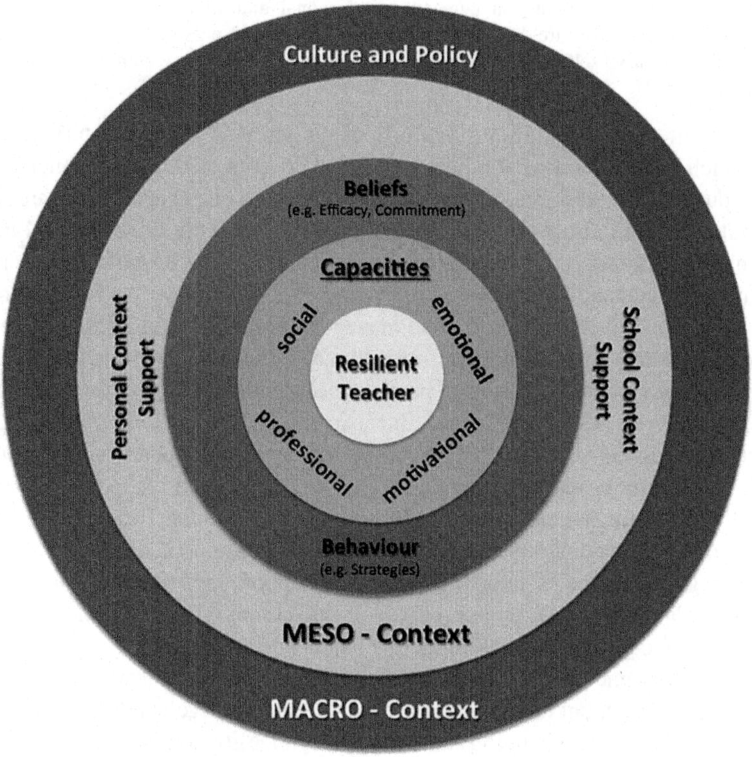

Fig. 5.1 Multilevel model developed by ENTREE (Wosnitza et al. 2014)

At the micro level and as suggested by Mansfield et al. (2012), one finds teachers' motivational, emotional, professional and social capacities. Capacities such as a teacher's intrinsic motivation (Kitching et al. 2009), competence to define professional goals (Sharplin et al. 2011), emotional competence (Chang 2009; Tait 2008) and emotional regulation (Jennings and Greenberg 2009; Morgan 2011; Tugade and Fredrickson 2004), as well as the capacity to adapt to a new social environment and communicate with colleagues and superiors (Schelvis et al. 2014; Sharplin et al. 2011), are considered. On the other hand, understanding resilience means not only identifying existing capacities but also means identifying behaviour dispositions like coping strategies to handle (potentially) stressful and challenging situations in a way that the outcome is satisfying, acceptable or at least manageable. It furthermore means to understand the teacher's beliefs on which her/his behaviour is built.

For this, the model also includes teacher beliefs like self-efficacy or commitment and their behaviour dispositions (e.g. coping strategies). Efficacy beliefs play an important role in teacher resilience (Bobek 2002; Day et al. 2007; Howard and Johnson 2004; Le Cornu 2009) and have also been found to be a strong predictor of teacher resilience (Ee and Chang 2010). The literature acknowledges that teachers with high levels of efficacy also possess high levels of resilience (Tschannen-Moran and Woolfolk Hoy 2007) and that teachers' efficacy beliefs "have a profound impact on resilience" (Kitching et al. 2009, p. 54). Self-efficacy is regarded as an interactive process and a key component of resilience that can be enhanced as teachers encounter and overcome challenges in their career. Also, teachers' sense of professional commitment is considered as another important factor contributing to their resilience (Day et al. 2007; Gu and Li 2013; Morgan 2011). The literature also underlines the importance of a sense of vocation in helping teachers to promote their personal resources, sustain their motivation and fuel their courage to face and overcome the challenges they meet (Day et al. 2007). Research shows that coping strategies are related to the construct of resilience (Connor and Davidson 2003; Sharplin et al. 2011).

On the meso-level of the model, contextual factors that are crucial for sustaining and maintaining teacher resilience are located. These factors include on the one hand the support a teacher gets at school, like support from colleagues, effective leadership, working in a good school atmosphere and caring and supportive relationships with colleagues (Cefai and Cavioni 2014; Ebersöhn 2012; Howard and Johnson 2004; Le Cornu 2013; Sumsion 2004). On the other hand, they also include the personal support outside school, which a teacher receives from family and friends (Mansfield et al. 2014). Research has shown that a lack of support from school leadership and poor relationships with colleagues, students or parents challenge teachers' capacity of resilience (Gu and Li 2013), outlining the importance of the contextual factors (Cefai 2007; Mansfield et al. 2012) and the personal and professional relationships for positively overcoming challenging situations and sustaining their passion and commitment to teaching (Brunetti 2006; Cefai and Cavioni 2014; Ebersöhn 2012; Morgan 2011; Papatraianou and Le Cornu 2014). The resilience literature also highlights the importance of seeking help or assistance as a coping strategy, when teachers face difficulties in handling the variety of stressors within the school context (Castro et al. 2010; Sharplin et al. 2011; Tait 2008).

Moreover, teachers are confronted with challenges that come with the continuing changes in policy and the increased pressure for teachers to improve their standards, which is a significant factor of stress in their work (Day and Gu 2014; Gu and Li 2013; Price et al. 2012). For this reason, the model proposed by ENTREE (Wosnitza et al. 2014) includes the policy aspects that interfere with teachers' resilience and well-being on the macro level.

Considering teacher resilience as a multidimensional construct and organised in different levels, in this chapter, we sought to identify which factors were most related to teacher resilience. Based on the heuristic model of teacher resilience proposed by ENTREE and presented above, we take into consideration the four levels considered by this model: capacities, beliefs, school and personal supportive contexts and culture and policy. More specifically, we analyse the role of perceived capacities (emotional competence, social competence, motivation, professional flexibility rumination and personal life); teacher commitment and teacher self-efficacy (beliefs); school support, institutional conditions for caring and supportive relationships, engagement in school community and conditions provided by institution for job satisfaction (school and personal supportive contexts); and administrative and policy demands (culture and policy) in pre-service teachers resilience.

In addition, taking into account the particularities of the teaching reality in different European countries, we aim to analyse differences in the relationship between teachers' resilience and the contributing contextual factors by country level.

Method

Participants

Pre-service teachers (N = 764) from Germany (n = 235, 69.8% female), Ireland (n = 154, 79.1% female), Malta (n = 262, 80.5% female) and Portugal (n = 113, 96.5% female) participated in the study. Participants age ranged from 18 to 48 (M = 25.2, SD = 5.7).

Measures

Measures used in this study comprised a global measure of teacher resilience, the Multidimensional Teacher Resilience Scale and scales measuring personal life, rumination, teacher commitment, teacher self-efficacy, social context, school support, conditions provided by institutions for job satisfaction and administrative and policy demands. In the following section, we briefly present each measure.

Global Measure of Teacher Resilience To assess resilience, we used the Teacher Resilience Scale (Morgan 2011), which encompasses nine items intended to assess how teachers deal with setbacks in school (e.g. "While things can upset me, I find I can bounce back"). Instead of the original 7-point scale, in this study, participants were asked to evaluate their level of confidence in a 5-point scale ranging from "Not confident at all" to "Absolutely confident".

Multidimensional Teacher Resilience Scale The Multidimensional Teacher Resilience Scale (MTRS) (Mansfield and Wosnitza 2015) comprises 16 items intended to assess 4 dimensions of teacher resilience: emotional (5 items, e.g. "When I feel upset or angry at school I can manage to stay calm"), social (4 items, e.g. "I am good at building relationships in new school environments"), motivational (8 items, e.g. "I like challenges in my work") and professional (2 items, e.g. "I can quickly adapt to new situations at school"). All items were answered in a 5-point Likert scale ranging from "completely agree" to "completely disagree".

Personal Life This is a four-item measure adapted from Morgan (2011) intended to assess the satisfaction with life outside school (e.g. "I have been happy with my social and personal life"). Participants' responses to each item were scored on a 5-point Likert scale ("strongly disagree" to "strongly agree").

Rumination The rumination scale (Morgan 2011) comprises four items assessing the extent to which teachers continue to think about problems that occurred at school (e.g. "When something upsets me at school, I find it hard to forget about it"). The response scale is a 5-point frequency scale ("Never" to "All the time").

Teacher Commitment Commitment is an eight-item measure adapted from Morgan (2011), assessing both commitment to profession (vocational commitment, e.g. "I feel that teaching is really right for me") and commitment to the school where teacher works (organisational commitment, e.g. "I am happy to continue working in this school"). Answers were given in a 5-point Likert scale ranging from "completely agree" to "completely disagree".

Teacher Self-Efficacy The Teacher Self-Efficacy (TSE) Scale was based on Morgan (2011), to which we added some new items assessing the feelings of competence in teaching (four items, e.g. "How confident you feel: Explaining difficult material in ways that the children will understand it") and behaviour management (four items, e.g. "How confident you feel: Managing inappropriate behaviour"). Items were rated on a 5-point scale ranging from "Not confident at all" to "Absolutely confident".

Social Context Social context is a three-dimensional measure adapted from Cefai and Cavioni (2014) intended to assess the perception of conditions provided by the school in terms of caring and supportive relationships (ICCSR) (nine items, e.g. "Our staff understands, supports and cares for one other"), the perception of support provided by the school administration (SPSA) (three items, e.g. "I am understood and supported by the administration" and the perception of collaborative partnerships in the school community (six items, e.g. "There are a number of teaching partnerships and/or mentoring schemes in our school"). Responses ranged on a 5-point Likert scale from "completely agree" to "completely disagree".

School Support The school support measure (Morgan 2011) has four items addressing the perception of support from colleagues at school (e.g. "When something goes wrong I can talk to some of the other teachers"). Items are rated on a 5-point Likert scale ranging from "Never" to "All the time".

Conditions Provided by Institutions for Job Satisfaction (CPIJS) This is a 12-item measure (Silva 2013) aiming to assess the perception of the presence of job satisfaction conditions in three dimensions: resources and working conditions (e.g. "To what extent these factors of job satisfaction are present in your teaching practice? School working conditions"), recognition and professional development (e.g. "To what extent these factors of job satisfaction are present in your teaching practice? Recognition and appreciation of teachers' performance by the school community") and school organisational climate (e.g. "To what extent these factors of job satisfaction are present in your teaching practice? Support and monitoring provided by school administration"). Participants rate each item on a 5-point scale ranging from "Never" to "Always". In this study, we used the global measure of job satisfaction by averaging the 12 items.

Administrative and Policy Demands This measure comprises six items assessing the perception of stress induced by changes in educational policies and in the educational system (e.g. "I find it frustrating that as soon as I become familiar with one policy directive another one replaces it"). The items were answered in a 5-point scale ranging from "Always" to "Never".

Procedure

All measures were included in the survey, which was hosted online between April and July 2014. In Portugal and Ireland, participants were recruited through email directed to higher education institutions that award teaching degrees. As an incentive, participants were entered into a prize draw to win a voucher for an online bookstore. In Germany, participants were recruited using two approaches: some teacher training students at a university were contacted via email and asked to do the online survey; teacher training students and pre-service teachers in the practical phase of their training were also asked to fill in the paper and pencil survey. In Malta, the online questionnaire was sent to all students following the Bachelor of Education course at a Faculty of Education.

At the beginning of the survey, all participants were informed about the aims of the project. Confidentiality and anonymity were assured since no identifying data were collected.

Data Analysis

For all the measures, confirmatory factor analyses (CFA) were carried out to confirm the factor structures. All CFA were conducted using the maximum likelihood estimator available in AMOS 24.0 (Arbuckle 2016). The models' goodness of fit was assessed using CFI, TLI and RMSEA. For CFI and TLI values, above 0.90 were considered as indicating a good fit of the models to the data, whereas for RMSEA values below 0.08 indicate an acceptable fit (Kline 2011). To assess reliability we used Cronbach's alpha.

Following the model proposed by the ENTREE project, we carried out a hierarchical regression analysis considering the global measure of resilience as dependent variable and all the other measures as independent variables. In the first step, we included the variables related to capacities: the four dimensions of the Multidimensional Teacher Resilience Scale (emotional competence, social competence, motivation and professional flexibility), personal life and rumination. In the second block, we added the variables related to the second level of the ENTREE model: the domain of beliefs. Thus, we included in the analysis the two dimensions of teacher commitment (profession and school) and the two dimensions of self-efficacy: self-efficacy for teaching and for behaviour management. In the third step, we added the variables considered in the meso-context, namely, those related to the school and personal supportive contexts (e.g. the two dimensions of social context measure – institutional conditions for caring and supportive relationships and engagement in school community; school support and the perception of conditions provided by institution for job satisfaction). The last block comprised the perception of administrative and policy demands as well as the variables considered previously. All measures were computed averaging the items.

Results

Confirmatory factor analyses were carried out for each measure separately showing an adequate fit to the data (CFI ranging from 0.935 to 0.999; TLI ranging from 0.922 to 0.996, respectively, for the Multidimensional Teacher Resilience Scale and the Personal Life Scale; and RMSEA ranging from 0.032 to 0.102, for the Personal Life scale and the Teacher Commitment Scale).

Table 5.1 shows the descriptive statistics, reliabilities for all the variables in the study and the correlations between them. With the exception of policy demands and rumination, all the variables relate positively with the global measure of resilience. Correlations with the global measure of resilience ranged from small to medium with the two dimensions of self-efficacy showing the highest correlations with the global measure of resilience.

Table 5.2 shows the results of the hierarchical regression analysis on the global measure of resilience. The first block of variables explains 27.4% of variance of teachers' resilience. From the variables included in this first step of analysis, social competence, professional flexibility and personal life are significantly associated with teachers' resilience. Concerning the variables added in the second step (teacher commitment and self-efficacy), only the dimensions of self-efficacy were significantly related to teachers' resilience. Moreover, when adding the beliefs-related variables, a significant association between rumination and resilience was found. This second block increased the explained variance of teachers' resilience by 13%. The third block has taken into consideration the variables related to schools' and personal supportive contexts. Adding those variables did not add much to the variance explained in teachers' resilience ($\Delta R^2 = 0.032$). However, the addition of the variables in the third block suppressed the significant association between professional flexibility and resilience but increased the explanation of emotional competence and teacher commitment in global resilience. Engagement in school community, school support and conditions provided by institution for job satisfaction are the variables added in the third step that were significantly related to resilience.

Table 5.1 Descriptive statistics, reliabilities and Pearson correlations between the variables of the study

	Variables	M	SD	Observed range	Cronbach's alpha	1	2	3	4	5	6	7	8	9	10	11	12	13	14	15	16
1	Resilience (global)	2.18	0.59	1–5	0.89																
2	MTRS – emotional competence	2.17	0.65	1–4.5	0.68	0.31															
3	MTRS – social competence	1.91	0.54	1–4.25	0.67	0.39	0.32														
4	MTRS – motivation	1.93	0.53	1–5	0.78	0.29	0.60	0.39													
5	MTRS – professional flexibility	2.01	0.70	1–5	0.75	0.36	0.38	0.36	0.37												
6	Personal life	1.90	0.79	1–4.75	0.83	0.26	0.29	0.18	0.27	0.12											
7	Rumination	2.22	0.86	1–5	0.87	−0.09	−0.18	−0.02	−0.06	−0.07	−0.05										
8	Teacher commitment – profession	1.77	0.74	1–5	0.88	0.32	0.32	0.26	0.39	0.28	0.34	−0.03									

9	Teacher commitment – school	1.98	0.93	1–5	0.89	0.27	0.28	0.23	0.28	0.28	0.24	−0.07	0.52								
10	TSE – teaching	2.08	0.63	1–4.25	0.82	0.45	0.20	0.28	0.28	0.28	0.17	0.07	0.22	0.13							
11	TSE – behaviour management	2.09	0.68	1–4.75	0.81	0.45	0.22	0.30	0.25	0.29	0.15	0.06	0.23	0.17	0.59						
12	ICCSR	2.22	0.70	1–4.67	0.90	0.32	0.26	0.36	0.28	0.31	0.24	−0.06	0.24	0.52	0.18	0.19					
13	SPSA	2.30	0.83	1–5	0.85	0.22	0.17	0.19	0.25	0.15	0.09	0.04	0.08	0.33	0.13	0.19	0.43				
14	Engagement in school community	2.43	0.67	1–4.67	0.77	0.40	0.30	0.39	0.35	0.41	0.17	−0.05	0.31	0.36	0.25	0.33	0.48	0.34			
15	School support	2.06	0.73	1–5	0.86	0.34	0.17	0.22	0.17	0.30	0.23	−0.04	0.21	0.42	0.19	0.16	0.64	0.27	0.41		
16	CPIJS	2.51	0.69	1–5	0.91	0.33	0.07	0.25	0.12	0.26	0.13	0.03	0.21	0.24	0.27	0.36	0.28	0.13	0.35	0.30	
17	Policy demands	2.63	0.71	1–5	0.81	−0.11	−0.07	−0.06	−0.06	−0.06	−0.06	0.22	−0.06	−0.04	−0.04	−0.02	−0.01	−0.06	−0.04	−0.09	0.06

MTRS multidimensional teacher resilience scale, *TSE* teacher self-efficacy, *ICCSR* institutional conditions for caring and supportive relationships, *SPSA* support provided by the school administration, *CPIJS* conditions provided by institution for job satisfaction. Correlations higher than 0.06 are significant at $p < 0.05$. Correlations higher than 0.09 are significant at $p < 0.01$

Table 5.2 Hierarchical multiple regression analyses for predictors of teachers' resilience scores

		Block 1			Block 2			Block 3			Block 4		
	Variables	*B*	*SE*	β	*B*	*SE*	β	*B*	*SE*	β	*B*	*SE*	β
Competencies	MTRS – emotional competence	0.08	0.04	0.09	0.06	0.04	0.07	0.08*	0.04	0.08*	0.08*	0.04	0.09*
	MTRS – social competence	0.29**	0.04	0.26**	0.20**	0.04	0.18**	0.16**	0.04	0.15**	0.16**	0.04	0.15**
	MTRS – motivation	0.02	0.05	0.02	−0.06	0.05	−0.06	−0.07	0.05	−0.07	−0.08	0.05	−0.07
	MTRS – professional flexibility	0.17**	0.03	0.20**	0.09**	0.03	0.11**	0.05	0.03	0.06	0.05	0.03	0.06
	Personal life	0.12**	0.03	0.15**	0.07**	0.03	0.09**	0.05*	0.03	0.07*	0.05*	0.03	0.07*
	Rumination	−0.04	0.03	−0.05	−0.06**	0.02	−0.09**	−0.06**	0.02	−0.09**	−0.06*	0.02	−0.08*
Beliefs	Teacher commitment – profession				0.06	0.03	0.08	0.07*	0.03	0.09*	0.07*	0.03	0.09*
	Teacher commitment – school				0.05	0.03	0.07	−0.01	0.03	−0.02	−0.01	0.03	−0.01
	Teacher self-efficacy – teaching				0.21**	0.04	0.22**	0.20**	0.04	0.21**	0.20**	0.04	0.21**
	Teacher self-efficacy – behaviour management				0.17**	0.04	0.19**	0.14**	0.04	0.16**	0.14**	0.04	0.16**
Meso-context	Institutional conditions for caring and supportive relationships							−0.02	0.04	−0.03	−0.02	0.04	−0.02
	Support provided by the school administration							0.04	0.03	0.05	0.03	0.04	0.05
	Engagement in school community							0.08*	0.04	0.09*	0.08*	0.04	0.09*
	School support							0.10**	0.04	0.13**	0.10**	0.04	0.12**
	Conditions provided by institution for job satisfaction							0.07*	0.03	0.08*	0.07*	0.03	0.08*
Macro-context	Policy demands										−0.03	0.03	−0.04
	R^2	0.249			0.379			0.411			0.413		
	F	33.4			36.5			27.6			26.0		
	ΔR^2	0.249			0.13			0.032			0.002		

MTRS multidimensional teacher resilience scale
$^*p < 0.05$; $^{**}p < 0.01$

In the last step, we added the perception of administrative and policy demands, which was not a significant predictor of pre-service teachers' resilience (Table 5.2).

In the final model, the strongest predictors of teachers' resilience were the two dimensions of self-efficacy (teaching and behaviour management) and social competence. Perception of school support, teacher commitment, emotional competence and engagement in school community are the variables that follow in the magnitude of the association with teachers' resilience. Finally, the only predictor that relates negatively and significantly with resilience is rumination, meaning that continuing to think about problems after their occurrence related negatively with resilience.

Four separate hierarchical regression analyses, one for each country, were carried out using only the variables of the two first levels of the model (competencies and beliefs) since data collection in Portugal did not include the measures for the meso- and macro-contexts. Table 5.3 shows the results for the last model tested in the hierarchical regression analyses for each country. For German pre-service teachers, the strongest predictors of resilience are teacher self-efficacy – teaching, emotional competence and teacher self-efficacy – behaviour management. The strongest predictor of Portuguese pre-service teachers' resilience is motivation followed by emotional competence and the teaching dimension of self-efficacy. For Maltese pre-service teachers, the strongest predictor of resilience is personal life followed by the teaching dimension of self-efficacy, social and emotional competence and self-efficacy in behaviour management. The two dimensions of self-efficacy are the only variables significantly related to resilience in Irish pre-service teachers.

Differences also arise when we look at the variance explained in resilience, with 55% of variance explained in the Portuguese sample, which is a value substantively higher than in the other samples.

Discussion

The first aim of this study was to analyse the factors that explain pre-service teachers' resilience. Based on the theoretical model developed by the ENTREE team (Wosnitza et al. 2013), we tested it through hierarchical regression analysis. Findings support the hypothesised model showing significant associations between variables at three of the four levels of the model and resilience. The results confirm the conception of resilience as a multidimensional construct, involving a dynamic relation between personal and contextual factors (Cefai and Cavioni 2014; Mansfield et al. 2012, 2016). On the one hand, it highlighted the relationship between social and professional competence and the capacity of resilience (Mansfield et al. 2012) but also the importance of personal life to deal with the demands of teacher profession. Also, being able to reflect about teacher experience and practice (Le Cornu 2009) and being highly committed to students are shown to have a significant impact in teacher resilience. When adding new personal variables in the model, the results show a significant impact of commitment and self-efficacy (both in teaching and behaviour management) in teacher resilience.

Table 5.3 Hierarchical multiple regression analyses for predictors of teachers' resilience scores

	German			Portuguese			Maltese			Irish		
Variables	*B*	*SE*	β	*B*	*SE*	β	*B*	*SE*	β	*B*	*SE*	β
MTRS – emotional competence	0.18**	0.06	0.21**	0.28*	0.11	0.26*	0.14*	0.06	0.14*	−0.03	0.09	−0.04
MTRS – social competence	0.10	0.07	0.09	0.16	0.11	0.14	0.15*	0.06	0.15*	0.09	0.10	0.09
MTRS – motivation	0.08	0.08	0.07	0.35*	0.14	0.27*	−0.04	0.07	−0.04	0.16	0.13	0.14
MTRS – professional flexibility	0.04	0.05	0.05	0.06	0.09	0.07	0.05	0.05	0.06	0.02	0.08	0.02
Personal life	0.05	0.04	0.10	[a]	[a]	[a]	0.16**	0.05	0.19**	0.07	0.07	0.08
Rumination	−0.02	0.04	−0.04	−0.09	0.07	−0.11	−0.07	0.04	−0.09	−0.03	0.04	−0.05
Teacher commitment – profession	0.03	0.05	0.04	0.14	0.09	0.17	0.07	0.05	0.09	0.05	0.08	0.05
Teacher commitment – school	0.04	0.03	0.09	0.13	0.07	0.19	0.05	0.04	0.07	0.07	0.08	0.07
Teacher self-efficacy – teaching	0.16*	0.06	0.18*	0.19*	0.09	0.20*	0.16**	0.06	0.18**	0.28**	0.09	0.32**
Teacher self-efficacy – behaviour management	0.18**	0.06	0.23**	0.06	0.09	0.07	0.11*	0.05	0.14*	0.20*	0.09	0.22*
R^2	0.39			0.55			0.37			0.44		
F	11.7			12.6			14.8			10.8		

MTRS multidimensional teacher resilience scale
$*p < 0.05$; $**p < 0.01$
[a]For Portuguese sample, data collection did not include the Personal Life measure

A sense of commitment, purpose, agency and vocation have been considered as aspects contributing to teacher effectiveness and fostering resilience (Day et al. 2007; Gu and Li 2013; Hong 2012; Morgan 2011; Tait 2008). Self-efficacy, globally, appears as the main predictor of teachers' sense of resilience. In previous studies (e.g. Bobek 2002; Ee and Chang 2010; Hong 2012; Howard and Johnson 2004), it was found that the beliefs about efficacy were reported to be the major components in teacher resilience and that self-beliefs about classroom management often constitute a personal risk factor (Beltman et al. 2011; Gu and Day 2013; Kitching et al. 2009). School support and engagement in school community were the contextual factors related to teacher resilience. In fact, when adding these aspects, a decline occurred in the significance of the previous factors, revealing that these contextual variables relate to personal resources (cf. Cefai and Cavioni 2014). Also, it gives strength to the conception of resilience as involving the context where teachers teach, rather than being an innate trait (Brunetti 2006). These results reveal the vital role of school organisation environment and support by colleagues and school leaders (Carmel and Cavioni 2014; Ebersöhn 2012; Gu and Day 2013; Le Cornu 2013; Papatraianou and Le Cornu 2014) in fostering teacher resilience and well-being and successful learning outcomes for all students (Gu and Day 2013).

Finally, no significant relationship was found between administrative and policy demands and teacher resilience, which can be explained by the fact that participants were pre-service teachers, who had not yet experienced the policy demands and the increased accountability imposed on teachers.

The second aim of the study was to analyse differences in the relationships between the variables considered and resilience in the various countries. The comparison of the pattern of associations between the variables considered and resilience showed similarities between the countries as well as some differences. Thus, despite self-efficacy being an influential predictor across the four countries as the global analysis showed, only for the Irish and German teachers it is the strongest predictor, whereas for the remaining countries it is emotional competence (Portuguese) or personal life (Maltese) that has the strongest relation with resilience.

Based on the evidence of these results, teacher resilience is not an innate state, but, rather, it is constituted and developed by the dynamic interaction of multiple aspects of teachers' personal and contextual competencies and resources that can be organised in different levels, from micro-level factors such as personal competencies to macro-level factors, acknowledging the crucial impact that the increased demands and policies exert on the teaching profession.

References

Arbuckle, J. L. (2016). *Amos (version 24.0) [Computer program]*. Chicago: IBM SPSS.

Beltman, S., Mansfield, C. F., & Price, A. (2011). Thriving not just surviving: A review of research on teacher resilience. *Educational Research Review, 6*, 185–207. https://doi.org/10.1016/j.edurev.2011.09.001.

Bobek, B. L. (2002). Teacher resiliency: A key to career longevity. *The Clearing House, 75*, 202–205. https://doi.org/10.1080/00098650209604932.

Brunetti, G. J. (2006). Resilience under fire: Perspectives on the work of experienced, inner city high school teachers in the United States. *Teaching and Teacher Education, 22*, 812–825. https://doi.org/10.1016/j.tate.2006.04.027.

Castro, A. J., Kelly, J., & Shih, M. (2010). Resilience strategies for new teachers in high-needs areas. *Teaching and Teacher Education, 26*, 622–629. https://doi.org/10.1016/j.tate.2009.09.010.

Cefai, C. (2007). Resilience for all: A study of classrooms as protective context. *Journal of Emotional and Behaviour Difficulties, 12*, 119–124. https://doi.org/10.1080/13632750701315516.

Cefai, C., & Cavioni, V. (2014). *Social and emotional education in primary school: Integrating theory and research into practice*. New York: Springer

Chang, M. (2009). An appraisal perspective of teacher burnout: Examining the emotional work of teachers. *Educational Psychology Review, 21*, 193–218. https://doi.org/10.1007/s10648-009-9106-y.

Connor, K., & Davidson, J. (2003). Development of a new resilience scale: The Connor-Davidson Resilience Scale (CD-RISC). *Depression and Anxiety, 18*, 76–82. https://doi.org/10.1002/da.10113.

Day, C., & Gu, Q. (2014). *Resilient teachers, resilient schools: Building and sustaining quality in testing times*. Oxon: Routledge.

Day, C., Sammons, P., Stobart, G., Kington, A., & Gu, Q. (2007). *Teachers matter: Connecting work, lives and effectiveness*. London: McGraw-Hill Education.

Ebersöhn, L. (2012). Adding 'flock' to 'fight and flight': A honeycomb of resilience where supply of relationships meets demand for support. *Journal of Psychology in Africa, 27*, 29–42. https://doi.org/10.1080/14330237.2012.10874518.

Ee, J., & Chang, A. (2010). How resilient are our graduate trainee teachers in Singapore? *The Asia-Pacific Education Researcher, 19*, 321–331.

Gu, Q., & Day, C. (2013). Challenges to teacher resilience: Conditions count. *British Educational Research Journal, 39*, 22–44. https://doi.org/10.1080/01411926.2011.623152.

Gu, Q., & Li, Q. (2013). Sustaining resilience in times of change: Stories from Chinese teachers. *Asia-Pacific Journal of Teacher Education, 41*, 288–303. https://doi.org/10.1080/1359866X.2013.809056.

Hong, J. Y. (2012). Why do some beginning teachers leave the school, and others stay? Understanding teacher resilience through psychological lenses. *Teachers and Teaching: Theory and Practice, 18*, 417–440. https://doi.org/10.1080/13540602.2012.696044.

Howard, S., & Johnson, B. (2004). Resilient teachers: Resisting stress and burnout. *Social Psychology of Education, 7*, 399–420. https://doi.org/10.1007/s11218-004-0975-0.

Ingersoll, R. M. (2003). *Is there really a teacher shortage?* [Report]. Retrieved from http://repository.upenn.edu/gse_pubs/133

Jennings, P. A., & Greenberg, M. T. (2009). The prosocial classroom: Teacher social and emotional competence in relation to student and classroom outcomes. *Review of Educational Research, 79*, 491–525. https://doi.org/10.3102/0034654308325693.

Kitching, K., Morgan, M., & O'Leary, M. (2009). It's the little things: Exploring the importance of commonplace events for early-career teachers' motivation. *Teachers and Teaching: Theory and Practice, 15*, 43–58. https://doi.org/10.1080/13540600802661311.

Kline, R. (2011). *Principles and practice of structural equation modeling* (3rd ed.). New York: Guilford Press.

Le Cornu, R. (2009). Building resilience in pre-service teachers. *Teaching and Teacher Education, 25*, 717–723. https://doi.org/10.1016/j.tate.2008.11.016.

Le Cornu, R. (2013). Building early career teacher resilience: The role of relationships. *Australian Journal of Teacher Education, 38*, 1–16. https://doi.org/10.14221/ajte.2013v38n4.4.

Mansfield, C. F., & Wosnitza, M. (2015). *Teacher resilience questionnaire – version 1.5*. Perth: Murdoch University, RWTH Aachen University.

Mansfield, C. F., Beltman, S., Price, A., & McConney, A. (2012). "Don't sweat the small stuff": Understanding teacher resilience at the chalkface. *Teaching and Teacher Education, 28*, 357–367. https://doi.org/10.1016/j.tate.2011.11.001.

Mansfield, C. F., Beltman, S., & Price, A. (2014). 'I'm coming back again!' The resilience process of early career teachers. *Teachers and Teaching: Theory and Practice, 20*, 547–567. https://doi.org/10.1080/13540602.2014.937958.

Mansfield, C. F., Beltman, S., Broadley, T., & Weatherby-Fell. (2016). Building resilience in teacher education: An evidenced informed framework. *Teaching and Teacher Education, 54*, 77–87. https://doi.org/10.1016/j.tate.2015.11.016.

Morgan, M. (2011). Resilience and recurring adverse events: Testing an assets-based model of beginning teachers' experiences. *The Irish Journal of Psychology, 32*(3–4), 92–104. https://doi.org/10.1080/03033910.2011.613189.

OECD. (2005). *Teachers matter: Attracting, developing and retaining effective teachers*. Paris: OECD.

Papatraianou, L. H., & Le Cornu, R. (2014). Problematizing the role of personal and professional relationships in early career teacher resilience. *Australian Journal of Teacher Education, 39*, 100–106. https://doi.org/10.14221/ajte.2014v39n1.7.

Price, A., Mansfield, C. F., & McConney, A. (2012). Considering 'teacher resilience' from critical discourse and labour process theory perspectives. *British Journal of Sociology of Education, 33*, 81–95. https://doi.org/10.1080/01425692.2011.614748.

Schelvis, R. M. C., Zwetsloot, G. I. J. M., Bos, E. H., & Wiezer, N. M. (2014). Exploring teacher and school resilience as a new perspective to solve persistent problems in the educational sector. *Teachers and Teaching, 20*(5), 622–637. https://doi.org/10.1080/135.

Schwarze, J., & Wosnitza, M. (2018a). How does apprentice resilience work? The conceptualisation of a generic process model of resilience and its application to vocational settings. In M. Wosnitza, F. Peixoto, S. Beltman, & C. F. Mansfield (Eds.), *Resilience in education: Concepts,contexts and connections* (pp. 35–51). New York: Springer.

Sharplin, E., O'Neill, M., & Chapman, A. (2011). Coping strategies for adaptation to new teacher appointments: Intervention for retention. *Teaching and Teacher Education, 27*, 136–146. https://doi.org/10.1016/j.tate.2010.07.010.

Silva, J. C. (2013). Clima escolar, satisfação, stresse profissional e colaboração entre professores: Que relações? (School climate, job satisfaction, professional stress and collaboration between teachers: What kind of relations?). Unpublished PhD thesis, Universidade Aberta, Lisboa, Portugal.

Sumsion, J. (2004). Early childhood teachers' constructions of their resilience and thriving: A continuing investigation. *International Journal of Early Years Education, 12*, 275–290. https://doi.org/10.1080/0966976042000268735.

Tait, M. (2008). Resilience as a contributor to novice teacher success, commitment, and retention. *Teacher Education Quarterly, 35*, 57–76.

Tschannen-Moran, M., & Woolfolk Hoy, A. (2007). The differential antecedents of self-efficacy beliefs of novice and experienced teachers. *Teaching and Teacher Education, 23*, 944–956. https://doi.org/10.1016/j.tate.2006.05.003.

Tugade, M. M., & Fredrickson, B. L. (2004). Resilient individuals use positive emotions to bounce back from negative emotional experiences. *Journal of Personality & Social Psychology, 86*, 320–333. https://doi.org/10.1037/0022-3514.86.2.320.

Wosnitza, M., Morgan, M., Nevralova, K., Cefai, C., Henkel, M., Peixoto, F., et al. (2013). *Keeping cool Europe – ENhancing Teacher REsilience in Europe*. Application lifelong learning programme. Submission number 539590-LLP-1-2013-1-DECOMENIUS-CMP.

Wosnitza, M., O'Donnell, M., Morgan, M., Mansfield, C. F., Beltman, S., et al. (2014). *Teachers resilience in Europe. A theoretical framework*. Aachen: ENTREE. Retrieved from http://entree-project.eu/wp-content/uploads/2014/11/ENTREE1-new-v2_EN-1.pdf.

Part III
Researching Resilience in Educational Contexts

Chapter 6
The Interplay Between the Motivation to Teach and Resilience of Student Teachers and Trainee Teachers

Lucas Lohbeck

Abstract This chapter focuses on the interplay of motivation to teach and resilience of pre-service teachers. A questionnaire study with two samples is presented: a group of students at the beginning of their teacher education programme ($n = 293$) and a group of trainee teachers ($n = 126$) in the transition between university and school. Both samples completed a questionnaire including the Teacher Resilience Questionnaire by Mansfield (Teacher resilience questionnaire. Murdoch University, Perth, 2013) and the Motivational Orientations to Teach Survey by Sinclair (Asia-Pac J Teach Educ 36:79–104, 2008a). Besides a significant correlation between resilience and the intrinsic motivation to teach, it became apparent both students and trainee teachers were distinctly driven more by intrinsic motives regarding the motivation to teach than by extrinsic motives. Whilst resilience was altogether equally pronounced in both groups, significant differences were apparent regarding the emotional dimension of resilience and regarding the kind of the motivation to teach. The fact that trainee teachers show significantly lower values regarding the emotional dimension of resilience and the intrinsic and extrinsic motivation could be the result of a "reality check" caused by first teaching experiences.

Research on resilience has greatly increased in recent years. Currently an overwhelming number of scientific studies exist which have theoretically conceptualised and empirically researched resilience in general (for an overview: Bengel and Lyssenko 2012) and especially teachers' resilience (e.g. Bobek 2002; Brunetti 2006; Castro et al. 2010; Gu 2014, 2018, Chap. 2, this volume; Mansfield et al. 2016; Oswald et al. 2003; Tait 2008). However, neither a uniform definition of resilience endorsed by all researchers nor a uniform concept of resilience exists. This confirms the complexity and multidimensionality of resilience and leads to significant

L. Lohbeck (✉)
RWTH Aachen University, Aachen, Germany
e-mail: Lucas.Lohbeck@rwth-aachen.de

M. Wosnitza et al. (eds.), *Resilience in Education*,
https://doi.org/10.1007/978-3-319-76690-4_6

differences regarding definition as well as to difficulties regarding communication between the groups of researchers (Mansfield et al. 2012a).

Nevertheless, there are some central aspects of resilience most scientists agree on. Resilience is to be seen as the effect of coping with stresses or, in more general terms, as the status after the confrontation with a stressor (Schwarze and Wosnitza 2018, Chap. 3, this volume). In the field of research on resilience of grown-ups, there is a research tradition which characterises resilience as a relatively stable personality trait (e.g. Block and Kremen 1996; Letzring et al. 2005). However, this view neither contributes to the explanation of the processes that form the basis of resilience nor is it helpful for the development of intervention strategies that enhance resilience (Luthar et al. 2000). Resilience is rather to be understood as the result of a complex interplay of individual characteristics, of the respective living environment and of the greater sociocultural context (Bengel and Lyssenko 2012). Resilience is dynamic, i.e. it develops processually in the course of and in the context of the man-environment interaction; it is variable, i.e. it can increase and decrease; it is specific to certain situations, i.e. certain stressors can be more easily dealt with than others; and it is multidimensional, i.e. it can be variably pronounced in different areas of life (Bengel and Lyssenko 2012). Resilience takes many forms and is exhibited differently in each person as its manifestations change over time depending on the person's success of dealing with situations where resilience is challenged (Oswald et al. 2003). It is to be assumed resilience also encompasses the capability to withstand stressful situations, to recover from them, to emerge stronger as well as more capable from them and to prosper, respectively (Walsh 2006). Research results indicate resilience can be promoted and enhanced (Cefai 2004; Gu 2014).

With regard to teacher resilience, Gu (2014) has also demonstrated that it is context-specific. Not only the individual school and classroom contexts influence the motivation and resilience of teachers but also the school management. Teacher resilience is also role-specific, i.e. there is an interrelation between a teacher's resilience and his or her "inner calling to teach" and "conviction of vocational commitment". After all, the teaching profession typically has to deal with significant stress and many daily stressors. Consequently, teacher resilience is not so much "bouncing back" after single traumatic experiences, but is rather distinguished by the ability to maintain one's balance and commitment in the face of daily challenges (Gu 2014).

Research on teacher resilience has identified a number of protective properties and competences that contribute to the formation of resilience. Amongst these are self-efficacy (Day 2008; Hong 2012), altruism (Chong and Low 2009), perseverance (Yost 2006), optimism (Le Cornu 2009), emotional intelligence (Chan et al. 2008), the willingness to take risks (Sumsion 2003) and flexibility (Le Cornu 2009). It also indicated certain skills contribute to becoming resilient. These include coping skills, like active problem-solving skills and the ability to seek assistance (Castro et al. 2010) as well as the ability to accept failures and to learn from them (Howard and Johnson 2004). Furthermore, interpersonal competences that enable us to build a social support network are of importance (Howard and Johnson 2004). Finally, it is evident there is a link between the ability to teach, teaching efficiency and the trust in one's own teaching ability and resilience (Klusmann et al. 2008).

Some research results also indicate that the kind of motivation for choosing the teaching profession and to work as a teacher has an impact on resilience (Flores 2006; Gu and Day 2007; Lipowsky 2003). Gu and Day (2007) exemplify the findings of a 4-year study on 300 teachers by portraying 3 resilient teachers and stress that "their inner motivation to serve called them into teaching" (Gu and Day, p. 1310) and that internal motivations "fuelled their capacities to exercise emotional strengths and professional competence and subsequently provided them with the resilience which enabled them to meet the challenges of the changing environments in which they worked" (Gu and Day, p. 1311). Flores (2006), in her study regarding the development of teachers and their professional identity during their first 2 years of professional work, found out that all teachers were overwhelmed by the amount and diversity of their tasks in school. Faced by a lack of support and guidance, they were forced into "learning while doing" (Flores 2006, p. 2047). There are accounts on two teachers who despite their very negative perception of school culture and school management preserved their enthusiasm and optimism. These teachers were characterised by the strong intrinsic motivation for their choice of profession: "a strong personal choice to become a teacher and the willingness to work with children" (Flores 2006, p. 2048). Through a survey of young professionals, Lipowsky (2003) found that from the four types of teachers, which were identified with the help of a cluster analyses, those teachers that were stressed the most had the lowest intrinsic motivation to choose their profession of all four groups.

Despite indications that there is a link between resilience and intrinsic motivation on the one hand and the great increase of research on resilience and protective factors within the past 10 years on the other, not very much attention has been paid to the connection between resilience and the kind of motivation to teach.

The question why people chose the teaching profession has been examined in view of both general career choice theories (e.g. Holland 1997) and of career choice models focusing on the teaching profession (e.g. Richardson and Watt 2006; Sinclair et al. 2006).

The current career choice models focusing on the teaching profession are based on theoretical frameworks. For example, Richardson and Watt's model (2006) is based on the expectancy-value theory and the model by Sinclair et al. (2006) on the self-concept theory. The self-determination theory (Deci and Ryan 2000) was used by Spittle et al. (2009) to better understand the career choice motivation of physical education teachers. The self-determination theory was also used for examining the relationship between goal orientation, intrinsic and extrinsic motivation and the performance of student teachers (Malmberg 2006).

In addition, findings of empirical research on career motives of teachers are drawn upon. Empirical research on the career choice of teachers has repeatedly reverted to the differentiation between intrinsic and extrinsic motives (e.g. Richardson and Watt 2006; Sinclair, 2008a). Thus, intrinsic and extrinsic factors were conceptualised. Sinclair (2008a) counts reasons like working with children, intellectual stimulation, altruism, authority and leadership, self-evaluation, personal and professional development amongst the intrinsic factors. He counts reasons like career change, working conditions, life-fit, influence of others and the nature of the teaching work amongst the extrinsic factors (Sinclair 2008a). Whilst Sinclair reckons altruism to be an intrinsic motive, Chong and Low (2009) deem this to be an independent category which includes the wish to work with children and the desire to make a contribution to society.

According to research findings, intrinsic and altruistic reasons are most crucial for the decision to become a teacher (Chong and Low 2009; Rothland 2011). In his meta-study on career choices by teachers in Germany, Rothland (2011) found that the reasons stated most often in all studies were the interest in children and youth and the happiness of being as well as working together with them, respectively. Intrinsic and, in this respect, especially people-and relationship-oriented motives generally predominate as the main motive for choosing the teaching profession (Rothland 2011). The predominance of intrinsic motives is to be deemed positive, because a high intrinsic motivation for choice of career comes along with higher self-esteem, a higher motivation to achieve and competence assessment as well as a stronger increase in competence when training to be a teacher (Rothland 2011). The question, if in addition there is also a link between intrinsic motivation to teach and the degree of resilience, shall be examined in the present study.

The Present Study

The present study addresses two central issues:

The first purpose of this study is to determine the interrelations between pre-service teacher resilience and work orientation. It especially aims to examine whether the kind of motivation to choose the profession is suitable as a predictor for the degree of resilience found in prospective teachers. In order to do so, the predictive capacity of the motivation to teach for the degree of resilience is to be compared to the predictive capacity of optimism, which is an empirically verified prediction variable for psychological well-being and resilience (Hoyer 2000; Scheier and Carver 1992).

The second question to be examined refers to the differences of the motivation to teach and the degree of resilience of student teachers and trainee teachers. Specifically if, motivation and resilience of prospective teachers, who have already made the transition into the practical phase of teacher training and have gained first teaching experiences, differ from the motivation and resilience student teachers show.

Methods

Participants

The sample consisted of 419 individuals. Two hundred ninety-three teacher students (70% female) between 19 and 36 years old ($M = 22.6$, SD = 4.28) attend a German university and 126 trainee teachers from a centre for practical teacher training (61% female) between 23 and 47 years old ($M = 27.6$, SD = 3.58). The teacher students were predominantly in the third semester of their university education (78%), whereas the trainee teachers were in the second half year of their practical training.[1]

Instruments

Participants of the study had the option to complete an online version or a paper-pencil version of the questionnaire. They were given time during a seminar session to participate in the study which resulted in a high response rate. Participation was anonymous and voluntary.

Whilst there is a well-validated German version of the Life Orientation Test (LOT) (Glaesmer et al. 2008), the Teacher Resilience Questionnaire (TRQ) and the Motivational Orientations to Teach Survey (MOT-S) needed to be translated into German first. For this purpose, the questionnaires were translated independently by two German native speakers. During the following review process, the two versions were compared with each other and discussed, and one version was chosen.

In a pretest with 85 students and 32 trainee teachers, the reliability of the scales and the subscales were scrutinised by determining internal consistency with the help of Cronbach's alpha. Whilst the internal consistency of the TRQ and of the intrinsic and extrinsic subscales were good ($\alpha > 0.75$), individual subscales did not show a sufficient internal consistency ($\alpha < 0.6$). Through the elimination of individual items, no sufficient values could be achieved, and they were excluded from the study.

Teacher Resilience For measuring resilience, the Teacher Resilience Questionnaire (TRQ) by Mansfield (2013) was used. This questionnaire had been developed by Mansfield for the purposes of a study which examined junior teachers' perceptions of resilience. This study utilises open-ended questions on what junior teachers believe to be the characteristics of resilient teachers. Mansfield et al. (2012a) have identified four dimensions of teacher resilience: a profession-related dimension, an emotional dimension, a motivational dimension and a social dimension. The

[1] In Germany, the practical training of teachers consists of two parts, a university part and a practical part. The practical part follows the Master's programme and lasts 18 months. During this time, the trainee teachers sit in on lessons given by their teaching mentors, teach under guidance and also teach independently.

profession-related dimension comprises the ability to teach effectively, organisational and reflection skills. The emotional dimension includes aspects like the ability to deflect negative things, to deal with work-related challenges and to advocate for one's own well-being. The motivational dimension comprises aspects like perseverance, self-confidence and optimism. The social dimension refers to the ability to seek and accept advice and to form support networks (Mansfield et al. 2012b). According to Mansfield et al. (2012b), a resilient teacher has characteristics belonging to all four dimensions. This multidimensional understanding of resilience reflects the various concepts as well as definitions of resilience mentioned above and emphasises the complex coaction of characteristics, skills and the use of resources in challenging situations. Based on these dimensions, Mansfield designed scales and included them in the TRQ. The profession-related dimension (four items) comprises aspects like flexibility and organisational skills. The emotional dimension scale (six items) includes aspects like humour and coping skills. With 12 of the altogether 28 items, the motivational dimension scale comprises the majority of the items. These include aspects like optimism, life goals and controlling conviction. Finally, the social dimension (six items) includes aspects like communication and problem-solving skills. The 28 items of the questionnaire are to be answered on the basis of a five-step Likert scale. The internal consistency reliability of the TRQ assessed by Cronbach's alpha was good: $\alpha = 0.85$. The subscales, however, partially only showed a satisfactory internal consistency (motivational dimension, $\alpha = 0.78$; emotional dimension, $\alpha = 0.68$; social dimension, $\alpha = 0.74$; and professional dimension, $\alpha = 0.50$). The professional dimension of teacher's resilience did not show a sufficient reliability in the pretest or in the study, and it was excluded from the evaluation.

Motivation to Teach To determine the motivation of student teachers for choosing their subject, the Motivational Orientations to Teach Survey (MOT-S) (Sinclair et al. 2006) was used.

The MOT-S is a slightly modified version of the Modified Orientation to Teach Survey (MOTS) which is based on the Orientations for Teaching Survey (OTS) devised by Ferrell and Daniel (1993). Sinclair et al. (2006) assume any motivation is either externally or internally referenced. Additionally, Sinclair et al. (2006) differentiate between adaptive and maladaptive motivation. The authors define adaptive motivation as "motivations that facilitate deep and lasting engagement in a task or activity. […] Conversely, maladaptive motivations are motivations that facilitate disengagement from, or 'shallow' (i.e. superficial) engagement in, tasks or activities" (Sinclair et al. 2006, p. 1138). Whilst Sinclair et al. (2006) view all intrinsic motives also as adaptive, they are of the opinion that extrinsic factors are partly adaptive (e.g. career considerations) and partly maladaptive (e.g. influence of others). The 80 items of the MOT-S are to be answered on the basis of a five-step Likert scale. The MOT-S comprises two main scales for measuring intrinsic and extrinsic motivation which are both divided into further subscales. The scales measure the subjectively perceived relevance of various aspects for the intrinsic and extrinsic motivation. The intrinsic subscale ($\alpha = 0.87$) measures the relevance of the following factors: working with children ($\alpha = 0.663$), intellectual stimulation ($\alpha = 0.71$), altruism ($\alpha = 0.63$), authority and leadership ($\alpha = 0.63$), self-evaluation ($\alpha = 0.77$) and personal and professional development ($\alpha = 0.60$). The extrinsic subscale ($\alpha = 0.78$) measures the following motives: career change ($\alpha = 0.796$), working conditions ($\alpha = 0.689$), life-fit ($\alpha = 0.58$), influence of others ($\alpha = 0.56$) and nature of teaching work ($\alpha = 0.58$) (Sinclair et al. 2006). Because of the small number of items of the individual subscales of the MOT-S, items with a Cronbach's alpha between 0.6 and 0.7 were also included in the analysis and discussion. The subscales professional development, life-fit, influence of others and nature of teaching work were excluded from the evaluation as they did not reach sufficient values in the pretest or in the study.

Optimism For the examination of generalised optimism, the Life Orientation Test by Scheier et al. (1994) was used. Scheier et al. (1994) have devised the Life Orientation Test for the determination of individual differences of generalised optimism and pessimism in the sense of a one-dimensional personality variable (Glaesmer et al. 2008). Of the ten items to be answered on a five-step Likert scale, three items form the value for optimism and three the value for pessimism. Four items are filling items. The internal consistency reliability of the scales assessed by Cronbach's alpha was satisfactory (optimism, $\alpha = 0.87$; pessimism, $\alpha = 0.87$). Glaesmer et al. (2008) have pointed out that the relevance of the construct optimism was impressively demonstrated in numerous studies and that in longitudinal studies positive correlations with psychological well-being, physical health, health-care behaviour, positive recuperation processes and low mortality could be shown.

Results

The primary aim of the study was to examine the correlation between the motivation to choose the teaching profession and teacher resilience. In order to do so, the correlations between the predictor variables and the criterion variables were calculated (see Table 6.1). Regarding the motivation to choose the teaching profession, a significant correlation between the intrinsic scale with teacher resilience can be

Table 6.1 Correlations (Pearson) and descriptive statistics ($334 \leq n \leq 419$)

	1	2	3	4	5	6	*N*	*M*	SD
1. Gender	–						419		
2. Teacher resilience	−0.13*	–					334	3.7	0.39
3. MOT-S-intrinsic	−0.13*	0.46**	–				353	3.4	0.47
4. MOT-S-extrinsic	−0.03	0.10	0.38**	–			355	2.7	0.46
5. Optimism	−0.08	0.51**	0.32**	0.05	–		375	3.7	0.38
6. Pessimism	0.05	−0.24	0.04	0.18**	−0.35**	–	371	2.4	0.75

$^{*}p < 0.05$; $^{**}p < 0.01$

observed ($r = 0.457$; $p < 0.01$). Further analysis of the intrinsic scale shows a medium to high correlation of the factors of the intrinsic motivation with the resilience scale: working with children ($r = 0.341$; $p < 0.01$), intellectual stimulation ($r = 0.411$; $p < 0.01$), altruism ($r = 0.260$; $p < 0.01$), authority and leadership ($r = 0.156$; $p < 0.01$) and self-evaluation ($r = 0.396$; $p < 0.01$).

Moreover, differences regarding male and female participants can be determined. Women showed a significantly higher degree of resilience ($r = 0.132$; $p < 0.01$) as well as a significantly higher intrinsic motivation to teach ($r = 0.132$; $p < 0.01$).

To examine common and specific effects of the predictors, multiple linear regression analyses were conducted in a next step. To begin with, it was examined to what extent optimism can be seen as a predictor for the degree of resilience. It is shown that through optimism ($\beta = 0.514$; $p < 0.001$), 26% ($R^2 = 0.262$; $p < 0.001$; F (1, 322) = 115, 59; $p < 0.001$) of the variance can be explained. When examining the influence of the motivation to choose the teaching profession on the variance of the degree of resilience, it became apparent that the explained variance of the degree of resilience increases if the intrinsic scale is not used as a whole ($\beta = 0.457$; $p < 0.001$) but only the factors intellectual stimulation ($\beta = 0.274$; $p < 0.001$), working with children ($\beta = 0.242$; $p < 0.001$) and self-evaluation ($\beta = 0.035$; $p < 0.001$). Whilst ($R^2 = 0.206$; $p < 0.001$; F (1, 306) = 80.88; $p < 0.001$) the variance can be explained with the help of the intrinsic scale, these three factors can be used to explain nearly 25% ($R^2 = 0.246$; $p < 0.001$; F (3, 304) = 33.93; $p < 0.001$) of the variance. In a next step, the optimism scale with the factors of the intrinsic motivation was examined as predictors for the degree of resilience. A hierarchical multiple regression (stepwise) showed that the 26% of the explained variance of the degree of resilience can be increased to more than 38% ($R^2 = 0.383$; F (3, 309) = 65.56 $p < 0.001$) through the optimism scale and the factors self-evaluation and intellectual stimulation. The factor self-evaluation explained another 9% of the variance of the degree of resilience (changes in $R^2 = 0.088$; changes in F (1, 310) = 42.15; $p < 0.001$), and the factor intellectual stimulation explained another 4% of the variance of the degree of resilience (changes in $R^2 = 0.037$; changes in F (1, 309) = 18.54; $p < 0.001$). In the final model, all three constructs were statistically significant. Generalised optimism showed the highest beta value ($\beta = 0.39$; $p < 0.001$), followed by the factor self-evaluation ($\beta = 0.24$, $p < 0.001$) and the factor intellectual stimulation ($\beta = 0.21$, $p < 0.001$).

The second aim of the study was to examine resilience and motives for choice of the teaching profession of student teachers and trainee teachers. A paired-samples t-test was conducted to evaluate the differences between the student teachers and the trainee teachers. It is apparent that resilience of the students and trainees was equally pronounced ($M = 3.7$; SD = 0.04). Also regarding the subscales for the motivational dimension (students: $M = 3.8$, SD = 0.05; trainees: $M = 3.8$, SD = 0.04), the social dimension (students: $M = 4.1$, SD = 0.06; trainees: $M = 4.1$, SD = 0.05) and the professional dimension (students: $M = 3.6$; SD = 0.06; trainees: $M = 3.7$; SD= 0.05), there are almost no differences. A significant difference showed, however, in the emotional dimension of the teachers' resilience scale. Thus, the teacher students showed a higher degree of the emotional dimension ($M = 3.3$; SD = 0.06)

Table 6.2 Teacher resilience and the motivation to teach of pre-service teachers

	Student teachers		Trainee teachers		
	M	SD	*M*	SD	*t*
Teacher resilience	3.7	0.40	3.7	0.33	0.338
Motivational dimension	3.8	0.46	3.8	0.39	0.406
Social dimension	4.1	0.56	4.1	0.53	0.599
Emotional dimension	3.3	0.56	3.1	0.48	1.99*
Professional dimension					
Intrinsic motivation	3.5	0.43	3.2	0.51	4.091***
Working with children	3.8	0.66	3.7	0.75	1.465
Intellectual stimulation	4.1	0.49	4.0	0.59	0.676
Altruism	3.8	0.67	3.3	0.74	5.644***
Authority and leadership	2.9	0.69	2.5	0.71	4.772***
Self-evaluation	3.4	0.76	3.3	0.89	1.201
Pers. and prof. development					
Extrinsic motivation	2.8	0.45	2.6	0.45	2.983**
Career change	1.7	0.79	1.4	0.65	3.117**
Working conditions	3.1	0.68	2.9	0.73	0.978
Life-fit					
Influence of others					
Nature of teaching work					

For the scales with a Cronbach's alpha <0.6 no data was calculated
$^{*}p < 0.05$; $^{**}p < 0.01$; $^{***}p < 0.001$

than the trainee teachers ($M = 3.1$; SD = 0.05), t (264) = 1.8, $p < 0.05$ (two-tailed) (see Table 6.2).

A comparison of the median made clear that the pre-service teachers were altogether driven more by intrinsic ($M = 3.4$; SD = 0.5) than by extrinsic motives to teach ($M = 2.7$; 0.5). Moreover, a significant positive correlation ($r = 0.377$; $p < 0.01$) of the intrinsic with the extrinsic motivation can be determined. Additionally, significant differences became apparent in the main scale for the intrinsic motivation (student teachers: $M = 3.5$, SD = 0.04; trainee teachers: $M = 3.2$, SD = 0.05), t (200) = 4.1, $p < 0.001$ and extrinsic motivation (student teachers: $M = 2.8$, SD = 0.04; trainee teachers: $M = 2.6$, SD = 0.05), t (194) = 3.0, $p < 0.01$ as well as for a majority of the subscales (see Table 6.2).

Discussion

The present study had two research interests. First of all, it was supposed to examine the correlation between the motivation to choose the teaching profession and resilience. Significant correlations between the kind of motivation and the degree of resilience could be shown. The determined significant correlations between resilience and intrinsic motivations to choose the teaching profession are consistent with findings of studies on intrinsic motivation by Kasser and Ryan (1993). Kasser and Ryan (1993) have found that highly intrinsically motivated individuals show a greater general adaptability and greater well-being than extrinsically motivated individuals. Advocates of the self-determination theory assume that the pursuit of intrinsic goals is beneficial for well-being, because they contribute to satisfying fundamental psychological needs (Sheldon 2002). Individuals pursuing intrinsic goals are thus more connected with their "human nature" and their fundamental needs. By contrast, individuals who are more focused on extrinsic goals overestimate the value of their goals for their well-being and neglect their fundamental psychological needs (Sheldon et al. 2010). Thus, studies have shown that individuals with strong extrinsic goals have more difficulties to fulfil their needs for competence, autonomy and social connectedness (e.g. Brdar 2006). Core elements of resilience are the perceived effectiveness when practicing certain behaviours (competence) and the perceived self-determination of one's behaviour (autonomy). Because of these conceptual interferences, correlations between resilience and intrinsic life goals were to be expected. It was shown that the factors of the intrinsic motivation for career choice scale (working with children, intellectual stimulation and personal and professional development) predict the degree of resilience nearly as well as optimism does. These factors appear to be especially important for the successful, long-term and healthy practice of the teaching profession. Thus, Schaarschmidt (2005) names liking to work with children and professional interest as basic requirements for the successful and motivated practice of the teaching profession. If these basic requirements are supplemented by the motivation to develop personally and professionally, the prospective teachers are probably well equipped for their job. In contrast to Rothland (2013), who has identified risky motivations to choose the teaching profession, it can be seen as beneficial motives for the choice of career.

The second part of the study dealt with the analyses of the differences regarding resilience and choice of career motives of pre-service teachers. Whilst both groups are equally resilient, trainee teachers show a significantly lower degree of the emotional dimension of resilience. The finding that work-related strains have an impact on the emotional resilience of trainee teachers is consistent with results of research on strains and stresses of prospective teachers. Thus, in a longitudinal study, Klusmann et al. (2012) found a significant increase of emotional exhaustion in trainee teachers. It is to be assumed that the transition to the practical part of the teacher training requires an adjustment which manifests itself in an increase of emotional exhaustion and challenges one's emotional resilience. These results are in concordance with models on the career paths of teachers (e.g. Hubermann 1989), which emphasise the challenges during the first phase of professional life, as well as with empirical studies which describe an increasing strain on young professionals (Drüge et al. 2014; Klusmann et al. 2012). Starting work is an especially challenging and stressful phase in the course of a teacher's professional life (Arnold 2005). However, the overall equal results of teacher resilience for both groups and the relatively small effect sizes indicate that the trainee teachers deal well with the start of their professional life and that there is no reason to assume the transition is marked by crisis (Klusmann et al. 2012). The fact that pre-service teachers are altogether driven decidedly more by intrinsic than by extrinsic motives correlates with the findings of other studies (Pohlmann and Möller 2010). The correlation of the intrinsic and extrinsic scales indicates that there are two independent factors for the choice of career. Thus, they are no dichotomous poles of a bipolar scale but two independent dimensions (Lipowsky 2003). Great intrinsic and extrinsic motivations for choice of career do not exclude each other. The decision to choose the teaching profession appears to be rather intrinsically motivated than extrinsically. This could be due to the generally positive profile of the teaching profession (Oesterreich 1987) and could be indicative of enthusiasm and idealism of pre-service teachers (Lipowsky 2003). On the other hand, the profession might have too few extrinsic incentives.

Finally, it should be considered that the prospective teachers might rate the intrinsic motivation of their choice of profession higher and therefore might have answered in a socially desirable way (Pohlmann and Möller 2010). Differences between the trainee teachers and the student teachers became apparent in the kind of motivation for their choice of profession. Thus, trainee teachers showed in all dimensions of the intrinsic and extrinsic MOTS scales lower results than the student teachers. The partially significant differences might point to the phenomenon of "reality check" as described by Sinclair (2008b). According to this, the initial motives for the choice of profession are being reevaluated after the first teaching experiences and the original ideas of the teaching profession are being compared with the new experiences. The fact that the differences for the intrinsic scales are more pronounced than for the extrinsic scales could indicate that trainee teachers that have become acquainted with professional practice have a more realistic view of the teaching profession. It could be shown by the present study that such a more realistic view goes along with a similarly high resilience.

Restrictively, it needs to be considered that the results of the study are based on self-evaluation and distortions cannot be ruled out. Other studies that also relied on self-evaluation showed a preference for intrinsic and therefore rather for the socially desired motivations for the choice of the teaching profession (Pohlmann and Möller 2010). In order to achieve a better understanding of the interrelation between resilience and the motives of choosing the teaching profession, longitudinal studies should be conducted, which depict the evolution of the motivation to choose the teaching profession and resilience over the entire time span of the training.

The findings of the present study have implications especially for the debate about the suitability diagnostics for the teaching profession. To stay healthy as a teacher over a long period of time, to teach with commitment and to motivate pupils to study require a high professional motivation. Even if good training can promote the motivation, certain basic requirements must be met. The findings of the study indicate that amongst these are a preference to work with children, professional interest and the conviction of one's suitability for the teaching profession resulting from an honest self-evaluation. The transition into professional practice is a complex adaptation for teachers which requires pedagogic optimism and drive. Wholesome motivations to choose the profession can contribute to the transition being resiliently successful.

References

Arnold, H. (2005). Beanspruchungsmuster und intervention. [Strain patterns and intervention]. In U. Schaarschmidt (Ed.), *Halbtagsjobber? Psychische Gesundheit im Lehrerberuf – Analyse eines veränderungsbedürftigen Zustandes. im Lehrerberuf – Analyse eines veränderungsbedürftigen Zustandes*. Weinheim: Belz.

Bengel, J., & Lyssenko, L. (2012). *Resilienz und psychologische Schutzfaktoren im Erwachsenenalter. Stand der Forschung zu psychologischen Schutzfaktoren von Gesundheit im Erwachsenenalter* [Resilience and psychological protective factors: Status of research on psychological protective factors of health in adulthood]. Köln: BZgA.

Block, J., & Kremen, A. M. (1996). IQ and ego-resiliency: Conceptual and empirical connections and separateness. *Journal of Personality and Social Psychology, 70*(2), 349–361.

Bobek, B. L. (2002). Teacher resiliency: A key to career longevity. *The Clearing House, 75*(4), 202–205.

Brdar, I. (2006). Life goals and well-being: Are aspirations important for happiness? *Društvena istraživanja, 15*(4–5), 671–691.

Brunetti, G. J. (2006). Resilience under fire: Perspectives on the work of experienced, inner city high school teachers in the United States. *Teaching and Teacher Education, 22*(7), 812–825.

Castro, A. J., Kelly, J., & Shih, M. (2010). Resilience strategies for new teachers in high-needs areas. *Teaching and Teacher Education, 26*(3), 622–629.

Cefai, C. (2004). Pupil resilience in the classroom. *Emotional and Behavioural Difficulties, 9*, 149–170.

Chan, W. Y., Lau, S., Nie, Y., Lim, S., & Hogan, D. (2008). Organizational and personal predictors of teacher commitment: The mediating role of teacher efficacy and identification with school. *American Educational Research Journal, 45*(3), 597–630.

Chong, S., & Low, E.-L. (2009). Why I want to teach and how I feel about teaching: Formation of teacher identity from pre-service to the beginning teacher phase. *Educational Research for Policy and Practice, 8*(1), 59–72.

Day, C. (2008). Committed for life? Variations in teachers' work, lives and effectiveness. *Journal of Educational Change, 9*(3), 243–260.

Deci, E. L., & Ryan, R. M. (2000). The "what" and "why" of goal pursuits: Human needs and the self-determination of behavior. *Psychological Inquiry: An International Journal for the Advancement of Psychological Theory, 11*(4), 227–268.

Drüge, M., Schleider, K., & Rosati, A. (2014). Psychosoziale Belastung im Referendariat – Merkmale, Ausprägungen, Folgen. [Psychosocial hazards of trainee teachers – characteristics, manifestations, outcomes]. *Die Deutsche Schule, 106*(4), 358–372.

Ferrell, C. M., & Daniel, L. G. (1993). *Construct validation of an instrument measuring teacher career motivations*. Paper presented at the Annual Meeting of the Mid-South Educational Research Association, New Orleans, LA. East Lansing: National Center for Research on Teacher Learning.

Flores, M. A. (2006). Being a novice teacher in two different settings: Struggles, continuities, and discontinuities. *Teachers College Record, 108*(10), 2021–2052.

Glaesmer, H., Hoyer, J., Klotsche, J., & Herzberg, P. Y. (2008). Deutsche Version des Life-Orientation-Tests (LOT-R) zum dispositionellen Optimismus und Pessimismus. [German version of the Life-Orientation-Test (LOT-R) for dispositional optimism and pessimism]. *Zeitschrift für Gesundheitspsychologie, 16*(1), 26–31.

Gu, Q. (2014). The role of relational resilience in teacher's career-long commitment and effectiveness. *Teachers and Teaching: Theory and Practice, 20*(5), 502–529.

Gu, Q. (2018). (Re)conceptualizing teacher resilience: A social ecological approach to understanding teachers' professional worlds. In M. Wosnitza, F. Peixoto, S. Beltman, & C. F. Mansfield (Eds.), *Resilience in education: Concepts, contexts and connections* (pp. 13–33). New York: Springer.

Gu, Q., & Day, C. (2007). Teachers resilience: A necessary condition for effectiveness. *Teaching and Teacher Education, 23*, 1302–1316.

Holland, J. (1997). *Making vocational choices: A theory of careers*. Englewood Cliffs: Prentice-Hall.

Hong, J. Y. (2012). Why do some beginning teachers leave the school, and others stay? Understanding teacher resilience through psychological lenses. *Teachers and Teaching, 18*, 417–440.

Howard, S., & Johnson, B. (2004). Resilient teachers: Resisting stress and burnout. *Social Psychology of Education, 7*(4), 399–420.

Hoyer, J. (2000). Optimismus und Gesundheit; Überblick Kritik und Forschungsperspektiven. [Optimism and health: Review, critique, and research perspectives]. *Zeitschrift für Gesundheitspsychologie, 8*(3), 111–122.

Huberman, M. (1989). The professional life cycle of teachers. *Teachers College Record, 91*, 31–57.

Kasser, T., & Ryan, R. M. (1993). A dark side of the American dream: Correlates of financial success as a central life aspiration. *Journal of Personality and Social Psychology, 65*, 410–422.

Klusmann, U., Kunter, M., Trautwein, U., Lüdtke, O., & Baumert, J. (2008). Teachers' occupational well-being and quality of instruction: The important role of self regulatory patterns. *Journal of Educational Psychology, 100*(3), 702–715.

Klusmann, U., Kunter, M., & Voss, T. (2012). Berufliche Beanspruchung angehender Lehrkräfte: Die Effekte von Persönlichkeit, pädagogischer Vorerfahrung und professioneller Kompetenz. [Emotional exhaustion and job satisfaction of beginning teachers: The role of personality, educational experience and professional competence]. *Zeitschrift für Pädagogische Psychologie, 26*(4), 275–290.

Le Cornu, R. (2009). Building resilience in pre-service teachers. *Teaching and Teacher Education, 25*(5), 717–723.

Letzring, T. D., Block, J., & Funder, D. C. (2005). Ego-control and ego-resiliency: Generalization of self-report scales based on personality descriptions from acquaintances, clinicians, and the self. *Journal of Research in Personality, 39*(4), 395–422.

Lipowsky, F. (2003). *Wege von der Hochschule in den Beruf. Eine empirische Studie zum beruflichen Erfolg von Lehramtsabsolventen in der Berufseinstiegsphase* [Pathways from university to the profession. An empirical study about the professional success of teacher education graduates at the career entry phase]. Bad Heilbrunn: Klinkhardt.

Luthar, S., Cicchetti, D., & Becker, B. (2000). The construct of resilience: A critical evaluation and guidelines for future work. *Child Development, 71*(3), 543–562.

Malmberg, L. E. (2006). Goal-orientation and teacher motivation among teacher applicants and student teachers. *Teaching and Teacher Education, 22*(1), 58–76.

Mansfield, C. F. (2013). *Teacher resilience questionnaire*. Perth: Murdoch University.

Mansfield, C. F., Beltman, S., Price, A., & McConney, A. (2012a). Don't sweat the small stuff: Understanding teacher resilience at the chalkface. *Teaching and Teacher Education, 28*(3), 357–367.

Mansfield, C. F., Beltman, S., & Wosnitza, M. (2012b). *Keeping cool. Embedding resilience in the initial teacher education curriculum*. Final report 2012. http://researchrepository.murdoch.edu.au/10522/1/PP9_1370_Mansfield_Report_2012_(1).pdf

Mansfield, C. F., Beltman, S., Broadley, T., & Weatherby-Fell, N. (2016). Building resilience in teacher education: An evidenced informed framework. *Teaching and Teacher Education, 54*, 77–87.

Oesterreich, D. (1987). *Die Berufswahlentscheidung von jungen Lehrern* [The career choice of young teachers]. Berlin: Max-Planck-Institut für Bildungsforschung.

Oswald, M., Johnson, B., & Howard, S. (2003). Quantifying and evaluating resilience promoting factors: Teachers' beliefs and perceived roles. *Research in Education, 70*, 50–64.

Pohlmann, B., & Möller, J. (2010). Fragebogen zur Erfassung der Motivation für die Wahl des Lehramtsstudiums (FEMOLA). [Motivation for choosing teacher education questionnaire (FEMOLA)]. *Zeitschrift für Pädagogische Psychologie, 24*(1), 73–84.

Richardson, P. W., & Watt, H. M. G. (2006). Who chooses teaching and why? Profiling characteristics and motivations across three Australian universities. *Asia-Pacific Journal of Teacher Education, 34*, 27–56.

Rothland, M. (2011). Warum entscheiden sich Studierende für den Lehrerberuf? Interessen, Orientierungen und Berufswahlmotivation angehender Lehrkräfte. [Why do students choose the teaching profession? Research on interests, orientations and career choice factors of preservice teachers]. In E. Terhart, H. Bennewitz, & M. Rothland (Eds.), *Handbuch der Forschung zum Lehrerberuf* (pp. 268–295). Münster: Waxmann.

Rothland, M. (2013). Riskante Berufswahlmotive und Überzeugungen von Lehramtstudierenden. ['Risky' motives of the career choices and beliefs of teacher students]. *Erziehung und Unterricht, 163*, 71–80.

Schaarschmidt, U. (2005). Potsdamer Lehrerstudie – ein erstes Fazit. [Potsdam teacher study – an initial conclusion]. In U. Schaarschmidt (Ed.), *Halbtagsjobber? Psychische Gesundheit im Lehrerberuf – Analyse eines veränderungsbedürftigen Zustandes*. Weinheim: Beltz.

Scheier, M. F., & Carver, C. S. (1992). Effects of optimism on psychological and physical well-being: Theoretical overview and empirical update. *Cognitive Therapy and Research, 16*(2), 201–228.

Scheier, M. F., Carver, C. S., & Bridges, M. W. (1994). Distinguishing optimism from neuroticism (and trait anxiety, self-mastery, and self-esteem): A re-evaluation of the Life Orientation Test. *Journal of Personality and Social Psychology, 67*, 1063–1078.

Schwarze, J., & Wosnitza, M. (2018). How does apprentice resilience work? The conceptualisation of a generic process model of resilience and its application to vocational settings. In M. Wosnitza, F. Peixoto, S. Beltman, & C. F. Mansfield (Eds.), *Resilience in education: Concepts, contexts and connections* (pp. 35–51). New York: Springer.

Sheldon, K. M. (2002). The self-concordance model of healthy goal-striving: When personal goals correctly represent the person. In E. L. Deci & R. M. Ryan (Eds.), *Handbook of self-determination research* (pp. 65–86). Rochester: University of Rochester Press.

Sheldon, K. M., Gunz, A., Nichols, C. P., & Ferguson, Y. (2010). Extrinsic value orientation and affective forecasting: Overestimating the rewards, underestimating the costs. *Journal of Personality, 78*(1), 149–178.

Sinclair, C. (2008a). Initial and changing student teacher motivation and commitment to teaching. *Asia-Pacific Journal of Teacher Education, 36*(2), 79–104.

Sinclair, C. (2008b). Attracting, training, and retaining high quality teachers: The effect of initial teacher education in enhancing student teacher motivation, achievement, and retention. In D. M. McInerney & A. D. Liem (Eds.), *Teaching and learning: International best practice* (pp. 133–167). Charlotte: Information Age Publishing.

Sinclair, C., Dowson, M., & McInerney, D. M. (2006). Motivations to teach: Psychometric perspectives across the first semester of teacher education. *Techers College Record, 108*(6), 1132–1154.

Spittle, M., Jackson, K., & Casey, M. (2009). Applying self-determination theory to understand the motivation for becoming a physical education teacher. *Teaching and Teacher Education, 25*, 190–197.

Sumsion, J. (2003). "Bad days don't kill you; they just make you stronger": A case study of an early childhood educator's resilience. *International Journal of Early Years Education, 11*(2), 141–154.

Tait, M. (2008). Resilience as a contributor to novice teacher success, commitment, and retention. *Teacher Education Quarterly, 35*(4), 57–76.

Walsh, F. (2006). *Strengthening family resilience*. New York: Guilford Press.

Yost, D. S. (2006). Reflection and self-efficacy: Enhancing the retention of qualified teachers from a teacher education perspective. *Teacher Education Quarterly, 33*(4), 59–76.

Chapter 7
Exploring Canadian Early Career Teachers' Resilience from an Evolutionary Perspective

Mylène Leroux

Abstract Recent research shows an increased interest in teacher resilience to promote positive adaptation to counteract negative consequences related to teacher induction hurdles. This chapter outlines some results (five participants) of a longitudinal study exploring the development of 23 Canadian novice teachers' resilience. Relying on questionnaires and a semi-structured interview, the risk and protective factors they experienced during their first 2 years of induction were identified, and different indicators of their psychological health as new teachers were analysed. After a thorough analysis of these five cases, it is possible to observe most of the participants are managing relatively well despite the challenges they face. Even if risk indicators are readily apparent for them, at least four of the beginning teachers seem to adapt quite positively. These outcomes provide a better understanding of the developmental process of novice teachers' resilience during their first years and suggest directions to improve teacher education and induction.

Professional insertion is often considered a difficult time that is nonetheless crucial to teachers' career (Portelance et al. 2008). Although novices often encounter unpredictable conditions (Blankenship and Coleman 2009) and go through a period of intense adaptation (Feiman-Nemser et al. 1999), they are generally expected to assume, almost right from the start, the same responsibilities as experienced teachers (LeMaistre and Paré 2010). These challenges have important impacts on early teachers' experiences, including high levels of stress (Klassen and Chiu 2010), emotional distress (Mukamurera et al. 2010), professional burnout (Fives et al. 2007), and even attrition (Tamir 2010).

Therefore, in recent years the retention of early career teachers has become a major issue in many countries (Mansfield et al. 2012). A number of researchers

M. Leroux (✉)
Université du Québec en Outaouais, Gatineau, QC, Canada
e-mail: mylene.leroux@uqo.ca

M. Wosnitza et al. (eds.), *Resilience in Education*,
https://doi.org/10.1007/978-3-319-76690-4_7

maintain the study of teacher resilience represents a solid basis for promoting "quality retention" (Gu and Day 2007, p. 1314).

Whilst many studies explore the characteristics of resilient teachers, and the ways to improve the teaching context in schools as well as the working conditions of teachers, there has been little investigation to date of teachers' resilience strategies in difficult contexts (Castro et al. 2010) or of their adaptive resilience process (Hong 2012). Thus, it appears more research is needed on teachers' resilience process rather than on risk and protective factors alone.

With this in mind, this research, subsidised by the Fonds de recherche du Québec – Société et culture, aimed to study the development of the participants' resilience just prior to entry into the profession, and subsequently during the first years of teaching, in connection with their reflection on their practice. It was conducted in Quebec, the sole province in Canada with a French-speaking majority, and carried out over a 3-year period with 23 early career teachers at the preschool and primary levels (children 5–12 years old). This chapter specifically describes the evolution of five teachers' resilience during their first 2 years of professional induction.

Conceptual Framework

This research hinges on two key concepts: teacher induction and teacher resilience.

Teacher Induction

Although teacher induction is considered a dynamic process of transition that generally covers the first 5 years of practice (Jeffrey and Sun 2008), this paper focuses on the first 2 years only. For Mukamurera et al. (2013), teacher induction is a multidimensional process consisting of five aspects: (1) employment integration characterised by job conditions in the profession (status, access to employment, etc.); (2) specific posting related to the conditions of the assigned task and the work (workload, correspondence to initial training, etc.); (3) organisational socialisation that includes integration into the milieu and the profession (appropriation of the culture, values, rules of functioning, etc.); (4) professionalism involving the consolidation of professional skills, knowledge, and the acquisition of efficiency; and (5) the personal and psychological dimension that overall refers to the emotional and affective aspects of induction, meaning the actual experiences early career teachers encounter.

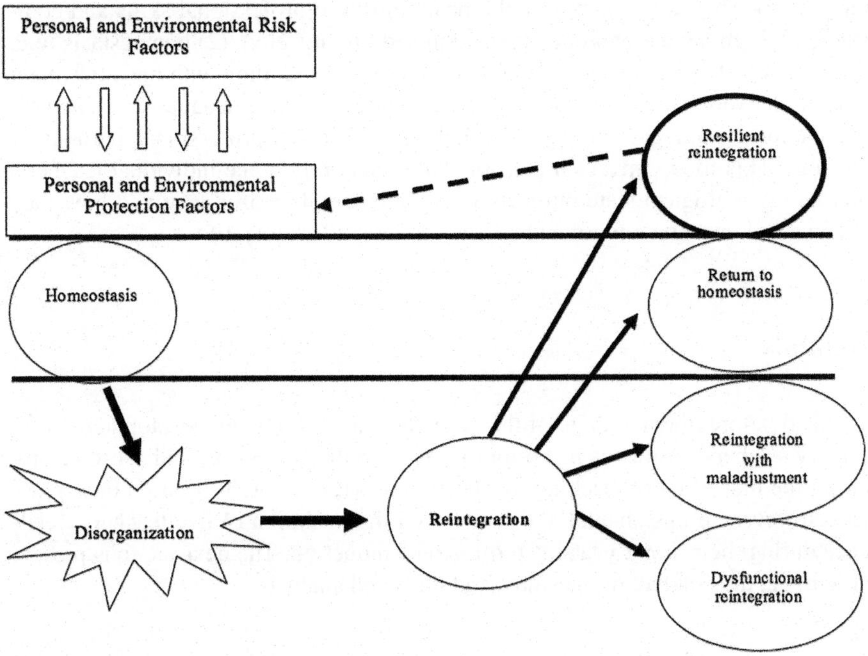

Fig. 7.1 Resilience process adapted from Richardson (2002)

Teacher Resilience

Although there is currently no common definition of resilience, several researchers have identified at least two key elements essential to the phenomenon: (1) the presence of significant risk or adversity and (2) positive adaptation (Théorêt 2005).

In recent decades, teacher resilience has been conceptualised in several ways (Yonezawa et al. 2011). Basically, the term "resilience" referred more to an individual capacity. However, "it has been subsequently shown that resilience is not solely a personal attribute, but is a complex construct resulting from a dynamic relation between risk and protective factors" (Beltman et al. 2011, p. 186). In consequence, a number of studies have attempted to identify the risk and protective factors (personal and environmental) for teachers, but researchers are increasingly interested in the adaptive processes that foster the development of resilience (Yonezawa et al. 2011).

According to Rutter (2012), resilience must be viewed as a process in order to recognise the progressive and non-definitive nature of this complex construct. Therefore, this chapter focuses on the conceptual model of the resilience process proposed by Richardson (2002), which offers an illustration of the dynamic interaction between risk and protective factors (Fig. 7.1). This model also has the advantage of presenting the various outcomes of the process, including (1) resilient reintegration (for teachers, this could mean improved professional skills and competencies, high degree of work satisfaction and vitality, etc.), (2) homeostasis (e.g. maintenance of competencies, comfort zone), (3) reintegration with maladjustment (loss of motivation, dissatisfaction, ongoing conflicts with colleagues, etc.), and (4) dysfunctional reintegration (e.g. psychological distress, professional burnout or attrition). This model makes it possible "to focus on how the individual teacher's internal psychological state interacts with the external environment and how they perceive and interpret environmental cues" (Hong 2012, p. 419).

Methods

As stated before, the main aim of this research was to study the development of 23 primary teachers' resilience just prior to entry into the profession, and subsequently during the first years of teaching, in connection with their reflection on their practice. However, in this chapter, the focus is on the evolution of five teachers' resilience during their first 2 years of professional induction. The next sections present the sample, the conduct of the study, and tools and analysis.

Sample

This chapter focuses on the five early career teachers in the preschool and primary sectors who participated in the study (questionnaires and interviews) during their first 2 years of induction (2012–2013 and 2013–2014). Four were working in the Outaouais region (southwest Quebec); one was teaching on the North Shore (northeast Quebec). There has been a shortage of teachers in the Outaouais region for some years. Many students do substitute teaching during their studies and manage to obtain contracts, even positions, fairly easily after graduation. This is hardly the case in other regions of Quebec, including the North Shore, where early career teachers often wait from 5 to 10 years to find work or a permanent position. A few personal and contextual details about each participant at the time of the study are provided below.

Cali was 23–25 years old. Immediately after graduating in December 2011, she obtained a short-term contract to teach preschool in a low-income area. For the 2012–2013 school year, her position was renewed. In the 2013–2014 school year, she was teaching at the same grade level but had changed schools. During the last interview (December 2013), she indicated she had been on sick leave for over a month owing to depression.

Grace was 22–24 years old. After graduating in January 2012, she worked as a substitute teacher and then taught third and fourth grades for a few months under contract. At the start of the 2012–2013 school year, and after substitute teaching for a few weeks in a first grade classroom, she received a contract to work for the remainder of the year. In the 2013–2014 school year, she was hired to teach fifth grade in another school in the same school district.

Michelle was 36–38 years old. As the only participant with teaching experience, she had taught for 10 years in Europe before studying in Quebec. In the 2012–2013 school year, she obtained a 100% contract as a special education teacher. She offered resource teaching to special needs pupils in five different schools. This same contract was renewed for the following school year.

Olivia was 22–24 years old. After graduating, she obtained various short-term contracts, ranging from a few weeks to a few months, in schools where she had interned. In the 2012–2013 school year, she began in one such school and then obtained a 100% contract to finish the last 100 days of fifth grade in a rural school in the same school district. For the 2013–2014 school year, she was hired to teach a multilevel classroom (first and second grades) in another school with a group that included children with behavioural problems.

Reese was 22–24 years old. After graduating, she returned to her native region, the North Shore, where she obtained a part-time contract teaching music in secondary school. In the 2012–2013 school year, she was given a 50% contract in special education, in collaboration with another teacher. She taught 12 special needs children (autism spectrum disorder, trisomy 21, attention-deficit disorder with hyperactivity, dysphasia, etc.) from preschool to sixth grade. She worked in a small locale shared with the school's daycare centre. In addition, she tutored one Anglophone and two Inuit pupils in French for a few hours each week (language support). For the 2013–2014 school year, she continued doing shared time in this school (1 day/week [20%] in one classroom) and then accepted an 82% contract from a small school consisting of 24 students. Here she worked as both a teacher and resource teacher for all cycles, gave lessons in drama, and taught mathematics to five students in the second cycle.

Conduct of the Study

Data were collected using a questionnaire on teachers' work experience and psychological health and an interview with the participants. Each year, teachers were invited to complete the questionnaire in October or November and to participate in the interview in November or December. There was only one point of data collection for questionnaires and interviews per school year, which could represent a limitation as the situation may have evolved by the end of the school year.

Tools and Analyses

According to Rutter (2012), the resilience process cannot be directly observed. Resilience must be evaluated based on its two core elements: risk or adversity and positive adaptation or competence (Luthar and Zelazo 2003).

In keeping with these considerations, this study was conducted using a mixed methodology on the basis of quantitative and qualitative data collection tools. First, the participants completed a questionnaire on teachers' work experience and psychological health (adapted from Houlfort and Sauvé 2010). Some scales in the evaluation questionnaire targeted risk or adversity and other positive adaptation. This paper focuses attention on three risk indicators (occupational stress factors, symptoms of professional burnout[1], and symptoms of psychological distress[2]) and four indicators of positive adaptation (mental health, subjective vitality[3], satisfaction of intrinsic needs[4], and work satisfaction[5]). The descriptive data in these questionnaires were analysed using Microsoft Excel.

The teachers then took part in a semi-structured interview lasting 45–60 min. This interview was divided into three parts: description of the teacher induction context, instruction to the double technique (Clôt 2001; Oddone et al. 1981), and self-assessment of professional competencies. The first two parts were coded using a coding grid for factors of risk (adversity) and protection (positive adaptation) (Leroux 2014). Thematic coding was done using QDA Miner, and intercoder agreements (about 80%) were conducted on 25% of the corpus to ensure coding validity. For the last part of the interview, the only element retained was self-assessment of overall level of competence (adaptation).

Main Findings

In keeping with Richardson's model (2002), the following sections first highlight the risk and protective factors identified in the interviews conducted. Then the felt risk is described and, finally, adaptation. This allows conclusions to be drawn about the participants and insert each one into the component of the resilience model that best describes their situation: (1) resilient reintegration, (2) homeostatic reintegration, (3) reintegration with maladjustment, and (4) dysfunctional reintegration.

Detailed Findings

Risk and Protective Factors

Table 7.1 presents the number of risk and protective factors identified in the interviews with each participant.

[1] French version of Maslach Burnout Inventory (MBI) (Maslach and Jackson 1986), adapted by Dion and Tessier (1994).

[2] Condensed French version of Psychiatric Symptom Index (Ilfeld 1976).

[3] French version of Subjective Vitality Scale (Ryan and Frederick 1997).

[4] French version of Intrinsic Need Satisfaction (Baard et al. 2004; Deci et al. 2001).

[5] French version of Satisfaction with Life Scale (Diener et al. 1985).

Table 7.1 Number of risk and protective factors identified for each participant

Risk factors	Year	Cali	Grace	Michelle	Olivia	Reese	Total factors/year
Personal	2012	9	10	8	9	6	42
	2013	14	11	7	5	5	42
Environmental	2012	14	9	8	11	14	56
	2013	12	12	10	12	12	58
Total risk factors/person	2012	23	19	16	20	20	98
	2013	26	23	17	17	17	100
Protective factors							
Personal	2012	19	15	10	13	15	82
	2013	14	17	15	18	11	75
Environmental	2012	12	10	7	14	14	57
	2013	11	11	11	12	10	55
Total protective factors/person	2012	31	25	17	27	29	139
	2013	25	28	26	30	21	130

First, it can be observed that there are generally more protective than risk factors for most teachers and that these protective factors include more personal than environmental factors. In terms of risk, environmental factors dominate. Between 2012 and 2013, an increase in the number of risk and protective factors is noted for three of the five participants.

Second, Tables 7.2 and 7.3 present the frequency of the main risk and protective factors identified in the interviews. To emphasise the relative importance of various factors, placed here in decreasing order of total frequency, only those factors identified four times or more during at least one participant's interview, or else mentioned by at least four of the five participants, were retained.

The personal risk factors most often identified are "lack of experience", which decreases in 2013, and "stress, burnout, fragile psychological health", which rises in 2013. With respect to environmental factors, it is possible to notice they are generally more frequent than personal factors. Factors "difficult relations with pupils" and "other nonspecific stressful school conditions" hold steady over time compared to "difficult relations with pupils' parents or problems related to family", "lack of cooperation or difficulties with colleagues", "heavy workload, lack of time, inappropriate task/assignment", and "lack of administrative support", which increase in frequency in 2013.

As for the personal protective factors, "well-developed competencies" largely dominate and rise in frequency sharply in 2013. Next in order are "sociability, altruism, involvement", "good life skills", "good organisational skills in classroom", "other personal protective factors", "interest in ongoing education", and "realistic expectations"; almost all of which increase in 2013. Regarding the main environmental factors, "colleagues' support, good collaboration", and "fair hiring practices" decrease in 2013, whilst "professional development opportunities", "access to ongoing education", and "good administrative support" increase. Although they are

Table 7.2 Frequency of main risk factors identified by participants

	Cali		Grace		Michelle		Olivia		Reese		Total frequency	
	2012	2013	2012	2013	2012	2013	2012	2013	2012	2013	2012	2013
Personal risk factors												
Lack of experience	4	2	4	9	0	2	1	1	6	0	15	9
Stress, burnout, fragile psychological health	2	8	1	4	1	0	1	2	1	2	6	16
Lack of preparation, deficient initial training	1	0	0	0	3	4	0	0	5	3	9	7
Negative feelings (e.g. sadness, anger)	4	3	2	2	0	1	1	1	1	0	8	7
Lack of involvement, difficulty socialising with others, self-isolation	0	5	1	1	3	1	0	0	1	2	5	9
Lack of competencies	0	3	2	3	1	0	1	0	0	0	4	6
Low self-efficacy, low self-confidence	0	1	2	3	0	0	1	0	0	1	3	5
Feeling out of place; fear of being judged	0	2	1	0	0	2	2	1	0	0	3	5
Environmental risk factors												
Difficult relations with pupils	5	9	12	12	5	5	17	17	11	7	50	50
Difficult relations with pupils' parents or problems related to family	6	4	2	9	1	10	7	4	6	4	22	31
Lack of cooperation or difficulties with colleagues	1	13	6	11	0	3	0	5	3	0	10	32
Other nonspecific stressful school conditions	2	4	1	1	6	7	3	2	5	4	17	18

(continued)

Table 7.2 (continued)

	Cali		Grace		Michelle		Olivia		Reese		Total frequency	
	2012	2013	2012	2013	2012	2013	2012	2013	2012	2013	2012	2013
Unfair hiring practices, job insecurity	0	2	3	2	2	2	2	1	10	7	17	14
Heavy workload, lack of time, inappropriate task/assignment	1	3	0	10	0	2	1	5	5	4	7	24
Lack of administrative support	1	1	1	1	2	8	4	7	4	2	12	19
No support system for professional induction	1	3	1	2	1	2	1	1	3	1	7	9
Dissatisfaction with support system for prof. induction	3	1	0	3	0	0	1	1	2	1	6	6
Inflexibility, lack of openness	1	5	0	0	1	3	0	1	1	0	3	9
Difficult relations with school team, poor work environment	3	0	1	0	0	0	1	1	2	0	7	1

not amongst those mentioned most often, factors relating to good relations with pupils and their parents rise in frequency. The following section examines each case.

Cali is the teacher with the highest number of risk factors in 2012 and 2013. She also has the most protective factors in 2012. However, their number falls in 2013, the personal protective factors in particular, whereas the number of risk factors increases. In 2013, she mentions more risk than protective factors in her interview, and it is possible to observe significantly more personal than environmental risk factors. These factors include, notably, "stress, burnout, fragile psychological health". Also, the frequency of the factor "lack of cooperation or difficulties with colleagues" rises sharply in 2013, as does the factor "lack of involvement, difficulty socialising with others, self-isolation"; conversely, the frequency of the protective factors "sociability, altruism, involvement" and "colleagues' support, good collaboration" decreases. This is no doubt due to the integration problems she mentions experiencing in her new school with colleagues characterised by "inflexibility, lack of openness":

Table 7.3 Frequency of main protective factors identified by participants

	Cali		Grace		Michelle		Olivia		Reese		Total	
	2012	2013	2012	2013	2012	2013	2012	2013	2012	2013	2012	2013
Personal protective factors												
Well-developed competencies	29	35	43	50	19	33	33	45	43	32	167	195
Sociability, altruism, involvement	14	8	6	5	1	1	4	10	8	7	33	31
Good life skills (e.g. problem-solving skills)	3	10	7	6	5	5	2	5	11	6	28	32
Good organisational skills in classroom	9	8	4	2	2	7	5	7	5	5	25	29
Other personal protective factors (e.g. creativity, punctuality)	5	2	2	7	0	1	3	10	3	4	13	24
Interest in ongoing education	3	7	4	1	3	4	0	2	5	7	15	21
Realistic expectations	4	4	3	13	0	1	2	3	0	0	9	21
Good psychological health	1	1	2	5	2	2	2	1	3	3	10	12
Sense of accomplishment	1	3	3	2	1	2	1	2	0	0	6	9
Feeling of being in the right place	2	0	0	3	0	2	2	3	0	0	4	8
Flexibility, open-mindedness	1	0	0	0	3	1	1	3	3	0	8	4
Good work-life balance	3	1	0	1	0	2	1	0	2	1	6	5
Motivation, optimism	1	0	1	1	0	0	0	3	1	1	3	5
Sense of humour	2	0	1	1	0	0	0	1	0	1	3	3
Networking	1	0	0	0	0	1	0	1	1	0	2	3

Environmental protective factors												
Colleagues' support, good collaboration	10	7	15	16	3	6	13	17	17	6	58	52
Professional dev. opportunities, access to ongoing education	2	4	2	4	1	5	6	9	5	8	16	30
Fair hiring practices	14	2	2	3	2	1	3	2	2	3	23	11
Good administrative support	3	5	1	4	3	4	4	0	3	3	14	16
Support system for professional induction	2	1	1	1	2	4	2	2	1	2	8	10
Good relations with pupils' parents or positive elements related to family	0	3	1	1	0	2	2	3	1	1	4	10
Family and friends' support and encouragement	3	1	4	2	0	0	1	1	2	0	10	4
Satisfaction with support system for prof. induction	1	1	0	0	1	1	1	2	3	2	6	6
Good relations with pupils	0	4	1	2	0	0	2	1	0	1	3	8
Good help and support from school	4	0	0	0	0	2	1	1	2	0	7	3
Other positive school conditions	0	0	1	1	0	1	1	1	0	3	2	6
Good relations with school team, good work environment	3	0	1	1	0	0	1	0	1	1	6	2

> There are certain differences of opinion concerning our vision of preschool [teaching five-year-olds to write]. Sometimes this can lead to fairly unpleasant situations [...] When things go against how I think of Kindergarten and what the program tells me [...], it can lead to small conflicts, which means you don't integrate too well, neither socially nor professionally, because the differences of opinion are an issue.[6]

However, she often mentions protective factors related to skills and competencies and interest in ongoing training. She was also the only teacher to be hired right out of university ("fair hiring practices").

For *Grace*, the number of risk and protective factors increases in 2013. She presents more personal risk factors than most of the others in 2012 and 2013 regarding "lack of experience" and "stress, burnout, fragile psychological health" in particular. As for environmental factors, the main point of contention involves difficult relations with pupils, parents, and colleagues. Regarding the pupils, she points out that she has several special needs children with behavioural problems. At times, she links the difficulties encountered with parents to her lack of experience:

> I'm being judged anyway because I'm a new teacher. Then, [the parents] try to interfere in everything we do. For example, telling me the way to do things, to change the dates of tests or things like that.

Grace also mentions the workload factor most often. Regarding personal protective factors, she cites professional competencies and "realistic expectations" in particular and to a greater degree than the other participants. With regard to environmental factors, she is one of two teachers who emphasises colleagues' support, and this factor holds steady over time.

Of the participants, *Michelle* presents the most significant increase in the number of protective factors in 2013, whereas her number of risk factors remains fairly stable. She is also amongst those with the lowest number of risk factors in 2012 and 2013. These risk factors include difficult relations with parents, "lack of administrative" support, and other stressful conditions such as working in five schools with pupils from first to sixth grades:

> While working in five different school teams, I'm present, but more discrete, because there are things that, since I'm not there every day, there are bits of information I don't have. I try to stay informed without being an imposition.

These elements are perhaps partly the reason she perceives a lack of administrative support. Michelle also mentions difficult relations with pupils, but much less frequently than the other teachers. She is also one of two teachers who identify lack of preparation in initial training. These findings can be explained by the fact that she works in special education rather than general education, offering resource teaching to only a few pupils at a time. For the time being, she appears to experience more difficulties with parents than do the other teachers. However, this appears to be because some parents know she is not qualified as a special education teacher, and she is responsible for developing and monitoring individualised education plans (IEP) for special needs pupils:

---

[6]All participants' quotes have been freely translated from French to English.

> In [IEP], we really try to accompany the parents because we're in a rather disadvantaged area. So we're not certain that some parents understand all the terms we use in the [IEP]. So it's for sure we have the role of accompanier to play at that level.

In regard to protective factors, she underscores competencies and skills, organisational skills (an aspect probably facilitated by resource teaching rather than classroom teaching), colleagues' support, and professional development opportunities. This last factor is particularly important for Michelle since she teaches in a field for which she has not been trained.

Olivia presents a small number of risk factors and a larger number of protective factors in 2013. She is amongst those with the fewest risk factors and the highest number of protective factors in 2013. Regarding risk factors – environmental in particular – difficulties with pupils stand out:

> [...] it's a group that needs to be very very tightly controlled. If I make the mistake of telling a joke, I lose control [...]. Otherwise, there's also the chance of a chain reaction, if somebody starts something silly, everybody jumps in and there's no end to it. The leaders I have aren't necessarily positive leaders.

She also mentions the lack of support by administrators and colleagues, as well as "heavy workload, lack of time, inappropriate task/assignment". For this last factor, she points out the following:

> We're in the field of education, that's how it is, but they often give us the most difficult classes, or the classes that teachers with the most seniority [don't want]...That's why I found myself with a multi[level] classroom, with difficult pupils and all that. I find that's a bit illogical, because in other professions, you get the most difficult dossiers when you have more experience, whereas in teaching, the opposite is true.

In regard to protective factors, Olivia strongly emphasises professional competencies and colleagues' support. She also talks about "sociability, altruism, involvement", "professional development opportunities", and other personal protective factors (e.g. joy, warmth, patience).

Finally, for *Reese*, it is possible to note a decrease in the number of risk and protective factors in 2013. She is the participant with the lowest number of protective factors in 2013, at both the personal and environmental levels. As for risk factors, although they fall in 2013, she specifies lack of experience, difficulties with pupils and their parents, lack of preparation in initial training, and "unfair hiring practices, job insecurity". These last two factors are hardly surprising, considering the highly complex tasks she was assigned in 2012 and 2013. In terms of protective factors, Reese, like the others, emphasises skills and competencies and the collaboration and support of colleagues but, unlike the others, mentions these less in 2013. She also evokes "sociability, altruism, involvement", "interest in ongoing training", and "professional development opportunities", which are essential in view of the tasks she was given:

> I had a lot of [training]. Last year, when I was in special education, they gave me all the training that was available, because I was working with autistic children, [with] trisomy [21] and everything.

Description of Risk

First, it should be recalled risk evaluation is done based on three scales: (1) sources of occupational stress, (2) symptoms of professional burnout, and (3) symptoms of psychological distress. The results for each participant are presented in Tables 7.4, 7.5, and 7.6.

These first results reveal workload followed by relations with parents and colleagues causes a higher level of stress in 2013 for at least three or four teachers. Workload presents the highest indices of stress, for Cali and Grace in particular, whilst those for classroom management and administrative relations decrease for three teachers. It can be pointed out that for Grace and Reese, classroom management and relations with parents generate moderate to significant stress.

Almost all participants experience symptoms of professional burnout more often in 2013. The results are particularly concerning for Olivia and Cali, who say they experience them between one and a few times per month or per week, respectively.

Finally, an increase can be observed in the frequency of symptoms of psychological distress in 2013 in terms of anxiety and irritability for a majority of the teachers. Grace says she experiences anxiety fairly to very often. For Cali, the situation is somewhat concerning; she reports experiencing cognitive symptoms very or fairly often, in addition to symptoms of anxiety and depression.

Table 7.4 Sources of occupational stress

Sources of occupational stress	Year	Cali	Grace	Michelle	Olivia	Reese
Workload	2012	2.00	2.13	1.83	1.67	3.00
	2013	4.33	3.00	2.50	2.00	2.70
Classroom management	2012	2.20	2.67	2.33	3.00	2.00
	2013	1.30	3.20	1.80	2.80	3.20
Relations with school leader/administrative support	2012	1.00	3.75	1.50	1.00	3.00
	2013	2.50	1.25	1.25	2.75	1.00
Relations with parents	2012	2.13	3.50	1.38	2.50	1.88
	2013	1.80	4.00	2.10	1.10	3.30
Relations with colleagues	2012	1.17	2.33	1.00	1.00	2.17
	2013	2.50	2.50	1.17	1.67	1.10

Data represent the average of the indicators of each source of stress evaluated according to the following scale: Not at all (1) – Mildly (2) – Somewhat (3) – Very much (4) – Always (5)

Table 7.5 Prevalence of burnout symptoms

Burnout symptoms	Year	Cali	Grace	Michelle	Olivia	Reese
	2012	2.75	2.00	1.63	2.13	2.88
	2013	5.50	2.50	1.80	3.40	2.00

Data represent the average of the indicators of burnout symptoms according to the following scale: Never (1) – A few times a year (2) – Once a month (3) – A few times a month (4) – Once a week (5) – A few times a week (6) – Every day (7)

Description of Adaptation

The analysis of adaptation is based on evaluation of mental health compared with others of the same age, evaluation of subjective vitality, perception of the satisfaction of intrinsic needs, perception of work satisfaction, and self-assessment of overall level of competence. Tables 7.7, 7.8, 7.9, 7.10, and 7.11 depict these results for each participant.

These first results reveal even if mental health deteriorates slightly for four of the five participants in 2013, it remains good or very good on the whole. This index seems worrisome only for Cali, since she considers her mental health to be poor.

Here, a decrease can be noted in subjective vitality for three participants, although four say they experience it often or fairly often just the same. Again, the situation is of concern for Cali especially, who shows a rather sharp decrease in this index in 2013.

For perception of intrinsic needs satisfaction, an improvement is observed in 2013 for a majority of the teachers in terms of the needs for belonging and

Table 7.6 Prevalence of symptoms of psychological distress

Symptoms of psychological distress	Year	Cali	Grace	Michelle	Olivia	Reese
Anxiety	2012	1.67	2.00	1.67	1.00	2.00
	2013	3.00	3.30	1.30	1.70	1.00
Cognitive symptoms	2012	2.00	1.00	1.00	1.00	2.00
	2013	4.00	2.00	1.00	1.00	2.00
Irritability	2012	1.00	1.00	1.25	1.00	1.00
	2013	2.00	1.80	1.00	1.50	1.30
Depression	2012	1.00	1.20	1.00	1.00	1.00
	2013	3.00	1.60	1.00	1.00	1.00

Data represent the average of the indicators of symptoms of psychological distress evaluated based on the following scale: Never (1) – Sometimes (2)

Table 7.7 Evaluation of mental health compared with others of the same age

Mental health	Year	Cali	Grace	Michelle	Olivia	Reese
	2012	2	2	1	1	1
	2013	5	2	2	2	3

Mental health was evaluated based on the following scale: Excellent (1) – Very good (2) – Good (3) – Average (4) – Poor (5)

Table 7.8 Evaluation of subjective vitality

Subjective vitality	Year	Cali	Grace	Michelle	Olivia	Reese
	2012	4	3.71	4.00	4.00	3.29
	2013	1.60	3.90	3.90	3.70	3.60

Data represent the average of the indicators of subjective vitality evaluated according to the following scale: Never (1) – Sometimes (2) – Fairly often (3) – Often (4) – Every day (5)

Table 7.9 Perception of intrinsic needs satisfaction

Intrinsic needs satisfaction	Year	Cali	Grace	Michelle	Olivia	Reese
Relatedness	2012	4.83	3.67	4.33	4.17	3.80
	2013	2.70	3.80	4.50	3.30	4.00
Competence	2012	4.67	4.17	4.00	4.67	4.17
	2013	2.80	3.50	4.20	4.80	4.50
Autonomy	2012	4.83	4.17	4.33	3.67	4.17
	2013	1.80	4.30	4.20	3.80	4.00

Data represent the average of the indicators of satisfaction of intrinsic needs evaluated according to the following scale: Strongly disagree (1) – Disagree (2) – Neither agree nor disagree (3) – Agree (4) – Strongly agree (5)

Table 7.10 Perception of work satisfaction

Work satisfaction	Year	Cali	Grace	Michelle	Olivia	Reese
	2012	5.38	4.60	6.20	5.40	4.80
	2013	3.80	4.40	5.60	5.00	4.60

Data represent the average of the indicators of work satisfaction evaluated according to the following scale: Disagree completely (1) – Strongly disagree (2) – Very slightly agree (3) – Somewhat agree (4) – Moderately agree (5) – Strongly agree (6) – Very strongly agree (7)

Table 7.11 Self-assessment of general level of competence (/10)

General level of competence	Year	Cali	Grace	Michelle	Olivia	Reese
	2012	8.0	6.0	7.0	8.5	6.5
	2013	7.5	6.5	7.0	8.5	7.5

competence. Michelle and Reese show a slight decrease in need for autonomy, but the index remains high. Again, only Cali's results are cause for concern, since her needs appear to be unsatisfied in 2013.

The indicator of work satisfaction is lower for all participants in 2013. However, with the exception of Cali, they say they are between moderately and very satisfied.

Finally, for most of the teachers, overall level of competence holds steady or improves during the second year of induction. The only teacher whose situation deteriorates is Cali, but her overall level of competence is amongst the highest nevertheless.

Portrait of Resilience for the Five Cases

For *Cali*, there is a lack of balance between her risk and protective factors, insofar as the protective factors do not outweigh the risk factors. Her risk indices are the highest, which translates into certain disorganisation. Since her adaptation indices are also rather weak, having fallen in 2013, and since she confirmed she was on sick leave for depression in her second interview, Cali matches the dysfunctional reintegration profile, at least during her second year of induction.

More protective factors than risk factors are observed for *Grace*. On the other hand, almost all her risk indices rise in 2013, although they are not always cause for concern. It is mainly the high indices of stress (especially relations with parents) and anxiety (symptom of psychological distress) that lead us to believe she is experiencing disorganisation. Her adaptation indices generally tend to be good, with the possible exception of sense of competence (satisfaction of needs and overall level of competence) and work satisfaction, which are slightly weaker than the others. Thus, she would fall within a profile of homeostatic reintegration or reintegration with maladjustment.

Michelle shows the greatest increase in number of protective factors in 2013 and mentions the fewest risk factors. Certain risk indices (sources of stress and symptoms of professional burnout) increase in 2013, but remain fairly weak in comparison to the others. Apart from that, the majority of these risk indices holds steady or improves, making it doubtful that she experiences disorganisation. Her adaptation indices are fairly good and are generally the highest of the five cases. Therefore, Michelle would match the resilient reintegration profile.

Olivia's results reveal risk factors decrease and protective factors increase in 2013. She is amongst the participants having the fewest risk factors and the most protective factors for this second year of induction. Regarding her risk indices, some increase in 2013 (particularly stress related to administrative support and symptoms of professional burnout), which suggests a certain disorganisation, whilst others hold steady or improve. As for adaptation indices, some improve and others decrease slightly, but most remain relatively good, except perhaps for the need for belonging, which falls sharply in 2013. Her overall level of competence holds steady and is the highest of all the teachers. All this suggests Olivia matches the profile of homeostatic, possibly even of resilient, reintegration.

For *Reese*, risk and protective factors decrease in 2013. This teacher presents the fewest protective factors in 2013, which, at first glance, appears troubling. However, many of her risk indices are fairly good, hold steady, or improve in 2013, with the exception of classroom management and relations with parents. This causes concern and leads us to note some disorganisation. Adaptation indices tend to be high overall, with improvement in 2013, except for the evaluation of mental health, which deteriorates and is slightly weaker than that of most other participants. These diverse results situate Reese within a homeostatic reintegration profile.

Discussion

After careful scrutiny of these results, it seems most of these novice teachers are managing relatively well despite the challenges they face. Analyses also allow certain observations, many of which are supported by the literature.

Regarding the challenges encountered, the risk factor "difficult relations with pupils" is generally the most frequent, whereas Grace and Olivia mention it more than the others; both cite pupils' behavioural problems, an element often seen as a challenge in terms of classroom management for novice teachers (Hong 2012). Difficult relations with parents are also an issue for all the teachers (Beltman et al. 2011; Tait 2008). These two aspects stand out as significant sources of stress for several of them. The majority also points out an important risk factor is difficult relations or lack of collaboration with colleagues (Castro et al. 2010); note the three persons for whom this factor occurs most frequently changed schools in 2013. For Cali, this challenge seems compounded by a conflict in values with certain colleagues and appears to interfere rather strongly with her integration and need for belonging. Another important risk factor is lack of administrative support, although the literature recurrently stresses the importance of the administration's role in teacher induction (Hong 2010; Huisman et al. 2010; Peters and Pearce 2012). Furthermore, whilst all the teachers cite the factor "unfair hiring practices, job insecurity", the latter is obviously of greatest importance to Reese, which confirms the unpredictability and complexity of the tasks novice teachers are often assigned (Hong 2012). Another significant risk factor is workload (Beltman et al. 2011), which was also identified as the strongest source of stress in the questionnaires. Two teachers in particular, Michelle and Reese, mention "lack of preparation, deficient initial training" (Huisman et al. 2010); however, it is possible to note they were not working in the field they had been trained for, which refers back to unpredictable working conditions (Gingras and Mukamurera 2008). Finally, at the personal level, several participants cite "stress, burnout, fragile psychological health" (Sharplin et al. 2011), whilst, at the same time, three teachers present heightened symptoms of burnout or psychological distress (Grace, Olivia, and, especially, Cali).

Regarding adaptation, "well-developed competencies" are undeniably the most important protective factor for all of the teachers (Beltman et al. 2011; Howard and Johnson 2004); four of them show this factor increases in frequency in 2013. Next in importance is colleagues' collaboration and support (Sharplin et al. 2011; Tait 2008), which is the first of the environmental protective factors for all participants, Grace and Olivia in particular. Now, this does not appear to be an external factor alone, since several also mention the personal factor "sociability, altruism, involvement". Thus, it is also important novice teachers make efforts to engage with colleagues, not simply wait for colleagues to come to them (Mansfield et al. 2012; Tait 2008). On a different note, professional development opportunities seem important (Huisman et al. 2010; Tait 2008), notably for Michelle, Olivia, and Reese. Recall Michelle and Reese teach in a field other than the one for which they were trained and Olivia teaches at a multiple level. Perception of work satisfaction also appears to play a relatively important role (Morgan et al. 2010; Sass et al. 2011) insofar as this index is high for all participants, with the exception of Cali, who experiences serious adaptation difficulties in 2013.

Returning now to the dimensions of teacher induction based on the model of Mukamurera et al. (2013), it would appear the main personal risks identified involve a sense of ill-being or lack of preparedness and may be linked to the personal/psychological and professionalism dimensions. As for the environmental level, the main risks involve, first, relational aspects (pupils, parents, colleagues, administration) and therefore the dimension of organisational socialisation and, second, elements related to hiring and assigned tasks, regarding employment and specific posting, respectively.

The key personal protective factors are professional skills and competencies – even certain personal characteristics – and therefore fall within the professionalism and personal/psychological dimensions (Mukamurera et al. 2013). Regarding environmental factors, they again involve support from colleagues and the administration (organisational socialisation), access to professional development opportunities (professionalism), hiring practices, and teacher induction structures (employment and specific posting). Those results highlight the interest of conceptualising resilience from an ecological perspective (Gu 2018, Chap. 2; Mansfield et al. 2018, Chap. 4; Peixoto et al. 2018, Chap. 5; Schwarze and Wosnitza 2018, Chap. 3 – all this volume).

Conclusion

Although this study is careful not to generalise considering the small sample, the findings presented here allow for a better understanding of beginning teachers' resilience and their needs. Also, even if all the data were collected during autumn for each school year, the study relies on a longitudinal approach that allowed for the consideration of an evolutionary perspective of the resilience process. In addition, findings offer solutions for improving initial and ongoing training and support at the time of induction, with a view to promoting teacher resilience.

Specifically, in order to better train teachers, teacher educators need to act more in harmony with the professionalism and personal/psychological dimensions (Mukamurera et al. 2013). The development of a greater sense of competence could be targeted by reinforcing, amongst other things, competencies for classroom management (especially the management of behavioural difficulties) and collaboration with colleagues and parents (Aitken and Harford 2011; Le Cornu 2009). For example, during initial training, it would help to work on the development of certain cooperative skills that are often taken for granted. Trainees could then be led to work not only together but with other professionals as well (resource teachers, special educators, psychologists, etc.) in a manner that reproduces the real interactions of a school team. Findings also emphasise the importance of improved psychological training for future teachers (Pelletier 2013; Théorêt 2011). They should be supported in developing their well-being and work satisfaction; managing their emotions, stress, and workload; finding a work-life balance; and maintaining realistic expectations (Théorêt and Leroux 2014; for other suggestions see Beltman et al. 2018, Chap. 14; Hazel 2018, Chap. 13 – both this volume).

Finally, with the aim of better supporting novice teachers and fostering "quality retention" (Gu and Day 2007), findings highlight the full importance of welcome and support by colleagues and the school administration (Beltman et al. 2011; Hong 2012; Peters and Pearce 2012). Participants strongly emphasise the need to be reassured, supported, acknowledged, informed, able to share and exchange, etc., which relates to the dimension of organisational socialisation (Mukamurera et al. 2013). Those findings emphasise the importance of relationships in the school (Crosswell et al. 2018, Chap. 8; Flores 2018, Chap. 10; Gu 2018, Chap. 2; Peixoto et al. 2018, Chap. 5 – all this volume).

In addition, access to professional development opportunities emerges as a key element (Aitken and Harford 2011; Henry et al. 2011). If teacher induction conditions are complex and often unpredictable, these opportunities may at least mitigate the negative impacts. It is also important to ensure all novices, who wish to do so, can benefit from such opportunities regardless of when they are hired (Duchesne and Kane 2010). To return to the issue of unpredictability, it would seem job security is not an absolute guarantee of satisfaction (e.g. Cali). For some teachers, what seems to have had a negative impact, more than the task itself, is changing schools at the end of a year, after they had forged bonds, developed a sense of belonging, learned the school's rules and functioning, etc. This may require another look. In conclusion, considering the strong emphasis on work overload by our participants, it appears they could use more free time for the various tasks they are often accomplishing for the first time (e.g. overall planning, report cards, meetings with parents, etc.). Another possible solution is a lighter workload (Duchesne and Kane 2010; Tait 2008). As a final consideration, we should remember that developing teacher resilience can not only rely on teachers' personal will and characteristics but also on environmental conditions (Gu 2018, Chap. 2, this volume) and sociocultural context (Crosswell et al. 2018, Chap. 8, this volume).

References

Aitken, R., & Harford, J. (2011). Induction needs of a group of teachers at different career stages in a school in the Republic of Ireland: Challenges and expectations. *Teaching and Teacher Education, 27*, 350–356.

Baard, P. P., Deci, E. L., & Ryan, R. M. (2004). Intrinsic need satisfaction: A motivational basis of performance and well-being in two work settings. *Journal of Applied Social Psychology, 34*, 2045–2068.

Beltman, S., Mansfield, C. F., & Price, A. (2011). Thriving not just surviving: A review of research on resilience. *Educational Research Review, 6*, 185–207.

Beltman, S., Mansfield, C. F., Wosnitza, M., Weatherby-Fell, N., & Broadley, T. (2018). Using online modules to build capacity for teacher resilience. In M. Wosnitza, F. Peixoto, S. Beltman, & C. F. Mansfield (Eds.), *Resilience in education: Concepts, contexts and connections* (pp. 237–253). New York: Springer.

Blankenship, T. B., & Coleman, M. (2009). An examination of "wash-out" and workplace conditions of beginning physical education teachers. *The Physical Educator, 25*(2), 97–111.

Castro, A. J., Kelly, J., & Shih, S. (2010). Resilience strategies for new teachers in high-needs areas. *Teaching and Teacher Education, 26*(3), 622–629.

Clôt, Y. (2001). Méthodologie en clinique de l'activité – L'exemple du sosie [Methodology in clinical activity – The example of the instruction to the double]. In M. S. Delefosse & G. Rouan (Eds.), *Les méthodes qualitatives en psychologie* (pp. 125–147). Paris: Dunod.

Crosswell, L., Willis, J., Morrion, C., Gibson, A., & Ryan, M. (2018). Early career teachers in rural schools: Plotlines for resilience. In M. Wosnitza, F. Peixoto, S. Beltman, & C. F. Mansfield (Eds.), *Resilience in education: Concepts, contexts and connections* (pp. 131–146). New York: Springer.

Deci, E. L., Ryan, R. M., Gagné, M., Leone, D. R., Usunov, J., & Kornazheva, B. P. (2001). Need satisfaction, motivation, and well-being in the work organizations of a former Eastern Bloc country. *Personality and Social Psychology Bulletin, 27*, 930–942.

Diener, E., Emmons, R. A., Larsen, R. J., & Griffin, S. (1985). The satisfaction with life scale. *Journal of Personality Assessment, 49*(1), 71–75.

Dion, G., & Tessier, R. (1994). Validation de la traduction de l'lnventaire d'epuisement professionnel de Maslach et Jackson [Validation of the translation of Maslach and Jackson's burnout inventory]. *Revue Canadienne des Sciences du Comportement, 26*(2), 210–227.

Duchesne, C., & Kane, R. (2010). Défis de l'insertion professionnelle et dispositifs d'encadrement [The challenge of teacher placement and follow-up support]. *McGill Journal of Education, 45*(1), 63–80.

Feiman-Nemser, S., Schwille, S., Carver, C., & Yusko, B. (1999). *A conceptual review of literature on new teacher induction*. Washington, DC: National Partnership for Excellence and Accountability in Teaching.

Fives, H., Hamman, D., & Olivarez, A. (2007). Does burnout begin with student-teaching? Analyzing efficacy, burnout, and support during the student-teaching semester. *Teacher and Teaching Education, 23*, 916–936.

Flores, M. A. (2018). Teacher resilience in adverse contexts: Issues of professionalism and professional identity. In M. Wosnitza, F. Peixoto, S. Beltman, & C. F. Mansfield (Eds.), *Resilience in education: Concepts, contexts and connections* (pp. 167–184). New York: Springer.

Gingras, C., & Mukamurera, J. (2008). S'insérer en enseignement au Québec lorsqu'on est professionnellement précaire: vers une compréhension du phénomène [Becoming a teacher in Quebec when you are professionally precarious: Towards an understanding of the phenomenon]. *Revue des Sciences de L'éducation, 34*(1), 203–222.

Gu, Q. (2018). (Re)conceptualizing teacher resilience: A social ecological approach to understanding teachers' professional worlds. In M. Wosnitza, F. Peixoto, S. Beltman, & C. F. Mansfield (Eds.), *Resilience in education: Concepts, contexts and connections* (pp. 13–33). New York: Springer.

Gu, Q., & Day, C. (2007). Teachers resilience: A necessary condition for effectiveness. *Teacher and Teaching Education, 23*, 1302–1316.

Hazel, G. (2018). Finding a place for resilience in teacher preparation. In M. Wosnitza, F. Peixoto, S. Beltman, & C. F. Mansfield (Eds.), *Resilience in education: Concepts, contexts and connections* (pp. 221–235). New York: Springer.

Henry, G. T., Bastian, K. C., & Fortner, C. K. (2011). Stayers and leavers: Early-career teacher effectiveness and attrition. *Educational Researcher, 40*(6), 271–280.

Hong, J. Y. (2010). Pre-service and beginning teachers' professional identity and its relation to dropping out of the profession. *Teaching and Teacher Education, 26*, 1530–1543.

Hong, J. Y. (2012). Why do some beginning teachers leave the school, and others stay? Understanding teacher resilience through psychological lenses. *Teachers and Teaching: Theory and Practice, 18*(4), 417–440.

Houlfort, N., & Sauvé, F. (2010). *Santé psychologique des enseignants de la Fédération autonome de l'enseignement* [Psychological health of teachers of the Autonomous Federation of Education]. Retrieved from Montréal, Québec: https://depot.erudit.org/bitstream/003212dd/1/30129826.pdf

Howard, S., & Johnson, B. (2004). Resilient teachers: Resisting to stress and burnout. *Social Psychology of Education, 7*, 399–420.

Huisman, S., Singer, N. R., & Catapano, S. (2010). Resiliency to success: Supporting novice urban teachers. *Teacher Development, 14*(4), 483–499.

Ilfeld, F. W. (1976). Further validation of a psychiatric symptom index in a normal population. *Psychological Reports, 39*, 1215–1228.

Jeffrey, D., & Sun, F. (2008). Persévérance et santé chez les enseignants en insertion professionnelle [Retention and health among teachers during teacher induction]. In L. Portelance, J. Mukamurera, S. Martineau, & C. Gervais (Eds.), *L'insertion dans le milieu scolaire: une phase cruciale du développement professionnel de l'enseignant* (pp. 163–183). Québec: Presses de l'Université Laval.

Klassen, R. M., & Chiu, M. M. (2010). Effects on teachers' self-efficacy and job satisfaction: Teacher gender, years of experience, and job stress. *Journal of Educational Psychology, 102*(3), 741–756.

Le Cornu, R. (2009). Building resilience in pre-service teachers. *Teaching and Teacher Education, 25*, 717–723.

LeMaistre, C., & Paré, A. (2010). Whatever it takes: How beginning teachers learn to survive. *Teaching and Teacher Education, 26*, 559–564.

Leroux, M. (2014). Surmonter les défis inhérents à l'insertion professionnelle: vers une exploration du processus de résilience d'enseignants débutants du préscolaire et du primaire [Overcoming the challenges inherent to teacher induction: Towards an exploration of the resilience process of beginning preschool and elementary school teachers]. In L. Portelance, S. Martineau, & J. Mukamurera (Eds.), *Développement et persévérance professionnels dans l'enseignement: oui mais comment?* (pp. 115–136). Québec: Presses de l'Université du Québec.

Luthar, S. S., & Zelazo, L. B. (2003). Research on resilience: An integrative review. In S. S. Luthar (Ed.), *Resilience and vulnerability: Adaptation in the context of childhood adversities* (pp. 510–549). New York: Cambridge University Press.

Mansfield, C. F., Beltman, S., Price, A., & McConney, A. (2012). "Don't sweat the small stuff": Understanding teacher resilience at the chalkface. *Teaching and Teacher Education, 28*(3), 357–367.

Mansfield, C. F., Ebersöhn, L., Beltman, S., & Loots, T. (2018). Great Southern Lands: Making space for teacher resilience in South Africa and Australia. In M. Wosnitza, F. Peixoto, S. Beltman, & C. F. Mansfield (Eds.), *Resilience in education: Concepts, contexts and connections* (pp. 53–71). New York: Springer.

Maslach, C., & Jackson, S. E. (1986). *Maslach burnout inventory: Manual* (2nd ed.). Palo Alto: Consulting Psychologists Press.

Morgan, M., Ludlow, L., Kitching, K., O'Leary, M., & Clarke, A. (2010). What makes teachers tick? Sustaining events in new teachers' lives. *British Educational Research Journal, 36*(2), 191–208.

Mukamurera, J., Bourque, J., & Ntebuste, J. G. (2010). La situation d'insertion professionnelle chez les enseignants du primaire au Québec [The induction situation of elementary school teachers in Quebec]. *Vivre le Primaire, 23*(2), 36–37.

Mukamurera, J., Martineau, S., Bouthiette, M., & Ndoreraho, J.-P. (2013). Les programmes d'insertion professionnelle des enseignants dans les commissions scolaires du Québec: Portrait et appréciation des acteurs [Teacher induction programs in Quebec school boards: Portrait and appreciation of the actors]. *Éducation et Formation, e–299*(Juin 2013), 13–35.

Oddone, I., Rey, A., & Birante, G. (1981). *Redécouvrir l'expérience ouvrière: Vers une autre psychologie du travail* [Rediscovering the worker experience: Towards another work psychology]. Paris: Éditions Sociales.

Peixoto, F., Wosnitza, M., Pipa, J., Morgan, M., & Cefai, C. (2018). A multidimensional view on pre-service teacher resilience in Germany, Ireland, Malta and Portugal. In M. Wosnitza, F. Peixoto, S. Beltman, & C. F. Mansfield (Eds.), *Resilience in education: Concepts, contexts and connections* (pp. 73–89). New York: Springer.

Pelletier, M.-A. (2013). *Faire face à la complexité du métier d'enseignant: Quels sont les besoins de formation psychologique à intégrer à la formation des futurs maitres?* [Facing the complexity of the teaching profession: What are the needs of psychological training to be included in future teachers' initial training?]. Paper presented at the Colloque international en éducation du CRIFPE, Montreal.

Peters, J., & Pearce, J. (2012). Relationships and early career teacher resilience: A role for school principals. *Teachers and Teaching: Theory and Practice, 18*(2), 249–262.

Portelance, L., Mukamurera, J., Martineau, S., & Gervais, C. (Eds.). (2008). *L'insertion dans le milieu scolaire: une phase cruciale du développement professionnel de l'enseignant*

[Induction in schools: A crucial phase in teacher professional development]. Québec: Presses de l'Université Laval.

Richardson, G. E. (2002). The metatheory of resilience and resiliency. *Journal of Clinical Psychology, 58*(3), 307–321.

Rutter, M. (2012). Resilience as a dynamic concept. *Development and Psychopathology, 24*(2), 335–344.

Ryan, M. R., & Frederick, C. (1997). On energy, personality, and health: Subjective vitality as a dynamic reflection of well-being. *Journal of Personality, 65*(3), 529–565.

Sass, D. A., Seal, A. K., & Martin, N. K. (2011). Predicting teacher retention using stress and support variables. *Journal of Educational Administration, 49*(2), 200–215.

Schwarze, J., & Wosnitza, M. (2018). How does apprentice resilience work? The conceptualisation of a generic process model of resilience and its application to vocational settings. In M. Wosnitza, F. Peixoto, S. Beltman, & C. F. Mansfield (Eds.), *Resilience in education: Concepts, contexts and connections* (pp. 35–51). New York: Springer.

Sharplin, E., O'Neill, M., & Chapman, A. (2011). Coping strategies for adaptation to new teacher appointments: Intervention. *Teaching and Teacher Education, 27*(1), 136–146.

Tait, M. (2008). Resilience as a contributor to novice teacher success, commitment, and retention. *Teacher Education Quarterly, 35*(Fall 2008), 57–75.

Tamir, E. (2010). The retention question in context-specific teacher education: Do beginning teachers and their program leaders see teachers' future career eye to eye. *Teacher and Teaching Education, 26*, 665–678.

Théorêt, M. (2005). La résilience, de l'observation du phénomène vers l'appropriation du concept par l'éducation [Resilience, from the observation of the phenomenon to the appropriation of the concept in education]. *Revue des Sciences de L'éducation, 31*(3), 633–658.

Théorêt, M. (2011). Contribution de la résilience éducationnelle à l'élaboration d'un modèle d'intervention sur la santé des enseignants [Contribution of educational resilience to the development of an intervention model on teacher health]. In P.-A. Doudin, D. Curchod-Ruedi, L. Lafortune, & N. Lafranchise (Eds.), *La santé psychosociale des enseignants et des enseignantes* (pp. 251–273). Québec: Presses de l'Université du Québec.

Théorêt, M., & Leroux, M. (2014). *Comment améliorer le bien-être et la santé des enseignants? Des ressources pour la résilience éducationnelle* [How to improve teachers' well-being and health? Resources for educational resilience]. Louvain-la-Neuve: De Boeck Supérieur.

Yonezawa, S., Jones, M., & Singer, N. R. (2011). Teacher resilience in urban schools: The importance of technical knowledge, professional community, and leadership opportunities. *Urban Education, 26*(5), 913–931.

Chapter 8
Early Career Teachers in Rural Schools: Plotlines of Resilience

Leanne Crosswell, Jill Willis, Chad Morrison, Andrew Gibson, and Mary Ryan

Abstract This chapter explores the plotlines of resilience as narrated by three early career teachers (ECTs) in rural schools and the deliberation process they undertook in response to their key challenges. Regular online reflections about their transition into rural teaching were collected through www.goingok.org, a digital tool (see Gibson A, Willis J, Morrison C, Crosswell L, Not losing the plot: creating, collecting and curating qualitative data through a web-based application. In The Australian Teacher Education Association (ATEA) 2013 Conference, July 2013, Queensland University of Technology, Brisbane, QLD. (Unpublished), 2013). Drawing on a transactional-ecological theory of resilience, the qualitative analysis was informed by current literature (see Day C, Gu Q, Resilient teachers, resilient schools: Building and sustaining quality in testing times. Routledge, Oxon, 2014; Mansfield CF, Beltman S, Broadley T, Weatherby-Fell N. Teach Teach Educ 54:77–87. https://doi.org/10.1016/j.tate.2015.11.016, 2016) that highlights the dynamic and ongoing process of interaction between the contextual and personal factors. The analysis was also informed by Archer's (2000) theories of social realism that enables the interplay between the personal powers of humans to act (PEPs), the affordances and constraints of the structural-material (SEPs) and cultural-discursive systems (CEPs). Rather than focusing solely on the capacities of individual ECTs, or structural and cultural conditions, together the transactional-ecological theories of resilience and

---

L. Crosswell (✉) · J. Willis
Queensland University of Technology, Brisbane, Australia
e-mail: l2.crosswell@qut.edu.au; jill.willis@qut.edu.au

C. Morrison
University of Tasmania, Hobart, Australia
e-mail: chad.morrison@utas.edu.au

A. Gibson
Sydney University of Technology, Ultimo, Australia
e-mail: Andrew.Gibson@uts.edu.au

M. Ryan
Macquarie University, Sydney, Australia
e-mail: mary.ryan@mq.edu.au

M. Wosnitza et al. (eds.), *Resilience in Education*,
https://doi.org/10.1007/978-3-319-76690-4_8

Archer's theoretical concepts enable a more nuanced analysis of the transition experiences for these rural ECTs. The data suggest the ECTs relied heavily on their available personal resources (PEPs) to maintain their resilience; however in doing so, they experienced strong fluctuations as they navigated the constant uncertainty inherent in the first year of teaching as well as the tensions of settling into a small rural community. Furthermore, the researchers recognised that these highly agentic early career teachers were seeking greater access to structural and cultural opportunities (SEPs and CEPs) within their resilience ecologies to affirm their own experiences, expectations and practice with colleagues and school leaders. The findings have implications for initial teacher preparation programs, school leadership and policy development in regard to retaining quality teachers in rural and remote schools.

The transition to teaching has historically been seen to be a period of intense challenge (Bezzina 2006). For early career teachers who choose to start their teaching practice in rural and remote schools, there are additional complexities to navigate, such as the separation from friends and family, adapting to living in the isolated community and working in an unfamiliar context with limited resources (Sharplin 2002; Yarrow et al. 1999). Successfully recruiting early career teachers to rural schools and supporting them in staying is a well-acknowledged issue (Sharplin et al. 2011; Sullivan and Morrison 2014; White and Kline 2012).

This chapter presents data from graduate teachers spending their first year in rural and remote Australian schools. They were graduates from a selective programme designed to develop a deep understanding of the potential challenges that face teachers in rural schools. A crucial part of this preparation was undertaking their final internship in a rural school, so these participants had been prepared for the challenges of working in rural schools and also had personal experience to draw on as they started their first year of teaching. Despite this, the data show that the early career teachers (ECTs) found themselves socially and professionally isolated and subsequently exhibited signs of emotional and physical fatigue. These experiences represent a disjuncture between what we know about effectively preparing preservice teachers (Darling-Hammond 2010) and the lived experiences of our ECTs.

Plotlines and digital journal entries from three graduate teachers are theorised within this paper as sociocultural narratives of teacher resilience. The participants chose the metaphor of "authoring" the plotlines of their professional identity to challenge deficit views of ECTs (Morrison et al. 2014. p. 10). Each plotline is a record of their personal experiences of transition over the first year of teaching in rural schools. The ECTs recorded regular reflections on their experiences, and this chapter explores how the ECTs activated their own resilience through their personal resources and contextual resources. Finally this paper concludes by theorising how the transitional experiences of ECTs can be enhanced and the challenges reduced through the intentional and strategic involvement of more experienced teaching colleagues and school leaders.

Teacher Resilience

Resilience is defined as the process an individual undertakes to adapt in positive ways to challenging circumstances (Fletcher and Sarkar 2013). Over time conceptualisations of resilience have shifted from being considered an innate element of an individual's personality to resilience being seen a transactional socioecological phenomenon (Johnson and Down 2013). It is transactional, because resilience involves various exchanges between the individual and the environments they are operating within. It is also socioecological, because resilience draws on the different resources and assets that are available within the socioecologies the individual is situated within and between. Within this situated understanding, it is evident that the rural school context and the isolated community played a critical role in the resilience of the ECTs involved in this project.

There has been intense interest in teacher resilience in recent years (see Gu and Day 2013; Johnson et al. 2016; Mansfield et al. 2016) arguably in response to high rates of teacher attrition, the intensification of the work of teaching and the increasing casualisation of the teaching workforce. The cognitive and emotional demands on teachers have become increasingly intense and complex (Hargreaves and Fullan 2012; Price et al. 2012) where teachers need to constantly draw on their reflexive, relational and decision capacities moment by moment throughout their teaching day. Day and Gu (2014) describe resilience as a daily requirement for all teachers to successfully navigate the constant uncertainty in today's dynamic classrooms. Resilient teachers adopt strategies that mobilise available personal and contextual resources in response to challenges (Mansfield et al. 2016). Personal resources that enhance resilient behaviours include intrinsic motivation or "inner drive" (Hong 2012), a sense of self-belief (Le Cornu 2009) and self-efficacy (Mansfield et al. 2016). Personal support networks are increasingly seen to be important for facilitating resilience, particularly those that are "mutually empathic and responsive" (Le Cornu 2013, p. 80). Contextual influences include school culture, school leaders (Mansfield et al. 2016) and strong supportive social networks (Gu and Day 2013; Le Cornu 2013). This chapter explores how early career teachers adapt to the challenges they encountered during their first year of rural teaching and how they sought to activate resources to support their resilience.

This chapter also uses Archer's (2000, 2003, 2012) ideas about how human exchanges in the social world are shaped by structural and cultural factors. Archer (2003) argues that whilst these structural and cultural factors emerge from people, they continue to be shaped and formed through people. As such, Archer identifies three categories of "emergent properties": structural emergent properties (SEPs), cultural emergent properties (CEPs) and personal emergent properties (PEPs). In other words, humans deliberate on and make choices within the existing structural and cultural factors they find themselves. For rural ECTS, the structural realities (SEPs) include limited public transport, subsidised and shared teacher accommodation and distance from family, whilst the cultural norms (CEPs) include differences in topics of conversation and new ways of relating between cultural or gender groups. ECTs experience these emergent properties as affordances or constraints depending on how they respond within their day-to-day social interactions. For example, being invited to play lawn bowls at the local "pub" (hotel) may be experienced as an affordance if the ECT is seeking to build social and cultural connections in a new community (activating CEPs) or a constraint if the ECT has an existing cultural perception that lawn bowls is for elderly people, and so declining the invitation misses out on a powerful local support network (depleting CEPs). It is through an individual's ongoing discernment and reflexive deliberation that new social roles are incorporated into an individual's sense of identity over time. This involves a constant process of self-evaluation, evaluating the new situations that arise and the relationships between them. Newcomers, with little experience of the cultural context and limited access to trusted others, become highly reliant on their personal properties as they engage in this ongoing evaluation process. To be successful in new social roles (such as rural teacher), the individual needs to access emergent properties from the structural (SEP), cultural (CEP) as well as their personal (PEP) contexts.

The combination of the transactional socioecological understanding of resilience with Archer's (2000, 2003) ideas affords a more nuanced understanding of the ways that the ECTs activated available personal and contextual resources to support their own resilience. The ECTs invested enormous time and energy into discerning the challenges and realities of their teaching lives whilst deciding what action they should take. Archer's concepts extended the way we understood the various ways that individual ECTs activated resources within their personal considerations (PEPs) and enabled some differentiation between the interrelated contextual resources, both cultural (CEPs) and structural (SEPs), that were available.

Research Design

The research was designed to answer the question: What social and individual practices enhance early career teacher resilience and identity formation in rural and remote settings? Whilst this chapter discusses three ECT plotlines in detail, the overall study included nine ECTs in their first year of teaching in rural and remote schools. Data were collected using the web application, goingok.org, enabling the creation of long-term reflexive accounts and plotlines in a simple and cost-effective way (Gibson et al. 2013). The web application generated a fortnightly email that asked "How are you going?" and participants responded by sliding the bar to indicate somewhere between "distressed" and "soaring", with "going ok" in the centre, with the option to write a reflection in the text box (Fig. 8.1).

The ECTs could access the application from their personal digital device which avoided situations where colleagues might inadvertently read these private reflections. The digital tool de-identified responses and generated a chart that documented the entries over time. The participants' deliberate use of the term "authoring" highlights their sense of agency in navigating the challenges of their early experiences

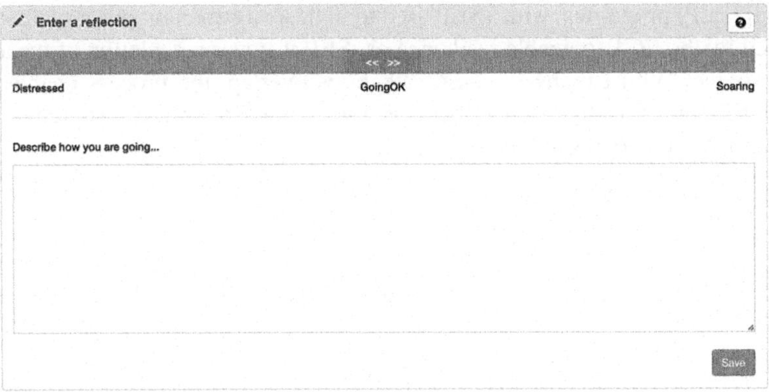

Fig. 8.1 going.ok.com prompt screen

of teaching (Morrison et al. 2014). Plotlines are "a type of conceptual scheme by which a contextual meaning of individual events can be displayed" (Polkington 1995, p. 7). Each dot represents the participant's self-score on a scale from 0% (distressed) to 100% (soaring) with an accompanying qualitative entry. Originally it was anticipated that significant factors influencing resilience would be easily identified within particularly high or low plot points. However, the accompanying text revealed more complex narrative plotlines that were a "linguistic form that preserves the complexity of human action with its interrelationship of temporal sequence, human motivation, chance happenings, and changing interpersonal and environmental contexts" (Polkington 1995, p. 7). Our research made visible these complex narratives by capturing the self-assessment of feelings on a quantitative scale, alongside the associated qualitative written text, so that we could ascertain those happenings and circumstances that prompted different ratings from different participants.

The narrative entries were first analysed using a grounded theory method (Charmaz 2006; Birks and Mills 2011) where the research team read through the plotlines in chronological order and coded entries line by line. The researchers questioned how or why a plot point might reflect a different tone than the accompanying entry and noted themes that were emerging both within and across various plotlines. These developing themes were interrogated and extended during research team meetings and in the co-writing of early interpretive memos. As researchers, we were conscious that we were also co-authors of the narratives as we reflexively worked with the plotlines, to bring contextual meaning to the data in this analysis. This "fluid, interactive and open ended" (Charmaz 2006 p. 178) analytical approach is typical of a grounded theory approach, where the interactions shape the analysis and interpretation.

Once the grounded themes were inductively identified within these data, a deductive approach was used to ascertain the reflexive mediation undertaken by the participants to manage their subjective and objective concerns and conditions (Archer 2003). The data were thus coded to indicate structural (SEP), cultural (CEP) and personal (PEP) properties, with +SEP used to indicate a structural property that was activated by the ECT to enable resilience or -SEP if it was a depletion of the available resource. Whilst many of these categories overlap, the process enabled the SEPs, CEPs and PEPs that were either available or not available as resources within their resilience ecologies to be more visible.

Data

Karen

Karen taught in a remote school over 1000 km from her home that catered for students from prep entry level (approximately 5 years old) to school exit (approximately 18 years old), with 90% of students from Indigenous communities. Karen's plotline (Fig. 8.2) reflected an ongoing struggle with a recorded mean score below 50%. As she came to the end of her first year, she was concerned that she had become the sort of teacher (pessimistic and negative) she never wanted to be.

Key Challenges

Karen was the only teacher in her curriculum area, and she was expected to teach multiage classes from early primary to upper secondary. She arrived to find there were no school planning documents to guide her, and she did not have access to the standard digital resources ("did not have access to the C2C or units that I was required to use"). On top of this, she had reduced non-contact time and no teacher aide. The complexity of such a workload became quickly apparent, "No time to get anything done the way I want it. I'm trying my very hardest but feel like I'm getting nowhere", and "I am exhausted all the time…school is frustrating and stressful at the moment…getting all the planning and assessment ready is OVERWHELMING!!!!" These challenges emerged from the existing structures (SEPs) of the school.

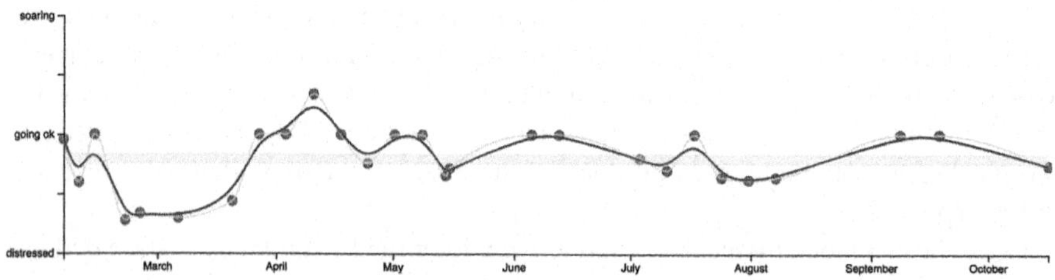

Fig. 8.2 Karen's plotline

Challenges from the cultural aspects of the school context (CEPs) included the negative student attitudes and behaviour. Karen found the students difficult to manage and became exhausted by the behaviours: "many of the students at this school hate [this subject] which is a bit disheartening ...and I take it personally at times. Also, some of the kids' behaviour is getting to me, the swearing and refusal to follow instructions ...is sooooooooo draining". The persistent student negativity eventually affected Karen's sense of efficacy, "I feel as though I am a much more negative person, which to me seems to be caused by the constant negative attitudes of many of the students at school".

In term 3 Karen needed to take a group of secondary students away on 5-day camp to an island (a drive of 11 h). She was expected to obtain her bus licence so she could drive the bus (SEPs). The prospect of spending 5 days supervising students who she struggled to manage in the classroom was daunting (CEPs): "This was probably the worst week yet...getting really nervous about taking students to [the] island. I'm not sure how they are going to behave and if I'll go crazy by being with them for 5 days non-stop!".

Activating Resilience

Karen adopted strategies to support her own resilience. These included strong self-care routines, "trying to exercise at least 30 mins a day to keep a clear head and to make sure I'm looking after myself...that's why I've been feeling good", and tending to her own spiritual care by attending the local church. She deliberately sought out social connection within the community: "I am really trying to get involved in the community...joined Bowls Club… playing netball on a Monday ...maybe Basketball on a Wednesday … and dinner with the teachers at least one night a week! The social life out here is lovely!". However, the analysis highlighted the burden on her individual energy and capacity (PEPs), working long hours to get on top of her workload, working consistently throughout her two first holiday breaks which eventually led to her feeling exhausted and depleted, "I'm home sick. I think that this year has really taken it out of me".

Whilst she initially enthused about her new colleagues, "The teaching staff at my school are AMAZINGLY helpful and caring! I love them all already!", there were few indications in later reflections that she was accessing CEP or SEP resources within the school context. Her colleagues rarely featured in her reflections, and she deliberated her dilemmas in isolation. It was not until a new deputy principal arrived that Karen again discussed support from more experienced others. The new deputy provided cultural support (CEPs) by acknowledging her "timetable is the worst that I've ever seen, particularly for a first-year teacher" and immediately provided structural support (SEPs) by reducing Karen's teaching load.

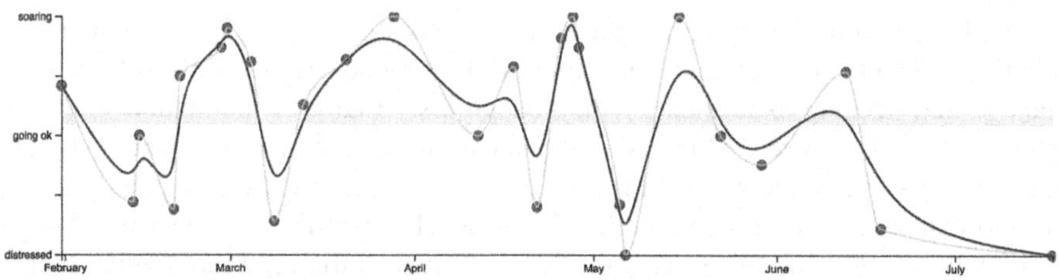

Fig. 8.3 Amanda's plotline

Amanda

Amanda taught a prep class in a primary to year 10 (approximately aged 15) school in a rural farming and mining community of 1500 people that was over 400 km from her hometown. She quickly established an effective working relationship with an experienced full-time teacher aide. Although she recorded a number of confident entries at the start of the year (and her overall mean score was above 50%), by the end of the year, she was making plans to leave the town and the schooling system (Fig 8.3).

Key Challenges

Amanda felt confident with her planning and teaching. Her challenges focused on managing challenging student behaviour, "I know behaviour change is a long process but it's just driving me up the wall!!!". When a student trashed Amanda's office and it took the principal over half an hour to respond to her frantic call for help, she felt "REALLY ANNOYED and ANGRY" and "incredibly unsupported" by the principal and "I decided I was not going to rely on him again". Amanda was also unsettled when a male student exposed himself to another student (CEPs), finding it difficult to reconcile her professional and personal responses: "At a professional level, I handled it fine... At a personal level though, I'm finding it hard to not feel creeped out". Amanda's personal health crumpled under this level of stress (PEPs), and she suffered three bouts of serious illness, "I'm feeling distressed about the fact that I haven't been at school with the kids... that I'm behind in my curriculum work...that I'm still experiencing temperatures 6 days into being sick".

Amanda received unwanted attention from a male parent, finding out through "comments that he has made to two other staff members". One of the senior teachers "positively supported me and told me not to worry", but Amanda reported feeling uncomfortable when he was waiting around outside her classroom. When the same parent then lodged a formal complaint that Amanda was not following his son's court-issued parenting plan, Amanda felt angry "that he would taint my professionalism in my school community". Amanda started feeling "incredibly isolated" in her rural context after a holiday spent visiting a capital city: "I am really missing coffee and good food and interesting events to go to". This heightened sense of social isolation, and the other challenges discussed above led to Amanda questioning her future in this rural community.

Activating Resilience

Amanda activated a number of effective personal strategies (PEPs) to enhance her resilience. These included normalising challenges ("Everyone keeps saying that first year teacher's often pick up a lot of colds because of the extra stress they are under"), optimistic perspective of her capacity ("finding myself being really confident about making certain decisions about what I need to do with the kids in order to get them achieving"), stoic persistence ("I went to school and I felt really unwell…HOWEVER....I did it. I made it through the day") and a capacity to reframe issues ("I probably don't have anything to worry about, it's just that it will be my first time"). Her personal philosophy (PEPs) of what makes a teacher effective focused on the academic progress of students, and she initiated ways of keeping track of her students' learning ("It's a great feeling looking through their pre-assessment and post-assessment data and seeing how much they've improved!!!").

She established a strong collaborative relationship with her teacher aide and sought a mentoring relationship with the year 1 teacher, thus accessing the available structural resources within the school (SEPs). When she became dissatisfied with the principal's level of support, she sought support from other colleagues. Amanda was also strategic in accessing a number of cultural resources (CEPs) to support her resilience. When her school colleagues appeared uninterested in socialising, she sought out connections to a wider social group again engaging in activities such as the local debutante ball, craft group, sporting fixtures and gym classes. However, all of these possible resources depended on Amanda's personal agency (PEPs) to maintain them and to integrate them into her understanding of her role as a rural ECT teacher.

Eleanor

Eleanor was employed as a year 1 teacher in a primary school in a small regional town, 600 km from home. Eleanor's moderately variable plotline became more turbulent with the arrival of a new student with significant behavioural issues, and then the death of a student in the middle of the year when Eleanor scored herself at 0% (distressed). From June onwards, Eleanor's overall plotline reflected her ongoing

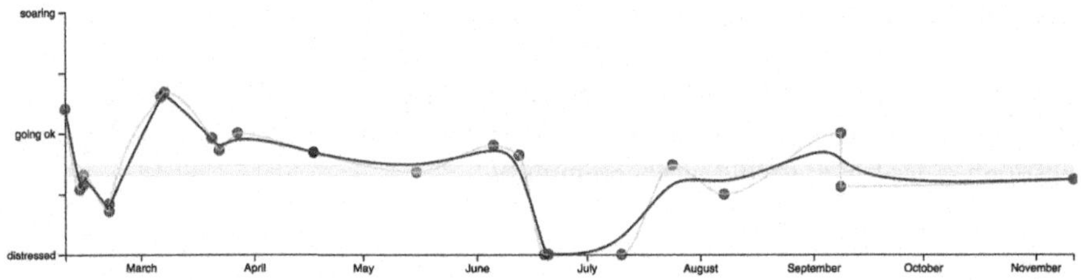

Fig. 8.4 Eleanor's plotline

scramble with a recorded mean score well below 50% (Fig 8.4). Eleanor held a strong belief that if she worked hard, she could be successful with clear evidence of her trying to problem-solve and toil her way out of this very challenging situation.

Key Challenges

Eleanor's early challenges were to do with workload, "feeling stressed about the workload" and later "struggling with the workload...trying to fit everything in". The pressure of the workload was exacerbated by the fact that Eleanor found herself responsible for training and supporting a new teacher aide (SEP); at the same time, she was grappling with the first weeks of beginning teaching herself: "she's finding it all new and difficult so I guess we are both new and are learning together!".

Managing challenging behaviours was also identified as an early issue. She was proactive in trying new approaches and found that "behaviour management is getting easier". However, when a new student arrived with high-level autism and ADHD, she records "feeling apprehensive...out of my depth and lacking strategies/skills". From a structural perspective, the school began training the teacher aide to provide support (SEP); however for the first month, she recorded, "it feels like I'm on my own". Eleanor scored herself at 0 (distressed) as the student's behaviour becomes increasingly violent: "He has been in detention every day for the past 4 days, has hit and punched kids and has sworn repetitively towards other students and teachers. It is hard to get him to do any work as he just says 'no', runs off and swears". With little expertise situated at the school, Eleanor turns to her personal networks (PEPs) to gather advice, "Am getting some great advice and support from friends who are very knowledgeable with students with autism". By the end of term 3, she was reported that she had "never been more exhausted and ...frustrated in my life".

During the September school holidays, one of the year 2 students in her class was killed in an accident. The trauma of this unexpected loss on top of the continuing demands of managing the challenging behaviours had a serious impact on Eleanor's resilience. During the final term of the year, Eleanor only recorded one journal entry in November in which she reflected that any other entries "would've all said 'distressed' or near that mark!!".

Activating Resilience

Eleanor's journal entries demonstrate her willingness to reflect on her professional practice to improve her outcomes. These comments include "lots of reflecting to do... lots of changing/adapting of my strategies", as well as identifying what she was trying, such as "explicit teaching and thinking space". She also demonstrated a consistent sense of personal optimism and hope (PEPs), reframing difficult circumstances to highlight the positives. Whilst she consistently reported feeling out of her depth and challenged by the new student with demanding behaviours, she continued to look for the positives in these experiences: "I am feeling out of my depth. I know this is a great experience for 1st year out, and will only make me stronger" and "He has taught me a lot this term and am really glad he is in my class". Her early-childhood philosophy focused on valuing every child, and this was foundational to her resilience; however she found herself depleted as she was supporting not only her own resilience but that of her students, teacher aide and parents.

Discussion

These three stories of transition into teaching are simultaneously unique and representative of experiences faced by other ECTs in the study. Whilst they did grapple with predictable common issues such as establishing social connections in small isolated communities (CEPs) and learning new school structures (SEPs), it was the situated issues such as the death of a student, unrealistic workload and perceived lack of support that required more sophisticated processes of adaptation and resilience (PEPs) from the ECTs. As graduates from a boutique preparation programme, it can be argued that these participants had been preselected for their resilient characteristics (Mansfield et al. 2016). These included the motivation (Hong 2012; Kitching et al. 2009) and sense of purpose (Day 2014) for teaching in isolated schools, along with having high expectations of themselves as ECTs, a sense of personal efficacy (Le Cornu 2009) and optimism (Day 2014). However, within a transactional socioecological framework of resilience, resilience is reliant not only on individual characteristics but also on prior experiences and the social strategies an individual adopts along with the sociocultural contexts (ecologies) the individual is working within.

These ECTs were agentic in relation to their own resilience and sought to resist deficit stories of becoming a rural ECT. They were aware that dominant scripts about ECTs psychologise and pathologise individuals who have struggled within the acknowledged complexity of rural teaching (Bezzina 2006; Johnson and Down 2013). They employed proactive approaches: establishing work-life balance, eating well, getting adequate sleep and scheduling sessions for regular exercise (Le Cornu 2013; Johnson et al. 2014), having clear professional goals (Sharplin et al. 2011), personal boundaries around the scope of work (Hong 2012) and active faith practices (Curry and O'Brien 2012). Whilst these types of strategies have been identified as having powerful impacts on an individual's capacity to be resilient (Mansfield et al. 2016), it is important to note that, from a transactional socioecological conception of resilience, these strategies are drawing heavily on the ECTs' personal ecologies rather than on the resources within the situated ecology, which seemed unavailable to them for much of the time.

There were limited indications of the ECTs successfully accessing resources within the situated ecology and the associated factors known to be supportive of resilience. These contextual resources include supportive relationships with school leaders (Day 2014), supportive relationships with experienced colleagues (Hong 2012; Papatraianou and Le Cornu 2014), supportive school cultures (Peters and Pearce 2012; Gu 2014) or a formal mentor (Mansfield et al. 2014). Whilst there are comments that indicate that the ECTs had accessed these factors at irregular points throughout the plotlines (e.g. Amanda consciously nurtured a supportive relationship with one colleague and Karen scheduled regular dinners with colleagues), it was not a consistent feature of any of the ECTs' experiences. The ECTs faced their emerging challenges without consistent access to the existing contextual resources. Significantly, all the ECTs recorded seeking support and guidance from experienced colleagues from the school site but with varying degrees of success. If little support was forthcoming, the ECTs recalibrated their expectations and returned to drawing heavily on their own personal resources to manage their circumstances. It is this overreliance on their personal resources to try and adapt to the unexpected challenges that had serious consequences for the long-term resilience of these participants.

Within a transactional socioecological understanding, teacher resilience is conceptualised as being able to mobilise available personal and contextual resources to navigate the dynamic challenges that the teaching environment continually throws up (Mansfield et al. 2016). Archer's theorisation extends the analysis into the ways that individual ECTs discerned and deliberated as they mediated the contextual resources (CEPs, SEPs) alongside their personal considerations (PEPs). The plotlines indicate that the ECTs spent a great deal of energy and time discerning the challenges and realities of their teaching lives whilst also deliberating about what to do about them and how to do it. In general this process was undertaken in isolation without productive input from more experienced others. Many of these participants' personal resources would have been extended by dialogue with a peer or leader, when reflecting and adapting strategies and when navigating boundaries between personal and professional identity. Structural factors that could have been more easily navigated through peer or leader support included responding to issues to do with teaching out of area, multiage teaching, training a teacher aide, managing a crowded curriculum and behaviour support for challenging students with disabilities. Similarly, cultural factors such as reconciling living near where a child has "trashed" your work office; supporting children, parents and self when a student dies; and accepting extra responsibilities when teaching in remote communities would have been highly challenging to negotiate in isolation. These are issues that would challenge experienced teachers with well-established histories and teaching identities.

ECTs who are experiencing contextual discontinuity (Archer 2003) would benefit from support in evaluating what is "usual" in this new role of rural teacher, what is unusual and what options an experienced teacher might consider as they make a way forward. Whilst the ECTs sought to activate structural and cultural support, this required additional demands on their personal resources to initiate the support. We argue that without this support being made available to them, the continual demand on their personal resources was a significant issue. A consequence of this constant drain on personal resources over time would be a negative impact on the way that the ECTs understand themselves as teachers and of how they present that image to others in their narration of professional identity. In the absence of more experienced interlocutors, an ECT with depleted PEPs may interpret their depleted state as an inability to manage the ECT role. The narrative that inevitably would emerge would be of the individual ECT failing to cope with teaching and searching for pathways out of teaching. Through the analysis of these plotlines, we argue that personal depletion is an inevitability in the absence of purposeful cultural and structural support.

Interactions between ECTs and their more experienced colleagues and leaders have been previously acknowledged to be particularly important (Gu and Day 2013; Le Cornu 2013; Peters and Pearce 2012), and Archer's (2000) concepts of structural emergent properties (SEPs) and cultural emergent properties (CEPs) help to ascertain why. As ECTs discern the challenges of their new roles and deliberate about how to respond through meaningful and productive interactions with colleagues, these colleagues provide access to the SEPs and CEPs that serve to fortify the PEPs. As the ECTs elaborate on their concerns, trusted colleagues identify structural and cultural resources that can be accessed or engaged whilst simultaneously shifting the emphasis away from personal assets as the sole determinant of success.

In these ways, leaders and more experienced teaching colleagues feature in the explanations of ECT resilience. Both SEPs and CEPs become evident in the interpretations of experience and influential in how individuals face new challenges. The school leader plays an important role in establishing and perpetuating the spoken and unspoken cultures of each school community. They legitimise the accepted practices and attitudes and privilege certain behaviours. A situated transactional-ecological approach to resilience is a more sophisticated understanding of this concept that has attracted intense interest from both researchers and policymakers in the past two decades. It is widely acknowledged that the transition into teaching is highly variable in terms of induction and ongoing mentoring (Owen et al. 2008). To ensure successful transition to teaching, it is imperative that schools and systems take responsibility for ensuring appropriate structural and cultural resources are available to support the resilience of ECTs.

Conclusion

The challenges of early career teaching in rural and remote locations have been a topic of study for decades (Plunkett and Dyson 2011; Ramsey 2000; Sharplin 2002; Yarrow et al. 1999). Often the challenges are associated with the remoteness of the locations in which ECTs live and teach which is an unchangeable geographic reality. The transition experiences of ECTs have been hard to capture as they often occur in isolation. This chapter adds to the evidence-based argument for greater structural and cultural support for rural and remote ECTs in two ways. Firstly, the digital plotlines collected high-quality personal quantitative and qualitative data from rural ECTs in their first year of teaching so that the resources and the ecologies that the ECTs activated could be traced over time. The ECTs were agentic in seeking out a range of strategies associated with personal resilience, yet there were persistent patterns of distress and underdeveloped social and cultural resources within their situated ecologies. Additional analysis drawing on Archer's concepts confirmed that initially ECTs drew on their PEPs without consistently accessing other ecological sources. These were soon depleted by demands of the first few months. When increased demands arrive, without secure sources within the ecology having been established, ECTs may struggle to establish an identity of competence. The second major contribution to this important focus for improvement in supporting early career teachers is the elaboration of the ecological-transactional theories of resilience with Archer's theories that connect the personal, cultural and structural resources to the process of ongoing identity formation. This analysis shows that personal depletion should not be a surprise but understood as inevitable if cultural and structural support is not made available. This cultural and structural support will not be the same for each ECT as they activate the emergent properties within the ecology differently. Neither should the support undermine the personal agency of the individual ECT but instead support the individual's ongoing discernment and reflexive deliberation over time. Understanding the process of this negotiation, and recognising the patterns of resilience within the ecology, enables more experienced leaders and mentors to support agentic ECTs in rural and remote schools (Figs. 8.2, 8.3 and 8.4).

Acknowledgements We would like to thank our participant-researchers for their contributions to the project. Their generous offerings of time and authentic input throughout their transitional phase into teaching have greatly enhanced our collective insights.

References

Archer, M. S. (2000). *Being human: The problem of agency*. Cambridge: Cambridge University Press.

Archer, M. (2003). *Structure, agency and the internal conversation*. Cambridge: Cambridge University Press.

Archer, M. (2012). *The reflexive imperative in late modernity*. Cambridge: Cambridge University Press.

Bezzina, C. (2006). Views from the trenches: Beginning teachers' perceptions about their professional development. *Journal of In-Service Education, 32*(4), 411430.

Birks, M., & Mills, J. (2011). *Grounded theory: A practical guide*. London: Sage Publications.

Charmaz, K. (2006). *Constructing grounded theory: A practical guide through qualitative research*. London: Sage.

Curry, J. R., & O'Brien, E. R. (2012). Shifting to a wellness paradigm in teacher education: A promising practice for fostering teacher stress reduction, burnout resilience, and promoting retention. *Ethical Human Psychology and Psychiatry, 14*(3), 178e191. https://doi.org/10.1891/1559-4343.14.3.178.

Darling-Hammond, L. (2010). Teacher education and the American future. *Journal of Teacher Education, 61*(1–2), 35–47.

Day, C. (2014). Resilient principals in challenging schools: The courage and costs of conviction. *Teachers and Teaching, 20*(5), 638e654. https://doi.org/10.1080/13540602.2014.937959.

Day, C., & Gu, Q. (2014). *Resilient teachers, resilient schools: Building and sustaining quality in testing times*. Oxon: Routledge.

Fletcher, D., & Sarkar, M. (2013). Psychological resilience. *European Psychologist, 18*(1), 12–23. https://doi.org/10.1027/1016-9040/a000124.

Gibson, A. P. (2017) *Reflective writing analytics and transepistemic abduction*. PhD thesis, Queensland University of Technology.

Gibson, A., Willis, J., Morrison, C., & Crosswell, L. (2013). Not losing the plot: Creating, collecting and curating qualitative data through a web-based application. In *The Australian Teacher Education Association (ATEA) 2013 Conference*, July 2013, Queensland University of Technology, Brisbane, QLD. (Unpublished).

Gu, Q. (2014). The role of relational resilience in teachers' career-long commitment and effectiveness. *Teachers and Teaching, 20*(5), 502–529.

Gu, Q., & Day, C. (2013). Challenges to teacher resilience: Conditions count. *British Educational Research Journal, 39*(1), 22–44. https://doi.org/10.1080/01411926.2011.623152.

Hargreaves, A., & Fullan, M. (2012). *Professional capital: Transforming teaching in every school*. New York: Teachers College Press.

Hong, J. Y. (2012). Why do some beginning teachers leave the school, and others stay? Understanding teacher resilience through psychological lenses. *Teachers and Teaching, 18*(4), 417. https://doi.org/10.1080/13540602.2012.696044.

Johnson, B., & Down, B. (2013). Critically re-conceptualising early career teacher resilience. *Discourse: Studies in the Cultural Politics of Education, 34*(5), 703–715.

Johnson, B., Down, B., Le Cornu, R., Peters, J., Sullivan, A., Pearce, J., & Hunter, J. (2014). Promoting early career teacher resilience: A framework for understanding and acting. *Teachers and Teaching, 20*(5), 530–546.

Johnson, B., Down, B., Le Cornu, R., Peters, J., Sullivan, A., Pearce, J., & Hunter, J. (2016). *Promoting early career teacher resilience: A sociocultural and critical guide to action*. London: Routledge.

Kitching, K., Morgan, M., & O'Leary, M. (2009). It's the little things: Exploring the importance of commonplace events for early-career teachers' motivation. *Teachers and Teaching: Theory and Practice, 15*(1), 43e58. https://doi.org/10.1080/13540600802661311.

Le Cornu, R. (2009). Building resilience in pre-service teachers. *Teaching and Teacher Education, 25*(5), 717–723.

Le Cornu, R. (2013). Building early career teacher resilience: The role of relationships. *Australian Journal of Teacher Education, 38*(4). https://doi.org/10.14221/ajte.2013v38n4.4.

Mansfield, C. F., Beltman, S., & Price, A. (2014). I'm coming back again!: The resilience process of early career teachers. *Teachers and Teaching: Theory and Practice, 20*(5), 547–567. https://doi.org/10.1080/13540602.2014.937958.

Mansfield, C. F., Beltman, S., Broadley, T., & Weatherby-Fell, N. (2016). Building resilience in teacher education: An evidenced informed framework. *Teaching and Teacher Education, 54*, 77–87. https://doi.org/10.1016/j.tate.2015.11.016.

Morrison, C., Willis, J., Crosswell, L., & Gibson, A. (2014). Turning points in narratives of research design: Research innovation stimulating unique responses to existing challenges for beginning rural teachers. *The Journal of Educational Enquiry, 13*(1). http://www.ojs.unisa.edu.au/index.php/EDEQ

Owen, S., Kos, J., & McKenzie, P. (2008). *Staff in Australia's schools: Teacher workforce data and planning processes in Australia*. Commonwealth of Australia, Canberra. http://research.acer.edu.au/tll_misc/17

Papatraianou, L. H., & Le Cornu, R. (2014). Problematising the role of personal and professional relationships in early career teacher resilience. *Australian Journal of Teacher Education, 39*(1), 100–106. https://doi.org/10.14221/ajte.2014v39n1.7.

Peters, J., & Pearce, J. (2012). Relationships and early career teacher resilience: A role for school principals. *Teachers and Teaching, 18*(2), 249–262.

Plunkett, M., & Dyson, M. (2011). Becoming a teacher and staying one: Examining the complex ecologies associated with educating and retaining new teachers in rural Australia. *Australian Journal of Teacher Education, 36*(1), 32–47.

Polkington, D. (1995). Narrative configuration in qualitative analysis. *International Journal of Qualitative Studies in Education, 8*(1), 5–23. https://doi.org/10.1080/0951839950080103.

Price, A., Mansfield, C. F., & McConney, A. (2012). Considering 'teacher resilience' from critical discourse and labour process theory perspectives. *British Journal of Sociology of Education, 33*(1), 81–95.

Ramsey, G. (2000). *Quality matters: Revitalising teaching: Critical times, critical choices: Report of the review of teacher education and training, New South Wales*. Sydney: NSW Department of Education and Training.

Sharplin, E. (2002). Rural retreat or outback hell: Expectations of rural and remote teaching. *Issues in Educational Research, 12*(1), 49–63.

Sharplin, E., O'Neill, M., & Chapman, A. (2011). Coping strategies for adaptation to new teacher appointments: Intervention for retention. *Teaching and Teacher Education, 27*(1), 136–146.

Sullivan, A., & Morrison, C. (2014). Enacting policy: The capacity of school leaders to support early career teachers through policy work. *The Australian Educational Researcher, 41*(5), 603–620.

White, S., & Kline, J. (2012). Developing a rural teacher education curriculum package. *Rural Educator: Journal for Rural and Small Schools, 33*(2), 36–42.

Yarrow, A., Ballantyne, R., Hansford, B., Herschell, P., & Millwater, J. (1999). Teaching in rural and remote schools: A literature review. *Teaching and Teacher Education, 15*(1), 1–13. https://doi.org/10.1016/s0742-051x(98)00036-5.

Chapter 9
Teachers' Narratives of Resilience: Responding Effectively to Challenging Behaviour

Katya Galea

Abstract This chapter explores the narratives of eight teachers who respond effectively to challenging behaviour in a boys' secondary school in Malta. The narrative exploration of teacher stories through in-depth interviews elicited the challenges faced by these teachers and the individual and contextual factors that have helped strengthen their resilience. Results show that each teacher's resilient story is unique as factors contributing to resilience interact in complex ways. However, common factors, such as a positive attitude, seeing mistakes as learning opportunities, accepting one's limitations, investing in firm but caring relationships, and remaining calm when responding to challenging behaviour, as well as contextual factors such as support within the school system contributed to their resilience. By investigating how resilient teachers respond to challenging behaviour in the dynamics of the classroom and in the wider context of the school, this study highlights what resilient teachers do to respond effectively to challenging behaviour in their everyday practices and how they do it, thereby also shedding light on what teacher education courses and continuous professional development sessions can focus on to enhance teacher resilience.

With working conditions over which they have little control, few opportunities to participate in the decision-making that affects their work, and the limited extent to which they can show their accountability in their students' learning, teachers have one of the most stressful professions (Kyriacou 2000). On top of stressors related to increased workload, emotional strain, excessive reforms, and lack of support from administration, teachers in countries across the globe also mention pupil behaviour as one of the factors that concerns them the most (Demetriou et al. 2009; Fantilli and McDougall 2009; Kyriacou 2011; Bricheno et al. 2009).

K. Galea (✉)
Secretariat for Catholic Education, University of Malta, Msida, Malta
e-mail: katya.galea@um.edu.mt

M. Wosnitza et al. (eds.), *Resilience in Education*,
https://doi.org/10.1007/978-3-319-76690-4_9

The work in the teaching profession brings considerable emotional demands on teachers (Hargreaves 1998, 2000; Bricheno et al. 2009; Nias 1996). Effective teaching involves substantial emotional investment to manage the dynamics of the classroom, and requires teachers to strive to engage with and build relationships with their students, not all of whom are eager to learn or have stable and secure lives at home. When teachers encounter students they cannot help, they go through different negative feelings including fear, frustration, guilt, anxiety, and anger (Nias 1996).

Role responsibility is another phenomenon that is continuously increasing for teachers. The need for teachers to deal with students' and parents' social problems (Scott et al. 2001) and the increasing accountability and pressure to perform (Ballard and Bates 2008; Bachkirova 2005; Dworkin 2009; Jamieson 2006) place extra demands on teachers' roles. Moreover, teachers' work in the present day is undoubtedly more complex and multifaceted; it leaves teachers with the need to update their work according to changing demands, policies, guidelines, and directives. For Baker (2005), the challenges are greater today than any other time, as teachers need to teach classes with students with individual educational needs, including those with social, emotional, and behavioural difficulties, and be able to meet curricular guidelines at the same time.

Whilst teachers are asked to give more input, however, they are being given less support (Hargreaves and Lo 2000). This condition has left some to argue how teaching is a paradoxical profession (Hargreaves 1998; Hargreaves and Lo 2000). Teachers are being required to update their teaching with a new kind of professionalism, that of developing classroom strategies to reach new learning goals, to meet all pupils' different needs, to commit themselves to their own lifelong learning, to work effectively with and learn from colleagues, to collaborate with parents, and to cope with the emotional demands of their work. Teachers are being held increasingly accountable for student performance and need to attain standards such as the ones posed by the Programme for International Student Assessment (PISA) (OECD 2012).

Academic pressures take the heart out of teaching, leading to less time for personal and collegial relationships, community development, and the flexibility to adapt the curriculum as one sees fit (Jamieson 2006; Oplatka 2006; Valli and Buese 2007). Teachers are expected to give better results in terms of their performance and effectiveness, but this is not always accompanied by a much-needed focus on their wellbeing and resilience, leaving them under further risk (Bullough 2009; Valli and Buese 2007).

Challenging Behaviour

"Acting out" or externalising behaviours, which may include disruptive and defiant behaviours, violence, as well as aggression (Cefai and Cooper 2009), are amongst the most stressful concerns experienced by teachers for numerous reasons. When externalising behaviours are present, students are more likely to have problems with academic achievement (Mattison et al. 1998; Benner et al. 2002). Furthermore, because of the changing social contexts in today's society, students with challenging behaviour have more social and emotional baggage. This may place extra pressure on teachers to be a source of support for their pupils (Gillham, as cited in Cefai and Cavioni 2014). This may lead to dissatisfaction with the profession, emotional exhaustion, and burnout (Day 2011; Day and Gu 2009; Kidger et al. 2010). Discipline problems within the classroom disrupt teaching and learning and serve as a threat to teachers' authority and capability of managing the classroom as well as the school's efforts to reach educational targets (Department for Education 2010; Farrell and Humphrey 2009).

Continued exposure to challenging behaviour can lead to a depletion of teachers' personal resources. This may cause teachers to doubt themselves, to lose the satisfaction they usually receive from teaching, and to teach at a lower quality than before (van der Wolf and Everaert 2003). Considering all these factors, it is not surprising that teachers often prefer to teach students with physical and intellectual disabilities, rather than working with pupils with challenging behaviour (Avramadis and Norwich 2002; Evans and Lunt 2002; Kalambouka et al. 2007; Tanti Rigos 2009).

The relational dynamics that take place when challenging behaviour is an issue in the classroom could also lead to what Jennings and Greenberg (2009) refer to as a 'burnout cascade', whereby the escalating misbehaviour in the classroom contributes to further teacher stress. In this respect, with the increase of child behaviour problems, teachers could resort to more negative and punitive classroom management strategies in an attempt to control the classroom, which gives rise to escalating conflict, and a self-sustaining cycle of classroom behaviour problems (Patterson and Yoerger 2002; Osher et al. 2007). In one study, burnout was found to increase negative perceptions of students' oppositional and defiant behaviours, which implies that as teachers' stress levels escalate, tolerance levels to these challenging behaviours decline (Kokkinos et al. 2005). This suggests a bidirectional relationship between teacher stress and escalating disruption in the classroom and continues to point towards how paramount it is to give attention to teacher resilience in the face of challenging behaviour.

Conceptual Frameworks

An Interactionist Resilience Perspective

Rather than seeing resilience as an innate trait of the individual, this study is guided by an interactionist model of resilience, which defines resilience as a dynamic and developmental process (Luthar et al. 2000). According to this framework, resilience results from "dynamic interactions within and between [the] organism and [the] environment" (Masten 2001, p. 233). Qualities that foster resilience in individuals are found both within the person and in their familial and environmental resources (Benard 1991; Oswald et al. 2003; Werner 1995). Although some may be more predisposed to possess such qualities, such as problem-solving skills and a sense of purpose (Benard 1995), the potential to be resilient in the face of negative circumstances can be enhanced or inhibited by the components of the setting (Benard 1991; Day et al. 2006; Oswald et al. 2003). Based on this approach, this study seeks to give value to the complex process that resilience is, to the continuous evolvement and development of resilience within the individual, and consequently to the individuality and uniqueness of each teacher's resilience process and story.

A Systemic Perspective

The eco-systemic theory devised by Bronfenbrenner (1979) provides the appropriate systemic backdrop that is used by this study. Such a theoretical framework considers the importance of the environment in the development of children and maintains that the different systems a child is embedded in influence the child's development and behaviour. In this study, teachers are considered to be key players in the child's microsystem, the system in which the child experiences interpersonal relations with key figures in his or her immediate environment, such as the school context (Bronfenbrenner 1994). In line with Bronfenbrenner's (1979) theoretical point of view, the research study takes on the assumption that teachers serve as significant and protective adults in the child's life (Masten and Obradović 2008). In order for them to be influential in the development of children's resilience, they need to be resilient themselves (Henderson and Milstein 2003). Therefore, a systemic perspective holds that in order to address challenging behaviour as one of the most stressful concerns for teachers, interventions need to also be aimed towards the teacher.

Teacher Resilience

The conceptualisation in this study encompasses resilience to be a dynamic and developmental process that arises through a complex interaction within the individual as well as between the individual and his or her environmental context (Bobek 2002; Day 2008; Sumsion 2003; Tait 2008). Resilient teachers bounce back after encountering challenges in their work and continue to persevere and thrive despite these difficult experiences (Malloy and Allen 2007). In this process, both individual factors, such as self-efficacy and a sense of agency (Castro et al. 2009), and contextual conditions, such as personal, professional, and peer relationships (Sammons et al. 2007), are influencing factors for the outcome of this process. Moreover, teachers' capacities to be resilient are mediated by personal, relational, and organisational conditions in their institutions, which can positively or negatively impact their sense of resilience (Gu and Day 2013). These definitions therefore suggest that resilience is distinguished by a developmental process that unfolds over time according to the stressors that emerge and that depends on personal, relational, and environmental conditions.

Design of the Study

This qualitative study incorporated a narrative method of inquiry to explore the individual and contextual factors that help teachers respond effectively in the face of challenging classroom behaviour. Such an approach was necessary to elicit the stories teachers tell about their professional and personal lives (Elbaz-Luwisch 2007) and to achieve an understanding of how teachers experience and manage emotions in their work (Nias 1996). A narrative research design also allows attention to be given to participants' contexts, whereby teachers are seen as being embedded within a school system and within a wider socio-cultural context (Elbaz-Luwisch 2007).

The setting of this study was an all-male secondary school for students between 10 and 15 years of age. The school was located in a disadvantaged area in the Mediterranean Island of Malta where social problems are more frequent than in other areas of Malta (Cefai et al. 2009). The choice of setting was based on research carried out in the Maltese context indicating behaviour problems are more prevalent in male students, secondary schools, schools run by the state, and in students that live in Malta's inner harbour region (Cefai et al. 2009). In order to identify resilient teachers, a screening device (Fig. 9.1) was created using Masten's (2001) definition of the construct of resilience, namely, that individuals would have (i) experienced a serious risk or threat (teachers in classrooms with challenging student behaviours) and (ii) demonstrated a successful outcome (teachers demonstrating traits of well-being (Yoon 2002) and employing an authoritative and proactive classroom management style) (Lewis 2001; Marzano et al. 2003; Watson and Battistich 2006).

Following a meeting with the school's senior management team to anonymously discuss the teachers that fit the criteria, eight teachers were identified and contacted.

Teachers who are dealing with challenging behaviour in their classrooms but need to be:

- Teachers who have students who exhibit challenging behaviour, such as, disruptive, oppositional, and defiant behaviour, in their classes
- Teachers who, in the last scholastic year, have taught at least one class in which challenging behaviour was present
- Teachers who, in this scholastic year, are teaching at least one class in which challenging behaviour is present

Teachers need to also display resilient behaviour:

- Teachers who do not have significant problems and disruptions with all or most classes despite having students with challenging behaviour in their classrooms
- Teachers who do not employ an excessively authoritarian or disciplinarian approach in behaviour management, such, as frequent and/or excessive use of punishment
- Teachers who do not frequently hand out reports and detentions to their students
- Teachers who do not frequently report their students for suspensions and exclusions
- Teachers who do not frequently refer students who are exhibiting challenging behaviour to support services such as those given by Inclusion coordinators, the School Psychological Services, counsellors, and so on, both within and outside of the school
- Teachers who do not repeatedly and frequently phone in sick
- Teachers who do not receive complaints about their behaviour management from parents and/or colleagues

Fig. 9.1 Screening device to identify resilient teachers

Table 9.1 Description of participants (names have been changed to protect the participants' anonymity)

Name	Subject	Years teaching	Currently teaching
Gail	English	17	Ages 10–12
Roberta	Maths	7	Ages 12–15
Claire	Maltese	15	Ages 10–13
Martin	Maltese	38	Ages 13–15
Joanne	English	17	Ages 13–15
Stephanie	Maths	8	Ages 10–12
Matthew	Maths	15	Ages 12–15
Diane	Maths	15	Ages 12–15

The eight teachers and their profiles are presented in Table 9.1. A pilot interview was carried out with the first participant who felt that the interview schedule did not need any modifications. Since no changes were adopted, the pilot interview was included as part of the data. To confirm that the chosen participants truly fit the criteria for the purpose of the study, the criteria were once more checked with the teachers prior to the start of the interview. In-depth interviews were guided by a semi-structured interview divided into two sections. The first set of questions concerned the teachers' backgrounds. Participants were asked about the classes and subjects they taught and the number of years they had been teaching. These questions also invited the participants to speak about the challenges presented by behavioural difficulties in the school system where they taught and their own wellbeing in the face of these challenges. The second section of the interview was focused on inquiring about the individual qualities and contextual factors that help teachers in their resilience when responding to challenging behaviour. The participants were also encouraged to recount some stories of when they felt they successfully dealt with stressful incidents involving challenging behaviour.

The interviews were transcribed by the author providing the opportunity to become even more familiar with the stories of the participants (Fraser 2004). Care was taken to note a variety of non-verbal factors including silences, pauses, and hesitations during the conduction of the interviews and their transcription. The tone of voice and emotions portrayed in the participants' stories were taken into account to gain a broader understanding of what the participants said (Fraser 2004; McCormack 2012).

The narratives were analysed using multiple lenses. After transcription, the recordings were listened to once more, and the author noted in a journal (Anderson and Jack 1991) the emotions expressed by the participants and felt by herself whilst hearing the narrated stories (Borland 1991; Kleinman and Copp 1993). Particular attention was paid to how the interviews started, unfolded, and ended (Plummer 2001). The author then interpreted individual transcripts. Each transcript was scanned for types and directions, contradictions, patterns and themes, tone of voice, and non-verbal communication (Fraser 2004). The transcript was divided into 'scenes', according to the different stories participants told, and then these were given a number and title (Fraser 2004). The language each participant used was also analysed by the author based on what was said, how it was said, and what was left unsaid (McCormack 2000a, b). After the context of the situation and the culture that the participants are embedded in were identified (McCormack 2000a, b), the transcripts were examined for the commonalities, differences, patterns, and themes across the participants' interviews (Fraser 2004).

A number of precautions were taken to ascertain a good standard of reliability and validity in the study. Acknowledgement was given to the author's own voice and position in the research (Creswell 2007). Hence, a reflexive journal was kept in which thoughts were written whilst the research process took place. The idea that the interview is a construct of the discourse between the interviewer and the interviewee was held throughout the entire process. Therefore, the voice of the author was included in the interpretation of the stories and was considered as another reconstruction of the stories (Mishler 1999). Furthermore, throughout the research process, frequent discussions with the research supervisor were held. The supervisor provided his own thoughts and reflections about the transcripts and their interpretations. Any suggestions that were elicited were then included in the constructions of the stories.

Teachers' Narratives of Resilience: Responding Effectively to Challenging Behaviour

The stories of resilience recounted by these teachers were all complex and unique to every participant. Although there were common themes and patterns throughout the narratives, which will be presented here, the dynamics that contribute towards teacher resilience interact in complex ways and are not so clear-cut. For the sake of clarity, the narratives of these teachers will be presented in five interrelated themes that were common across all participants. The following attitudes, beliefs, dispositions, practices, as well as relational and contextual protective factors are what have helped Diane, Stephanie, Roberta, Matthew, Gail, Martin, and Claire sustain their resilience in the face of challenging behaviour.

Being Driven by a Sense of Vocation: "We Can See it in Your Eyes!" (Joanne)

Some of the teachers spoke about an inner disposition that has led them to teach and that has given them the strength to overcome certain difficulties. This was true for Joanne and Gail, but they spoke about it in different ways:

> Joanne: "...it's within you I think, it's within you. It's useless not feeling a certain something within to do it, you won't succeed without that. That's why it's not easy to just choose to

work as a teacher because if you're not good for certain things, no way. That's what they tell me usually those that I talk to, for example, headmistresses ... the heads and the assistant [head]... they say 'we can see it in your eyes that what you're telling us comes from the heart!'"

The inner disposition to teach students with difficulties was also a factor that helped Gail: "... I still prefer teaching the basic skill students than the higher achievers. I find myself more comfortable with these kinds of students". Both Gail and Joanne therefore showed how their vocational selves help maintain their satisfaction and happiness in teaching these students.

Getting to Know Students: "Conducting a Certain Analysis" (Martin)

Attempting to understand and consider students' backgrounds helped these teachers change how they respond to challenging behaviour. Martin, for example, conducts "a certain analysis" before taking disciplinary measures:

Martin: "What is important is to set clear boundaries. But it is also important to know what the boundary of the child is...you need to do a form of analysis, too. If I am going to confront him in class and I shout at him in class, I know what his reaction is going to be, and so I don't confront him in class."

In Joanne's narrative, the issue of students' backgrounds was a theme that she turned back to at different points during the interview. For her, getting to know about her students' backgrounds "really makes a difference". When talking about a challenging student, Joanne believes that a teacher should see "what kind of environment he is coming from, the type of child, the family he lives with and then you try to adapt, and even how you behave, you see a bit the emotional background of this person. It makes a big difference!" Joanne also takes a proactive approach and asks other teachers about the backgrounds these students have: "And I go ask the Guidance teachers about them as it helps me a lot".

On a similar vein, both Gail and Diane recounted how taking an interest in the lives of their students has helped them tailor the curriculum to their needs which minimised discipline problems:

Gail: "For example, I ask them 'What topics would you like to tackle?' And most of them like sports, they like bikes, they like music. And I tell them 'OK, I don't know a lot of sports, what do you suggest?' I ask them to give me ideas. I ask them [about] their favourite teams, their favourite sports, and I try as far as possible to try to create material which I think they would enjoy."

Diane: "That particular class was quite difficult, was quite tough as well. I had to really get to them, I had to get examples from their real lives. For example, I did measuring. I was hearing them speak about birds and hunting and things like that ... I thought 'OK' let me get a handout for them with different birds and a presentation on the birds, and they would come out and literally measure the wing span of each bird and things like that. As soon as I put a picture on the screen I grabbed their attention. That was OK. They told me what the bird was, and where you find it and things like that. And then a consequence was 'OK let's come measure it now that you know that's the bird, and we move on to the next so that we can see what the next bird is'. You know you have to find ways and means how to get to them because otherwise their resistance is very, very impenetrable. If they say they don't want, they wouldn't do anything!"

Learning about their students has helped these teachers gain their students' respect and build relationships with them:

> Martin: "I enjoy football, for example and the fact that I am involved in a local football club and the children see me on the bench ... that works miracles with the children. Teachers who involve themselves in sports activities are seen in a different light by the children. It's like you're dismantling a lot of barriers."

These teachers employed different strategies to learn about the realities of the students they teach. All of the participants also noted that although they formed caring and understanding relationships with the children, these relationships were embedded within limits and boundaries, as Roberta explains in her description of how a teacher needs to be:

> Roberta: "calm, patient ... but at the same time she means business ... even though I have a very good relationship with them they know that, for example, if someone comes in class with an earring, I am going to take it ..."

Getting closer to the socio-cultural contexts of their students was useful for these teachers. This helped them respond to challenging behaviour, adjust the curriculum accordingly, and build relationships with them.

Keeping It from Escalating: "...I try to talk to him using words of encouragement" (Claire)

Many of the teachers showed a proactive approach to behaviour management in their narratives. Teachers sought ways of preventing challenging behaviour from occurring and escalating further. Martin finds a sense of humour helps him because:

> Martin: "...if you take situations in the classroom too seriously, it's like a referee that within the first, in the first minute took out a red card is going to lose the game completely. It cannot be. You have just started a lesson and you have already asked two children to leave the classroom. A sense of humour is needed so as to diffuse the situation. An experienced teacher is able to predict what might happen."

Whilst Diane finds that "a time-out from the room" helps to contain challenging behaviour, Matthew handles challenging behaviour by talking to the student one-on-one:

> Matthew: "One of the strategies I use is to firstly talk to the child on his own, so I take him aside and I talk to him on his own".

Roberta believes it is important for the teacher not to shout and to respond to challenging behaviour as calmly as possible:

> Roberta: "...[do] not shout" ... a lot of them tell you "Don't shout" or "I don't like that teacher because she shouts!"

Therefore, either through easing situations with humour or by using words of encouragement, these teachers worked to avoid confrontations with students and sought to prevent challenging behaviour from getting worse.

Looking at the Challenge Differently: "Look I made a mistake in this, next time I'll adapt, act differently ..." (Joanne)

What was common amongst these participants' narratives was the hopeful and optimistic outlook they adopted in the face of their challenges and the way they persevered during tough times. When asked about any suggestions she would give to other teachers, Joanne recommended others:

> Joanne: "... not to give up and when there is certain behaviour that makes them think they're failing ... not to give up. Trying to find a solution to the problem. Because if you give up, then you're not fit for this job because you will face these things all the time."

Stephanie not only adopted a positive attitude in the way she looked at challenges in her work, she also tried to transmit this outlook to her students when they also encounter setbacks at school:

> Stephanie: "Come on don't give up. Everybody was like this." And sometimes I put it on me. I say "Even I. Who knows how many times I used to get mixed up in this subject? Don't be afraid." And you continue to encourage them. Even if they don't understand. "Come on. I will explain again. It's OK."

The importance of experience emerged quite strongly from the teachers' narratives. In some way or another, all of the participants mentioned how they have learned to manage behaviour and deal with the challenges it has presented during the years they have been teaching. Teachers like Roberta learnt that:

> Roberta: "...sometimes you have something that works, something that doesn't work ... until you find their ways and means."

For Martin, looking at the challenge differently also meant finding other causes to explain why challenging behaviour occurs:

> Martin: "And being either a man or a woman also makes a difference. And being either a man who has no hair or a woman [who] has just started teaching. Everything counts. The same children behave differently with different teachers, at different times of the day. In the morning it's one thing, in the evening it's another thing. If it's after a Physical Education lesson it's one thing, if it's after an English lesson it's another thing. So everything counts."

These teachers looked at the setbacks in their work as challenges that can be worked through rather than barriers that cannot be overcome. Because of this, they reflected on their experiences, learned from their mistakes, and set new goals.

Receiving Whole-School Support: "Giving backup and support to one another" (Stephanie)

All of the teachers referred to the importance of collegial and managerial support in responding effectively to challenging behaviour. Stephanie finds that when she discusses some of the strategies others have found to work with children help her in her work:

> Stephanie: "And you talk to your friends. You say "Listen, with this student if I do this it's better than doing this"... Giving backup and support to one another. Because the students I teach are the same ones my friends teach, and so it comes natural to share ideas about what is best and what is worst, what is working, and what doesn't with certain children."

Whilst Stephanie finds that support from colleagues helps her to bounce off ideas on the teaching practices and behaviour management strategies that are best suited for her students, Roberta appreciates the support she gets from other teachers because it helps her realise:

> Roberta: "... that you don't feel alone I think. Because you say 'He's not doing this just to me' for example ... 'He doesn't just treat me in this way'".

One the other hand, Diane explained how responding to challenging behaviour also entails having the backup of other teachers and the leadership team:

> Diane: "... All the teachers need to pull on the same rope. So if I don't accept a certain type of behaviour, then the boy cannot, after he goes out of my classroom, go to someone else who accepts it ... To have help, there needs to be the [administration team] backing you in every word you say."

Discussion

Being Driven by a Sense of Vocation

For the teachers in this study, one of the factors that contributed to their resilience was having an inner calling to teach. Joanne's sense of vocation helped her develop caring relationships with her students. Joanne brought love to her teaching role, which helped her persevere even in the most difficult of circumstances. Whilst Joanne spoke of love and respect, Gail referred to the importance of kindness and patience with these kinds of students. These teachers had inner natural qualities that made them good at teaching students with challenging behaviour and helped them persevere in challenging times.

A strong sense of vocation as a protective factor in the development of teacher resilience has already been documented in the literature (Day and Gu 2007; Flores 2018, Chap. 10, this volume; Gu 2018, Chap. 2, this volume; Gu and Day 2013; Patterson et al. 2004). Moreover, these teachers experienced positive emotions including love and care for their students (Nieto 2003), as well as "endless patience"

(Nieto 2009, p. 11). Strong emotions such as these kept teachers going, particularly with hard-to-reach students (Nieto 2009), whilst positive emotions may have led to stronger resilience (Fredrickson 2001; Sutton and Wheatley 2003).

Getting to Know Students

Another commonality amongst these teachers' narratives was the fact that they took the time to learn about their students. They gave due consideration to students' backgrounds and kept these in mind as they responded to challenging behaviour, an element of teacher resilience that also emerged from Howard and Johnson's study (2004). Teachers who appraise challenging behaviour as having an uncontrollable cause, such as a difficult family background, are more likely to express sympathy and pity, rather than get angry about the behaviour (Clark and Artiles 2000; Reyna and Weiner 2001). The consideration and thought that go behind this endeavour were exemplified in Martin's story, who, with 38 years of teaching experience, sought to carry out a meticulous "analysis" in order to be able to appropriately handle the challenging behaviour. Joanne takes a more proactive approach and asks guidance teachers about students' backgrounds to be able to adapt to their needs. Joanne's willingness to understand students' backgrounds was clearly one of the reasons that enabled her to develop caring relationships with these students.

In a similar vein, both Gail and Diane recounted how taking an interest in the lives of their students has helped them tailor the curriculum to their needs minimising discipline problems. Inquiring about "the socio-cultural realities" (Nieto 2009, p. 12) of students made a difference to how Diane and Gail responded to the behaviour. One of the ways they did this was by designing lessons that were appealing to their students. These teachers demonstrated humble and flexible qualities that helped them to look for new ways to allow their students to learn. This ultimately contributed to their own resilience (Tait 2008).

Getting to know students also entailed building caring relationships with them. Martin, for example, used his passion for football to "dismantle the barriers" between teacher and pupil. Just as Roberta expressed, all of the participants also noted that although they formed understanding relationships with the children, these relationships were embedded within limits and boundaries. Balancing compassion, understanding, and respect with firm expectations, guidance, discipline, and structure was a way for Roberta to successfully establish a supportive and positive teacher-student relationship which ultimately left a positive impact on student behaviour (Darling-Hammond et al. 2002; Marzano et al. 2003; Morrison et al. 2010). This skill was a marker of her resilience (Benard 1991; Johnson et al. 2012) and socio-emotional competence (Jennings and Greenberg 2009).

Keeping It from Escalating

The teachers showed a proactive approach to behaviour management in their narratives. For Martin, humour was one of the ways to lighten up tense situations and minimise discipline problems (Bobek 2002; Fovet 2009; Nieto 2009; Patrick et al. 2003; Prosser et al. 2009). On the other hand, Matthew, Roberta, and Diane made use of calm strategies in dealing with misbehaviour. Whilst Matthew was more direct in handling the behaviour by having a word with the student one-on-one, Diane preferred to give a time-out until the student had calmed down. Similarly, Roberta found that refraining from shouting was an effective way of dealing with the behaviour. Remaining calm when responding to challenging behaviour signifies an effective classroom management style (Jennings and Greenberg 2009) and has an effective impact on defiant behaviours (Rogers 2009, 2011). The teachers in this study can also be said to be socially and emotionally competent. They can be considered as role models of appropriate emotional and social behaviour for their students (Jennings and Greenberg 2009) showing them that in order to deal with a problem, one must talk about it calmly, directly, and honestly with the other person.

Looking at the Challenge Differently

Despite experiencing challenging behaviour and other setbacks in their work, these teachers were successful at keeping an optimistic view on the difficulties they encountered. Teachers, like Joanne, approached challenges with persistence and perseverance and did not give up easily. Hope and perseverance kept appearing throughout Stephanie's narrative, too. Stephanie's inner hope and perseverance, as well as the encouragement and enthusiasm she gave to her students, were important factors that helped her in her career (Nieto 2003). Taking up a hopeful and optimistic attitude has been found to leave a positive impact on teacher resilience (Johnson et al. 2012; Tait 2008; Nieto 2003).

Roberta emphasised that she learns from the challenges she experiences in teaching. She looks at the setbacks in her work as challenges that can be worked through rather than barriers that cannot be overcome. In all, the teachers placed importance on learning and always sought to better themselves (Bobek 2002; Gu 2018, Chap. 2, this volume; Patterson et al. 2004). Rather than keep on worrying about their mistakes, they chose to learn from them and move on (Howard and Johnson 2004; Tait 2008). Similar to the experiences of the participants in this study, the teachers in Howard and Johnson's study (2004) did not see mistakes as their fault, sought to find other explanations for why something went wrong, and maintained a realistic understanding of their own power and limitations.

Receiving Whole-School Support

All of the teachers referred to the importance of collegial and managerial support in responding effectively to challenging behaviour. The relational conditions within the school have been found to be a source of support for teachers and contribute towards the development of teacher resilience (Day and Gu 2007; Flores 2018, Chap. 10, this volume; Gu and Day 2007, 2013; Howard and Johnson 2004; Johnson et al. 2012; Prosser et al. 2009). Realising that other teachers are dealing with the same behavioural problems helped Stephanie and Roberta feel like they were not alone (Howard and Johnson 2004). Stephanie's resilience also came from the fact that she fostered good relationships with other teachers, whom she asked for suggestions and strategies on how to respond to children's challenging behaviour (Bobek 2002; Day and Gu 2007).

Supportive leadership was a theme Diane referred to as a factor that made a difference to teachers when managing student misbehaviour. A strong and supportive leadership has been documented in various studies as a key feature in teacher resilience (Bobek 2002; Day and Gu 2007; Howard and Johnson 2004; Gu and Day 2007, 2013; Johnson et al. 2012).

Conclusion

The findings in this study continue to suggest that resilience is a multifaceted process (Oswald et al. 2003). When it comes to the development of resilience in the context of challenging behaviour, the process is dependent on the multifactorial and complex phenomenon challenging behaviour poses, as well as how it evolves and meets other mediating factors that contribute to resilience. The evidence firstly indicates that these teachers' resilience was deeply rooted in their inner calling to teach and in what Gu and Li (2013) call their "educational purposes and moral values" (p. 300). Unsurprisingly, other individual qualities, such as a positive attitude, seeing mistakes as learning opportunities, and accepting one's limitations, helped teachers grow and improve their ability to respond adequately to the challenging behaviour with each year that passed.

Secondly, these teachers continued to consistently show that teaching is "about relationships" (Johnson et al. 2012, p. 542; Gu 2018, Chap. 2, this volume; Le Cornu 2013). A highly relational profession has required them to develop a high level of social and emotional competence (Jennings and Greenberg 2009) and build respectful and compassionate relationships with their pupils coupled with firm expectations. The teachers also carried out their teaching duties in ways that sought to prevent challenging behaviour from occurring by making an effort to evaluate students' backgrounds before responding to the behaviour, adapting lessons to student needs, and remaining calm when handling challenging behaviour. The importance of social support in facilitating the resilience of these teachers also emerged as a strong contributing factor and goes on to show how resilience can be moulded by organisational and relational processes.

Contribution of the Study

This research study continues to contribute to the existing body of literature on resilience. Although it not only addresses the scarcely researched topic that is teacher resilience, it investigates it in a new light. For example, whilst the number of studies regarding the resilience of novice teachers has been growing in recent years (Bowles and Arnup 2016; Castro et al. 2009; Ee and Chang 2010; Johnson et al. 2012; Le Cornu 2013; Mansfield et al. 2014; Papatraianou and Le Cornu 2014; Pearce and Morrison 2011; Peters and Pearce 2012), the issue of challenging behaviour has been rarely addressed from this unique point of view of teacher resilience. By studying the specific concern of responding to challenging behaviour in the dynamics of the classroom and in the wider context of the school, this study gives a closer look at what resilient teachers *do* to respond effectively to challenging behaviour in their everyday practices, and *how* they do it, thereby also shedding light on what teacher education courses and continuous professional development sessions could focus on to enhance teacher resilience.

The Linkage Between Challenging Behaviour and Teacher Resilience

These findings emphasise the possibility that when teachers are resilient, challenging behaviour can be managed better, and negative effects on the teacher are minimised. Through being resilient in their ways of responding to challenging behaviour, these teachers stopped what could have led to the "burnout cascade" mentioned by Jennings and Greenberg (2009) previously. The more experience these teachers gained, the better they became at overcoming challenges in their profession, and the more resilient they became in the face of challenging behaviour in the classroom. Consequently, it could be said that their resilience contributed to another cycle, this time a positive one, by which their resilience decreased challenging behaviour in the classroom, minimising their levels of stress and burnout. The less stressed and burnt out they became, the better they became at being able to respond to challenging behaviour. Therefore, the evidence continues to show how teachers, and hence their resilience, constitute an important level of the school system and the child's life. When aiming for change to happen within pupils' behaviour and resilience, the resilience of their educators, those who give their 'heart' to teaching and learning, cannot be overlooked. After all, if they are at the "heart" of teaching, they are the ones who can make a difference in the "hearts" of their students.

References

Anderson, K., & Jack, D. C. (1991). Learning to listen: Interview techniques and analyses. In S. Berger Gluck & D. Patai (Eds.), *Women's words: The feminist practice of oral history* (pp. 11–26). New York: Routledge.

Avramadis, E., & Norwich, B. (2002). Teachers' attitudes towards integration/inclusion: A review of the literature. *European Journal of Special Needs Education, 17*(2), 129–147.

Bachkirova, T. (2005). Teacher stress and personal values: An exploratory study. *School Psychology International, 26*(3), 340–352.

Baker, P. H. (2005). Managing student behaviour: How ready are teachers to meet the challenge? *American Secondary Education, 33*(3), 51–64.

Ballard, K., & Bates, A. (2008). Making a connection between student achievement, teacher accountability, and quality classroom instruction. *The Qualitative Report, 13*(4), 560–580.

Benard, B. (1991). *Fostering resiliency in kids: Protective factors in the family, school, and community*. Portland: Northwest Regional Educational Laboratory.

Benard, B. (1995). *Fostering resilience in children.* ERIC Digest (ERIC Document Reproduction Service No. ED 386 327).

Benner, G. J., Nelson, J. R., & Epstein, M. H. (2002). Language skills of children with EBD. *Journal of Emotional and Behavioural Disorders, 10*(1), 43–57.

Bobek, B. L. (2002). Teacher resiliency: A key to career longevity. *The Clearing House, 75*(4), 202–205.

Borland, K. (1991). That's not what I said: Interpretive conflict in oral narrative research. In S. Berger Gluck & D. Patai (Eds.), *Women's words: The feminist practice of oral history* (pp. 63–76). New York: Routledge.

Bowles, T., & Arnup, J. L. (2016). Early career teachers' resilience and positive adaptive change capabilities. *The Australian Educational Researcher, 43*(2), 147–164.

Bricheno, P., Brown, S., & Lubansky, R. (2009). *Teacher wellbeing: A review of the evidence.* London: Teacher Support Network.

Bronfenbrenner, U. (1979). *The ecology of human development.* Cambridge, MA: Harvard University Press.

Bronfenbrenner, U. (1994). Ecological models of human development. In M. Gauvain & M. Cole (Eds.), *Readings on the development of children* (pp. 37–43). New York: Freeman.

Bullough, R. V. (2009). Hope, happiness, teaching and learning. In C. Day & J. C.-K. Lee (Eds.), *New understandings of teacher's work, professional learning and development in schools and higher education 6.* London: Springer.

Castro, A. J., Kelly, J., & Shih, M. (2009). Resilience strategies for new teachers in high needs areas. *Teaching and Teacher Education, 26*(3), 622–629.

Cefai, C., & Cavioni, V. (2014). *Social and emotional education in primary school: Integrating theory and research into practice*. New York: Springer.

Cefai, C., & Cooper, P. (Eds.). (2009). *Promoting emotional education. Engaging children and young people with social, emotional and behaviour difficulties.* London: Jessica Kingsley Publishers.

Cefai, C., Cooper, P., & Camilleri, L. (2009). Social, emotional and behavior difficulties in Maltese schools. *The International Journal of Emotional Education, 1*(1), 8–49.

Clark, M. D., & Artiles, A. J. (2000). A cross-national study of teachers' attributional patterns. *Journal of Special Education, 34*(2), 7–89.

Creswell, J. W. (2007). *Qualitative inquiry & research design. Choosing among five approaches.* Thousand Oakes: Sage Publications.

Darling-Hammond, L., Ancess, J., & Ort, S. W. (2002). Reinventing high school: Outcomes of the coalition campus project. *American Educational Research Journal, 39*(3), 639–673.

Day, C. (2008). Committed for life? Variations in the conditions for teachers' professional learning and development: Sustaining commitment and effectiveness over a career. *Oxford Review of Education, 33*(4), 423–443.

Day, C. (2011). Uncertain professional identities: Managing the emotional contexts of teaching. In C. Day & J. C.-K. Lee (Eds.), *New understandings of teachers' work: Emotions and educational change* (pp. 45–64). London: Springer.

Day, C., & Gu, Q. (2007). Variations in the conditions for teachers' professional learning and development: Sustaining commitment and effectiveness over a career. *Oxford Review of Education, 33*(4), 423–443.

Day, C., & Gu, Q. (2009). Teacher emotions: Well being and effectiveness. In P. Schutz & M. Zembylas (Eds.), *Advances in teacher emotion research: The impact on teachers' lives* (pp. 15–32). Dordrecht: Springer.

Day, C., Stobart, G., Sammons, P., Kington, A., Gu, Q., & Smees, R. (2006). *Variation in teachers' work, lives and effectiveness*. London: DfES.

Demetriou, H., Wilson, E., & Winterbottom, M. (2009). The role of emotion in teaching: Are there differences between male and female newly qualified teachers' approaches to teaching? *Educational Studies, 35*(4), 449–473.

Department for Education. (2010). *The Importance of Teaching. The Schools White Paper 2010.* Paper Presented to Parliament by the Secretary of State for Education by Command of Her Majesty. Retrieved from https://www.gov.uk/government/uploads/system/uploads/attachment_data/file/175429/CM-7980.pdf

Dworkin, A. G. (2009). Teacher burnout and teacher resilience: Assessing the impacts of the school accountability movement. In L. J. Saha & A. G. Dworkin (Eds.), *International handbook of research on teachers and teaching* (pp. 491–501). New York: Springer.

Ee, J., & Chang, A. (2010). How resilient are our graduate trainee teachers in Singapore? *The Asia-Pacific Education Researcher, 19*(2), 321–331.

Elbaz-Luwisch, F. (2007). Studying teachers' lives and experience: Narrative inquiry into K-12 teaching. In D. J. Clandinin (Ed.), *Handbook of narrative inquiry: Mapping a methodology* (pp. 357–383). Thousand Oakes: Sage Publications.

Evans, J., & Lunt, I. (2002). Inclusive education. *European Journal of Special Needs Education, 17*(1), 1–14.

Fantilli, R. D., & McDougall, D. E. (2009). A study of novice teachers: Challenges and supports in the first years. *Teaching and Teacher Education, 25*(6), 814–825.

Farrell, P., & Humphrey, N. (2009). Improving services for pupils with social, emotional and behavioural difficulties: Responding to the challenge. *The Journal of Emotional Education, 1*(1), 164–182.

Flores, M. A. (2018). Teacher resilience in adverse contexts: Issues of professionalism and professional identity. In M. Wosnitza, F. Peixoto, S. Beltman, & C. F. Mansfield (Eds.), *Resilience in education: Concepts, contexts and connections* (pp. 167–184). New York: Springer.

Fovet, F. (2009). The use of humour in classroom interventions with students with social, emotional and behavioural difficulties. *Emotional & Behavioural Difficulties, 14*(4), 275–289.

Fraser, H. (2004). Doing narrative research. *Qualitative Social Work, 3*(2), 179–201.

Fredrickson, B. L. (2001). The role of positive emotions in positive psychology: The broaden-and-build theory of positive emotions. *American Psychologist, 56*(3), 218–226.

Gu, Q. (2018). (Re)conceptualizing teacher resilience: A social ecological approach to understanding teachers' professional worlds. In M. Wosnitza, F. Peixoto, S. Beltman, & C. F. Mansfield (Eds.), *Resilience in education: Concepts, contexts and connections* (pp. 13–33). New York: Springer.

Gu, Q., & Day, C. (2007). Teachers' resilience: A necessary condition for effectiveness. *Teaching and Teacher Education, 23*(8), 1302–1316.

Gu, Q., & Day, C. (2013). Challenges to teacher resilience: Conditions count. *British Educational Research Journal, 39*(1), 22–44.

Gu, Q., & Li, Q. (2013). Sustaining resilience in times of change: Stories from Chinese teachers. *Asia-Pacific Journal of Teacher Education, 41*(3), 288–303.

Hargreaves, A. (1998). The emotional practice of teaching. *Teaching and Teacher Education, 14*(8), 835–854.

Hargreaves, A. (2000). Mixed emotions: Teachers' perceptions of their interactions with students. *Teaching and Teacher Education, 16*, 811–826.

Hargreaves, A., & Lo, L. (2000). The paradoxical profession: Teaching at the turn of the century. *Prospects, 30*(2), 1–16.

Henderson, N., & Milstein, M. (2003). *Resilience in schools: Making it happen for students and educators*. Thousand Oaks: Corwin Press.

Howard, S., & Johnson, B. (2004). Resilient teachers: Resisting stress and burnout. *Social Psychology of Education, 7*, 399–420.

Jamieson, B. (2006). *State of the teaching profession 2006: Back in the day...* Retrieved from http://professionallyspeaking.oct.ca/september_2006/survey.asp

Jennings, P. A., & Greenberg, M. T. (2009). The prosocial classroom: Teacher social and emotional competence in relation to student and classroom outcomes. *Review of Educational Research, 79*(1), 491–525.

Johnson, B., Down, B., Le Cornu, R., Peters, J., Sullivan, A., Pearce, J., & Hunter, J. (2012). *Early career teachers: Stories of resilience.* South Australia: University of South Australia. Retrieved from http://www.ectr.edu.au/

Kalambouka, A., Farrell, P., Dyson, A., & Kaplan, I. (2007). The impact of placing pupils with special educational needs in mainstream schools on the achievement of their peers. *Educational Research, 39*(4), 365–382.

Kidger, J., Gunnell, D., Biddle, L., Campbell, R., & Donovan, J. L. (2010). Part and parcel of teaching? Secondary school staff views on supporting student emotional health and wellbeing. *British Educational Research Journal, 36*(6), 919–935.

Kleinman, S., & Copp, C. (1993). *Emotions and fieldwork.* London: Sage Publications.

Kokkinos, C. M., Panayiotou, G., & Davazoglou, A. M. (2005). Correlates of teacher appraisals of student behaviors. *Psychology in the Schools, 42*(1), 79–89.

Kyriacou, C. (2000). *Stress-busting for teachers*. Cheltenham: Stanley Thornes.

Kyriacou, C. (2011). Teacher stress: From prevalence to resilience. In J. Langan-Fox & C. L. Cooper (Eds.), *Handbook of stress in the occupations* (pp. 161–173). Cheltenham: Edward Elgar.

Le Cornu, R. (2013). Building early career teacher resilience: The role of relationships. *Australian Journal of Teacher Education, 38*(4), 1–16.

Lewis, R. (2001). Classroom discipline and student responsibility: The students' view. *Teaching and Teacher Education, 17*(3), 307–319.

Luthar, S. S., Cicchetti, D., & Becker, B. (2000). The construct of resilience: A critical evaluation and guidelines for future work. *Child Development, 71*(3), 543–562.

Malloy, W. W., & Allen, T. (2007). Teacher retention in a teacher resiliency-building rural school. *Rural Educator, 28*(2), 19–27.

Mansfield, C. F., Beltman, S., & Price, A. (2014). 'I'm coming back again!' The resilience process of early career teachers. *Teachers and Teaching, 20*(5), 547–567.

Marzano, R. J., Marzano, J. S., & Pickering, D. J. (2003). *Classroom management that works.* Alexandra: ASCD.

Masten, A. S. (2001). Ordinary magic: Resilience processes in development. *American Psychologist, 56*(3), 227–238.

Masten, A. D., & Obradović, J. (2008). Disaster preparation and recovery: Lessons from research on resilience in human development. *Ecology and Society, 13*(1), 9. Retrieved from http://www.ecologyandsociety.org/

Mattison, R. E., Spitznagel, E. L., & Felix, B. C. (1998). Enrolment predictors of the special education outcome for SED students. *Behavioral Disorders, 23*(4), 243–256.

McCormack, C. (2000a). From interview transcript to interpretive story: Part 1 – Viewing the transcript through multiple lenses. *Field Methods, 12*(4), 282–297.

McCormack, C. (2000b). From interview transcript to interpretive story: Part 2 – Developing an interpretive story. *Field Methods, 12*(4), 298–315.

McCormack, C. (2012). Storying stories: A narrative approach to in-depth interview conversations. *International Journal of Social Research Methodology, 7*(3), 219–236.

Mishler, E. G. (1999). *Storylines. Craftartists' narratives of identity*. Cambridge, MA: Harvard University Press.

Morrison, F. J., Ponitz, C. C., & McClellan, M. (2010). Self-regulation and academic achievement in the transition to school. In S. D. Calkins & M. A. Bell (Eds.), *Child development at the intersection of emotion and cognition* (pp. 203–224). Washington, DC: American Psychological Association.

Nias, J. (1996). Thinking about feeling: The emotions in teaching. *Cambridge Journal of Education, 26*(3), 293–306.

Nieto, S. M. (2003). What keeps teachers going? *Keeping good teachers, 60*(8), 14–18.

Nieto, S. M. (2009). From surviving to thriving. *How Teachers Learn, 66*(5), 8–13.

OECD. (2012). *PISA 2009 technical report*. PISA: OECD Publishing. Retrieved from https://doi.org/10.1787/9789264167872-en

Oplatka, I. (2006). Going beyond role expectations: Towards an understanding of the determinants and components of teacher organizational citizenship behavior. *Educational Administration Quarterly, 42*(3), 385–423.

Osher, D., Sprague, J., Weissberg, R. P., Axelrod, J., Keenan, S., Kendziora, K., & Zins, J. E. (2007). A comprehensive approach to promoting social, emotional, and academic growth in contemporary schools. In A. Thomas & J. Grimes (Eds.), *Best practices in school psychology* (Vol. 5, 5th ed., pp. 1263–1278). Bethesda: National Association of School Psychologists.

Oswald, M., Johnson, B., & Howard, S. (2003). Quantifying and evaluating resilience-promoting factors: Teachers' beliefs and perceived roles. *Research in Education, 70*, 50–64.

Papatraianou, L. H., & Le Cornu, R. (2014). Problematising the role of personal and professional relationships in early career teacher resilience. *Australian Journal of Teacher Education, 39*(1), 100–116.

Patrick, H., Meyer, D. K., Turner, J. C., & Midgley, C. (2003). How teachers establish psychological environments during the first days of school: Associations with avoidance in mathematics. *Teachers College Record, 105*(8), 1521–1558.

Patterson, G. R., & Yoerger, K. (2002). A developmental model for early- and late-onset antisocial behavior. In J. B. Reid, J. Snyder, & G. R. Patterson (Eds.), *Antisocial behavior in children and adolescents: A developmental analysis and model for intervention* (pp. 147–172). Washington, DC: American Psychological Association.

Patterson, J. H., Collins, L., & Abbott, G. (2004). A study of teacher resilience in urban schools. *Journal of Instructional Psychology, 31*(1), 3–11.

Pearce, J., & Morrison, C. (2011). Teacher identity and early career resilience: Exploring the links. *Australian Journal of Teacher Education, 36*(1), 48–59.

Peters, J., & Pearce, J. (2012). Relationships and early career teacher resilience: A role for school principals. *Teachers and Teaching, 18*(2), 249–262.

Plummer, K. (2001). The call of life stories in ethnographic research. In P. Atkinson, A. Coffey, S. Delamont, J. Lofland, & L. Lofland (Eds.), *Handbook of ethnography* (pp. 395–406). London: Sage Publications.

Prosser, B., Tuckey, M., & Wendt, S. (2009). *The personal domain: Exploring what sustains professionals in urban fringe communities*. Paper presented at the Australian Association for Research in Education Conference, Canberra.

Reyna, C., & Weiner, B. (2001). Justice and utility in the classroom: An attributional analysis on the goals of teachers' punishment and intervention strategies. *Journal of Educational Psychology, 93*(2), 309–319.

Rogers, B. (2009). *How to manage children's challenging behaviour*. London: Sage.

Rogers, B. (2011). *Classroom behaviour: A practical guide to effective teaching, behaviour management and colleague support*. London: Sage.

Sammons, P., Day, C., Kington, A., Gu, Q., Stobart, G., & Smees, R. (2007). Exploring variations in teachers' work, lives and their effect on pupils: Key findings and implications from a longitudinal mixed-method study. *British Educational Research Journal, 33*(5), 681–701.

Scott, C., Stone, B., & Dinham, S. (2001). "I love teaching but…" international patterns of teacher discontent. *Education Policy Analysis Archives, 9*(28), 1–19.

Sumsion, J. (2003). 'Bad days don't kill you: They just make you stronger': A case study of an early childhood educator's resilience. *International Journal of Early Years Education, 11*(2), 141–154.

Sutton, R. E., & Wheatley, K. F. (2003). Teachers' emotions and teaching: A review of the literature and directions for future research. *Educational Psychology Review, 15*(4), 327–358.

Tait, M. (2008). Resilience as a contributor to novice teacher success, commitment, and retention. *Teacher Education Quarterly, 35*(4), 57–75.

Tanti Rigos, V. (2009). *Maltese teachers; causal attributions, cognitive and emotional responses to students with emotional and behavioural difficulties*. Unpublished M.Ed. dissertation. Faculty of Education, University of Malta.

Valli, L., & Buese, D. (2007). The changing roles of teachers in an era of high-stakes accountability. *American Education Research Journal, 44*(3), 519–558.

van der Wolf, K., & Everaert, H. A. (2003). Teacher stress, challenging parents and problem students. In S. Castelli, M. Mendel, & B. Ravn (Eds.), *School, family, and community partnership in a world of differences and changes* (pp. 135–146). Gdansk: University of Gdansk.

Watson, M., & Battistich, V. (2006). Building and sustaining caring communities. In C. S. Weinstein & C. M. Evertson (Eds.), *Handbook of classroom management: Research, practice, and contemporary issues* (pp. 253–280). Mahwah: Lawrence Erlbaum.

Werner, E. E. (1995). Resilience in development. *Current Directions in Psychological Science, 4*(3), 81–85.

Yoon, J. S. (2002). Teacher characteristics as predictors of teacher-student relationships: Stress, negative affect, and self-efficacy. *Social Behavior and Personality, 30*, 485–494.

Chapter 10
Teacher Resilience in Adverse Contexts: Issues of Professionalism and Professional Identity

Maria Assunção Flores

Abstract Teacher resilience is a construct, that is, relative, developmental and dynamic; it is socially constructed and depends on personal and professional dispositions. Issues of commitment, professionalism and professional identity, for instance, need to be taken into account if teacher resilience is to be fully understood. In this chapter I draw upon a larger piece of research aimed at investigating teachers' work and lives in challenging circumstances. Data were collected through a national survey ($n = 2702$ teachers), focus group ($n = 99$ teachers) and interviews to 11 school principals. Findings suggest the connection between teacher commitment and resilience which are associated with issues of school culture and leadership, a sense of vocation and teachers' beliefs and professional values. Factors and sources of teacher motivation and resilience are also identified within a context marked by teacher intensification, lack of trust, worsening of teaching conditions, lower social and economic status and legislative "tsunami". The chapter ends with the discussion of the importance of relationships in the teaching profession and issues of motivation and professionalism which entails given ways of being and feeling as a teacher.

Over the last 15 years or so, resilience has emerged as a field of research, not only in countries that experience high rates of attrition but also in contexts in which the teaching profession has gone through changing policy and social circumstances affecting its social and economic status (Beltman et al. 2011; Flores 2014; Gu 2014; Gu and Li 2013; Mansfield et al. 2012). According to Le Cornu (2009, p. 717), "one of the main reasons for the increased attention to teacher resilience is the considerable attention paid in recent years to the high proportion of teachers who leave the profession in the first years". However, as the author stressed, resilience is not only important for early career teachers but for enhancing teacher effectiveness. Similarly,

M. A. Flores (✉)
University of Minho, Braga, Portugal
e-mail: aflores@ie.uminho.pt

M. Wosnitza et al. (eds.), *Resilience in Education*,
https://doi.org/10.1007/978-3-319-76690-4_10

Gu and Day (2007, p. 1302) state that "A shift in focus from teacher stress and burnout to resilience provides a promising perspective to understand the ways that teachers manage and sustain their motivation and commitment in times of change". Although resilience has evolved as a research topic over the last 15 years or so, there is a scarcity of studies in this field, especially as far as experienced teachers are concerned. According to Mansfield et al. (2012, p. 366), "research specifically focused on teacher resilience is in its infancy". Also, Gu and Day (2007) state that "the question of promoting resilience in teachers in times of change remains overlooked" (p. 1303). It is possible, however, to identify some studies that deal with resilience as an important construct to understand teachers' predispositions, behaviours and attitudes in adverse teaching contexts. Existing literature suggests that teacher resilience is complex and dynamic and it involves a range of personal and contextual factors (Galea 2018, Chap. 9, this volume; Mansfield et al. 2012, 2014). It is within this perspective that the study reported in this chapter was carried out in a context which has been, over the last few years, particularly challenging for Portuguese teachers. Over the last decade research has shown that rather than being seen as an "innate quality", resilience is understood as "relative, developmental and dynamic, manifesting itself as a result of a dynamic process within a given context" (Gu and Day 2007, p. 1305). Although there is a growing body of literature that deals with teacher resilience, it is possible to identify a wide range of definitions of resilience, most of which emphasise both individual and contextual factors and its multidimensionality and complexity (Mansfield et al. 2012). In the next section, the key features highlighted in teacher resilience literature are identified.

Understanding Teacher Resilience

A recent review by Beltman et al. (2011) points to the emergence of resilience as a field of research. However, the authors identify a wide range of conceptualisations of resilience which demonstrates the complex and multifaceted nature of the concept but also raises issues of ambiguity and consistency.

As a matter of fact, teacher resilience has been described in various ways in the literature. It has been related to "the capacity to successfully overcome personal vulnerability and environmental stressors" (Oswald et al. 2003, p. 50) and to "specific strategies that individuals employ when they experience an adverse situation" (Castro et al. 2010, p. 263). For instance, Brunetti (2006, p. 813) defines resilience as "a quality that enables teachers to maintain commitment to teaching and their teaching practices despite challenging conditions and recurring setbacks".

Literature on resilience has evolved from identifying personal traits to looking at the factors that influence the resilience process. This implies understanding resilience not only as a psychological construct but as a multidimensional and socially constructed concept (Gu and Day 2007). Therefore, context plays a key role in the development and demonstration of resilience (Mansfield et al. 2012) as well as support, both formal and informal (Papatraianou and Le Cornu 2014). As such, "resilience is not a quality that is innate. Rather, it is a construct that is relative, developmental, dynamic, connoting the positive adaptation and development of individuals in the presence of challenging circumstances" (Gu and Day 2007, p. 1305).

Drawing upon existing definitions and understandings of resilience, Mansfield et al. (2012) identify the following key themes: it involves a dynamic process, it is associated with the interaction between person and context, and it is related to the ways in which individuals respond to challenging or adverse situations. In addition, there are (individual and contextual) protective and risk factors that determine the resilience process. Personal strengths such as particular characteristics, attributes and assets have also been identified (Mansfield et al. 2012). As such, resilience is not only an outcome but also a process involving the "interactions between early career teachers and the social, cultural, political and relational contexts of their new profession" (Pearce and Morrison 2011, p. 48). As the contributions to this volume highlight, it is important to conceptualise teacher resilience in the light of a social ecological approach (Gu 2018, Chap. 2, this volume) and to develop perspectives to foster resilience based on a self-reflection and professional development perspective (Mansfield et al. 2018, Chap. 4, this volume; Wosnitza et al. 2018, Chap. 16, this volume).

As Gu and Day (2007) assert, resilience, as a multidimensional, socially constructed concept, is situated in the discourse of teaching as emotional practice, and it is relative, dynamic and developmental in nature. The authors define resilience as the "capacity to continue 'bounce back', to recover strengths or spirit quickly and efficiently in the face of adversity, is closely allied to a strong sense of vocation, self-efficacy and motivation to teach which are fundamental to a concern for promoting achievement in all aspects of students' lives" (Gu and Day 2007, p. 1302).

A recent study by Mansfield et al. (2012) shows that graduating and early career teacher associate resilience with multidimensional and overlapping features. The authors identified 23 interrelated aspects of resilience which were organised according to four overarching dimensions: the emotional (managing emotions, enjoying teaching, etc.), the profession-related (commitment to students, being reflective and flexible, etc.), the motivational (motivation and enthusiasm, being positive and optimistic, etc.) and the social (interactions with students and colleagues, interpersonal and communication skills, etc.).

Research literature has also identified the risk factors related to contexts of teaching seen as adverse contexts such as heavy workload, classroom management, feelings of unpreparedness, lack of support, lack of resources, etc. (Jenkins et al. 2009; McCormack and Gore 2008; Sumsion 2004). Also, Le Cornu (2009) has identified the complex and dynamic interactions between individuals and their student teaching contexts. Writing in the context of a study of pre-service teachers in their practicum, the author identified three main features that contribute to build resilience: opportunities for peer support; explicit teaching of particular skills and attitudes; and adoption of particular roles by pre-service teachers, mentors at school and university supervisors. In a similar vein, Pearce and Morrison's (2011) study has investigated the impact of professional, individual and relational conditions on the resilience of early career teachers and has highlighted the importance of understanding how they engage in the formation of professional identities.

Gu and Days's study (2007, p. 1311) of three resilient teachers demonstrated the "sense of meaning and moral purpose" in the "pursuit and exploration of their professional values and ideologies". The authors conclude that "these internal values and motivation, fuelled their capacities to exercise emotional strengths and professional competence and subsequently provided them with the resilience which enabled them to meet the challenges of the changing environments in which they worked". In this way, the negative effects of stressful working conditions and life events were managed as positive personal and professional resources in their life trajectories. Similarly, Flores et al. (2014) found that what kept teachers going in challenging circumstances were the students as well as the positive relationships at school and supportive and encouraging school culture and leadership.

Individual protective factors include intrinsic motivation, persistence, optimism, emotional intelligence, sense of humour and willingness to take risks, whereas environmental protective factors include mentor support, peer support, family and friends' support and school administration support (see Mansfield et al. 2012). Also, Castro et al. (2010) showed that novice teachers utilised a variety of strategies, including help-seeking, problem-solving, managing difficult relationships and seeking rejuvenation/renewal in building additional resources and support. The authors conclude that resilient teachers demonstrated agency in the process of overcoming adversity.

The review by Beltman et al. (2011) of studies related to early career teachers' resilience has shown that resilience is the outcome of a dynamic relationship between individual risks and key individual protective factors. The authors identified individual attributes such as altruistic motives and high self-efficacy as key individual protective factors. Different sources for contextual supports and contextual challenges were identified such as school administration, colleagues and pupils. In a study in the USA, Brunetti (2006) found that teachers who remain in inner city classrooms for more than 12 years were resilient and able to overcome difficult challenges. Three main factors were identified: the students; professional and personal satisfaction; and support from administrators, colleagues and the organisation of the school.

Beltman et al. (2011, p. 196) state that resilience is a "complex, idiosyncratic and cyclical construct, involving the dynamic processes of interaction over time between person and environment" and it "is evidenced by how individuals respond to challenging or adverse situations and the contexts in which they work have been shown to provide both protective and risk factors".

A recent review of existing literature on veteran teachers reveals that most of the studies focused on veteran teachers' resilience and that issues concerning veteran teachers' identities are key to understanding why they remain in the profession and are able to sustain their motivation and commitment over time (Carrillo and Flores 2017). Their sense of vocation, the relationships with the students and support from school administration and colleagues contributed positively to their identities and to their feelings of self-efficacy. Conversely, the increasing measures of accountability, problematic classroom management, adverse personal factors, excessive paperwork and heavy workload impacted negatively on their identities. The authors also state that veteran teachers were able to build on their confidence regarding their professional competence and relied on internal and external factors to maintain their commitment to teaching. The role of emotions in the transformation of veteran teachers' identities and the permeable boundaries of the contexts were also identified.

Key Issues in Teacher Professionalism in Challenging Times

Recent literature on teacher professionalism has highlighted its complex and dynamic nature which relates not only to policy environment but also to the ways in which teachers see themselves as professionals and the conditions for them to exercise their profession. In general, issues such as intensification and bureaucratisation, increased forms of managerialism, and greater accountability and public scrutiny are but a few examples of the changes in the teaching profession identified in the literature (Day 1999; Day et al. 2007; Flores 2012; Helsby 2000; Kelchtermans 2009; Osborn 2006). This situation has implications for teachers' sense of professionalism and for their professional identities as it impacts upon the ways in which they experience their daily work at school as well as their public image in society.

In many countries, teachers' work became characterised by "ruptures rather than continuities" (Carlgren 1999, p. 44). Issues such as the existence of greater control over teachers' work and performance of schools (Ball 2003) through accountability mechanisms led to more pressure upon schools and teachers to increase standards of teaching, learning and achievement (Osborn 2006; Day and Smethem 2009). A culture of managerialism and performativity (Ozga 2000) and standardisation and overregulation (Hargreaves 2003) of teaching and teachers' work have been widely discussed internationally. Such changes in teaching and in teachers' work have led to a decrease in their motivation, job satisfaction and sense of professionalism leading to feelings of tiredness (Flores 2012), teacher stress, fatigue and burnout (see, for instance, Esteve 1991; Flores 2014). Looking at the opportunities and threats in teaching, amongst other features, Hargreaves and Fullan (2012, p. 43) noted that there was "more interactive professionalism among teachers", but they also warned that it "can turn into hyperactive professionalism as teachers are thrown into hurried meetings to devise quick-fix solutions that will lead to instantaneous gains in student achievement results".

In a nationwide survey carried out in Portugal, in which 2702 teachers participated, Flores et al. (2014) concluded that recent policy initiatives, associated with a context of austerity and economic crisis, led to a decrease in teachers' motivation, to a greater control of their work, to an increase of their workload and bureaucracy and to a deterioration of their working conditions including their social economic status. The same nationwide study also indicated that teachers have been subject to greater public scrutiny and that the image of teaching and teachers in the media has contributed to the deterioration of the teaching profession.

It is within this context that the study reported in this chapter was carried out framing resilience as a key factor to analyse the ways in which teachers in Portugal perceive changes in their profession and working conditions in adverse times. The economic and financial crisis that has been affecting several sectors in the Portuguese society has led to increases in unemployment, salary cuts and higher taxes. These have impacted upon teachers and the teaching profession. Along with these are also changes at a policy level amongst which are new mechanisms for teacher evaluation, new protocols for school governance, reduction in the school curriculum and introduction of national exams from the primary school upward. In general, more pressure is placed on schools and teachers to increase teaching standards and student achievement. In addition, changes in their workload and working conditions have been implemented. Drawing from the major research project, this chapter addresses the following research questions:

1. How do Portuguese teachers view their experience as teachers in current challenging circumstances?
2. How do they describe the contexts in which they work?
3. What kinds of factors influence their resilience and professionalism in adverse times?

The Context and Design of the Study

This chapter reports on data drawn from a broader 3-year piece of research (January 2011 to June 2014) funded by *Fundação para a Ciência e a Tecnologia* (National Foundation for Science and Technology) (PTDC/CPE-CED/112164/2009) aimed at examining existing conditions for teacher leadership and professional development in challenging circumstances. A mixed-method research design was devised (see Table 10.1).

Table 10.1 Phases and methods of data collection

Phases	Methods	Participants
Phase I	Online survey nationwide	2702 teachers
February–April 2012		
Phase II	Semi-structured interviews	11 schools
		11 head teachers
November 2012–April 2013	Focus group	45 focus groups
		99 teachers
		108 students
Phase III	Professional development courses	5 schools
	Questionnaires with open-ended questions	
	Portfolios	
May 2013–May 2014	Reflective tools	66 teachers
	Artefacts	
	Reflective journals	

The project included three phases of data collection (see Table 10.1), including a national survey in which 2702 teachers participated (phase I), semi-structured interviews to principals in 11 schools located in different regions of the country, focus groups with 99 teachers and focus groups with 108 students (phase II) and a professional development programme in 5 schools located in northern Portugal, in which 66 teachers participated (phase III). In this chapter some data gathered from teachers in phases I and II will be reported. Phase I was carried out between February and April 2012, and phase II was conducted between November 2012 and April 2013.

Participants

In total, in phase I, 2702 teachers from mainland Portugal responded to the questionnaire which was administered online: 78.5% were female. Also, 42.8% of the participants were between 40 and 49 years old, 28.6% were between 50 and 59 years old and 25.5% were between 30 and 39 years old. Only 1.7 were between 20 and 19 years of age. As far as the qualifications of the teachers participating in the study are concerned, the majority of them hold a *licenciatura* degree (59. 3%), and 21. 4% hold a master's degree (21.4%). The majority of the participants have between 11 and 20 years of experience (37.6%) and between 21 and 30 years (34.9%). Most of the participants have between 1 and 10 years of experience in their present school (65.8%). The majority of the participants have a permanent post at school (83.3%). In addition, the majority of the participants taught in urban schools (51.1%) and in all sectors of teaching (from pre-school to secondary school: 3–18-year-old students). Most teachers taught in third cycle (41.9%) (students aged 12–15) and in secondary education (33.2%) (students aged 16–18).

As far as the 99 teachers participating in the focus group are concerned, the majority of them were female teachers (76.8%). As for their age, 31.3% were between 51 and 60 years old and 27.3% between 41 and 50 years old. The participating teachers came from all levels of teaching, from pre-school to secondary school, and taught various subjects. In regard to their experience as teachers, 36.4% have between 21 and 30 years of service, 26.3% between 31 and 40, and 22.2% between 11 and 20 years of experience. In general, the age of the teachers participating in the survey and in the focus group is in line with the "General profile of the teachers 2014/2015" published by the Ministry of Education (Direção-Geral de Estatísticas da Educação e Ciências, July 2016). According to these statistics, only 1.4% of the Portuguese teachers are younger than 30 years of age.

Data Collection and Analysis

A nationwide survey was conducted through an online questionnaire (using the surveymonkey device) which was sent to the principals of all elementary and secondary schools in mainland Portugal. The questionnaire was then distributed to the teachers in each school. Permission for administering the questionnaire in public schools was previously obtained from the Ministry of Education. The questionnaire was devised by the author and colleagues based upon earlier work (see Day et al. 2007; Flores et al. 2007). It included both closed- and open-ended questions according to two main dimensions: (i) motivation and job satisfaction (including questions about current motivation, areas in which teachers experienced the greatest increase in satisfaction and the most dissatisfaction, etc.) and (ii) leadership, autonomy and school culture (e.g. factors that hinder or promote teacher leadership, opportunities and motives for engaging in professional development opportunities).

In order to further analyse issues of teacher professionalism associated with the effects of policy initiatives on teachers' work arising from the quantitative data, focus group were carried out with 99 teachers in 11 schools throughout the country. Each focus group comprised three to seven participants. Teachers participating in the focus group were recruited by the head teacher in each of the 11 participating schools. All of them were volunteers. The focus group protocol aimed at analysing in a deeper way preliminary findings arising from the survey data, but it also aimed at giving voice to teachers to talk about their experience as teachers in challenging circumstances especially in regard to the ways in which their professionalism has been affected. The focus group protocol included questions related to perceptions of school culture and leadership, changes in teachers' work and issues related to being a teacher and teaching as a profession. The focus groups were conducted in each of the schools by at least two researchers participating in the wider research project.

Quantitative data were analysed statistically with the use of SPSS (version 20). The process of qualitative data analysis was undertaken according to two phases: an analysis of data gathered in each school through the voices of teachers, students and the principal. A second phase was then carried out according to a comparative or horizontal analysis (cross-case analysis) (Miles and Huberman 1994). In this phase, it was possible to look for common patterns as well as differences. A semantic criterion was used to look for key themes arising from the qualitative data by the research team. This chapter presents the main findings from the survey (phase I) and data from the focus group with teachers (phase II) in order to illustrate quantitative data.

Findings

Findings are presented according to three main key themes: (i) changing teaching contexts, massive legislation and deterioration of working conditions; (ii) working in challenging contexts, motivation and sense of vocation; and (iii) resilience, professionalism and identity.

Changing Teaching Contexts: Massive Legislation and Deterioration of Working Conditions

Teachers reported the adverse times and challenging circumstances in Portugal as a result of the economic and financial crisis with implications for education in general and for teachers' work in particular which is in line with previous empirical work (Flores and Ferreira 2016). They spoke of salary cuts, higher taxes and unemployment affecting teaching in particular. Added to this are changes in the policy environment with massive legislation which impacted upon a wide range of dimensions in Portuguese schools, namely, new mechanisms for teacher evaluation, new protocols for school governance, reduction in the school curriculum and the introduction of national exams from the primary school upward. In general, teachers felt that more pressure has been placed upon schools and upon them in order to increase teaching standards and student achievement. These issues are highlighted in the focus group interviews: "Bureaucratic procedures (...) administrative and bureaucratic records have been increasing in recent years"; "I see my work a bit of in a schizophrenic way. It is really how I feel. You have to comply with curricula and programs and all the paperwork that is required… it is difficult to manage it".

Along with this is the deterioration of the teaching profession which, according to the participants, is due, at least to a certain extent, to the negative image of teaching and teachers in the media (90% agree and strongly agree): "Our image as teachers has been deteriorated in terms of social recognition and economic status."; "My main concerns relate to the crisis and its effects in the school (number of students per class, workload, changes in curriculum, etc.,)."; "Your work as a teacher has been more and more technical and bureaucratic, and it does not leave room for creativity and innovation".

By and large teachers claim that their working conditions deteriorated over the last few years including an increase in workload and in bureaucracy, greater public accountability and greater control over their work (see Table 10.2). The following quotes from the focus groups illustrated this claim:

> Over the last years, there has been a negative image of teachers in the media and in the society in general… (Secondary school female teacher, 35 years of experience)
>
> As a teacher you have to work harder, your workload has increased, bureaucracy has increased, paperwork has increased, etc. (Secondary school female teacher, 28 years of experience)
>
> The most problematic factor is the news, the lack of safety and instability in economic terms, the reduction of the salary (…) you never know what tomorrow will bring (Secondary school female teacher, 21 years of experience)

All of these external factors have affected their sense of professionalism and their daily work in schools. Issues such as lack of motivation, tiredness and disappointment emerged from their accounts. Teachers participating in both the survey

Table 10.2 Changes in teachers' perceptions of their work (2009–2012)

	Strongly agree/ agree	I don't agree nor disagree	Disagree/strongly disagree
Teacher individualism has increased	50.3% (916)	25.1% (464)	24.2% (439)
Teachers' workload has increased over the past 3 years	96.7% (1772)	2.3% (43)	1% (18)
The bureaucracy in teaching has increased	95.4% (1752)	2.9% (54)	1.7% (31)
There was an increase of teachers' public accountability	74.6% (1371)	19.8% (363)	5.6% (103)
There was an accentuation of criticism to teachers	92.2% (1694)	5.9% (109)	1.9% (35)
There was greater control over teachers' work	75.6% (1383)	17.4% (318)	7% (129)

and the focus group talked about the increasing challenges and demands that they had to deal with, stemming not only from the policy environment but also from the social, cultural and economic factors that have affected their work.

Working in Challenging Circumstances: Motivation and Sense of Vocation

One of the issues which became very clear in teachers' accounts was their motivation as teachers. In the survey, they were asked about their current levels of motivation (in 2012). They reported that their motivation (in 2012) was moderate (45.5%), although 27.4% admit that their motivation was high and for 17.4% of the participants was low. Interestingly, when asked about their job satisfaction and motivation over the last 3 years (2009–2012) (during which major reforms in education and in teaching have been put into place in schools), the majority of the participants reported that their motivation and their job satisfaction decreased (61.6% and 44.5%, respectively). Issues such as salary cuts, increase of bureaucracy, the deterioration of the social image of teaching, lack of motivation from the part of students, lack of valorisation of school from the part of parents and lack of career prospects, along with massive legislation that has been published and recent policy initiatives, were at the forefront of their accounts. Amongst the policy initiatives that have affected teachers' work are teacher evaluation, a new system for school governance (the merging of schools in big clusters of schools), increase of number of pupils per class and of classes per teacher and the increase of workload. However, some of the teachers, despite all the changes and challenges that they have to deal with in their schools, resist and try to become more resilient in order to keep their motivation and joy of teaching despite "all the things that go wrong in education". The following quotes from the focus groups illustrate this theme:

> As a teacher you feel unmotivated with all that is going on in Education, but you need a positive attitude in order to motivate your students for learning. (Secondary school male teacher, 21 years of experience)
>
> I try to make an effort to carry on keeping in mind the goal that has made me choose this profession, I mean, my students! (Elementary school female teacher, 22 years of experience)

As this last quote illustrates, teachers draw upon their sense of vocation (their commitment and willingness to make a difference in their students' lives) in order to face adverse contexts of teaching. In other words, what keeps teachers going, despite everything, are their students which became sources of motivation in challenging working contexts. The participating teachers in the focus group refer to external factors which lead to lack of motivation and dissatisfaction, such as policy initiatives, deterioration of working conditions, heavy workload, changes in teacher career (no career prospects), increase in bureaucracy, etc. But they also spoke of the ways in which they overcome the difficulties in their daily work focusing on their students and on the classroom practice:

> There is heavy workload… Nowadays you need to do more in schools without fewer resources. This means extra work for you as a teacher… and you need to do your best against the odds. (Elementary school male teacher, 27 years of experience)
>
> There is more and more paperwork and you have less time to devote to your students. (Primary school female teacher, 15 years of experience)
>
> I try to focus on my students and on my work with them in the classroom. That is why I became a teacher in the first place! (Elementary school teacher, 16 years of teaching)

The context of economic and social crisis has impacted upon school and families, and teachers are concerned with this situation and with its implications for their work which becomes even more demanding and tiring. They show concern with students' learning in more demanding and complex contexts of teaching which is in line with recent research (Flores and Ferreira 2016).

Added to their efforts to keep themselves motivated as professionals and their focus on their students in adverse working conditions were their views of school culture and leadership which explain differences in teachers' accounts of resilience to which I now turn.

Resilience, Professionalism and Identity

Some teachers who participated in the research project were able to remain in teaching despite the heavy workload, the pressure in regard to student achievement and the massive changes in policy and school organisation and governance. They claim that their willingness and motivation to continue to be a teacher are due to a great extent to their students ("what keeps me in teaching are my students"). This is to be related to teachers' sense of professionalism and their capacity for resilience, which are linked to their professional values as teachers and to their beliefs and sense of identity. The following quotes from the focus groups illustrate these points:

> As a teacher you may lack motivation in regard to everything, to salary cuts, to what has been taken away from you, but as far as your work with the students is concerned and your family you do everything you can. You do your best. (Elementary school female teacher, 17 years of experience)
>
> All this [massive changes in legislation] leads to the lack of motivation. I don't feel that this has an impact on my work. It is a great concern but it doesn't affect my work as a teacher. (Secondary school female teacher, 21 years of experience)
>
> I really enjoy being with the kids. Coming to school is not a pleasure to me anymore, but I still enjoy being with my students. (Female pre-school teacher, 33 years of experience)
>
> It is professionalism that makes you do what you do and leading… nobody is able to deal with so much work… it is because teachers are professionals that they do what they do. (Elementary school male teacher, 33 years of experience)

These professional attitudes and motivational responses are in line with another question included in the survey. Teachers were asked about the most important dimensions of their work (see Table 10.3). They identified collaborating with colleagues (63.4%), supporting students (58.7%), reflecting on one's own work (51.1%), planning teaching (49.1%) and continuous professional learning (45.1%) as the most important ones (see Table 10.3). The least valued dimensions are performing administrative tasks (7.5%), involvement within the local community (14.5%), developing teamwork (18.7%), using ICT (19.7%) and participating in decision-making process (19.7%).

Teachers responding to the survey identified "collaborating with colleagues" as the most important dimension of their work. However, and interestingly, they also agreed that over the last 3 years, there was an increase in teacher individualism. In addition, "developing teamwork" and "participating in the decision-making process" are amongst the least valued dimensions of teachers' work. There is ambiguity in their perceptions as if, on the one hand, they value collaboration with colleagues

Table 10.3 Dimensions of teachers' work

	Frequency	%
Collaborating with colleagues	1140	63.4
Supporting students	1056	58.7
Reflecting on one's own work	919	51.1
Planning teaching	882	49.1
Continuous professional learning	810	45.1
Developing innovative practices	801	44.5
Monitoring student behaviour	801	44.5
Accessing educational resources	497	27.7
Communicating with parents	463	25.8
Participating in decision-making process	355	19.7
Using ICT	354	19.7
Developing team work	337	18.7
Involvement within the local community	260	14.5
Performing administrative tasks	134	7.5

and, on the other hand, they do not value as much teamwork and participation in the decision-making process. This ambivalence may be related to top-down initiatives in order for teachers to do (compulsory) meetings at school. Issues of structural and comfortable collaboration (in many cases drawn from top down initiatives) and authentic collaboration (initiated and fostered by teachers themselves at school) might explain some of the findings (Hargreaves 1998; Williams et al. 2001).

Both internal and external factors explain teachers' resilience and sense of professionalism. They spoke of issues such as joy of teaching, commitment to students' learning, willingness to grow professionally despite the negative and less encouraging external working environment, but they also talked about the positive "ethos" of their workplace, supportive and encouraging leadership, trust and positive relationships with colleagues. In fact, the importance of relationships in teaching was at the forefront of their accounts in the focus groups:

> Maybe you learn more when you have a chat with a colleague in the staffroom having a cup of tea or coffee rather than in those compulsory in-service activities that you have to do in order to get credits... but your day-to-day experience is important... trying to figure out what and why you are doing so and so. This is very important for your professional growth as a teacher as well as sharing materials with colleagues and working closely with them. (Secondary school female teacher, 33 years of experience)
>
> For me what is important is the relationship with colleagues... working together. Then you also have those training activities, but in my view what promotes professional development is really the relationship and interaction with colleagues, working together, sharing, etc. (Secondary school female teacher, 33 years of experience)

In other words, in teachers' accounts it was possible to identify issues of professionalism (in which care, dedication and commitment to learning were key elements) and a sense of identity with clear images of themselves as professionals with strong professional values and awareness of their role in making a difference in their students' lives. So despite the negative policy environment and the deterioration of their working conditions, they remain committed to their students and to the social and moral purposes of teaching which, in turn, relates to their sense of vocation. They have clear and strong ideas about what it means for them to be a teacher, which relate to their professionalism and sense of identity and, thus, to their capacity for being resilient in the adverse contexts in which they work.

Discussion and Conclusion

Existing literature suggests that teacher resilience is a construct, that is, relative, developmental and dynamic; it is socially constructed and depends on personal and professional dispositions as well as on contextual factors. It entails a sense of purpose and meaningful actions particularly in adverse circumstances (Day and Gu 2014) as it is the case of Portuguese teachers over the last few years. The present study adds to existing literature in shedding additional light upon the factors that influence teachers' capacity to be resilient (Gu 2014), not only in their early stages, as much of extant literature focuses on (see, for instance, Johnson et al. 2015; Mansfield et al. 2014), but in all phases of the teaching career, especially experienced teachers, and particularly in adverse circumstances. It is important not only to look at teacher attrition and resilience in the early years of the teaching, especially in countries in which there is a teacher shortage, but also to all phases of the teaching career, particularly veteran teachers, and focusing on what keeps them motivated in their job and why they remain in teaching despite the increasing challenges and changes in their working conditions.

By and large, issues such as bureaucracy, intensification, the deterioration of social image of the teaching profession, unemployment amongst teachers due to the financial and economic crisis and endless reforms in education (such as external evaluations for teachers, schools and students) are amongst the external factors that account for teachers' lack of motivation and dissatisfaction. However, key factors and sources of personal and professional motivation helped teachers remain in the teaching profession despite everything and were derived from factors such as teacher collaboration, classroom work and the relationship with students. This is in line with earlier empirical work which has shown devotion to students, pursuit of personal and professional fulfilment and support from administration, colleagues and the organisation of the school as key elements in understating teacher resilience (Brunetti 2006). Other studies have highlighted the importance of internal factors such as autonomy and personal involvement on teachers' levels of job satisfaction in detriment to externally imposed measures (Butt et al. 2005).

The study reported in this chapter has demonstrated that teachers' strong professional values, their sense of professionalism and their capacity for resisting and for being resilient (despite negative policy environment and the challenging social and economic context) as well as their sense of identity as teachers emerged from the data in explaining the ways in which some teachers became more resilient than others. This is in line with Day and Gu's (2014, p. xvii) idea of "persistence of hope and endeavour among teachers to do their best" and their notion of "everyday resilience". The authors stress that "being a resilient teacher goes beyond mere survival on an everyday basis. Teaching to their best across a career span of 30 years or more requires that teachers are able to exercise 'everyday resilience' that classroom conditions inherently demand".

The factors and sources of teacher motivation and job satisfaction were analysed in challenging contexts ranging from feelings of frustration and low morale to resilience and professionalism. In particular, the "relational resilience" (Day and Gu 2014) was explored in the light of evidence from the study taking into account the context of teacher intensification, lack of trust, worsening of teaching conditions, lower social and economic status and the legislative "tsunami" that has invaded schools and teachers' work.

Teachers' accounts in this study point to issues that are related to the ways in which they experience their professionalism, in particular issues of commitment, engagement, care and attention to pupils. This may be associated with their resilience which in turn relates to school culture and leadership, a sense of vocation and strong beliefs and professional values as teachers. As Gu and Day's study (2007, p. 1314) demonstrated, "underlying resilient teachers endeavours to exert control over difficult situations is their strength and determination to fulfil their original call to teach and to manage and thrive professionally".

Issues of commitment, professionalism, professional identity and professional values need to be taken into account in order to understand differences in teacher resilience. As such, professional development opportunities as well as conditions for teachers to exercise their professionalism in supportive and encouraging school cultures are of paramount importance if teachers are to be resilient, motivated and engaged in their profession. Also relevant are opportunities for teachers to develop their sense of vocation, their values as professionals and their views of teaching and learning as well as their care for the students, as this study also demonstrated. Gu and Day (2007) identified professional assets for teachers, namely, sustaining a sense of vocation (teaching as more than just a job) and developing a sense of efficacy as a key component of teacher resilience. The authors also identified the influence of external factors such as external policy contexts and school contexts. In other words, Gu and Day (2007, p. 1314), reiterate that resilience is determined by "the *interaction* between the internal assets of the individual and the external environments in which the individual lives and grows (or does not grow)" (original emphasis).

This study, which took place in especially challenging circumstances, provided evidence of the multidimensional, dynamic and complex nature of teacher resilience. Not only does it relate to issues of teacher commitment, self-efficacy, effectiveness and agency, as earlier research has demonstrated (Day and Gu 2009; Ebersöhn 2014; Gu and Day 2007; Mansfield et al. 2012, 2014; Vance et al. 2015), but it is also dependent upon teachers' professional values, their sense of professionalism and their identity as teachers as well as the contextual factors that hinder or support the exercise of their profession. Resilient teachers spoke of positive atmosphere at school, encouraging leadership and supportive colleagues, but they also claim that their remaining in teaching is to be related to their strong professional values as teachers, to their sense of vocation and to their professionalism and identity as teachers.

Limitations of this study are that resilience was not the main focus of the larger study and that it relies on teachers' self-perceptions. Nevertheless, it contributes to better understanding teachers' work in challenging circumstances, particularly experienced teachers as they make sense of the tensions and challenges in their daily work. Findings have implications for teacher education, particularly for in-service teacher education and professional development providers. Creating spaces for teachers to discuss and build their professionalism, to share and discuss the core features of their work and of their professional values and identities as teachers as well as to frame and interpret their current working conditions in a context of greater accountability and performativity becomes a key issue for professional development providers if teacher resilience is to be fostered.

This study supports earlier work on teacher resilience, for instance, Day and Gu (2014, p. 11) when they advocate for resilience as a relational concept which "recognizes the interactive impact of personal, professional and situated factors on teachers' work and lives and contextualizes teachers' endeavours to sustain their professional commitment". The relational and affective dimensions of teaching were highlighted in teachers' accounts and, despite the external factors leading to lack of motivation such as lack of career prospects, salary cuts, worsening of working conditions and unemployment, were of paramount importance as key sources of motivation, resilience and hope in teaching.

References

Ball, S. (2003). The teacher's soul and the terrors of performativity. *Journal of Education Policy, 18*(2), 215–228.

Beltman, S., Mansfield, C. F., & Price, A. (2011). Thriving not just surviving: A review of research on teacher resilience. *Educational Research Review, 6*(3), 185–207.

Brunetti, G. J. (2006). Resilience under fire: Perspectives on the work of experienced, inner city high school teachers in the United States. *Teaching and Teacher Education, 22*(7), 812–825.

Butt, G., Lance, A., Fielding, A., Gunter, H., Rayner, S., & Thomas, H. (2005). Teacher job satisfaction: Lessons from the TSW pathfinder project. *School Leadership & Management, 25*(5), 455–471.

Carlgren, I. (1999). Professionalism and teachers as designers. *Journal of Curriculum Studies, 31*(1), 43–56.

Carrillo, C., & Flores, M. A. (2017). Veteran teachers' identity. What does research literature tell us? *Cambridge Journal or Education*. https://doi.org/10.1080/0305764X.2017.1394982.

Castro, A. J., Kelly, J., & Shih, M. (2010). Resilience strategies for new teachers in high-needs areas. *Teaching and Teacher Education, 26*, 622–629.

Day, C. (1999). *Developing teachers. The challenges of lifelong learning*. London: Falmer Press.

Day, C., & Gu, Q. (2009). Veteran teachers: Commitment, resilience and quality retention. *Teachers and Teaching: Theory and Practice, 15*(4), 441–457.

Day, C., & Gu, Q. (2014). *Resilient teachers, resilient schools*. London: Routledge.

Day, C., & Smethem, L. (2009). The effects of reform: Have teachers really lost their sense of professionalism? *Journal of Educational Change, 10*, 141–157.

Day, C., Flores, M. A., & Viana, I. (2007). Effects of national policies on teachers' sense of professionalism: Findings from an empirical study in Portugal and in England. *European Journal of Teacher Education, 30*(3), 249–266.

Direção-Geral de Estatísticas da Educação e Ciências (2016). *Perfil do Docente* [Teacher profile].

Ebersöhn, L. (2014). Teacher resilience: Theorizing resilience and poverty. *Teachers and Teaching Theory and Practice, 20*(5), 568–594.

Esteve, J. M. (1991). Mudanças Sociais e Função Docente. In A. Nóvoa (Ed.)., (org) *Profissão professor*. Porto: Porto Editora.

Flores, M. A. (2012). Teachers' work and lives: A European perspective. In C. Day (Ed.), *The Routledge international handbook of teacher and school development*. London: Routledge.

Flores, M. A. (Ed.) (2014). *Profissionalismo e liderança dos professores* [Teacher professionalism and leadership]. Santo Tirso: De Facto Editores.

Flores, M. A., & Ferreira, F. I. (2016). Education and child poverty in times of austerity in Portugal: Implications for teachers and teacher education. *Journal of Education for Teaching*., special issue, *42*(4), 404–416.

Flores, M. A., Day, C., & Viana, I. C. (2007). Profissionalismo Docente em transição. As identidades dos professores em tempos de mudança. Um estudo com professores ingleses e portugueses [Teacher professionalism in transition: Teacher identities in times of change. A study of English and Portuguese teachers]. M. A. Flores, e I. C. Viana (Orgs.) *Profissionalismo docente em transição. As identidades dos professores em tempos de mudança* [Teacher professionalism in transition. Teachers identities in times of change]. Braga. CIEd.

Flores, M. A., Ferreira, F. I., & Parente, C. (2014). Conclusões e Recomendações [Conclusions and recommendations]. In M. A. Flores (Ed.), *Profissionalismo e liderança dos professores [Teacher professionalism and leadership]* (pp. 217–236). Santo Tirso: De Facto Editores., 2014.

Galea, K. (2018). Teachers' narratives of resilience: Responding effectively to challenging behaviour. In M. Wosnitza, F. Peixoto, S. Beltman, & C. F. Mansfield (Eds.), *Resilience in education: Concepts, contexts and connections* (pp. 147–166). New York: Springer.

Gu, Q. (2014). The role of relational resilience in teachers' career-long commitment and effectiveness. *Teachers and Teaching Theory and Practice, 20*(5), 502–529.

Gu, Q. (2018). (Re)conceptualizing teacher resilience: A social ecological approach to understanding teachers' professional worlds. In M. Wosnitza, F. Peixoto, S. Beltman, & C. F. Mansfield (Eds.), *Resilience in education: Concepts, contexts and connections* (pp. 13–33). New York: Springer.

Gu, Q., & Day, C. (2007). Teachers resilience: A necessary condition for effectiveness. *Teaching and Teacher Education, 23*, 1302–1316.

Gu, Q., & Li, Q. (2013). Sustaining resilience in times of change: Stories from Chinese teachers. *Asia-Pacific Journal of Teacher Education, 41*(3), 288–303.

Hargreaves, A. (1998). *Os professores em tempos de mudança: o trabalho e a cultura dos professores na idade pós-moderna.* [Teachers in times of change: Teachers' work and culture in the post-modern age] Lisboa: McGraw-Hill.

Hargreaves, A. (2003). *Teaching in the knowledge society: Education in the age of insecurity.* Maidenhead: Open University Press.

Hargreaves, A., & Fullan, M. (2012). *Professional capital. Transforming teaching in every school.* London: Routledge.

Helsby, G. (2000). Multiple truths and contested realities. The changing faces of teacher professionalism in England. C. Day, A. Fernandez, T. E Hauge, J. Moller The life and work of teachers. International perspectives in changing times. London: Falmer Press.

Jenkins, K., Smith, H., & Maxwell, T. (2009). Challenging experiences faced by beginning casual teachers: Here one day and gone the next! *Asia-Pacific Journal of Teacher Education, 37*(1), 63–78.

Johnson, B., Down, B., Le Cornu, R., Peters, J., Sullivan, A., Pearce, J., & Hunter, J. (2015). *Early career teachers. Stories of resilience*. Singapore: Springer.

Kelchtermans, G. (2009). O comprometimento profissional para além do contrato: Autocompreensão, vulnerabilidade e reflexão dos professores [Teacher commitment beyond contract: Self-understanding, vulnerability and teacher reflection]. In: M. A. Flores, & A. M. Veiga Simão (Eds.), *Aprendizagem e desenvolvimento profissional de professores: contextos e perspectivas* [Teacher learning and professional development: Contexts and perspectives]. Mangualde: Edições Pedago.

Le Cornu, R. (2009). Building resilience in pre-service teachers. *Teaching and Teacher Education, 25*, 717–723.

Mansfield, C. F., Beltman, S., Price, A., & McConney, S. (2012). Don't sweat the small stuff: Understanding resilience at the chalkface. *Teaching and Teacher Education, 28*(3), 357–367.

Mansfield, C. F., Beltman, S., & Price, A. (2014). 'I am coming back again!' The resilience process of early career teachers. *Teachers and Teaching Theory and Practice, 20*(5), 547–567.

Mansfield, C. F., Ebersöhn, L., Beltman, S., & Loots, T. (2018). Great southern lands: Making space for teacher resilience in South Africa and Australia. In M. Wosnitza, F. Peixoto, S. Beltman, & C. F. Mansfield (Eds.), *Resilience in education: Concepts, contexts and connections* (pp. 53–71). New York: Springer.

McCormack, A., & Gore, J. (2008). *"If only I could just teach": Early career teachers, their colleagues, and the operation of power.* Paper presented at the annual conference of the Australian Association for Research in Education.

Miles, M., & Huberman, A. M. (1994). *Qualitative data analysis* (2nd ed.). Thousand Oaks, Sage.
Osborn, M. (2006). Changing the context of teachers' work and professional development: A European perspective. *International Journal of Educational Research, 45*, 242–253.
Oswald, M., Johnson, B., & Howard, S. (2003). Quantifying and evaluating resilience-promoting factors: Teachers' beliefs and perceived roles. *Research in Education, 70*, 50–64.
Ozga, J. (2000). Education: New labour, new teachers. In J. Clark, S. Gewirtz, & E. McLaughlin (Eds.), *New managerialism, new welfare?* London: Sage.
Papatraianou, L. H., & Le Cornu, R. (2014). Problematizing the role of personal and professional relationships in early career teacher resilience. *Australian Journal of Teacher Education, 39*(1), 100–116.
Pearce, J., & Morrison, C. (2011). Teacher identity and early career resilience: Exploring the links. *Australian Journal of Teacher Education, 36*(1), 48–59.
Sumsion, J. (2004). Early childhood teachers' constructions of their resilience and thriving: A continuing investigation. *International Journal of Early Years Education, 12*(3), 275–290.
Vance, A., Pendergast, D., & Garvis, S. (2015). Teaching resilience: A narrative inquiry into the importance of teacher resilience. *Pastoral Care in Education, 33*(4), 195–204.
Williams, A., Prestage, S., & Bedward, J. (2001). Individualism to collaboration: The significance of teacher culture to the induction of newly qualified teachers. *Journal of Education for Teaching, 3*(27), 253–267.
Wosnitza, M., Delzepich, R., Schwarze, J., O'Donnell, M., Faust, V., & Camilleri, V. (2018). Enhancing teacher resilience – From self-reflection to professional development. In M. Wosnitza, F. Peixoto, S. Beltman, & C. F. Mansfield (Eds.), *Resilience in education: Concepts, contexts and connections* (pp. 275–288). New York: Springer.

Chapter 11
An Exploratory Interview Study of University Teacher Resilience

Kerstin Helker, Caroline F. Mansfield, Marold Wosnitza, and Hendrieke Stiller

Abstract Although teacher resilience research has blossomed in the last 5–10 years, the resilience of schoolteachers and principals has been the main focus of research. There is little research exploring the resilience of university teachers. This chapter presents findings from an exploratory study regarding university teacher resilience. Participants were 26 university teachers, 17 from Germany and 9 from Australia. Semi-structured interviews were conducted to explore the challenges, coping strategies and work-related emotions of participants and how they view resilience in the context of their work. Findings revealed challenges such as heavy workload, interpersonal relationships, time management and finding the right balance between teaching and research activities. Strategies include social support, time management and consciously maintaining a healthy work-life balance. The findings are discussed in light of a model of university teacher resilience, which is adapted to take into account specific aspects of university work.

Recent studies regarding the work of university teachers have argued that "academia is no longer a comparatively low-stress working environment" (Watts and Robertson 2011, p. 34), and reports of high stress and burnout are increasingly frequent. Significant changes in the university context through massification and corporatisation of higher education (e.g., Research Institute for Higher Education

K. Helker (✉) · H. Stiller
RWTH Aachen University, Aachen, Germany
e-mail: kerstin.helker@rwth-aachen.de; hendrieke.stiller@rwth-aachen.de

C. F. Mansfield
School of Education, Murdoch University, Perth, WA, Australia
e-mail: Caroline.Mansfield@murdoch.edu.au

M. Wosnitza
Institute of Education, RWTH Aachen University, Aachen, Germany

School of Education, Murdoch University, Perth, WA, Australia
e-mail: marold.wosnitza@rwth-aachen.de

M. Wosnitza et al. (eds.), *Resilience in Education*,
https://doi.org/10.1007/978-3-319-76690-4_11

Hiroshima University 2008; Ryan 2012) have led to increases in student-staff ratios, quality assurance and performance measures and competition for global market share. Such changes have in turn resulted in increased pressures, demands and challenges for university teachers around the world (Teichler et al. 2013). Although the research regarding university teachers' stress, motivation and job satisfaction (e.g., Bentley et al. 2013; Shin and Jung 2014; Wosnitza et al. 2014) has revealed aspects and conditions that influence stress and burnout (risk factors), there is a silence in the literature regarding those that mitigate negative outcomes and might promote positive outcomes (protective factors). Research regarding teacher resilience has helped elucidate the relationship between risk and protective factors for school teachers, and recommendations have been made to support resilience in those contexts (see e.g., Day and Gu 2014). Teacher resilience, being a multidimensional and dynamic process by which individuals negotiate challenges and use adaptive coping strategies to enable outcomes such as professional engagement, commitment, growth, well-being and job satisfaction (Beltman 2015; Mansfield et al. 2016a), could be a useful lens with which to explore university teacher resilience.

Even though there has been much research regarding teacher resilience over the past 15 years, this research has focused on *schoolteachers* and the personal factors, strategies and contextual characteristics that help them cope with challenging experiences in their everyday professional life (e.g., Beltman et al. 2011; Ebersöhn 2014; Gu and Day 2007; Mansfield et al. 2012). Whilst insights from this research have informed training programmes to foster schoolteachers' resilience (e.g., Mansfield et al. 2016b; Peixoto et al. 2018, Chap. 5, this volume), other groups of professional educators, like university teachers, have been left somewhat disregarded. The study presented in this chapter therefore draws on interviews with different university teachers to explore the relevant aspect of teachers' resilience with university teachers. Whilst the working situation of university teachers has globally been identified as changing and challenging (Teichler et al. 2013), this study seeks to draw on data from multiple and significantly different working situations of university teachers to explore challenges, coping strategies, emotions and sense of resilience in university teachers.

In the German context, university graduates starting an academic career enter a full or half time position as junior researchers in an externally funded research project or a temporary position, which usually includes working on research projects of the institute or school, teaching, and working on their qualification (PhD and then habilitation) project. Work contracts run for a maximum of six years at each qualification stage. Except for professors, who usually are employed permanently, the proportion of researchers and lecturers with permanent positions is only 25.2% (Statistisches Bundesamt 2016). Recent studies on the work situation of academics in Germany found 10% of senior and 16% of junior academics express low job satisfaction (Jacob and Teichler 2011; Kwieck and Antonowicz 2013). Of the surveyed university teachers, 17% of senior and 19% of junior academics, respectively, stated that they would not become an academic if they had to do it over again, and 48% of senior and 36% junior academics describe their job as a source of considerable personal strain.

In Australia, many university teachers begin their academic careers working on short-term contracts either whilst completing their PhD or following recent completion. Workloads are typically teaching intensive (80% of load) until individuals have enough research outcomes to be deemed "research active" and have their teaching load reduced to a minimum of 40% (see Cole 2015). Arguably, early career academics experience the highest teaching load of their career whilst also establishing a research profile and track record. The casualisation of the academic workforce (Ryan et al. 2013) and challenges of working in academia in Australia (Rainnie et al. 2013), along with the ageing academic workforce (Bexley et al. 2012), are of concern.

Research involving 5525 Australian university teachers (Bexley et al. 2011) reported that about half of the participants described their workload as unmanageable and a source of personal stress. Furthermore, approximately half the respondents intended to leave the Australian higher education context to move to an overseas university or retire in the following ten years. Those intending to leave cited reasons such as lack of job security, income, and research funding as key factors influencing their decision.

Given findings such as these, Watts and Robertson (2011) conclude in their thorough literature review on burnout in university teaching staff that "the extent of burnout in university teaching staff is comparable with other education and medical professionals" (p. 46). For university teachers, the most frequently mentioned challenging factors contributing to this situation were "budget cuts, excessive weekly hours of work, lack of time to respond to the work load, lack of resources, conflictive and ambiguous role, little control over issues affecting tasks that are part of the job position, little opportunity to promote and control one's professional career, relationships with students, little social acknowledgement and reward for their professional labour, low salaries and job insecurity" (Navarro and Más 2010, p. 69).

Studies focusing on the work environment of university teachers found the competing obligations of academia to be its most prominent characteristic. University teachers name a multitude of conflicting goals, including goals for their career at university, their research, teaching, self-development or their qualification (Wosnitza et al. 2014). Optimally, teaching and research should be complementary (cf. Geschwind and Broström 2014; Visser-Wijnveen et al. 2010); however, for most academics they compete for the same time resources (Bexley et al. 2011; Cretchley et al. 2013). Research is also often prioritised over teaching and is deemed to have a greater influence on promotion opportunities (Bloch et al. 2013). Whilst teaching may be a major component of university teachers' job satisfaction (Visser-Wijnveen et al. 2009), student variables (number of students, care required by them) have been strongly linked to burnout in academic staff (Watts and Robertson 2011). University teachers furthermore experience many different emotions in their interactions with their students (Hagenauer and Volet 2014). But whilst Hagenauer et al. (2016) found in a study with German and Australian university teachers that all supported emotion display in university teaching, differences between countries could be identified.

In an international comparative study of higher education working conditions, Jacob and Teichler (2011) examined overall work conditions of university teachers. Comparing Germany and Australia, they found that whilst 96% of German professors have tenure, whilst only 19% of academics at the lecturer stages below the professorship work on permanent positions. In Australia, 76% of professors and 51% of lecturers have a permanent position (Jacob and Teichler 2011). The tendency to employ academic staff on short-term contracts has risen in Australia over the last years (Bexley et al. 2011), and academics experience a strong uncertainty (Welch 2005) and insecurity of academic employment (May et al. 2013).

So why do some university teachers stay in the profession and positively continue with their work, whilst others experience considerable stress and burnout or intend to leave? Resilience provides a useful lens to explore this question. Resilience is a multidimensional and dynamic process by which individuals negotiate challenges by mobilising personal and contextual resources and using adaptive coping strategies to enable outcomes such as professional engagement, commitment, growth, well-being and job satisfaction (Beltman 2015; Mansfield et al. 2016a). The resilience process involves managing risk factors and promoting protective factors over time (Beltman et al. 2011). Protective factors can be personal qualities from which a person may benefit such as self-efficacy, optimism, sense of purpose, hope, spirituality and contextual resources including positive relationships, social and emotional support, recognition and work culture. In addition, the use of coping strategies such as problem-solving, help seeking, time management, reflection, faith practices and mindfulness helps the individual positively cope with the challenges they experience (e.g. Beltman et al. 2011; Bengel and Lyssenko 2012; Mansfield et al. 2016a, b; Ungar 2004; Werner 2011; Windle 2011).

In their empirical study exploring teachers' views of resilience, Mansfield et al. (2012) described four distinct dimensions: profession-related, social, motivational and emotional. Profession-related aspects of resilience included being organised and well prepared, having effective teaching skills and being flexible and reflective. Social aspects included building and maintaining supportive relationships, seeking help, taking advice and communicating effectively. The motivational dimension focused on efficacy, persistence and improvement, whilst emotional aspects incorporated managing emotion, coping with stress, enjoying teaching and depersonalising stressful situations.

Even though school contexts and the work profile of school teachers is somewhat different to that of university teachers, there are similarities in reports of stress and burnout, the general nature of teaching and its demands and the broader contexts of educational institutions. The research regarding teacher resilience therefore provides a sound basis to inform a study of university teachers' resilience.

This exploratory study in an under-researched field focuses on what general challenges, coping strategies, emotions and sense of resilience can be identified with university teachers. Accordingly, the following research questions were developed based on the above theoretical background and inspired the development of the interview questions:

1. What challenges do university teachers face in their position?
2. What coping strategies do university teachers apply to deal with these challenges?
3. Do the university teachers experience positive/negative emotions in their teaching – which, when and why?
4. How do university teachers describe a resilient university teacher?

Method

Participants

Twenty-six university teachers from different Australian and German universities and different subject areas volunteered to participate in this study. Data was gathered through one semi-structured interview. Interviews lasted around 30 min and were conducted either face to face or by phone, depending on participant's availability and location. Seventeen participants were from Germany (nine female), and nine participants were from Australia (nine female). The participants were researching and teaching in the following areas: humanities ($n = 9$), health ($n = 8$), maths and science ($n = 4$), engineering ($n = 4$) and others ($n = 1$). The German participants had been working as university teachers for between 1.5 and 28 years, the Australian participants for 3–60 years (missing data $n = 1$).

Procedure

Interviews were conducted by research assistants using an interview schedule that included questions on different aspects of the role and motivation of university teachers. Interviews lasted around 30 min and were conducted in the interviewees' main language. Within the part that focused on university teachers' resilience, participants were asked to describe the challenges they face in their current position and which coping strategies they use to help deal with those challenges. Participants were furthermore asked to describe which positive and negative emotions they experience and manage in their teaching and to elaborate on the concrete situations that may evoke these emotions. A final question asked participants to describe the qualities of "resilient" university teacher.

Data Analysis

Interviews were transcribed and then analysed by researchers speaking both German and English. Coding units were translated from German to English after the final categorisation.

The analyses applied Mayring's (2010) qualitative content analysis to answer the research questions. The first stage in the analysis process involved the determination of categories by one researcher. In the second step, a second researcher recoded 40% of the data (11 interviews, intercoder agreement, 85%). In a third step, the two researchers shared and compared findings and agreed on interpretation of the data to enhance reliability (Fraenkel et al. 2011). For the first three research questions, categories were built inductively in order not to have findings influenced by categories identified in research with school teachers. The analysis of the fourth research question used the method of deduction. Here the resilience dimensions (social, emotional, professional, motivational) found in the literature (Kumpfer 1999; Mansfield et al. 2012) were used as main categories to ensure the comparability of the results.

Results

The results will be presented in response to each of the above research questions.

Research Question 1: What Challenges Do University Teachers Face in Their Position?

University teachers in this study experienced a range of challenges (47 statements) that can be classified into four main categories deriving from *academic work environment*, *teaching*, *research* and *other* sources. Table 11.1 provides numbers of interviewees mentioning each of the identified aspects, category definition and sample quotes.

Considering the whole sample of university teachers, most participants (73%) mentioned challenges related to the *academic working environment.* The most adverse factors described in this category were a heavy workload (mentioned by 42%; "the pile just does not get smaller" (#D9)), challenging interpersonal relationships like "not getting on with the boss" (#A2; 30%) and time management issues (30%; "everything revolves around the time factor" (#D17)). Although sometimes structuring the work was up to the university teachers themselves ("The way of working is very open, free. You can arrive when you like, you can leave as you like"), this also revealed disadvantages—"but that leads to postponing tasks"

Table 11.1 Challenges of university teachers

Categories		DE	AUS	Total
Challenges	Sample quotes	($n = 17$)	($n = 9$)	($n = 26$)
Academic work environment	Get overloaded (#A5); to sort out interpersonal issues (#D7); time management is a big thing (#A8); inequities in the work (A8); meet different needs (#A2); I can't switch off completely (#D17); work on a weekend (#A3); all problems of a big bureaucratic organisation (#A5)	13 (76.5%)	6 (66.7%)	19 (73.1%)
Work area teaching	Responsibility to make sure I teach it well (#A3); trying to get them to do it (#A9); confidence will come with experience (#D14); staff, who is not here for the right reasons (#A5); to revise lectures, bringing in new ideas (#D6); getting new impulses for teaching (#A4)	7 (41.2%)	7 (77.8%)	14 (53.8%)
Work area research	Find time for research (#D5); research has the least priority (#D10); intellectual challenge (#D6); impulses for research (#A4); to apply for a professorship (#D1); focus on habilitation (#D13); you have to get the money (#D5); need to bring in grant money (#D7); cooperate with other institutes (#D6)	9 (52.9%)	3 (33.3%)	12 (46.2%)
Others	Officially I only have the authority to issue directions in the medical staff, not in the nursing staff (#D4); I don't have a Masters or a PhD… I don't fit in (#A1)	1 (5.9%)	1 (11.1%)	2 (7.7%)

(#D15). Work-life balance (15%) and administrative tasks (11%) were also mentioned as challenging aspects in the academic work environment.

Over half (54%) of participants experienced challenges derived from *teaching*. Here, a significant focus was on the problem of student needs-orientated teaching (30%), e.g. to adapt to students' differences in prior knowledge. Also, university teachers mentioned struggles with teaching conditions (19%; "teaching is not rewarded. Teaching is just a subordinated evil" (#D2)), their role (12%; "the role that you're in as a casual tutor" (#A6)) and keeping course content up to date (8%).

Just less than half (46%) of the university teachers also mentioned challenges related to *research*. The biggest challenge in this category was finding the time to actually do research (23%), e.g. "less and less time for research" (#D10) in a context of the "publish or perish sort of mentality" (#A8). Conducting research itself ("Finding the right questions to ask" (#A4) and "facing a tough nut to crack" (#D3)) was perceived as another big challenge by 19% of university teachers. Furthermore, participants perceived challenges resulting from their academic career, pursuing research grants and cooperation with other institutes or industry (all 8%). One university teacher mentioned the struggle to "not lose all your excitement" (#D6). Other aspects that were named by two participants were having to deal with ambiguous authority (#D4) as well as lack of qualification for the job (#A1).

Research Question 2: What Coping Strategies Do University Teachers Apply to Deal with These Challenges?

Regarding the second research question, participants described a number of different strategies like *structuring their work*, *seeking social support*, *caring for their work-life balance*, *emotion regulation* and *self-improvement*, whilst some also reported *no use of strategies* (Table 11.2).

Overall, half of the interviewed university teachers (50%) talked about *seeking social support* when asked about their coping strategies. This included support of colleagues (27%; "talking to (…) colleagues, sharing problems" (#A8)) but also support of family and friends (19%; "talking to my husband" (#A8)). These supportive relationships were deemed important for sharing their frustration (19%; "I moan to my husband" (#A1)).

Participants described coping strategies that addressed the *structuring of their work* (46%). Most of these concerned instructional planning (19%; "to be as prepared as possible" (#A9)), structuring their different tasks (15%; "prioritising" (#A7)) as well as using planning tools (12%; "daily schedule, calendars" (#D8)). Working from home was a useful strategy (12%; "I stay a day at home" (#D7)) along with time management (8%), spontaneity and flexibility. Seven university teachers talked about their work-life balance when asked about coping strategies.

Table 11.2 Coping strategies of university teachers

Categories		DE	AUS	Total
Coping strategies	Sample quotes	(*n* = 17)	(*n* = 9)	(*n* = 26)
Seeking social support	Ask for help (#D4); talking to other academics (#A9); I just rant (#A7); talking to friends, sharing problems (#A8); I always can consult my superior (#D1)	8 (47.1%)	5 (55.6%)	13 (50%)
Structuring work	Think ahead, plan ahead (#A1); structure (#D4); prioritise (#A7); lots of lists, whiteboards, calendars (#A7); do stuff at home (#A7); clear time structure (#D4); spontaneity (#D11); finding a different way (#A2)	8 (47.1%)	4 (44.4%)	12 (46.2%)
Work-life balance	To have something outside (#A2); garden, read a book on the weekend (#A7); periodical holidays (#D7); sports (#D9); have exercise (#A2); something nice with my family (#A8)	4 (23.5%)	3 (33.3%)	7 (26.9%)
Self-improvement	Continuing education, trainings, seminars (#D4); learn from it (#A8)	2 (11.8%)	1 (11.1%)	3 (11.5%)
Emotion regulation	Realise when it is too much (#D17); live in that moment and enjoy that moment (#A8)	4 (23.5%)	2 (22.2%)	6 (23.1%)
No use of strategies	Determined by externals (#D9); no strategies (#D16); use the ostrich (#A8); spend more time working than I should (#A7); eat too much (#A7); I turned my hobby into a career (#D6); there is no need for strategies (#D13)	7 (41.2%)	5 (55.6%)	12 (46.6%)

Hobbies ("doing things that are a lot of fun" (#D17)), holidays and sports (both mentioned by 12%) as well as time spent with the family (8%) were mentioned.

Emotion regulation was another strategy mentioned by 23% of participants. Emotion regulation involved distancing oneself from the problem (8%; "to put problems behind, reflect" (#D17)), knowing one's own limits (8%; "recognize this is a waste of time, energy and anxiety to continue (#A2)) and generally showing a positive attitude (8%; "to focus on the things I really like to do" (#D4)). About half of the participants (47%) described no particular coping strategies. Whilst 23% stated they were kept from using strategies by external circumstances ("accept that it is what it is, it cannot change" (#A2)), for others, it was more personal behaviour in the face of stress. Whilst some university teachers stated not using particular strategies (12%; "I don't take breathers" (#D9)), others tried to avoid problems (12%; "try to forget it all" (#A6)), work more (12%; "work weekends, work here late at night (#A8)) or react physically ("grind my teeth" (#A7)) or with gallows humour. Two university teachers explicitly stressed that there was no need for them to use any coping strategies ("I turned my hobby into a career" (#D6); "there is no need for strategies" (#D13)).

Research Question 3: Do the University Teacher Experience Positive/Negative Emotions in Their Teaching: When, Which and Why?

Positive Emotions

In their replies to the third research question and interview question, respectively, the participants mostly talked about situations that raised general positive emotions. The responses can be classified in three main categories: positive emotions deriving from *positive interaction with students*, positive emotions because of *positive self-reflection* and positive emotions relating to positive *working conditions*. Table 11.3 provides an overview.

Specific emotions are only mentioned in the context of the interaction with students. Nine participants named the emotions "fun"/"pleasure" and one talked about "inspiration". In the main category (*interaction with students*, 80%), perceived engagement and motivation of the students (35%; "students are engaged and they are interested" (#A9)) and positive feedback by the students (35%; immediate positive feedback" (#A5)) were the two themes mentioned most often to give rise to positive emotions in university teachers. Furthermore, 31% of university teachers described enjoying seeing the "eureka moment" (#A1) and "someone's light bulb switch on" (#A5). Working in small groups and positive personal relationships with students are each mentioned by 12% of interviewees as raising positive emotions. With regard to their *positive self-reflection*, seven university teachers (27%) talked about the enthusiasm they feel during lectures: "It is the kick" (#D13); "I can tell you that sometimes when I get carried away in a lecture, if somebody stood up in

Table 11.3 Situations that evoke positive emotions in university teachers

Categories		DE	AUS	Total
Positive emotions	Sample quotes	(n = 17)	(n = 9)	(n = 26)
Positive interaction with students	When the students really join in (#D2); when they ask questions; you realise that they think (#D7); teaching awards (#D13); clicked on a light bulb for them or they can relate to it or they can apply it to themselves (A3); the biggest fun is to work in small groups (#D17); lovely interactions with students (#A1); they are greeting me from far away (#D5)	14 (82.3%)	7 (77.8%)	21 (80.1%)
Positive self-reflection	It is really fun during a lecture. I always feel as if I am in my own world (#D5); I really feel good about that I'm teaching (#A9)	4 (23.5%)	3 (33.3%)	7 (26.9%)
Positive framework conditions	Technological opportunities you have today (#D3)	1 (5.9%)	–	1 (3.8%)

the middle of the room naked I wouldn't notice it" (#A4). Four university teachers stated they enjoy when their lesson plans work out: "When a seminar concept works very well" (#D13).

Negative Emotions

The participants extensively described 48 situations evoking negative emotions which can be organised in three main categories: *negative interactions with the students*, *adverse organisational conditions* and *negative self-reflection*. Table 11.4 provides an overview of categories, subcategories and how many university teachers mentioned the respective aspects in their interview.

Negative emotions mostly derive from *negative interactions with the students*, with 80% of the university teachers mentioning this factor. The main subcategories are the opposites of the factors that make university teachers experience positive emotions in their interactions with their students: lack of engagement and motivation (39%), i.e. if teachers feel that "the students are really good but lazy" (#D10) and "trying to do the bare minimum to get through" (#A7); students not showing any learning outcomes (31%; "sometimes I think you cannot be *that* stupid" (#D15)); and negative feedback by students (15%; "you get all these great comments and then you just get one or two not really great comments and you just think about them" (#A9)). Further aspects were students' behaviour (12%; "you want them to be adult learners but they are not adult learners yet" (#A1)), the interaction with failing students (8%; "hardest thing is having a conversation with someone who has failed" (#A2)), post-exam review (8%; "if students think they have the right for more points" (#D12)), and the interactions within groups of students (4%; "they really had a bad way to interact with each other" (#D15)).

Table 11.4 Situations that evoke negative emotions in university teachers

Categories		DE	AUS	Total
Negative emotions	Sample quotes	($n = 17$)	($n = 9$)	($n = 26$)
Negative interactions with students	Where a student hasn't even tried, after you've put so much work into it to try (#A3); students not even have basic knowledge (#D7); only the frustrated students use the evaluation tool (#D4); I hate ETIs, I hate those (#A8); some students don't seem to be very interested in taking control of their learning (#A5); when students fail the disappointment changes into grief, because you see how they destroy themselves (#D11); if they haggle for half a point (#D9)	13 (76.5%)	8 (88.9%)	21 (80.1%)
Organisational conditions	Sometimes the courses are too full (#D5); you cannot change the meta dimension (D2)	8 (47.1%)	1 (11.1%)	9 (34.6%)
Negative self-reflection	When I get the feeling you talked to a wall because they don't get it (#D11); if the concept doesn't work (#D17); is this something that I'm not doing correctly? (#A3)	4 (23.5%)	4 (44.4%)	8 (30.7%)
Others	It's frustrating that the medical studies in *city* is like secondary school (#D4)	1 (5.9%)	–	1 (3.8%)

Negative emotions emerged during *self-reflection* after unsuccessful teaching experiences (27%; "you think you did something wrong" (#D8)) and because of the lack of personal enthusiasm for their own work (i.e. "getting bored with the topic" (#D17)). Furthermore, negative emotions because of *adverse organisational conditions* (mentioned by 35% of university teachers) include the limited possibilities for changing conditions and the organisational difficulties in the infrastructure and policy of the university: "you can't do anything about it" (#A6).

Research Question 4: How Do University Teachers Describe a Resilient University Teacher?

The last question in the interview was posed to explore which factors university teachers themselves considered helpful to protect them from the various challenges of university teaching. The emerging factors could be assigned to each of the dimensions suggested by Mansfield et al. (2012): *emotional*, *professional*, *motivational* and *social*. Table 11.5 provides an overview of all mentioned factors (Fig. 11.1).

Almost three quarters of university teachers (72%) named aspects that can be ascribed to the *emotional dimension*, with distancing oneself from problems ("not taking problems back home" (#D16)) as the most frequently mentioned factor. Further aspects are serenity and calmness (28%; "to stay calm even in stressful situations" (#D13)), successfully managing the crisis (20%), emotion regulation (12%),

Table 11.5 Aspects that characterise a resilient university teacher

Categories		DE	AUS	Total
Factors of resilience	Sample quotes	($n = 17$)	($n = 8$)	($n = 25$)
Emotional dimension	Don't get wound up in what's happening at work (#A8); serenity (#D6); work with defeats (#D8); control one's feelings and keep one's temper (#D13); you have got to know your own limits (#D14); being able to say "no" (#D10); walking away and just forgetting about it (#A7); taking sufficient sleep (#D12)	14 (82.4%)	4 (44.5%)	18 (72%)
Professional dimension	Strong organisational skills (#D14); to put personal matters behind the goal of what has to be taught (#D4); distance from your role (#D15); sometimes turning a blind eye (#D11); accept that there is a bell curve of students (#A1); who is reflective, is happy to reflect on both, the good and bad aspects (#A1); to be able to take feedback, whether it's positive, negative, constructive (#A3); find out how to cope with these loads (#A4); someone who is very knowledgeable, who has a good broad knowledge of their content (#A1); you have got to have a hand basket or a handbag of different teaching tools you can use to engage those very different learning styles (#A2)	11 (64.7%)	7 (77.8%)	18 (72%)
Motivational dimension	You need to be intrinsically motivated (#A8); to have teeth (#D8); working towards improvement for own satisfaction (#A9); understanding yourself (#A8); I have a plan, I do my thing (#D2)	10 (58.8%)	4 (44,5%)	14 (56%)
Social dimension	Give help where it's asked for (#A1); meet the needs of your colleagues (#A2); work as a team (#A3); support from your colleagues (#A4); you really need support from the senior people, and especially from the ones who are administrative, and especially the ones in charge of the money (#A4); families help, partners help (#A7); support from students (#A4)	–	7 (77.8%)	7 (28%)

setting limits for oneself and others (12%) and taking time off work (12%). Few university teachers talked about self-care ("ensure that your needs are getting met as well" (#A8), humour (#A1) and confidence (#A1)).

Regarding the *professional dimension*, a resilient university teacher's planning abilities (24%; "time management" (#D10, #D14)), sense of responsibility towards his or her students (20%) and a clear definition of their role (20%; "balancing closeness and distance" (#D13)) were the most often mentioned factors. The participants furthermore described a resilient university teacher as someone who is not too perfectionistic (16%; "remember that the world is not perfect and neither are you"

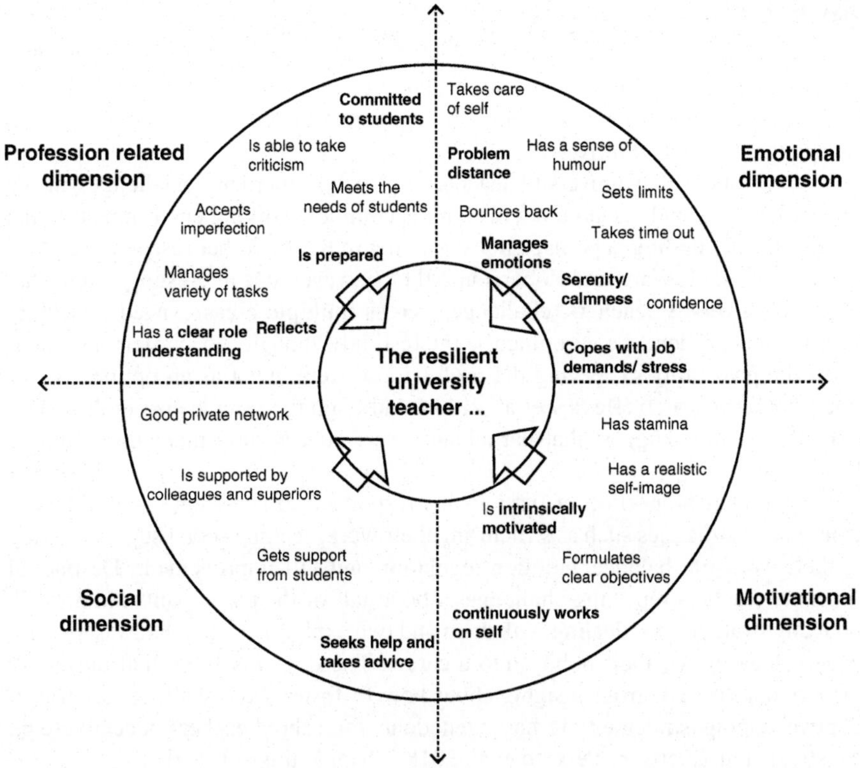

Fig. 11.1 Aspects that characterise a resilient university teacher (figure developed in reference to Mansfield et al. 2012; most commonly mentioned aspects in each quarter are printed in bold)

(#D11)), engages in constructive self-reflection (16%; "who is reflective, is happy to reflect on both, the good and bad aspects (#A1)), and is open to criticism (12%; #A9). This university teacher is able to manage the plurality of tasks, has a good content knowledge and is able to adapt the teaching requirements to students.

In the *motivational dimension*, which 56% of participants mentioned, resilient university teachers are described as never losing their enthusiasm (#D5), showing perseverance (#D3), working on self-improvement, and having goals ("resilient people have a clear picture of themselves" (#D14)).

In the *social dimension* (28%), resilient university teachers give help in order to receive help from others (e.g., colleagues, superiors, private networks) and are not afraid to ask for help (#A1). This dimension is only mentioned by Australian university teachers.

Discussion

This study aimed to explore university teacher resilience and in doing so considers the challenges, emotions and coping strategies that enable university teachers to manage their work and thrive.

Findings show that university teachers not only experience challenges in the areas of teaching and research but also in the complex working environment of the university. This finding is perhaps not surprising in light of other research (see e.g., Bexley et al. 2011; Watts and Robertson 2011); however, it is interesting to note that for some university teachers, challenges across multiple areas existed (teaching, research and academic environment). Interestingly though, no participants mentioned the possibility of leaving the profession or retirement as an option, as was done in other research (Bexley et al. 2011). Although the sample size in this study is small, this may suggest that participants were successfully managing multiple challenges.

A significant proportion of participants responded to challenges with the conscious use of strategies such as structuring their work, seeking social support, caring for their work-life balance, emotion regulation and self-improvement. Despite all university teachers reporting challenges, about half of the participants did not talk about any strategies for dealing with them and two explicitly stated that was the case because they turned their hobby into a career. These results show that university teachers may benefit from insights about how to foster their resilience by use of adaptive coping strategies, as has been done for schoolteachers recently (e.g., Mansfield et al. 2016a, b; Peixoto et al. 2018, Chap. 5, this volume).

Findings furthermore suggest that the emotional well-being of university teachers is strongly affected by their interactions with their students, with 80.1% of university teachers stating their emotional well-being was related to positive and negative interactions with students (see also Hagenauer and Volet 2014, 2016). The same holds true for university teachers' self-evaluation regarding their teaching. It might be surprising that university teachers' emotions are strongly affected by their teaching experiences when expressing a stronger preference for teaching (Teichler et al. 2013), but perhaps university teachers are more affected by their teaching experiences because of their interpersonal nature. These findings illustrate the importance of viewing resilience of university teachers as an interactive and dynamic process, whereby the interaction between individual and contextual factors can have constraining or supportive effects on the individual person.

From a theoretical perspective, the findings highlight the importance of context at the micro and macro levels (Mansfield et al. 2018, Chap. 4, this volume) in understanding resilience. Perhaps not surprisingly, there were unique risk factors and yet similar protective factors for university teachers in each context. How university teachers describe a resilient university teacher reflects many of the resilience factors described in the literature regarding resilience of adults and schoolteachers. Consequently, they can reflect the four-dimensional model of resilience (social, emotional, motivational, and professional). Additional factors found in the interviews, such as balancing the variety of tasks, are attributable to the differing working conditions of schoolteachers (Mansfield et al. 2012) and university teachers. This emphasises the relevance of the context, in which resilience of individuals and groups is examined.

Although the analyses includes data that were collected in interviews with self-selected university teachers, the present investigation is a useful exploratory study to provide initial contributions to the discourse on the under-researched field of university teacher resilience and should be understood as a starting point for future research efforts. Whilst the data in this study do not allow for further analyses of contextual, discipline specific, age, experience-related and gender-specific differences between the university teachers, some differences between German and Australian university teachers could be identified. The differences in both university systems (e.g., Jacob and Teichler 2011; Teichler and Höhle 2013) and university teacher attrition, however, suggest researching differences in larger samples.

In sum, this exploratory study produces initial insight into challenges and supports that university teachers experience that contribute to their resilience. With the ongoing worldwide change in university systems, increase in student numbers and stronger emphasis on teaching as part of academic careers, there are potential benefits for individuals and systems in better understanding the resources and strategies that support university teacher resilience.

References

Beltman, S. (2015). Teacher professional resilience: Thriving not just surviving. In N. Weatherby-Fell (Ed.), *Learning to teach in the secondary school* (pp. 20–38). Melbourne: Cambridge University Press.

Beltman, S., Mansfield, C. F., & Price, A. (2011). Thriving not just surviving: A review of research on teacher resilience. *Educational Research Review, 6*, 185–207.

Bengel, J., Lyssenko, L. (2012). *Resilienz und psychologische Schutzfaktoren im Erwachsenenalter. Stand der Forschung zu psychologischen Schutzfaktoren von Gesundheit im Erwachsenenalter* [Resilience and psychological protection factors during adulthood. State of research on psychological protection factors of health during adulthood]. Köln: BZgA.

Bentley, P. J., Coates, H., Dobson, I. R., Goedegebuure, L., & Meek, V. L. (2013). Academic job satisfaction from an international comparative perspective: Factors associated with satisfaction across 12 countries. In P. J. Bentley, H. Coates, I. R. Dobson, L. Goedegebuure, & V. L. Meek (Eds.), *Job satisfaction around the academic world* (pp. 239–262). Netherlands: Springer.

Bexley, E., James, R., & Arkoudis, S. (2011). *The Australian academic profession in transition. Addressing the challenge of reconceptualising academic work and regenerating the academic workforce*. Melbourne: Centre for the Study of Higher Education.

Bexley, E., Arkoudis, S., & James, R. (2012). The motivations, values and future plans of Australian academics. *Higher Education, 65*(3), 385–400. https://doi.org/10.1007/s10734-012-9550-3.

Bloch, R., Lathan, M., & Würmann, C. (2013). Trotz allem zufrieden mit der Lehre. Subjektive Lage und Haltung der Lehrenden an Universitäten [Despite everything happy with teaching. Subjective situation and view of university teachers]. *Zeitschrift für Hochschulentwicklung, 8*(3), 42–58.

Cole, B. (2015). *Academic workload guide*. Retrieved from http://www.nteu.org.au/article/Academic-Workload-Guide--18230

Cretchley, P. C., Edwards, S. L., O'Shea, P., Sheard, J., Hurst, J., & Brookes, W. (2013). Research and/or learning and teaching: A study of Australian professors' priorities, beliefs and behaviours. *Higher Education Research and Development, 33*(4), 649–669. https://doi.org/10.1080/07294360.2013.863836.

Day, C., & Gu, Q. (2014). *Resilient teachers: Resilient schools. Building and sustaining quality in testing times*. Oxon: Routledge.

Ebersöhn, L. (2014). Teacher resilience: Theorizing resilience and poverty. *Teachers and Teaching, 20*(5), 568–594. https://doi.org/10.1080/13540602.2014.937960.

Fraenkel, J. R., Wallen, N. E., & Hyun, H. (2011). *How to design and evaluate research in education*. Columbus: McGraw-Hill Higher Education.

Geschwind, L., & Broström, A. (2014). Managing the teaching–research nexus: Ideals and practice in research-oriented universities. *Higher Education Research and Development, 34*(1), 60–73. https://doi.org/10.1080/07294360.2014.934332.

Gu, Q., & Day, C. (2007). Teachers resilience: A necessary condition for effectiveness. *Teaching and Teacher Education, 23*, 1302–1316.

Hagenauer, G., & Volet, S. (2014). 'I don't think I could, you know, just teach without any emotion': Exploring the nature and origin of university teachers' emotions. *Research Papers in Education, 29*(2), 240–262. https://doi.org/10.1080/02671522.2012.754929.

Hagenauer, G., Gläser-Zikuda, M., & Volet, S. E. (2016). University teachers' perceptions of appropriate emotion display and high-quality teacher-student relationship: Similarities and differences across cultural-educational contexts. *Frontline Learning Research, 4*(3), 44–74. https://doi.org/10.14786/flr.v4i3.236.

Jacob, A. K., & Teichler, U. (2011). *Der Wandel des Hochschullehrerberufs im internationalen Vergleich – Ergebnisse einer Befragung in den Jahren 2007/08* [The change in university teachers' profession in international comparison – Results of a survey in the years 2007/2008. Retrieved from: https://www.uni-kassel.de/einrichtungen/fileadmin/datas/einrichtungen/incher/T_12__BMBF_Hochschullehrerstudie_2011.pdf

Kumpfer, K. L. (1999). Factors and processes contributing to resilience: The resilience framework. In M. D. Glanz & J. L. Johnson (Eds.), *Resilience and development: Positive life adoptions* (pp. 179–223). New York: Kluwer Academic.

Kwieck, M., & Antonowicz, D. (2013). Academic work, working conditions and job satisfaction. In U. Teichler & E. A. Höhle (Eds.), *The work situation of the academic profession in Europe: Findings of a survey in twelve countries*. Dodrecht: Springer.

Mansfield, C. F., Beltman, S., Price, A., & McConney, A. (2012). "Don't sweat the small stuff:" Understanding teacher resilience at the chalkface. *Teaching and Teacher Education: An International Journal of Research and Studies, 28*(3), 357–367.

Mansfield, C. F., Beltman, S., Broadley, T., & Weatherby-Fell, N. (2016a). Building resilience in teacher education: An evidenced informed framework. *Teaching and Teacher Education, 54*, 77–87. https://doi.org/10.1016/j.tate.2015.11.016.

Mansfield, C. F., Beltman, S., Broadley, T., & Weatherby-Fell, N. (2016b). *BRiTE: Building resilience in teacher education* (ID13-2924). Office of Learning and Teaching. Retrieved from http://www.olt.gov.au/resource-brite

Mansfield, C. F., Ebersöhn, L., Beltman, S., & Loots, T. (2018). Great Southern lands: Making space for teacher resilience in South Africa and Australia. In M. Wosnitza, F. Peixoto, S. Beltman, & C. F. Mansfield (Eds.), *Resilience in education: Concepts, contexts and connections* (pp. 53–71). New York: Springer.

May, R., Peetz, D., & Strachan, G. (2013). The casual academic workforce and labour market segmentation in Australia. *Labour & Industry: A Journal of the Social and Economic Relations of Work, 23*(3), 258–275. https://doi.org/10.1080/10301763.2013.839085.

Mayring, P. (2010). *Qualitative Inhaltsanalyse: Grundlagen und Techniken*. Beltz: Weinheim.

Navarro, M. L. A., & Más, M. B. (2010). Job stress and burnout syndrome at university: A descriptive analysis of the current situation and review of the principal lines of research. *Annuary of Clinical and Health Psychology, 6*, 67–72.

Peixoto, F., Wosnitza, M., Pipa, J., Morgan, M., & Cefai, C. (2018a). A multidimensional view on pre-service teacher resilience in Germany, Ireland, Malta and Portugal. In M. Wosnitza, F. Peixoto, S. Beltman, & C. F. Mansfield (Eds.), *Resilience in education: Concepts, contexts and connections* (pp. 73–89). New York: Springer.

Rainnie, A., Goods, C., Bahn, S., & Burgess, J. (2013). The challenges of working in Australian academia: An introduction. *Labour & Industry: A Journal of the Social and Economic Relations of Work, 23*(3), 191–199. https://doi.org/10.1080/10301763.2013.839080.

Research Institute for Higher Education Hiroshima University (RIHE). (2008). *The changing academic profession in international comparative and quanititative perspectives. Foreword.* Retrieved from http://rihejoho.hiroshima-u.ac.jp/pdf/95244.pdf

Ryan, S. (2012). Academic zombies: A failure of resistance or a means of survival? *Australian Universities Review, 54*(2), 3–11.

Ryan, S., Burgess, J., Connell, J., & Groen, E. (2013). Casual academic staff in an Australian University: Marginalised and excluded. *Tertiary Education and Management, 19*(2), 161–175. https://doi.org/10.1080/13583883.2013.783617.

Shin, J. C., & Jung, J. (2014). Academics job satisfaction and job stress across countries in the changing academic environments. *Higher Education, 67*, 603–620. https://doi.org/10.1007/s10734-013-9668-y.

Statistisches Bundesamt. (2016). *Hochschulen auf einen Blick* [Universities at a glance]. Retrieved from: https://www.destatis.de/DE/Publikationen/Thematisch/BildungForschungKultur/Hochschulen/BroschuereHochschulenBlick0110010167004.pdf?__blob=publicationFile

Teichler, U., & Höhle, E. A. (2013). *The work situation of the academic profession in Europe: Findings of a survey in twelve countries*. Heidelberg: Springer.

Teichler, U., Arimoto, A., & Cummings, W. K. (2013). *The changing academic profession – Major findings of a comparative survey*. Dordrecht: Springer.

Ungar, M. (2004). Theorie in die Tat umsetzen. Fünf Prinzipien der Intervention [Put theory into practice. Five principles of intervention]. In M. Zander (Ed.), *Handbuch Resilienzförderung* (pp. 157–178). Wiesbaden: VS.

Visser-Wijnveen, G. J., Van Driel, J. H., Van der Rijst, R. M., Verloop, N., & Visser, A. (2009). The relationship between academics' conceptions of knowledge, research and teaching – A metaphor study. *Teaching in Higher Education, 14*(6), 673–686. https://doi.org/10.1080/13562510903315340.

Visser-Wijnveen, G. J., Van Driel, J. H., Van der Rijst, R. M., Verloop, N., & Visser, A. (2010). The ideal research-teaching nexus in the eyes of academics: Building profiles. *Higher Education Research and Development, 29*(2), 195–210. https://doi.org/10.1080/07294360903532016.

Watts, J., & Robertson, N. (2011). Burnout in university teaching staff: A systematic literature review. *Educational Research, 53*(1), 33–50. https://doi.org/10.1080/00131881.2011.552235.

Welch, A. (2005). Challenge and change: The academic profession in uncertain times. In A. Welch (Ed.), *The professoriate: Profile of a profession* (Vol. 7, pp. 1–19). Dordrecht: Springer.

Werner, E. E. (2011). Risiko und Resilienz im Leben von Kindern aus multiethnischen Familien [Risk and resilience in the life of children from multiethnic families]. In M. Zander (Ed.), *Handbuch Resilienzförderung* (pp. 32–46). Wiesbaden: VS.

Windle, G. (2011). What is resilience? A review and concept analysis. *Reviews in Clinical Gerontology, 21*, 152–169. https://doi.org/10.1017/S0959259810000420.

Wosnitza, M., Helker, K., & Lohbeck, L. (2014). Teaching goals of early career university teachers in Germany. *International Journal of Educational Research, 65*, 90–103. https://doi.org/10.1016/j.ijer.2013.09.009.

Chapter 12
Teacher Championship of Resilience: Lessons from the Pathways to Resilience Study, South Africa

Linda C. Theron

Abstract Resilience, or the process of adjusting well to adversity, is a process that requires input from social ecologies. The resilience literature is unambiguous that a crucial source of such social-ecological support is teachers. However, most accounts of how teachers enable resilience are drawn from Global North studies (i.e. studies in the more developed countries of the Northern hemisphere). To address this gap, my chapter reports how high school teachers from rural, disadvantaged contexts in South Africa informed the resilience of their students. To do so, I draw on phenomenological data generated by 230 Sesotho-speaking adolescents who participated in the Pathways to Resilience Study. Using the lens of Ungar's Social Ecology of Resilience Theory, I extrapolate teacher actions that enabled students to accommodate structural adversities. I then draw attention to resilience-supporting actions that teachers did not advance. I use both these teacher actions and apathies to theorise changes to teacher education if teachers are to champion resilience in Global South contexts.

Psychological resilience is the process of maintaining, regaining, or improving one's functioning despite challenges that threaten to upset positive functioning and/or normative development (Masten 2014a). From a social-ecological perspective, the environment in which a young person is situated is likely to have a significant influence on the process of psychological resilience (Cicchetti 2013; Masten 2014b; Panter-Brick 2015; Ungar 2011). School ecologies form a key part of the environment of most young people – because adolescents spend a considerable amount of time at school, schools have the power to influence resilience processes quite extensively (Theron 2016a). Based mainly on studies in developed contexts (i.e. those parts of the world where societal challenges are less pervasive and resources more readily available), it seems that teachers, in particular, are central to how schools facilitate

L. C. Theron (✉)
University of Pretoria, Pretoria, South Africa
e-mail: Linda.Theron@up.ac.za

M. Wosnitza et al. (eds.), *Resilience in Education*,
https://doi.org/10.1007/978-3-319-76690-4_12

resilience (Sanders and Munford 2016; Ungar et al. 2014). Accordingly, I use this chapter to document how high school teachers from rural, resource-poor contexts in South Africa facilitated resilience amongst Sesotho-speaking students. In doing so, this chapter draws attention to the relatively underreported explanations of how teachers in underdeveloped contexts champion resilience (Acevedo and Hernandez-Wolfe 2014; Theron 2016a). Given the increasing understanding that specific socio-cultural contexts shape how teachers (and other stakeholders) facilitate resilience (Masten 2014a, b), it is important to explore how teachers in developing and/or resource-poor contexts facilitate the resilience of the young people they teach.

A Social-Ecological Approach to Resilience

The Social Ecology of Resilience Theory (Ungar 2011) – which forms the theoretical framework of this chapter – emphasises the role that social ecologies (i.e. social and organisational systems) play in supporting young people to develop positively. This emphasis does not mean that young people themselves do not play a meaningful role in maintaining, regaining, or improving their functioning in the face of adversity. Instead, it means that social ecologies may not hold young people exclusively responsible for the outcomes they achieve in the face of adversity – the family, community, and other environments in which young people are nested have a duty to support vulnerable young people well enough that it is possible for them to achieve positive outcomes (Ungar et al. 2015). For example, why Sesotho-speaking young people from South Africa adjusted well to the risks of being orphaned related partly to their own agency and partly to accessible teachers who helped them access social supports and solve other problems (Theron et al. 2014). In other words, achieving and maintaining functional outcomes in the presence of significant stressors draws on the strengths of young people (e.g. intelligence, a sense of humour, tenacity) as well as on social-ecological resources (e.g. caring adults, extramural programmes, resilience-supporting cultural values).

Based on an 11-country (Canada, United States, China, India, Israel, Palestine, Russia, Gambia, Tanzania, South Africa, Colombia) 2003–2005 study of the positive adjustment of vulnerable young people, a social-ecological approach to resilience posits that family and micro/macro community environments need to facilitate seven processes of resilience (Ungar et al. 2007). These include constructive relationships, a powerful identity, access to material resources (including education), a sense of social and/or spiritual cohesion, experiences of control and efficacy, adherence to cultural norms and beliefs, and social justice (see Table 12.1 for a definition of each). Social-ecological input is key to all of these mechanisms. For example, young people's investment in education implies that their social ecologies have made it possible for them to access education resources and have staffed education systems with competent and caring professionals. Similarly, young people's sense of efficacy when they succeed at solving problems is associated with others in their environment having scaffolded problem-solving skills and modelled resource use.

A Social-Ecological Approach to How Schools Facilitate Resilience

There is a solid body of literature on schools and resilience (e.g. Esquivel et al. 2011; Henderson 2012; Theron 2016a; Ungar et al. 2014). Still, to date, only two published studies (i.e. Kumpulainen et al. 2016; Theron and Theron 2014) have applied the seven social-ecological mechanisms to shed light on how school ecologies enable resilience. Although the two studies had vastly disparate participants (i.e. vulnerable first graders in Finland and South Africa; vulnerable rural and urban South African university students), they both reported that resilience was associated with schools facilitating (i) constructive relationships, (ii) a powerful identity, and (iii) access to material resources. Neither study reported a sense of social and/or spiritual cohesion as informing resilience. The studies differed in terms of social justice, experiences of control and efficacy, and adherence to cultural norms. As recounted by vulnerable rural and urban South African university students, social justice experiences (facilitated by teachers in school contexts) supported psychological resilience during their school-going years (Theron and Theron 2014). The study by Kumpulainen et al. (2016) offered no evidence that social justice mattered for resilience. Instead, experiences of control and efficacy and adherence to cultural norms were linked to the resilience of the first graders who participated in the study.

Given these similarities and differences, I became curious as to which of the above-mentioned social-ecological mechanisms account for how teachers enable the resilience of Sesotho-speaking adolescents who participated in the Pathways to Resilience Study. A prior publication (i.e. Theron 2016c) explored which of the mechanisms reported by Ungar et al. (2007) account for the resilience of the Sesotho-speaking adolescents who participated in the Pathways to Resilience Study. This article implied that teachers were important resilience role players. However, because this publication was not focused on teachers, it could not detail which social-ecological mechanisms were implicated in how teachers enabled the resilience of Sesotho-speaking adolescents who participated in the Pathways to Resilience Study.

Pathways to Resilience, South Africa: A Summary of the Methodology

The Pathways to Resilience Study, South Africa, was part of a 5-year, five-country study of the formal and informal mechanisms and resources that support vulnerable young people to avoid negative developmental outcomes (see http://www.resilienceresearch.org/ for detail of the greater project). In South Africa, 1209 young people living in the Thabo Mofutsanyana district participated. The Thabo Mofutsanyana district, like much of the Free State province that it forms part of, is characterised by multiple structural disadvantages which manifest as poverty, joblessness, violence, substandard infrastructure, widespread HIV and AIDS, and other communicable diseases and adolescents who are orphaned (Theron 2016c). At the time of the study (2009–2014), around 60% of Free State young people – majority black – subsisted on approximately $50 per month (Hall 2012).

Participants

The project was guided by a panel of local adults who served local youth (i.e. a Community Advisory Panel or CAP including four provincial education department representatives, a young motivational speaker, three adults from child-focused non-government organisations, one clergyman, one representative from the provincial department of social development, and four adults who worked in child welfare institutions; see Theron 2013 for detail about the CAP). As explained in Theron (2016b), the CAP facilitated recruitment of young people who were made vulnerable by structural inequities. For the purposes of this chapter, suffice it to say that the CAP-facilitated recruitment resulted in participants typically being drawn from no-fee and reduced-fee schools (i.e. schools reserved for the poorest of South African children – Hall and Giese 2012). The mean age of participants was 16 (SD 1.64). The majority (97.6%) self-identified as black (predominantly Sesotho-speaking) and female (52.7%). On average, the highest grade completed was Grade 8 (SD 1.4). The 230 young people who generated the qualitative data being reported in this chapter formed a subset of the participants described above.

Qualitative Methods

The qualitative methods are described at length in Jefferis and Theron (2015) and Theron (2016b). For the purposes of this chapter, these methods can be summarised as young people participating in semi-structured interviews and visual participatory methods (draw-and-write, participatory video, and/or clay modelling). All of these were vetted by the CAP as culturally acceptable and safe and guided by a central question: ‘What has helped you to do well in your life so far, even though you face difficulties?’ The visual participatory methods prompted informal group discussions during which researchers could further explore young people’s accounts of what had enabled their resilience.

Data Analysis

For the purpose of this chapter, data analysis was done in three steps. First, a research psychology intern and I perused the Pathways qualitative data set to locate data segments (if any) that included accounts of school staff facilitating resilience processes.

In the current data set, there was no mention of janitors or other supportive school staff; teachers predominated. Second, using a deductive approach (Creswell 2012), we independently analysed the identified segments to understand how teachers enabled resilience processes. The deductive analysis was based on Ungar et al.'s (2007) seven resilience mechanisms. As in Theron and Theron (2014), we coded for teachers facilitating/obstructing any of these seven mechanisms. There were no instances of teachers obstructing resilience processes. Following Saldana (2009), we used a consensus discussion to finalise our analyses. Our codes seldom differed, but when they did we debated until we agreed on a code. Third, I critically interpreted what the coded mechanisms suggested about teachers' facilitation of resilience and used these to group the mechanisms into two overarching themes (as presented below). I presented the findings to education researchers and psychologists at two conferences and used their feedback to fine-tune the findings and increase trustworthiness (Creswell 2012). For example, a conference attendee asked whether the championship of resilience was a whole school endeavour and this alerted me to the importance of clarifying that teacher championship of resilience typically related to the actions of individual teachers (see below).

Teacher Championship of Resilience

As summarised in Table 12.1, analysis revealed that teachers facilitated resilience amongst their students by leveraging most of the mechanisms described by Ungar et al. (2007). However, in this process, resilience was typically championed by individual teachers and in ways that enabled individual students (rather than the student corps or the community in which students were rooted). Furthermore, the championship of resilience neglected social justice pathways.

Individual Teachers Enable Individuals

Teacher championship of resilience included six of the seven mechanisms of resilience: access to material resources, constructive relationships, a powerful identity, experiences of control and efficacy, a sense of social and/or spiritual cohesion, and adherence to cultural norms and beliefs (see Table 1). As noted previously in relation to different South African studies of how school ecologies facilitate resilience (Theron and Engelbrecht 2012; Theron and Theron 2014), these teacher actions were both ordinary (e.g. enabling adolescents by supporting them to master literacy skills) and extraordinary (e.g. using personal finances to support the wellbeing of students). Put differently, teachers' support of resilience related to what they did as part of the everyday task of being a teacher and to what they did above and beyond these expected tasks.

Table 12.1 Teacher-mediated resilience-supporting mechanisms

Resilience mechanism (Ungar 2015; Ungar et al. 2007)	Teacher-related definition (adapted from Ungar 2015)	Evidence (three examples for each; for additional teacher-related examples from the Pathways to Resilience study, see Theron 2016c and Theron et al. 2013)
Access to material resources (i.e. getting what is necessary to satisfy basic physical [e.g. food, shelter] and psychological [e.g. self-actualisation via education or employment] needs)	Teacher-facilitated support to obtain sufficient food, clothing, education, employment, etc.	*They* [teachers] *give us food, even if I don't have money for lunch I know there will be food*
		I didn't have an ID [identity document]. *My teachers told me about this service* [Department of Home Affairs that provided him with an ID]
		Participant: *I live with my teacher*
		Researcher: *Can I ask, why do you live with your teacher?*
		Participant: *Teacher loves me* [and then she explained in Sesotho that her teacher took her in when her grandparents died and she was homeless]
Constructive relationships (i.e. having relationships with significant others that support positive development)	Positive connections between teachers and students	*My teachers tell me to work hard this year, encourage me, and I promise you I will do that*
		They [teachers] *ask us what's wrong ... do we have problems – if we have a problem, we must go to them and talk about the problem*
		My register teacher – she is a comforting person ... when someone listens to me when I need something or when I cry about something... then I take you as a person that really cares ... she listens to me
A powerful identity (i.e. having a sense of personal competence and enjoying acknowledgement of this competence along with opportunities to develop personal capacity)	Teacher-enabled sense of competence; teacher facilitation of learning opportunities that support the development of competencies	*Teachers did well for me – they boosted my future. I will become something in this world because of teachers*
		Teachers, education, and sport teach me a lot. Even now I am brilliant at what I do in life and I know I am going to achieve
		When you want education, teachers help you so that when you grow up you can be something better in life

Experiences of control and efficacy (i.e. being listened to and being supported to overcome challenges in ways that facilitate a sense of having control over difficulties)	Teacher-mediated sense of being able to control current challenges	*My teacher at school helped me to do well in life because she taught me how to write and read and about many things in the world and how to take care of myself. I know how to handle my problems in life because of school and teachers*
		For me to be strong, Ms X [teacher] gives me advice and I take her advice, and when something makes me sad I go to [teachers X & Y], and talk to them, and then they give me advice and that makes me strong
		At school we get messages from teachers that if you want to change your life, it's possible. This one teacher used to observe the naughty things we used to do. And she asked me why I used to take money from younger children. She told me never to hit younger children and take their money, but rather to come to her if I need any money. I listened to her and I changed...I used to go to her as she said, and she bought me boots, soccer boots... I was glad because then I could move away from my bad friends and play football
Sense of cohesion (i.e. a sense of belonging to a specific community as well as the sense that life has meaning and purpose, despite adversity)	Teacher-facilitated sense of belonging (at school and to the community) and/or teacher encouragement to believe that life has or will have meaning despite daily challenges	*I will go to school feeling sad, but I will forget about things that are happening at home...Teachers used to encourage us to forget experiences and focus on the future...*
		They [teachers] *taught me to work with people and to communicate with other people*
		Teachers teach me about life...So that I don't have to think about crying, but come to school...Learning is important and learning to have a career...Because if you haven't finished your grade twelve, there's nothing in life for you

(continued)

Table 12.1 (continued)

Resilience mechanism (Ungar 2015; Ungar et al. 2007)	Teacher-related definition (adapted from Ungar 2015)	Evidence (three examples for each; for additional teacher-related examples from the Pathways to Resilience study, see Theron 2016c and Theron et al. 2013)
Cultural adherence (i.e. identifying with/endorsing and enacting group beliefs or values)	Teacher-aided enactment of convention of traditionally African values (e.g. interpersonal respect and interdependence	*School teaches me how to respect others...When the teacher talks in the class you must listen, and he tells you '[Do] not talk when I talk, that thing is not right, so you shall listen, you have to know more'. It helps me because I don't want to be a naughty girl – then people [would] talk about me, 'Oh that girl she's so naughty she doesn't respect'. That would be bad for me*
		From my teacher I have learnt that we should work together so that we don't have difficulties
		At school I get more help because some of the lessons that you are taught is about reality, so they [teachers] help you to see what life is, and how you must treat people well so that they can treat you the same way

Significantly, whether ordinary or extraordinary, teacher actions were directed at young people as individuals. What participants reported was devoid of any suggestion that teacher actions were aimed at altering the systemic factors which put young people at risk. This person-directed focus could be an artefact of the individual-focused method of data generation (i.e. asking young people to recount what had supported them as individuals to do well in life). I am, however, more inclined to suggest that this focus relates to how foundational ecological theories of human development position the individual as central to all interactions (e.g. Bronfenbrenner 2005). Consequently, services and interventions are typically aimed at an individual, rather than at changing systems (Hart et al. 2016). Resilience guidelines for teachers generally follow suit and offer a range of individual-directed actions (e.g. Oades-Sese et al. 2013). In addition, it is also possible that teachers – who, in South Africa, constitute an undervalued and underpaid group of professionals with relatively little power to effect systemic change – directed their attention at individual adolescents because this was an achievable target. Moreover, when individuals welcome and make good use of offered supports, support is more likely to be sustained (Zautra 2014) and so the evidence that their actions were making a meaningful difference probably spurred teachers to sustain individual-directed supports.

Although there were no accounts of teachers obstructing resilience, participants made statements that suggested that teacher championship of resilience was not true of all teachers. For example, participants referred to a single teacher (e.g. 'There is a teacher at school that I approach when I have problems at home'). Other participants clarified that some teachers were uncaring (e.g. 'Teachers are helpful, but not all of them ... [some] don't really connect with children, they just don't care') or unapproachable (e.g. 'I was scared to go to the teacher to tell him what happened'). These occasional statements underscore that individual teachers – and not the teaching staff as a whole – were enabling vulnerable young people. This implies that resilience-enabling teacher actions were not part of a formal, school-wide approach to support the resilience of young people (as in, e.g. health promoting schools – see Stewart and Wang 2012).

Teachers Neglect Social Justice Pathways to Resilience

Allied to teachers' focus on supporting young people to beat the structural odds that were stacked against them (e.g. by providing food or encouraging educational aspirations), there was an absence of teacher actions aimed at changing these odds. As Seccombe (2002) noted, 'changing the odds' (p. 384), or addressing the social determinants of risk, is crucial to resilience. It requires a social justice agenda (Hart et al. 2016; Masten 2014b). Nothing in Pathways participants' accounts suggested that teachers challenged the social injustices that were at the root of what was putting them at risk. Prilleltensky and Prilleltensky (2005) equate actions aimed at undoing social injustices with 'distal caring' (p. 89). In comparison, 'proximal caring' (p. 89) is expressed in the interaction between a professional (e.g. teacher) and young person – although resilience-enabling, proximal acts of care are insufficient to sustain positive outcomes in contexts of chronic adversity. In the interests of resilience, teachers (see Theron 2016a) and other professionals and service providers (see Wessells 2015) need to enact both types of caring. This was illustrated, for example, in a study by Acevedo and Hernandez-Wolfe (2014) with 21 Colombian teachers who enabled the resilience of young people challenged by structural disadvantage: these teachers connected constructively with the vulnerable young people they were teaching. Simultaneously, they also advocated for systemic change that would alleviate the structural inequities that underpinned what was placing these young people at risk (Acevedo and Hernandez-Wolfe 2014).

Moving Forward: Augmenting Teacher Championship of Resilience

As mentioned in the introduction, this chapter was prompted by the relative underreporting of how teachers in underdeveloped contexts champion resilience. Interestingly, compared to reviews of how teachers globally enable resilience (e.g. Theron 2016a; Ungar et al. 2014), the above account of how some South African teachers championed resilience does not provide evidence of unique teacher-facilitated pathways of resilience. Globally teachers enable resilience by caring for, connecting with, and capacitating their students. The commonalities between the findings of this chapter and other accounts of how teachers enable resilience direct attention to how more teachers can be supported to champion resilience. As detailed below, four potential leverage points for augmenting teacher championship of resilience are implicated in the preceding account of how some South African teachers in rural, resource-poor schools supported young people to beat the myriad odds of being structurally disadvantaged.

Acclaim and Maintain Teacher Championship of Resilience

Clearly, with regard to resilience, teacher actions matter. As previously noted (Theron and Engelbrecht 2012), these actions need to be celebrated and publicised (even though they are limited to 'proximal caring'). Public acknowledgement of teacher contributions to the resilience of vulnerable young people is likely to buffer the compassion fatigue that has recently become associated with teacher championship of resilience (e.g. Acevedo and Hernandez-Wolfe 2014). Furthermore, social ecologies will need to invest in formal ways to sustain teachers' resilience-enabling actions, both at pre- and in-service stages (e.g. via programmes that capacitate the personal resilience of teachers or via school-based supports – see Beltman et al.

2016; Mansfield et al. 2012, 2014). Sustaining teacher championship of resilience is crucial, given the growing understanding that it is 'enduring commitment to the young person' rather than haphazard support that really matters (Sanders and Munford 2016).

Champion Resilience Systemically

The resilience of vulnerable young people needs more than the inputs of individual teachers. It needs whole school and education system responses. A carefully planned systemic response – one that includes inputs at the level of the individual, the classroom, and the system (Fazel et al. 2014) – will amplify what individual teachers are already managing to achieve, as well as legitimise resilience agendas. It will probably also sensitise teachers towards understanding that enabling resilience should be every teacher's business. The Health Promoting Schools (HPS) initiative provides an example of a whole school approach aimed at capacitating the health and wellbeing of all students. Similar to other whole school approaches (see Mallin et al. 2013), it draws on teacher, student, and parent inputs and mobilises links between parents, young people, and community resources. A systematic review of the literature showed that HPS is an effective way of enabling resilience (particularly amongst teachers and students) (Stewart and Wang 2012).

As part of a systemic response, young people need to understand that they form part of the school system and need to be involved in resilience-enabling initiatives. In addition, they need to be sensitised to the importance of personal agency and reciprocity (Sanders and Munford 2016). For instance, because teachers' capacity to act is curtailed when they are unaware that young people need support, young people need to communicate support needs to teachers (Theron and Engelbrecht 2012). They also need to reciprocate, including making good use of offered supports as well as contributing to the efficiency of the school system (by, e.g. contributing to fund-raising schemes initiated by teachers) (Theron and Theron 2014).

Equip Teachers to Mobilise Social Justice

In addition, teacher actions (both individual and school-wide) need to be augmented in ways that will challenge the social injustices (such as structural inequities) which perpetuate the risks which make young people vulnerable. The resilience literature includes robust calls for greater attention to social change agendas that, ultimately, will reduce threats to young people's wellbeing (e.g. Hart et al. 2016; Masten 2014b; Seccombe 2002; Theron 2016c), but this call is faint in the literature on teachers and resilience (Theron 2016a). One way of addressing this is to emphasise a social justice mandate in pre- and in-service teacher training. Along with this, teachers need to be taught participatory action research skills that will capacitate them to confront higher-level structural influences that place young people at risk. A South African study with 33 teachers in 4 geographically disparate, resource-poor schools produced evidence that teaching in-service teachers participatory action research skills prompted benefits not only for the teachers themselves but also for their schools (Ebersöhn et al. 2015). In particular, vulnerable students benefitted because action research skills aided teachers' use of group-facilitated problem-solving (e.g. accessing government grants for vulnerable families and youth) and enhanced teachers' networking capacity (e.g. collaborating with individuals and organisations to provide psychosocial support to students).

Form University-School Partnerships

The successes of the above-mentioned study by Ebersöhn et al. (2015) reflect university-school partnerships. So too does the success of Boingboing, a not-for-profit, a social enterprise that works with communities (including school communities) and the statutory sector to advance resilience (http://www.boingboing.org.uk/; see Hart et al. 2016). This implies that augmenting in-service teacher championship of resilience will require a commitment from higher education institutions to develop research agendas that leverage teacher and school capacity to co-facilitate positive outcomes for young people. Importantly, these partnerships should not blindly reproduce documented pathways to resilience but co-produce contextually and culturally relevant ways of advancing the wellbeing of vulnerable young people (Hart et al. 2016; Theron 2016c).

Conclusion

The four leverage points suggested above are not extraordinary. Their commonplaceness is reminiscent of Masten's seminal statement: 'Resilience does not come from rare and special qualities, but from the everyday magic of ordinary, normative human resources in the minds, bodies and brains of children, in their families and relationships and in their communities' (2001, p. 235). Accordingly, using these leverage points to capacitate teachers in South Africa (and elsewhere) to champion the resilience of vulnerable adolescents should be achievable. Empirical follow-up to test this concluding assumption and to refine how best to support teachers to champion resilience should, therefore, be expedited.

References

Acevedo, V. E., & Hernandez-Wolfe, P. (2014). Vicarious resilience: An exploration of teachers and children's resilience in highly challenging social contexts. *Journal of Aggression, Maltreatment & Trauma, 23*(5), 473–493. https://doi.org/10.1080/10926771.2014.904468.

Beltman, S., Mansfield, C. F., & Harris, A. (2016). Quietly sharing the load? The role of school psychologists in enabling teacher resilience. *School Psychology International, 37*(2), 172–188.

Bronfenbrenner, U. (Ed.). (2005). *Making human beings human: Bioecological perspectives on human development*. Thousand Oaks: Sage.

Cicchetti, D. (2013). Annual research review: Resilient functioning in maltreated children-past, present and future perspectives. *Journal of Child Psychology and Psychiatry, 54*, 402–422.

Creswell, J. W. (2012). *Educational research: Planning, conducting, and evaluating quantitative and qualitative research* (4th ed.). Boston: Pearson.

Ebersöhn, L., Loots, T., Eloff, I., & Ferreira, R. (2015). In-service teacher training to provide psychosocial support and care in high-risk and high-need schools: School-based intervention partnerships. *Journal of Education for Teaching, 41*(3), 267–284.

Esquivel, G. B., Doll, B., & Oades-Sese, G. V. (2011). Introduction to the special issue: Resilience in schools. *Psychology in the Schools, 48*(7), 649–651. https://doi.org/10.1002/pits.20585.

Fazel, M., Hoagwood, K., Stephan, S., & Ford, T. (2014). Mental health interventions in schools in high-income countries. *The Lancet Psychiatry, 1*(5), 377–387. https://doi.org/10.1016/S2215-0366(14)70312-8.

Hall, K. (2012). Income poverty, unemployment and social grants. In K. Hall, I. Woolard, L. Lake, & C. Smith (Eds.), *South African child gauge 2012* (pp. 95–97). Cape Town: Children's Institute, University of Cape Town.

Hall, K., & Giese, S. (2012). Addressing quality through school fees and school funding. In K. Hall, I. Woolard, L. Lake, & C. Smith (Eds.), *South African child gauge 2012* (pp. 35–40). Cape Town: Children's Institute, University of Cape Town.

Hart, A., Gagnon, E., Eryigit-Madzwamuse, S., Cameron, J., Aranda, K., Rathbone, A., & Heaver, B. (2016). Uniting resilience research and practice with an inequalities approach. *SAGE Open, 6*(4), 2158244016682477.

Henderson, N. (2012). Resilience in schools and curriculum design. In M. Ungar (Ed.), *The social ecology of resilience: Culture, context, resources and meaning* (pp. 297–306). New York: Springer.

Jefferis, T., & Theron, L. C. (2015). Community-based participatory video: A vehicle for exploring, and advocating for, girls' resilience. *Perspectives in Education*.

Kumpulainen, K., Theron, L. C., Kahl, C., Mikkola, A., Salmi, S., Bezuidenhout, C., Khumalo, T., & Uusitalo-Malmivaara, L. (2016). Positive adjusting to first grade in risk-filled communities in South Africa and Finland: The role of school ecologies. *School Psychology International, 37*, 121–139. https://doi.org/10.1177/0143034315614687.

Mallin, B., Walker, J. R., & Levin, B. (2013). Mental health promotion in the schools: Supporting resilience in children and youth. In S. Prince-Embury & D. H. Saklofske (Eds.), *Resilience in children, adolescents, and adults. Translating research into practice* (pp. 91–112). New York: Springer.

Mansfield, C. F., Price, A., McConney, A., Beltman, S., Pelliccione, L., & Wosnitza, M. (2012). *Keeping cool: Embedding resilience in the initial teacher education curriculum*. Final report. Australian Government: Office for Learning and Teaching. Retrieved from http://researchrepository.murdoch.edu.au/10522/

Mansfield, C. F., Beltman, S., & Price, A. (2014). 'I'm coming back again!' The resilience process of early career teachers. *Teachers and Teaching, 20*(5), 547–567.

Masten, A. S. (2001). Ordinary magic: Resilience processes in development. *American Psychologist, 56*(3), 227–238. https://doi.org/10.1037/0003-066X.56.3.227.

Masten, A. S. (2014a). *Ordinary magic. Resilience in development*. New York: Guilford.

Masten, A. S. (2014b). Global perspectives on resilience in children and youth. *Child Development, 85*(1), 6–20. https://doi.org/10.1111/cdev.12205.

Oades-Sese, G. V., Kitzie, M., Velderman, C., Rubic, W. L., Rutstein, S., & Waltuck, M. (2013). Cultural considerations for building social–emotional and academic resilience in Hispanic preschool children. In S. Prince-Embury & D. H. Saklofske (Eds.), *Resilience in children, adolescents, and adults. Translating research into practice* (pp. 279–298). New York: Springer.

Panter-Brick, C. (2015). Culture and resilience: Next steps for theory and practice. In L. C. Theron, L. Liebenberg, & M. Ungar (Eds.), *Youth resilience and culture: Commonalities and complexities* (pp. 233–244). Dordrecht: Springer.

Prilleltensky, I., & Prilleltensky, O. (2005). Beyond resilience: Blending wellness and liberation in the helping professions. In M. Ungar (Ed.), *Handbook for working with children and youth: Pathways to resilience across cultures and contexts* (pp. 89–103). London: Sage.

Saldana, J. (2009). *The coding manual for qualitative researchers*. London: Sage.

Sanders, J., & Munford, R. (2016). Fostering a sense of belonging at school – Five orientations to practice that assist vulnerable youth to create a positive student identity. *School Psychology International, 37*, 155–171. https://doi.org/10.1177/0143034315614688.

Seccombe, K. (2002). "Beating the odds" versus "changing the odds": Poverty, resilience, and family policy. *Journal of Marriage and Family, 64*(2), 384–394. https://doi.org/10.1111/j.1741-3737.2002.00384.

Stewart, D., & Wang, D. (2012). Building resilience through school-based health promotion: A systematic review. *International Journal of Mental Health Promotion, 14*(4), 207–218. https://doi.org/10.1080/14623730.2013.770319.

Theron, L. C. (2013). Community-researcher liaisons: The pathways to resilience project advisory panel. *South African Journal of Education, 33*(4), 1–19.

Theron, L. C. (2016a). The everyday ways that school ecologies facilitate resilience: Implications for school psychologists. *School Psychology International, 37*, 87–103. https://doi.org/10.1177/0142723713503254.

Theron, L. C. (2016b). Researching resilience: Lessons learned from working with rural, Sesotho-speaking South African young people. *Qualitative Research*, in press.

Theron, L. C. (2016c). Towards a culturally- and contextually-sensitive understanding of resilience: Privileging the voices of black, South African young people. *Journal of Adolescent Research, 31*(6), 635–670. https://doi.org/10.1177/0743558415600072.

Theron, L. C., & Engelbrecht, P. (2012). Caring teachers: Teacher-youth transactions to promote resilience. In M. Ungar (Ed.), *The social ecology of resilience: Culture, context, resources and meaning* (pp. 265–280). New York: Springer.

Theron, L. C., & Theron, A. M. C. (2014). Education services and resilience processes: Resilient black South African students' experiences. *Child and Youth Services Review, 47*(3), 297–306. https://doi.org/10.1016/j.childyouth.2014.10.003.

Theron, L. C., Liebenberg, L., & Malindi, M. J. (2014). When schooling experiences are respectful of children's rights: A pathway to resilience. *School Psychology International, 35*(3), 253–265. https://doi.org/10.1177/0142723713503254.

Ungar, M. (2011). The social ecology of resilience: Addressing contextual and cultural ambiguity of a nascent construct. *American Journal of Orthopsychiatry, 81*, 1–17. https://doi.org/10.1111/j.1939-0025.2010.01067.

Ungar, M., Brown, M., Liebenberg, L., Othman, R., Kwong, W. M., Armstrong, M., & Gilgun, J. (2007). Unique pathways to resilience across cultures. *Adolescence, 42*(166), 287–310. Retrieved from http://www.ncbi.nlm.nih.gov/pubmed/17849937.

Ungar, M., Russell, P., & Connelly, G. (2014). School-based interventions to enhance the resilience of students. *Journal of Educational and Developmental Psychology, 4*(1), 66–83. https://doi.org/10.5539/jedp.v4n1p66.

Ungar, M., Theron, L., Liebenberg, L., Tian, G., Restrepo, A., Sanders, J., Munford, R., & Russell, S. (2015). Patterns of individual coping, engagement with social supports, and use of formal services among a five-country sample of resilient youth. *Global Mental Health, 2*, 1–10. https://doi.org/10.1017/gmh.2015.19.

Ungar, M. (2015). Resilience and culture: The diversity of protective processes and positive adaptation. In L. C. Theron, L. Liebenberg, & M.Ungar (Eds.), *Youth resilience and culture: Commonalities and complexities* (pp. 37-49). Dordrecht: Springer.

Wessells, M. G. (2015). Commentary: A social environment approach to promotive and protective practice in childhood resilience – Reflections on Ungar (2014). *Journal of Child Psychology and Psychiatry, 56*(1), 18–20. https://doi.org/10.1111/jcpp.12367.

Zautra, A. J. (2014). Resilience is social, after all. In M. Kent, M. C. Davis, & J. W. Reich (Eds.), *The resilience handbook: Approaches to stress and trauma* (pp. 185–196). New York: Routledge.

Part IV
Connecting to Practice

Chapter 13
Finding a Place for Resilience in Teacher Preparation

Gavin Hazel

Abstract Australian school systems are moving towards a more systematic and comprehensive recognition of the interrelationships between academic outcomes, wellbeing, resilience and personal development. Against this background it seems timely to examine how teacher education can most effectively integrate concepts like resilience into teacher education. When there are so many competing demands on pre-service training, it can be difficult to see how one more area could possibly be added to an already crowded programme. However, making teachers aware of their role in developing resilient students does not require the addition of something 'new' to their training. It involves instead an explicit acknowledgement that encouraging resilience in students is the fundamental outcome of a meaningful connection with the students. Resilience is a bridging concept that links together the cognitive, emotional, social and physiological domains of wellbeing. Examples, strategies and lessons will be drawn from the Response Ability National Teacher Education project.

School systems are shifting towards a more systematic and comprehensive appreciation of the interrelationships between academic outcomes, wellbeing, resilience and personal development. Against this background it is timely to think about how concepts like resilience and wellbeing can be most effectively integrated into initial teacher education (ITE). With so many competing demands on ITE, it can be difficult to see how one more area could possibly be added to an already crowded curriculum. However, making teachers aware, during their initial professional preparation, of their role in developing and supporting students does not require the appendage of something 'new' to their training. It involves instead an explicit acknowledgement that encouraging resiliency in students can be a fundamental outcome of a meaningful connection and communication with students. It is the

---

G. Hazel (✉)
Everymind, Newcastle, Australia

University of Newcastle, Callaghan, Australia
e-mail: Gavin.Hazel@hnehealth.nsw.gov.au

M. Wosnitza et al. (eds.), *Resilience in Education*,
https://doi.org/10.1007/978-3-319-76690-4_13

relational, interpersonal reflective and metacognitive components of teaching practice that are central to enabling the resilience building capacity of educational settings and educators.

This chapter will describe the application of a resilience and strengths informed capability development intervention, called Response Ability (www.responseability.org), to the pre-service preparation of Australian teachers. Firstly, a broad brush stroke picture of current ITE context, and the impact of resilience and wellbeing thinking, will be provided. This will be followed by an outline of how resilience principles and practices can be fitted within ITE. Then an overview of the Response Ability intervention will be set out. As part of this account key lessons gathered during the development, dissemination and implementation of this intervention will be reported. The chapter will close with a reflection, based on these lessons, on how teacher education programs in Australia specifically, and internationally more generally, could most effectively integrate wellbeing and resilience into ITE.

Initial Teacher Education in the Context of Resilience and Wellbeing

Clearly, the wealth of international and national work being undertaken in regard to students' wellbeing, resilience and learning in educational settings shows the potential of educators to support positive outcomes for children and young people. It also makes clear that wellbeing and resilience will continue to be a cornerstone of education and care practices for many years to come (Bridgeland et al. 2013; Graetz et al. 2008; Hawkins et al. 2008; Mansfield et al. 2016; Ransford et al. 2009; Roffey 2016; Weissberg et al. 2015; Weston et al. 2008). The literature and Australian policy and practice also suggest that the promotion of social and emotional wellbeing, as well as a focus on early intervention and prevention, will increasingly be adopted as a core activity for schools and teachers.

A key implication of this is that all teachers, ranging from new graduates through to more experienced practitioners, will need to be able to demonstrate an understanding of resilience and wellbeing and its implications for professional practice (Collaborative for Academic, Social and Emotional Learning 2003, 2012; Durlak et al. 2010; Hazel 2014; Ikesako and Miyamoto 2015; Macklem 2014; Schonert-Reichl et al. 2015; Sheppard et al. 2015; Weston et al. 2008; Zins et al. 2004). Although expert opinion, professional teacher standards and research indicate that an understanding of wellbeing, resilience and the social and emotional dimensions of learning are indispensable to the role of all teachers, there are varying levels of adoption in ITE, to date, across the Australian tertiary sector. Recently pockets of excellence and progress have emerged, but the need remains for significant transformation to be undertaken across the ITE sector as a whole.

To bring about sustained change in a profession requires the adoption of a new way of carrying out previous activities (Broadley et al. 2014; Davis et al. 2012; Hazel 2012; Vincent et al. 2005). Importantly, this often entails the revision of skills, knowledge and beliefs. This is a complex process, and there are significant inhibitors to change at the personal, group and system levels (Sheppard et al. 2015). One of the fundamental questions in the development of a university-based ITE programme is: Which elements should be addressed in pre-service or initial education and which would be better dealt with in later professional development? In practical and service-oriented professions, this is particularly an issue and has seen a shift over time from predominantly workplace-based models of professional preparation to university-awarded qualifications and professional placements, practicums and internships. In many such professions there remain tensions about what can and should be learned at a university or college and what must be absorbed 'on the job' or through formal professional development activities (Billett 2009; Deed et al. 2011; Hammerness 2006; Ingvarson et al. 2014).

Difficulties arise for professions when knowledge or skills that are fundamental to current professional practice are devalued by being marginalised or omitted from pre-service programs. This can lead to graduates being poorly prepared for, or becoming disenchanted with, some aspects of their roles once they enter the workforce. The solution to balancing a multitude of pressures and priorities within a constrained ITE programme is often to try to touch on 'a little of everything' in the limited time available. Whilst this is an understandable response to the circumstances, it becomes important to be strategic about the key messages emphasised in each selected area that makes up the programme. It is also critical to introduce topics in such a way that their importance is understood and graduates are able to integrate them in a meaningful way into their beginning practice, while building on them further through workplace experience and professional development (Beltman et al. 2011; Darling-Hammond and Bransford 2005; Ingvarson et al. 2014; Mansfield 2012). Building capability and scaffolding of teacher educators are two important enablers in these circumstances (Hazel 2015; Hunter Institute of Mental Health 2010).

The organisation of ITE programs in the Australian tertiary education sector is shaped by a broad range of factors (Aspland 2006; Ingvarson et al. 2014; Norton and Cherastidtham 2014) including professional standards; accrediting and employment requirements; research and best practice; educational policy and curriculum; and the professional interests and strengths of the faculty or school, programme planners and individual lecturers. These factors affect the relative emphasis that is placed upon different content areas. These decisions are also bound within the technical requirements of degree regulations, length of programme, modes of delivery, quality assurance practices and funding mechanisms. When looking to influence university, teacher preparation awareness of this context is critical to understanding what is both possible and practical.

Including Resilience in Initial Teacher Education: Some Basic Principles

That resilience and wellbeing need to be addressed as a priority is increasingly accepted; yet the best way to do this on a day-to-day basis in teacher training, understandably, remains an open question. A deeper understanding of wellbeing and resilience, in the context of education, is needed to inform the ways in which prospective teachers are prepared (Beltman 2015; Clarke et al. 2015; Collaborative for Academic, Social and Emotional Learning 2003; Durlak et al. 2011; Franklin et al. 2012; Graetz et al. 2008; Rowe et al. 2007; Weston et al. 2008; Zins et al. 2007). The key operational questions for ITE are: How can graduates be best prepared to contribute to the complementary outcomes of learning, resilience and wellbeing? And how should current knowledge about wellbeing and resilience be blended with the other professional knowledge that makes up ITE?

Resilience is a highly malleable, and increasingly ubiquitous, idea that has tended to be shaped by its applications to a wide variety of contexts and disciplines. It has also undergone, and continues to undergo, phases of theoretical and empirical refinement. Baggio et al. (2015) proposed that when we consider the breath of meanings attributed to resilience, there appears to be a consistent and common emphasis on persistence in the face of disturbance or disruption and within some contexts a focus on the link between this persistence, adaption and learning. It is this adaptive construction that has most practical salience and application to educators. Resilience, perceived in this way, is sympathetic with a holistic approach to mental health and wellbeing. In this chapter, resilience is conceived as a bridging concept (Baggio et al. 2015) that links together the domains of cognitive, emotional, social and physiological wellbeing and learning.

Concordantly, resilience is most effectively conceptualised in ITE, as cross-disciplinary, not belonging exclusively to any particular domain or area (Hazel and Vincent 2005; Schonert-Reichl et al. 2015; Stafford et al. 2007; Weston et al. 2008). In this sense it is akin to other foundational principles of education, such as inclusion, diversity and equity. Ideally such principles are taught explicitly to all pre-service teachers at some point in a given programme but can also be reinforced in connection with other topic areas and related to students' personal and practical experiences.

Graduates need to be cognisant of two key messages in regard to resilience and wellbeing (Hunter Institute of Mental Health 2010; Kay-Lambkin et al. 2007; Stafford 2007; Stafford et al. 2007; Response Ability 2007b, 2010) and should be provided with fundamental skills in these domains. (1) Young people's wellbeing has an impact upon their learning, behaviour and success at school; teachers and schools can create environments that promote the wellbeing, resilience and learning of young people. (2) Teachers have a duty of care towards any young person who is at risk of harm as a result of social or emotional difficulties; this requires the capacity to recognise troubled young people and refer them to appropriate support agencies (Hunter Institute of Mental Health 2010; Response Ability 2007a, b, 2014a, b, 2015).

For example, Response Ability advocates that a comprehensive integration of wellbeing and resilience into ITE programs (Foggett et al. 2007; Hazel and Vincent 2005; Kay-Lambkin et al. 2007; Stafford 2007; Stafford et al. 2007; Vincent et al. 2005; Weatherby-Fell and Vincent 2005; Weatherby-Fell and Kean 2004) would be comprised of the following components being provided throughout a programme:

- Exploring the two key principles suggested above in early foundation units to be taken by all pre-service teachers in the programme, whilst providing them with supporting and extension materials that they can retain for further reference
- Providing a more detailed exploration of resilience, social and emotional wellbeing and learning in a unit and/or in an elective unit
- Taking the opportunity to reinforce the importance of this issue by integrating a consideration of wellbeing and resilience when discussing other relevant topics such as learning, diversity/inclusion, behaviour management and professional responsibilities
- Integrating considerations of young people's wellbeing and resilience as part of professional experience or practicum components – either by setting relevant tasks whilst in the school setting (such as reviewing policies and partnerships) or discussing relevant issues in follow-up tutorials or seminars
- Modelling pedagogic practices and assessment that explicitly acknowledge social and emotional dimensions of learning and resilience (i.e. 'two-way pedagogies', 'supportive learning environments' and 'assessment of affective characteristics')
- Planning using a curriculum alignment approach to ensure a cohesive and consistent structure between goals, approaches and assessments

Such comprehensive integration aims to ensure that all graduates have some appreciation of the interrelationship between wellbeing, resilience and education and the implications for the teacher's role (Beltman et al. 2011; Stafford et al. 2007). Consistent with the principles of curriculum integration, such an approach is likely to be more effective in shaping graduates' beliefs and practice than a brief, isolated exposure. The challenge is how is this achieved across the tertiary education sector as a whole?

Response Ability: An Example

Since 2000 the Australian government has actively supported, ITE and in-service preparation of, teachers to contribute through their day-to-day practice to the wellbeing and learning of children and young people. Response Ability is the pre-service element of this activity, and its purpose is to support tertiary education institutions in their training of education and care professionals. Its scope includes early childhood, primary and secondary teacher training in university and vocational education. Response Ability aims to enable tertiary educators (e.g. lecturers, tutors and course coordinators) to raise awareness and build the capacity of the future teacher workforce.

As part of the initial consultation for the development of Response Ability project, conducted in the late 1990s, substantial and practical differences were identified between the contexts of the ITE with prospective teachers and school-based in-service professional development. The development of a tailored approach that was sensitive to the practical nuances of the tertiary education system, the nature of prospective student's knowledge and skills and the variety of content and instructional modalities would be critical for successful development, dissemination, adoption and maintenance of the programme. To ensure continuity across the tertiary education sector in general and the in-service initiatives in particular, Response Ability worked closely during resource development and implementation phases with both peek bodies and peer programs within the mental health and schooling space, including *MindMatters*, *KidsMatter* and *KidsMatter Early Childhood*.

Since the launch of Response Ability's first resource in 2001 (complementing *MindMatters*, the national in-service resource the government commissioned during the same period), the challenge of being 'fit for purpose' and responsive to developments within the tertiary education context has remained constant with substantial reforms occurring both in schools, systems and teacher accreditation and in the tertiary education sector, in particular in teacher education. For instance, the landscape of ITE in Australia is currently undergoing some of the biggest regulatory and structural changes in its history (Aspland 2006; Ingvarson et al. 2014). The uncapping of the number of initial teacher enrolments, the introduction of national systems of accreditation and the development of a national school curriculum are anticipated to lead to significant changes in ITE courses and programs. This is combined with an expanding role for public health initiatives in the educational setting, the emergence of major national health promotion, prevention and early intervention mental health initiatives and significant technological and communication advances. In short, the instructional, practical and policy environment for schoolteachers, and those who train them, is providing both significant opportunities for innovation and substantive practical challenges.

Concordantly, as a domain of intervention, Australian ITE is a structured but dynamic environment reflecting a spectrum of approaches, students, educators, programs and levels of study (Kay-Lambkin et al. 2007). The content of ITE programs is typically organised around the thematic areas of professional experiences, curriculum and pedagogic studies and foundational studies, but there is a significant degree of institutional autonomy on how these themes are represented in specific programs. Whilst the national accreditation process is refining this situation, there continue to be distinctive and practical differences between institutions' approaches to preparing prospective teachers.

In responding to these circumstances, Response Ability is deliberately designed to provide a framework for communicating critical resilience and social and emotional wellbeing principles, knowledge and skills to the ITE sector (Hazel 2012). By targeting a common core of capacities and concepts that are essential to mental health, resilience and wellbeing, Response Ability is intended to firstly empower teacher educators and their students, secondly to build capacity in initial teacher educators and their students' professional capabilities and finally to transform the behaviour and culture of ITE programs so that the inclusion of social and emotional wellbeing in education becomes a regular feature of teacher preparation (Kemp and Hazel 2013).

The Response Ability resources are based on the principles of co-creation and evidence-informed practice and employ the design values of being:

1. Multidimensional: Allows for sequential or simultaneous implementation, used in both core and elective subjects and applicable to both generic and applied context
2. Multimodal: Allows for use in direction instruction, guided/supported learning, rehearsal, problem-solving or experiential learning
3. Flexible: Explicitly allows for educator autonomy in the choice/design of implementation, sequencing and focus

Using these principles Response Ability has produced four custom-designed multimedia resources covering the promotion of social and emotional wellbeing and learning from birth–18 years and nationally disseminated these resources to all universities, technical and further education (TAFE) institutions and the majority of private registered training organisations (RTO). In overview the core Response Ability resources consist of the following components:

- Short films made in authentic early childhood and school settings in Australia
- Interviews with experienced early education and care educators and school teachers
- Genuine interactions with children and families
- Realistic case study scenarios for students to examine
- Over 300 practical student activities linked to the early education and care competencies and teaching practices
- Notes for facilitators accompanying all student activities
- Practical advice on promoting mental health and supporting early intervention
- Student handouts on key issues

Response Ability intentionally uses a mix of multimedia stimulus and support materials to evoke problem-solving scenarios and encourage critical thinking, reflection and problem-solving (Cavanagh et al. 2014; Kay-Lambkin et al. 2007). This is an approach that allows for both rehearsal and debriefing around a range of situations, issues and concerns that are germane to social and emotional development, education and care. It provides prospective teachers with both knowledge and experience which can then be applied to their practicums and ongoing work within schools. Through its unique position in the ITE environment, Response Ability creates a first point of contact for future teachers and educators with wellbeing and resilience. In doing so Response Ability lays the foundation for national in-service programs, *KidsMatter Early Childhood*, *KidsMatter* and *MindMatters* mental health promotion initiatives, that teachers and educators will encounter in schools and early childhood and care services.

The underlying logic model of this approach is that by increasing the capability of educators to engage with resilience, social and emotional wellbeing and learning, we can make progress on some of the broader intractable challenges that confront child and youth wellbeing. One of the fundamental assumptions behind the Response Ability intervention is that appropriately equipped and supported teachers can actively contribute to strengthening children and families wellbeing and resilience (Response Ability 2007a). By seeking to implement common concepts, principles and approaches across child and youth professionals, Response Ability seeks to develop an acute understanding of the direct contribution that teachers, schools and learning make to resilience, wellbeing and learning. In summary, Response Ability supports not just specific job-related skills, like observing student behaviour, but enables a new way of thinking about education from the perspectives of resilience and social and emotional wellbeing (Hazel 2012).

There are many critical variables within the dynamic context of the classroom that teachers can influence. During their initial education, prospective teachers begin to establish attitudes, beliefs, behaviours, knowledge and skills that are central to this work. As we have discussed, a key component of this professional growth should be a firm appreciation of resilience, wellbeing, learning and schooling. To develop teachers competent in the domain of resilience, social and emotional wellbeing, mental health and learning requires knowledge, experience and resources to support practice. An effective method for building capability is to provide prospective teachers with tools that assist them in figuring out what is important as opposed to just 'nice to know' – essential to help them unpack key concepts, rehearse core skills and both build confidence and competence. With this in mind, Response Ability developed a range of guidelines, translation tools and extension materials for supporting teaching practice and decision-making across the spectrum of teaching qualifications, settings and learning areas.

The CHILD framework (Response Ability 2014b) provides practical guidance for supporting children's resilience, mental health and wellbeing in the context of teachers' day-to-day work (Kay-Lambkin et al. 2007). It has two applications in ITE. Firstly, CHILD summarises the practical strategies that teachers can use to support children and young peoples' social and emotional development, wellbeing, resilience and learning. Secondly, it provides a scaffold to support lecturers' examination of social and emotional learning and a method through which they can inspect their own discipline/content areas to identify where social and emotional wellbeing is either part of their existing curriculum design or alternatively where there may be opportunities to strengthen this element. The CHILD framework (Hunter Institute of Mental Health 2010) is shaped by a set of fundamental assumptions:

- Children and young people have a strong sense of identity.
- Children and young are connected with and contribute to their world.

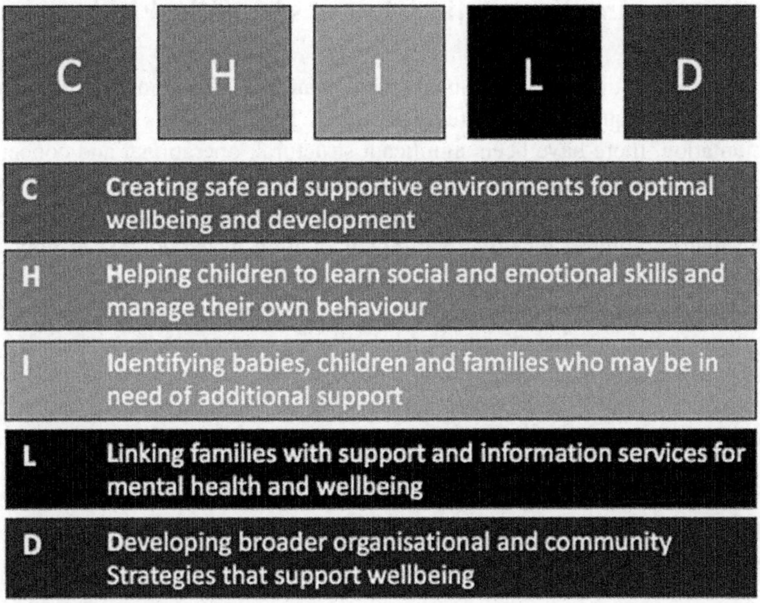

Fig. 13.1 CHILD framework

- Children and young have a strong sense of wellbeing.
- Children and young are confident and involved learners.
- Children and young are effective communicators.

CHILD (Fig. 13.1) aligns with the key principles of mental health promotion, prevention and early intervention, as they apply to people who work with children and young people. By synthesising a range of research and theory in the areas of mental health promotion, resilience, education, positive psychology, public health, development and mental health, the CHILD framework is designed to complement and not replace existing programs, frameworks and resource; CHILD conveys heuristic teachers can apply directly to their practice in whatever role, situation or type of position they find themselves in. It also forms a means of relating their work with the national ongoing professional development and in-school programs of KidsMatter Early Childhood, KidsMatter and MindMatters.

The instructional resources constructed around the CHILD framework are intended to provide lecturers with multiple points of access and connection for ITE programs to the concepts of social and emotional wellbeing regardless of type of programme, level of qualification, curriculum orientation or instructional mode. They translate the broad evidence base on resilience and wellbeing into discrete but complementary domains of professional practice (Kay-Lambkin et al. 2007). These domains can then be used to locate opportunities within existing ITE courses to include these principles and practices as part of the preparation of teachers.

Reflections on Implementation: Lessons from the Field

The dissemination, uptake, adoption and maintenance of innovations in highly regulated professional qualifications are challenging. Throughout its development and implementation, there have been significant structural, operational and conceptual challenges for Response Ability. At the same time, there have also been a growth in the research behind resilience and wellbeing and a deepening of our practical understanding that is required for effective implementation in the context of education (Durlak et al. 2010, 2011; Weissberg et al. 2015).

The long-term adoption of the Response Ability initiative has relied upon tertiary education making social and emotional wellbeing and resilience principles and practices part of their regular and ongoing preparation of teachers (Stafford et al. 2007). Response Ability has worked in partnership with tertiary educators with the aim of building organisational and individual capacity for this integration (Kemp and Hazel 2013). The key lessons learnt working towards this goal are as follows (Allen and Vincent 2005; Cavanagh et al. 2014; Foggett et al. 2007; Kay-Lambkin et al. 2007; Kemp and Hazel 2013; Weatherby-Fell and Vincent 2005; Weatherby-Fell and Kean 2004).

Social and Emotional Wellbeing and Resilience Can Be Challenging to Teach in ITE

Teaching and learning of resilience, mental health and wellbeing material are demanding. Lecturers and students value the opportunity to work on these domains, but they need practical ways to do so that respond to the constraints of time, levels of organisational buy-in, differing levels of enthusiasm for 'upskilling' in this area of teacher education (mainly at the level of lecturers) and differing programs, opportunities and student cohorts.

Multidisciplinary Interventions Are Challenging but Possible Within ITE

The culture of tertiary education, embodied in the organisational structure and the processes to recruit staff to teaching and research positions, seeks out and encourages, to a degree, specialisation in discrete areas. Response Ability brings by design multidisciplinary knowledge and requires lecturers to value information that is being drawn from the knowledge domains in which they may have limited professional interest. Initially those educators who are most closely aligned to health, psychology or child development disciplines were typically the most sympathetic or open to inclusion of resilience and wellbeing.

This has been both a strength and barrier. It means that there has been a cohort of academics who are willing to create a point of access into ITE programs, but this has also meant that other academic cohorts saw this area as being owned by particular staff or specialisations as opposed to something that has universal relevance and application to all prospective teachers. This circumstance has introduced the need to break down assumptions about area, as well as the potential stigma around mental health, before progress can be made with late adopters of the project. The combination of iterative co-designed resources and support, alongside of significant changes in public and professional perception and understanding of social and emotional wellbeing in education, has allowed progress; but this remains an ongoing challenge.

Support for the Inclusion of Resilience in ITE Comes from Building Capability

Even considering the practical, conceptual and cultural challenges in fostering professional learning for tertiary staff and ensuring dissemination occurred independently of direct on-site input from project staff, Response Ability has demonstrated that this approach can bring about change (Kay-Lambkin et al. 2007; Stafford et al. 2007). Where Response Ability has been taken up in a deep and well-thought-out way, it has led to important impacts on university course curriculum, lecturer practice and student sense of confidence and competence in regard to mental health and wellbeing (Allen and Vincent 2005; Cavanagh et al. 2014; Foggett et al. 2007; Kay-Lambkin et al. 2007; Weatherby-Fell and Vincent 2005; Weatherby-Fell and Kean 2004). The implementation of Response Ability has corroborated the original logic model and the decision made to bring lecturers actively into the process of delivering the content rather than providing a discrete, static and closed resource that was simply distributed. Moreover lecturers have made use of the flexibility and adaptability of the resource to find a wide range of locations within their teaching programs.

Pathways to Mastery: Preparing Graduates

There is an implicit understanding in the teaching standards and competencies that ITE programs do not produce full formed experts who have mastered all domains of their professional skill set. Graduates need experience to mature in their capabilities and progress towards mastery. Response Ability initiates the professional learning and development required by prospective teachers, but this learning and development needs to continue through workplace professional development and reflection. The goal of intervention is to build capability and confidence as foundation for mastery and for this to be carried forward into career-long professional development and learning.

Conclusion

There is sufficient research, policy, professional and public support for the proposition that theories of resilience are central to the work of teachers and that there remains no question of whether student wellbeing and resilience should be a key element of the role of the teaching profession. The only remaining questions relate to how best to represent and support this key element of professional practice, through elements such as professional standards, initial training, teacher registration and ongoing professional learning.

The answers to these questions will require more than the translation of multidisciplinary knowledge about resilience and wellbeing into the context of schooling. We will need to continue to consider innovative mechanism and strategies to support professional learning at every stage of a teacher's career – from initial training forwards. To do this involves an appreciation of the opportunities and limitations afforded by way teachers are prepared for their profession and learn in the workplace. Effective and integrated inclusion of resilience, wellbeing and learning in ITE is a critical component in supporting teachers to understand how they can expand the learning experiences of all students; to encourage the use of different and innovative teaching methods to support social and emotional learning, wellbeing and engagement; and to develop whole of school planning and accountability for wellbeing. One promising pathway to realising this goal is sector-wide capability development interventions, like Response Ability, MindMatters and KidsMatter, which focus on promoting and fostering core professional competences and skills. By working with, and building the capacity of, all teachers and teacher educators we can embed resilience at the core of education and schooling.

References

Allen, J., & Vincent, K. (2005, November). *Journeys: Supporting innovation in teacher education throughout Australia*. Paper presented at the Australian Association for Research in education conference: 'Creative dissent: Constructive solutions', University of Western Sydney, Australia.

Aspland, T. (2006). Changing patterns of teacher education in Australia. *Education Research and Perspectives, 33*(2), 140–163.

Baggio, J. A., Brown, K., & Hellebrandt, D. (2015). Boundary object or bridging concept? A citation network analysis of resilience. *Ecology and Society, 20*(2), 2. https://doi.org/10.5751/ES-07484-200202.

Beltman, S. (2015). Teacher professional resilience: Thriving not just surviving. In N. Weatherby-Fell (Ed.), *Learning to teach in the secondary school* (pp. 20–38). Melbourne: Cambridge University Press.

Beltman, S., Mansfield, C. F., & Price, A. (2011). Thriving not just surviving: A review of research on teacher resilience. *Educational Research Review, 6*, 185–207.

Billett, S. (2009). Realising the educational worth of integrating work experiences in higher education. *Studies in Higher Education, 34*(7), 827–843. https://doi.org/10.1080/03075070802706561.

Bridgeland, J., Bruce, M., & Hariharan, A. (2013). *The missing piece: A national survey on how social and emotional learning can empower children and transform schools*. Washington, DC: Civic Enterprises.

Broadley, T., Mansfield, C. F., Beltman, S., & Weatherby-Fell, N. (2014). Innovating resilience resources through BRiTE online modules. In J. Herrington, J. Viteli, & M. Leikomaa (Eds.), *Media world conference on educational media and technology 2014* (pp. 2432–2434). Chesapeake: Association for the Advancement of Computing in Education.

Cavanagh, S., Cole, J., Hazel, G., Gilson, K.-M., & Kynaston, J. (2014). Building the capacity of early childhood educators to promote children's mental health: Learnings from three new programs. In S. Garvis & D. Pendergast (Eds.), *Health and wellbeing in the early years* (pp. 331–348). Melbourne: Cambridge University Press.

Clarke, A. M., Morreale, S., Field, C. A., Hussein, Y., & Barry, M. M. (2015). *What works in enhancing social and emotional skills development during childhood and adolescence? A review of the evidence on the effectiveness of school-based and out-of-school programmes in the UK*. A report produced by the World Health Organization Collaborating Centre for Health Promotion Research. Galway: National University of Ireland.

Collaborative for Academic, Social, and Emotional Learning. (2003). *Safe and sound: An educational leader's guide to evidence-based social and emotional learning (SEL) programs*. Chicago: Collaborative for Academic and Social and Emotional Learning.

Collaborative for Academic, Social, and Emotional Learning. (2012). *2013 CASEL guide: Effective social and emotional learning programs – Preschool and elementary* (school ed.). Chicago: Collaborative for Academic and Social and Emotional Learning.

Darling-Hammond, L., & Bransford, J. (Eds.). (2005). *Preparing teachers for a changing world: What teachers should learn and be able to do*. San Francisco: Jossey-Bass.

Davis, E., Hazel, G., & Clark, S. (2012). *Building the capacity of early childhood educators to promote children's mental health: Learnings from three new programs*. Paper presented at the Seventh World Conference on the Promotion of Mental Health and Prevention of Mental and Behavioral Disorders, held at the Perth convention and exhibition centre, Australia.

Deed, C., Cox, P., & Prain, V. (2011). Enablers and constraints in achieving integration in a teacher preparation program. *Australian Journal of Teacher Education, 36*(8), 68–96.

Durlak, J. A., Weissberg, R. P., & Pachan, M. (2010). A meta-analysis of after-school programs that seek to promote personal and social skills in children and adolescents. *American Journal of Community Psychology, 45*, 294–309. https://doi.org/10.1007/s10464-010-9300-6.

Durlak, J. A., Weissberg, R. P., Dymniciki, A. B., Taylor, R. D., & Schellinger, K. B. (2011). The impact of enhancing students' social and emotional learning: A meta-analysis of school-based universal interventions. *Child Development, 82*, 405–432. https://doi.org/10.1111/j.1467-8624.2010.01564.x.

Franklin, C. G. S., Kim, J. S., Ryan, T. N., Kelly, M. S., & Montgomery, K. L. (2012). Teacher involvement in school mental health interventions: A systematic review. *Children and Youth Services Review, 34*(2012), 973–982. https://doi.org/10.1016/j.childyouth.2012.01.027.

Foggett, K., Kemp, E., & Stafford, K. (2007). *The response ability initiative: Resources for social and emotional health education*. Paper presented at 25th international/biennial Australian Council of Health, Physical Education and Recreation (ACHPER) Conference, Freemantle, Australia.

Graetz, B., Littlefield, L., Trinder, M., Dobia, B., Souter, M., Champion, C., Boucher, S., Killick-Moran, C., & Cummins, R. (2008). KidsMatter: A population health model to support student mental health and well-being in primary schools. *International Journal of Mental Health Promotion, 10*(4), 13–20. https://doi.org/10.1080/14623730.2008.9721772.

Hammerness, K. (2006). From coherence in theory to coherence in practice. *Teachers College Record, 108*(7), 1241–1265.

Hawkins, J. D., Kosterman, R., Catalano, R. F., Hill, K. G., & Abbott, R. D. (2008). Effects of social development intervention in childhood 15 years latter. *Archives of Paediatric and Adolescent Medicine, 162*, 1133–1141. https://doi.org/10.1001/archpedi.162.12.1133.

Hazel, G. (2012). *Enabling knowledge transfer by influencing professional practice dissemination planning in a tertiary education system*. Paper presented at the Seventh World Conference on the Promotion of Mental Health and Prevention of Mental and Behavioral Disorders, Perth, Australia.

Hazel, G. (2014). *A question of fundamentals: Teacher standards and teacher preparation*. Paper presented at the Australian Teacher Education Association Conference, ACU North Sydney, Australia.

Hazel, G. (2015). *Driving change through capability development: Early childhood and teacher workforce preparation for supporting children and families*. Paper presented at the Ninth World Congress on the Promotion of Mental Health and the Prevention of Mental and Behavioural Disorders, Columbia Metropolitan Convention Center, Columbia, South Carolina, USA.

Hazel, G., & Vincent, K. (2005). Adolescents' social and emotional wellbeing: Finding a place in teacher education. *Education Connect, 3*, 3–9.

Hunter Institute of Mental Health. (2010). *Response ability vocational education and training resources: Children's services background reading for teachers*. Newcastle: Hunter Institute of Mental Health.

Ikesako, H., & Miyamoto, K. (2015). *Fostering social and emotional skills through families, schools and communities: Summary of international evidence and implication for Japan's educational practices and research* (OECD Education Working Papers, No. 121). Paris: OECD Publishing. https://doi.org/10.1787/5js07529lwf0-en

Ingvarson, L., Reid, K., Buckley, S., Kleinhenz, E., Masters, G., & Rowley, G. (2014). *Best practice teacher education programs and Australia's own programs*. Canberra: Department of Education.

Kay-Lambkin, F., Kemp, E., Stafford, K., & Hazell, T. (2007). Mental health promotion and early intervention in early childhood and primary school settings: A review. *Journal of Student Wellbeing, 1*(1), 31–56.

Kemp, E., & Hazel, G. (2013). *Creating skilled educators through pre-service teacher training in mental health promotion*. Paper presented at Australian Teacher Education Association Conference, Brisbane.

Macklem, G. L. (2014). *Preventive mental health at school: Evidence-based services for students*. New York: Springer.

Mansfield, C. F. (2012, September). Promoting resilience for teachers and their students: A four dimensional view. Presentation at the Children's Hospital Educational Research Institute (CHERI) conference. Sydney.

Mansfield, C. F., Beltman, S., Broadley, T., & Weatherby-Fell, N. (2016). Building resilience in teacher education: An evidenced informed framework. *Teaching and Teacher Education, 54*, 77–87.

Norton, A., & Cherastidtham, I. (2014). *Mapping Australian higher education, 2014–15*. Melbourne: Grattan Institute.

Ransford, C. R., Greenberg, M. T., Domitrovich, C. E., Small, M., & Jacobson, L. (2009). "The role of teachers" psychological experiences and perceptions of curriculum supports on the implementation of social and emotional learning curriculum. *School Psychology Review, 38*(4), 510–532.

Response Ability. (2007a). *Research and evidence* [Fact sheet]. Retrieved April 20, 2016, from http://www.responseability.org/__data/assets/pdf_file/0019/4933/Research-and-Evidence.pdf

Response Ability. (2007b). *Response ability – Resources for teacher education: Early childhood and primary*. Canberra: Australian Government Department of Health and Ageing.

Response Ability. (2010). *Response ability: Vocational education and training resources: Children's services*. Canberra: Australian Government Department of Health and Ageing.

Response Ability. (2014a). *Promoting resilience and wellbeing* [Fact sheet]. Retrieved April 17, 2018, from http://www.responseability.org/__data/assets/pdf_file/Fact-sheet-Promoting-Resilience-and-Wellbeing.pdf

Response Ability. (2014b). *CHILD framework* [Fact Sheet]. Retrieved April 17, 2018 from http://www.responseability.org/__data/assets/pdf_file/0014/10535/CHILD-Framework-Final.pdf

Response Ability. (2015). *GRIP framework* [Fact Sheet]. Retrieved April 17, 2018, from http://www.responseability.org/__data/assets/pdf_file/Fact-sheet-GRIP-framework.pdf

Roffey, S. (2016). Building a case for whole-child, whole-school wellbeing in challenging contexts. *Educational & Child Psychology, 33*(2), 30–42.

Rowe, F., Stewart, D., & Patterson, C. (2007). Promoting school connectedness through whole school approaches. *Health Education, 107*(6), 524–542.

Schonert-Reichl, K. A., Hanson-Peterson, J. L., & Hymel, S. (2015). SEL and preservice teacher education. In J. A. Durlak, C. E. Domitrovich, P. Weissberg, & T. P. Gullotta (Eds.), *Handbook of social and emotional learning: Research and practice* (pp. 395–405). New York: Guilford Press.

Sheppard, J., Pickett, K., Dewhisrt, S., Byrne, Speller, V., Grace, M., Almond, P., & Roderick, P. (2015). Initial teacher training to promote health and well-being in schools – A systematic review of effectiveness, barriers and facilitators. *Health Education Journal.*, Advanced online publication. https://doi.org/10.1177/0017896915614333.

Stafford, K. (2007). Mental health promotion in schools. *Issues, 80*(Sept), 4–6.

Stafford, K. Moore, C., Foggert, K., Kemp, E. Hazell, T. (2007). *Proving and improving: Exploring the links between resilience, behaviour and academic outcomes*. Paper presented at Australia Association for Research in Education Annual Conference, Fremantle.

Vincent, K., Hazell, T., Allen, J., & Griffiths, T. (2005). New times, new teachers: Valuing social and emotional wellbeing in teacher education. In M. Cooper (Ed.), *Teacher education: Local and global*. Proceedings of the 33rd annual Australian teacher education association conference held at the Crowne plaza surfers paradise, Australia, 6–9 July 2005 (pp. 447–453). Surfers Paradise: Griffith University.

Weatherby-Fell, N., & Vincent, K. (2005). Social and emotional wellbeing in teacher education: Reflections by early career teachers. In *Proceedings of the Australian Teacher Education Association (ATEA) conference*.

Weatherby-Fell, N., & Kean, B. (2004). Mental health and teacher education – Implications of the rural perspective for beginning teachers. *International Journal of Practical Experiences in Professional Education, 8*, 6–18.

Weissberg, R. P., Durlak, J. A., Domitrovich, C. E., & Gullotta, T. P. (2015). Social and emotional learning: Past, present and future. In J. A. Durlak, C. E. Domitrovich, P. Weissberg, & T. P. Gullotta (Eds.), *Handbook of social and emotional learning: Research and practice* (pp. 3–19). New York: Guilford Press.

Weston, K. J., Anderson-Butcher, D., & Burke, R. W. (2008). Developing a comprehensive curriculum framework for teacher preparation in expanded school mental health. *Advances in School Mental Health Promotion, 1*(4), 25–41. https://doi.org/10.1080/1754730X.2008.9715737.

Zins, J. E., Bloodworth, M. R., Weissberg, R. P., & Walberg, H. J. (2007). The scientific base linking social and emotional learning to school success. *Journal of Educational & Psychological Consultation, 17*(2/3), 191–121.

Zins, J. E., Weissberg, R. P., Wang, M. C., & Walberg, H. J. (Eds.). (2004). *Building academic success on social and emotional learning: What does the research say?* New York: Teachers College Press.

Chapter 14
Using Online Modules to Build Capacity for Teacher Resilience

Susan Beltman, Caroline F. Mansfield, Marold Wosnitza, Noelene Weatherby-Fell, and Tania Broadley

Abstract Teacher resilience is regarded as a complex, multidimensional, dynamic construct. Enhancing teacher resilience can potentially increase teacher commitment, yet interventions to build resilience in pre-service programmes are scarce. This chapter examines the effectiveness of the BRiTE (*Building Resilience in Teacher Education*) online modules to develop pre-service teachers' capacity for resilience in Australia. The modules are briefly described. Perceptions of 146 final year pre-service teachers were gathered regarding resilience, self-efficacy, commitment and coping before completing the BRiTE modules and their final professional experience school placement. Both pre- and post-school placement measures were completed by 49 participants. To determine the impact of using the modules, matched data sets were divided with "users" (n = 32) scoring significantly higher scores than "non-users" (n = 17) on five post-placement survey scales. Despite some limitations, there was an indication that using the online modules assisted pre-service teachers develop their capacity for resilience. Adapting the modules for use with in-service teachers and other professionals is an avenue for future research.

S. Beltman (✉)
School of Education, Curtin University, Perth, WA, Australia
e-mail: s.beltman@curtin.edu.au

C. F. Mansfield
School of Education, Murdoch University, Perth, WA, Australia
e-mail: Caroline.Mansfield@murdoch.edu.au

M. Wosnitza
Institute of Education, RWTH Aachen University, Aachen, Germany

School of Education, Murdoch University, Perth, WA, Australia
e-mail: marold.wosnitza@rwth-aachen.de

N. Weatherby-Fell
University of Wollongong, Wollongong, Australia
e-mail: noelene@uow.edu.au

T. Broadley
Queensland University of Technology, Brisbane, Australia
e-mail: tania.broadley@qut.edu.au

M. Wosnitza et al. (eds.), *Resilience in Education*,
https://doi.org/10.1007/978-3-319-76690-4_14

This study has significance, given the importance of teacher professional resilience, and suggests that interventions developed for pre-service contexts can make a difference.

Teacher education programmes have a role in assisting beginning teachers to develop capacity for resilience (Beltman et al. 2011), but the question of how this may occur is largely unanswered. Teacher resilience has been associated with positive outcomes such as commitment, wellbeing and job satisfaction (Gu and Li 2013), and teacher educators and researchers have argued the need for resilience-related skills to be developed during teacher education experiences (Buchanan et al. 2013). Recommendations include using scenarios, videos and observations (Tait 2008), as well as case studies, action research and teaching advanced problem-solving (Castro et al. 2010). Nevertheless, few interventions provide evidence on how best to incorporate activities into teacher education programmes.

Drawing on literature regarding suggested topics and activities, online modules (BRiTE, *Building Resilience in Teacher Education*; https://www.brite.edu.au/) were created that could be implemented in multiple ways in pre-service teacher education settings and beyond. Such an approach is consistent with a focus on using new technologies and blended learning to support teaching and learning in higher education (Johnson and Broadley 2012). A design-based research framework provided an evolving method of effective evaluation and redesign of educational tools (Reeves 2006). Expertise of researchers, teacher educators, psychologists, teachers and instructional designers was drawn upon within the process.

Once the design of the modules was completed, feedback about their effectiveness was obtained through the evaluation of an intervention where the modules were implemented in a teacher education programme in Australia. The aim of this chapter is to present the findings of the evaluation and to determine the impact of engaging with the modules.

Conceptualisation of Teacher Resilience

As indicated in the Introduction, conceptualisations of resilience may differ (Beltman and Mansfield 2018, Chap. 1, this volume). Resilience is conceptualised in this chapter as a *capacity*, a *process* as well as an *outcome* (Beltman 2015). There is agreement in the literature that resilience is a multidimensional and complex concept (Mansfield et al. 2012) or a “composite construct” (Gu and Li 2013, p. 292). Figure 14.1 illustrates the multidimensional and dynamic nature of resilience where personal and contextual resources are harnessed through the use of various strategies which then enable resilience outcomes. Based on Biggs and Moore’s (1993) model showing the complexity of the learning process, the figure uses bidirectional arrows between all components indicating that process is complex, interrelated and dynamic. This conceptualisation endeavours to draw together potentially disparate

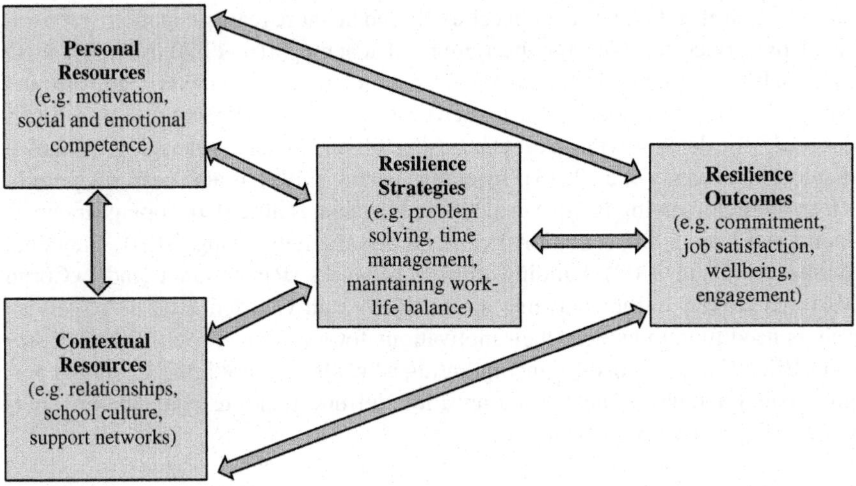

Fig. 14.1 The teacher resilience process. (Adapted from Mansfield et al. 2016b)

views of resilience focusing on individual capacity, on contextual risk and resources, on dynamic adaptation processes or on resilience as a desirable outcome.

As shown in Fig. 14.1, resilience is shaped by a mixture of personal and contextual resources. Personal resources can include those which are profession-, motivation-, social-, and emotion-related (Mansfield et al. 2012). Contextual resources could include relationships with school leaders (Peters and Pearce 2012). As illustrated in the centre, capacity for resilience is not simply a set of characteristics, but involves the ability to *use* one's own personal resources as well as those in one's contexts (Gu and Li 2013). Harnessing resources involves the use of various strategies, and so resilience is also seen as a process (Castro et al. 2010). For example, networking and collaboration can help create important networks for beginning teachers (Schlichte et al. 2005).

Resilience is also an outcome which "enables teachers to maintain their commitment to teaching … despite challenging conditions and recurring setbacks" (Brunetti 2006, p. 813). Teacher resilience has been described as being "closely allied to a strong sense of vocation, self-efficacy and motivation to teach which are fundamental to a concern for promoting achievement in all aspects of pupils' lives" (Sammons et al. 2007, p. 694). The outcome then, shaped by these resources and strategies, is teachers who are committed to and developing in the profession.

Resilience in Teacher Education

The literature regarding teacher resilience often points to the role teacher education programmes may play in assisting aspiring teachers to develop particular skills that will make a positive contribution to their resilience in the profession. Buchanan et al. (2013) argued that teacher educators should be more realistic in their "preparation of preservice teachers for the rigours of teaching" (p. 115). Such "rigours" could include working in challenging rural and remote contexts (Sullivan and Johnson 2012) or in resource constrained areas of poverty (Ebersöhn 2014). Skills are needed for dealing with particular groups of students and managing unwanted behaviour (Buchanan et al. 2013). Teaching specific skills has also been suggested - such as problem-solving (Castro et al. 2010; Huisman et al. 2010), coping strategies (Chong and Low 2009), emotional competence (Ee and Chang 2010), emotional intelligence (Chan 2008), building support networks (Papatraianou and LeCornu 2014) and strategies for managing stress (Curry and O'Brien 2012). Pre-service teachers need time to explore their motivations for teaching (Prosser 2008). Curry and O'Brien (2012) argued for incorporating a "wellness paradigm," including personal goals for physical health and nutrition, leisure, relationships and work pursuits within pre-service programmes.

Resilience Interventions

Even though the literature makes recommendations for teacher education, there are limited examples of how such recommendations may be implemented, particularly with pre-service teachers. In one study located, Le Cornu (2009) used a learning community model of professional experience to positively contribute to pre-service teacher resilience. It included opportunities for peer and collegial support, explicit teaching of interpersonal skills for developing relationships and a focus on nurturing wellbeing.

Despite the paucity of interventions with pre-service teachers, there are some examples of interventions with practicing teachers. Stress management training (Siu et al. 2014) and classroom management strategies (Dicke et al. 2015) have had a positive impact on beginning teacher wellbeing. Relaxation therapy has been used to reduce teacher stress (Kaspereen 2012). Mindfulness development programmes such as Cultivating Awareness and Resilience in Education (CARE) (Jennings et al. 2013) have resulted in improved teacher wellbeing, as well as reducing risk of burnout. Likewise, a gratitude-focused intervention (Chan 2011) positively influenced teachers' life satisfaction and sense of personal accomplishment as well as reducing emotional exhaustion and depersonalisation.

Online interventions to promote wellbeing could be a useful way to assist university students who may be reluctant to seek formal help (Ryan et al. 2010). One programme of a 90-min seminar with follow-up individual activities reported a positive influence on university students' wellbeing (Stallman 2011). It focused on six building blocks of resilience: realistic expectations, balance, connectedness, positive self-talk, stress management and taking action.

The Intervention: The BRiTE Modules

One of the challenges in developing interventions is the complex, dynamic and idiosyncratic nature of resilience. Gu and Li (2013, p. 300), for example, referred to "the uncertain and unpredictable circumstances and scenarios which form the main feature of teachers' everyday professional lives". Personal and contextual resources available to a particular individual in a particular setting will also vary as highlighted by Yonezawa et al. (2011) who wrote about "the conflation of resilient characteristics of teachers and the environmental supports" (p. 915). Addressing this complexity was an important issue to address in designing and evaluating the modules for this intervention. The BRiTE modules, described below, focused on highlighting and developing strategies that pre-service teachers could use to harness their unique personal resources and resources in their varied contexts.

To develop the modules, an evidence-based resilience framework was developed (Mansfield et al. 2016a, b) to inform module content around five main themes: *understanding and building resilience* (e.g. why teacher resilience is important; the resilience process), *relationships* (e.g. developing support networks; communicating effectively), *wellbeing* (e.g. responding to stress; achieving work-life balance), *motivation* (e.g. self-efficacy; help-seeking) and *emotions* (e.g. optimistic thinking; managing emotions). These themes formed the basis of the five BRiTE modules. Figure 14.2 shows the main findings from the literature and BRiTE module topics.

Rationale for Online Modules

Having developed the content for the modules, a set of self-paced online learning experiences was developed. The process of learning through a digital experience has been given various terms such as distance learning, distributed learning, e-learning and online learning. Increasingly researchers and developers are grappling with understanding the specific characteristics of these learning environments (Garrison 2011; Moore et al. 2011). Nevertheless, online learning generally means accessing learning experiences through using some type of technology connected to the Internet (Moore et al. 2011). In the present intervention, online modules are explicitly defined as the organising principle for guiding learners through self-paced, asynchronous learning experiences, hosted on the Internet.

In online learning, the technology is simply a delivery mechanism for the provision of authentic learning experiences, materials or instruction (Broadley et al. 2013). The use of online learning materials can be highly effective in increasing student achievement and engagement when there is a focus on quality content, on the instructional strategies built into the learning materials and on the learner at the core (Naveh et al. 2010). Social interaction and discourse are key components of online learning (Anderson 2008).

module	literature informed concepts	examples of module topics
B Building resilience	resilience is a dynamic, multifaceted process where individuals mobilise personal and contextual resources and use coping strategies to enable resilience outcomes	what is resilience? why is resilience important for teachers? resilience in schools what makes a resilient teacher? the resilience process – bouncing back and bouncing forward
R Relationships	social competence (for building relationships, support networks and working collaboratively), setting boundaries, communication	understanding relationships and resilience building relationships in schools working in a professional team building personal and professional support networks using social media support networks communicating effectively
I Wellbeing	seeking renewal, work-life balance, time management	understanding personal wellbeing and mental health responding to and managing (dis)stress healthy living managing work-life balance time management
T Taking initiative	efficacy, value, sense of purpose, sense of vocation, initiative, high expectations, problem solving, professional learning, goal setting, help seeking, reflection, persistence	maintaining motivation persistence and efficacy problem solving processes goal setting and management help seeking ongoing professional learning
E Emotions	emotional competence, optimism empathy, hope, courage, humour, emotion regulation, mindfulness	emotional awareness optimistic thinking enhancing positive emotions managing emotions

Fig. 14.2 Building Resilience in Teacher Education: the BRiTE concepts and topics. (Adapted from Mansfield et al. 2016a)

In relation to teacher resilience, there are suggestions in the literature that online resources can support resilience, but this previous work has been through online synchronous and asynchronous networking rather than online learning, such as casual teachers accessing support through a social networking site (Papatraianou and Le Cornu 2014). Whilst the use of social networking sites can "foster resiliency amongst the younger teachers entering the workforce" (Muller et al. 2011, p. 553), many learning management systems already cater for collaboration through discussion boards and web conferencing technologies. For this reason, the BRiTE modules were not developed with a collaboration feature for social interaction.

The modules were specifically designed to focus on learning outcomes associated with identified topics of resilience, with the intention that teacher educators would follow up with discussion in class time or embed these modules within their learning management system. Suggested implementation strategies for teacher educators are included in the BRiTE website, where a range of strategies explain their use either through independent access or to complement face-to-face courses where aspects of resilience may not be covered.

Four design principles informed the creation of the modules. The modules are *personalised* with each user provided with "content or an experience which has been tailored to suit their specific needs based on implicit or explicit information about that user" (O'Donnell et al. 2015, p. 23). Through the use of an initial quiz, the learning topics are prioritised and orchestrated for the individual user based on the responses gathered in the quiz and to suit the unique needs of each user. Further personalisation is available to users as they pin and save learning objects into a personalised toolkit for future reference as required. Modules are *interactive*, as users respond to scenarios, have opportunities for reflection and contribute ideas regarding useful additional strategies. Dynamic principles mean the modules include nonlinear navigation, multimedia links and further resources. Modules are *practice-based* with teacher voices frequently "heard" through videos as well as direct quotes from research featuring pre-service and early career teachers. Finally, modules are *evidence-informed*, with reference to supporting research and literature a key feature of each topic.

Teacher education courses include field-based practical or professional experience components where pre-service teacher education students are placed in schools under the supervision of mentor teachers. These are an important learning experience for pre-service teachers (Zeichner 2010) and can be stressful for a number of reasons (Caires et al. 2009; Gardner 2011). For example, the realities of teaching might contrast with previously idealised images of teaching (Goldstein 2005). In the BRiTE modules, reference is made to these experiences and to possible knowledge, skills and strategies that could be used to overcome or ameliorate stressful situations. The study aimed to determine whether pre-service teachers who completed the BRiTE modules, and used the related knowledge and skills during their final professional experience placement in schools, reported higher levels of teacher resilience, commitment to the profession and coping strategies than students who said they did not use the modules.

Method

Procedure and Participants

The evaluation of the implementation of the BRiTE modules occurred in a series of phases (Fig. 14.3). Final year pre-service teachers from two universities in two Australian states were invited to complete the BRiTE modules and asked to complete an online survey, including a set of scales, before gaining access to the modules. Informed ethical consent at university and individual level was obtained. Invitations were made by staff known to the participants but not currently teaching them.

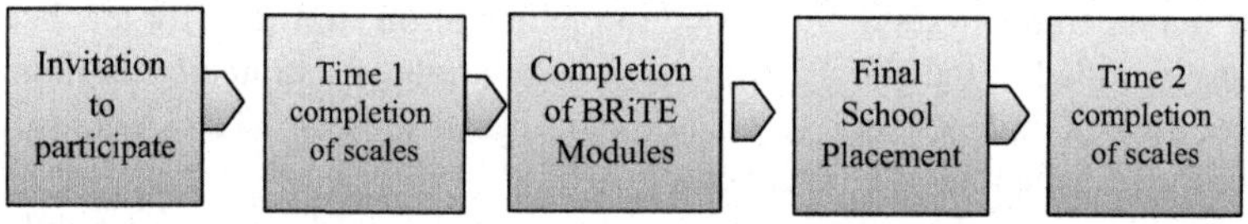

Fig. 14.3 Design of implementation evaluation

Interested participants were provided via email with information on registering for module access and accessing the pre-module survey. The pre-module survey (Time 1) was completed by 146 pre-service teachers (average age 32.1 years; 79.5% female) prior to beginning the modules. The modules were available for 8 weeks and participants were able to engage with as few or as many as they wished.

The majority ($n = 100$) of those completing the Time 1 survey were from one of the two universities and were in a Graduate Diploma of Education (primary or secondary) delivered across four campuses. These 100 students were contacted again after their final professional experience (PEX) placement. This was a supervised placement in a different school location and different context from their previous placements including city schools, major regional centres and remote regional areas. Schools were government and non-government. Although it was suggested that completion of the modules should be undertaken during the week prior to their final 5-week block placement in schools, a number of participants completed the modules during or at the completion of their PEX. At the end of the placement, students who had agreed to participate were contacted by email and invited to complete another survey (Time 2) and 49 participants did this. This did represent a drop out of around 50%. As Time 2 was at the completion of the professional experience placement and the teacher education programme, a number of students commenced casual teaching or accepted additional opportunities to work in non-teaching capacities. This impacted on their availability and focus. In addition, some students were reticent to undertake the T2 survey as they had not completed all the modules and were unwilling to provide feedback based on their perceived limited knowledge and engagement with the modules. Some had explained that they were busy completing required assessments before their placement so had not prioritised the modules which were not compulsory.

Instruments

Scales (Time 1 and Time 2)

The survey administered at Time 1 included demographic questions and a set of scales. The same scales were administered at Time 2 (after completing PEX). Table 14.1 provides the number of items and a sample item for each scale administered at T1 and T2.

The first set of four scales, TRP (teacher resilience profession; 6 items), TRM (teacher resilience motivation; 10 items), TRE (teacher resilience emotion; 6 items)

Table 14.1 Scale details, means, standard deviations and reliabilities at Times 1 and 2

				T1			T2		
	Scale	# Items	Sample item	M	SD	α	M	SD	α
TRP	Teacher resilience – profession	6	I reflect on my teaching and learning to make future plans	25.5	2.7	0.77	27.1	2.4	0.81
TRM	Teacher resilience – motivation	10	I like challenges in my work	41.4	4.4	0.83	43.6	5.2	0.91
TRE	Teacher resilience – emotion	6	When something goes wrong at school I don't take it too personally	24.1	3.1	0.75	26.0	3.3	0.86
TRS	Teacher resilience – social	4	When I am at work I can generally resolve conflicts with others	16.8	1.9	0.70	17.6	2.0	0.77
TCG	Teacher commitment – general	5	I feel pleased that I decided to be a teacher	21.9	3.2	0.91	22.5	3.8	0.95
RUM	Rumination	7	When something upsets me at school, I find it hard to forget about it	24.3	3.4	0.68	23.1	3.1	0.56
TRG	Teacher resilience – general	9	(Confidence re) getting over setbacks in school	34.0	6.0	0.93	36.8	5.8	0.94
TEF	Teacher efficacy	12	(Confidence re) teaching in a way that my students will remember important information	44.4	8.3	0.94	48.7	8.0	0.94
CAP	Coping appraisal	7	Analyse my reaction to the problem	28.4	3.5	0.82	29.6	3.2	0.78
CSO	Coping social	4	Seek advice from others	15.3	2.3	0.81	15.8	2.4	0.79
CCH	Coping challenge	4	Take a positive approach and see it as a challenge	15.1	2.3	0.66	15.4	2.3	0.57
CAV	Coping avoidance	4	Pray for it to go away	9.3	3.1	0.74	8.7	2.1	0.79

and TRS (teacher resilience social; 4 items), were newly developed scales (Mansfield and Wosnitza 2014) based on earlier work on teacher resilience (Mansfield et al. 2012). Ratings were on a 5-point scale (1, strongly disagree; 2, disagree; 3, neutral; 4, agree; 5, strongly agree).

The second set of four scales, TCG (teacher commitment general; 5 items), RUM (rumination; 7 items), TRG (teacher resilience general; 9 items) and TEF (teacher efficacy; 12 items), were taken from Morgan (2011) where the factors most likely to facilitate beginning teacher resilience were identified, based on an asset model of resilience. Items were rated on a 5-point scale (1, strongly disagree/never; 5, strongly agree/always). In the RUM scale the positive and negative aspects were reversed as rumination was considered to be a "factor that could aggravate the adverse events" (Morgan 2011, p. 96). The final two scales in this set (TRG and TEF) used the same stem: "*How confident do you feel about succeeding in each of the following on a regular basis*?" Ratings were again on a 5-point scale (1, not confident; 2, somewhat confident; 3, moderately confident; 4, mostly confident; 5, absolutely confident) (see also Wosnitza et al. 2018, Chap. 16, this volume).

The third set of scales was the Deakin Coping Scales (CAP, coping appraisal; CSO, coping social; CCH, coping challenge; and CAV, coping avoidance) (Moore 2003). Developed in a nursing context, these scales include four factors involving *appraisal* of a situation or problem and its demands (CAP), seeking out and using available *social* resources (CSO), seeing a situation as a *challenge* (CCH) and *avoiding* action such as hoping for a solution to emerge (CAV). The stem for each scale was "Please indicate which response shows how you address demands or problems that arise in general" and a 5-point scale was used (1, never; 2, rarely; 3, sometimes; 4, often; 5, always).

Post-Placement Scales (Time 2)

The survey completed at T2 after the final PEX comprised the same three sets of scales as administered at T1, with an additional 14 items rated on a 5-point scale (1, never/not at all; 5, definitely/always) regarding use of the modules in the previous placement as well as in their future career. Items included, for example, "During your PEX, to what extent did you use items from your BRiTE toolkit?" and "To what extent do you think you will refer to the BRiTE modules in the early stages of your career?"

After placement, 24 students were interviewed and asked whether they had consciously used the modules during their placement and to explain how this had helped them. Although these data are not reported here, two illustrative comments are provided to indicate what participants meant when they said they had "used" the modules. For example, two interviewees said:

> One of the children…had behavioural issues and I found that confronting and challenging and just…to have, just to go back to the module especially in the area of not taking it personally. In talking to a mentor, in finding out how other people deal with it. It made me feel I wasn't needing to cope alone. That there was the support out there and there was things I could do with it out there. I went back into that classroom the next day after having reprised [sic] that and I had a much better day with him and I felt much better within myself that I was capable. [Participant 12]
>
> I remember one day in particular where I had a REALLY bad day…It was the worst class I have ever had…I guess working through the BRiTE stuff for me was more about reminding me about options because when you are in the moment you feel a bit trapped … it can feel really overwhelming… and then you catastrophise it….doing the modules straight before [PEX] was good because it reminded you not to do that. Not to catastrophise…take a minute, speak to someone… which for me is an important thing as I don't naturally speak to people when I have a problem. [Participant 14]

Data Analysis

All scales showed acceptable to good reliabilities at T1 (see Table 14.1). The scales from Morgan (2011) and Moore (2003) showed a similar reliability structure to the originally published instruments. For T1 and T2 the Cronbach alphas for all scales ranged between $\alpha = 0.70$ and $\alpha = 0.95$ (see Table 14.1) with two exceptions – rumination ($\alpha_{t1} = 0.68$; $\alpha_{t2} = 0.56$) and coping challenge ($\alpha_{t1} = 0.66$; $\alpha_{t2} = 0.57$). Therefore these two scales were not considered further in the analysis. For each scale at T1 and T2, a scale mean was calculated. The resulting scale means were used for further analysis. Matched data sets for T1 and T2 were available for 49 participants.

Results

No significant group differences were found for gender or university for all scales and both measurement points. However, paired sample t-tests showed significant differences with medium effect sizes between the two measurement points for 8 of the 10 scales (see Table 14.2). A significant increase occurred in all resilience measures for those who completed both sets of scales before and after the BRiTE implementation and PEX. Furthermore there was a significant increase for teaching efficacy and two of the coping scales, namely, appraisal (CAP) and social (CSO) at T2.

To determine to what extent the use of the items from the BRiTE toolkit had an impact on these changes, participants who completed the survey at both measurement points were divided into two groups based on the feedback they gave to the question "During your PEX to what extent did you use items from your BRiTE toolkit?". Those who answered "never" or "rarely" were categorised as "non-users" (n = 17) the others (n = 32) as "users". No significant group differences between users and non-users could be identified at T1. At T2 after the module implementation and PEX, the scales showed significant group mean differences between users

Table 14.2 Changes in measures over time

		Time 1		Time 2					
	Scale	M	SD	M	SD	t (df 48)	p		d
TRP	Teacher resilience – profession	4.2	0.46	4.5	0.77	−3.97	<.001	↗	0.48
TRM	Teacher resilience – motivation	4.1	0.44	4.4	0.52	−2.83	<.001	↗	0.35
TRE	Teacher resilience – emotion	4.0	0.52	4.3	0.54	−3.90	0.007	↗	0.40
TRS	Teacher resilience – social	4.2	0.49	4.4	0.51	−2.64	0.011	↗	0.37
TCG	Teacher commitment – general	4.4	0.65	4.5	0.77	−1.88	0.066		
TRG	Teacher resilience – general	3.8	0.66	4.1	0.65	−2.92	0.005	↗	0.38
TEF	Teacher efficacy	3.7	0.69	4,1	0.67	−4.59	<.001	↗	0.51
CAP	Coping appraisal	4.0	0.50	4.2	0.45	−3.17	0.003	↗	0.46
CSO	Coping social	3.8	0.59	3.9	0.61	−2.72	0.009	↗	0.38
CAV	Coping avoidance	2.3	0.89	2.2	0.77	0.94	0.351		

Table 14.3 Users and non-users at Time 2

Scale	Non-users		Users					
	M	SD	M	SD	SD	*t* (df = 47)	*p*	*d*
TRP: teacher resilience – profession	4.4	0.42	4.6	0.36	0.36	−2.15	0.037	0.52
TRM: teacher resilience – motivation	4.1	0.53	4.5	0.47	0.47	−2.61	0.012	0.81
TRE: teacher resilience – emotion	4.1	0.62	4.5	0.46	0.46	−2.38	0.022	0.77
TRS: teacher resilience – social	4.2	0.42	4.5	0.52	0.52	−2.21	0.032	0.61
TCG: teacher commitment – general	4.1	0.90	4.7	0.61	0.61	−2.46	0.008	0.83
TRG: reacher resilience – general	3.9	0.69	4.2	0.60	0.60	−1.46	0.151	
TEF: teacher efficacy	3.8	0.70	4.1	0.67	0.67	−1.79	0.079	
CAP: coping appraisal	4.1	0.46	4.3	0.44	0.44	−1.12	0.269	
CSO: coping social	3.9	0.58	3.9	0.63	0.63	0.02	0.988	
CAV: coping avoidance	2.1	0.76	2.2	0.78	0.78	−0.34	0.739	

and non-users on four scales. As seen in Table 14.3, users scored significantly higher scores than non-users on the post-placement survey scales of differentiated teacher resilience (TRM, TRE, TRS, TRP), although not on the general measure of resilience (TRG). Users also scored significantly higher than non-users on teacher commitment (TCG). No significant differences were found for efficacy (TEF) or the coping measures.

Discussion

The findings showed that pre-service teachers who completed the BRiTE modules independently and reported using them during their professional experience placement scored significantly higher on some measures of resilience than participants who completed the modules but reported not using them in their placement. The significant increases on all four resilience scales are a positive finding as the scales and BRiTE modules were based on the same literature highlighting the key components of resilience (Beltman et al. 2011; Mansfield et al. 2012, 2016). In this small study it was also promising to see that those who used the modules reported increased commitment to teaching. They scored significantly higher than non-users on the TCG scale which included items such as: "*I am likely to be teaching in ten years' time*" and "*I feel that teaching is really right for me*".

The modules specifically targeted skills such as building relationships in schools, communicating effectively, time management, maintaining motivation, help-seeking and managing emotions (see Fig. 14.2). Such skills are consistent with the noncognitive skills like "communication skills", "motivation" and "resilience" that teacher education programmes in Australia are recommended to assess in order to select suitable candidates to become teachers (AITSL 2015). Whilst this synergy is positive, what our study also shows is that such skills can be developed using suitable interventions during pre-service programmes. This position is consistent with the literature that shows that resilience, rather than being an innate attribute, can be learnt (Beltman et al. 2011). As illustrated in Fig. 14.1, skills and attributes continue to develop over time, as individuals live and work in different contexts that can support their professional growth (Cameron and Lovett 2015; Meister and Ahrens 2011). Likewise the ongoing support of others in their professional work contexts plays an important role:

> The nature and sustainability of resilience in teachers over the course of their professional lives is not a static or innate state, but influenced, individually and in combination, by the strength of their vocational selves, the commitment of those whom they meet as part of their daily work and the quality of leadership support within the school as well as their capacities to manage anticipated as well as unanticipated personal events. (Gu and Day 2013, p. 40)

The study reported in this chapter has several limitations. The number of participants who used the modules and agreed to participate in the Time 2 round of data collection was small. One key aspect of resilience is a positive sense of personal agency (Day 2008), and it is possible that many of the participants who did not persist with the modules needed more assistance and support from others. In this intervention the responsibility was on an individual to engage with and complete the modules. It is also difficult to disentangle the effect of the modules and the placement which was an important component of the course. Measures of context were not included even though contexts can present challenges and are a key resource for developing resilience. The scales used were largely newly developed, and two had low reliability and were removed from the analysis. A further limitation is that the possible long-term effect of the modules has not been investigated in this study. The period between completing the modules and the post-questionnaire was about 8 weeks, and follow-up would be needed once the participants commenced work as teachers, in a potentially less supported context, to examine longer-lasting impact. The overall findings therefore need to be interpreted cautiously. Measuring resilience presents challenges as it is a multidimensional and dynamic construct and more work is needed in this area.

The implementation evaluated in this study was based on participants accessing the modules independently in their own time. Whilst they were encouraged by the university staff to do so, this was not part of their standard course or assessed components. Guidelines have been developed for teacher educators to implement the modules in different ways within their course. One way could be as in this intervention with a simple recommendation to engage independently with the modules. The other extreme would be to embed the modules into a learning management system and require their completion with related assessment tasks. In between these extremes, educators could select relevant aspects of the modules and use them as prior reading, class discussion topics or assessments. Whilst the flexibility of the ways the modules could be used is a strength and makes them suitable for various settings, it also means that further research is needed to determine whether different types of implementation are more suitable for different individual pre-service teachers, for teacher educators, for different programmes or at different times of the pre-service programme.

It may also be that such modules would be of use in the early years of teaching when teachers are most likely to leave the profession (Gallant and Riley 2014). Another important area to examine is whether interventions maintain their impact over time and if they make any difference to the academic and wellbeing outcomes of those teachers' pupils. According to Day and Gu (2010), teacher resilience, well-being and commitment are key outcomes of the resilience process and lead to increased teacher effectiveness and pupil progress. The implementation of one evidence-based programme focusing on social and emotional learning needed to be supported through ongoing training such as coaching as well as the support of the organisation (CASEL 2015). Do teacher education programmes have the room and resources to provide such support in a global trend of increasing accountability (Day and Gu 2014; Mayer 2014)? Can these modules be adapted for teachers at different levels of experience, for different countries or even across different professions?

In conclusion, this chapter has briefly outlined evidence-informed online modules that represent an innovative resource in the field. Although further work is needed, initial findings regarding the potential impact of such an intervention are promising for developing the capacity of pre-service teachers to meet the demands of the profession and to continue to grow and develop as professionals who are committed and effective.

Acknowledgements The Building Resilience in Teacher Education [BRiTE] project was funded by an Australian Government, Office for Learning and Teaching grant.

References

AITSL [Australian Institute for Teaching and School Leadership]. (2015). *Action now: Selection of entrants into initial teacher education*. Melbourne: AITSL. Retrieved from http://www.aitsl.edu.au/initial-teacher-education/ite-reform/selection.

Anderson, T. (2008). *The theory and practice of online learning* (2nd ed.). Edmonton: Athabasca University Press (AU Press). Retrieved from http://www.ebrary.com.

Beltman, S. (2015). Teacher professional resilience: Thriving not just surviving. In N. Weatherby-Fell (Ed.), *Learning to teach in the secondary school* (pp. 20–38). Melbourne: Cambridge University Press.

Beltman, S., & Mansfield, C. F. (2018). Resilience in education: An introduction. In M. Wosnitza, F. Peixoto, S. Beltman, & C. F. Mansfield (Eds.), *Resilience in education: Concepts, contexts and connections* (pp. 3–9). New York: Springer.

Beltman, S., Mansfield, C. F., & Price, A. (2011). Thriving not just surviving: A review of research on teacher resilience. *Educational Research Review, 6*, 185–207. https://doi.org/10.1016/j.edurev.2011.09.001.

Biggs, J., & Moore, P. J. (1993). *The process of learning* (3rd ed.). Sydney: Prentice Hall.

Broadley, T., Ledger, S., & Sharplin, E. (2013). Portals and platforms: Does the technology matter when developing an online community? In J. Herrington et al. (Eds.), *Proceedings of World Conference on Educational Media and Technology 2013* (pp. 1408–1413). Association for the Advancement of Computing in Education (AACE).

Brunetti, G. J. (2006). Resilience under fire: Perspectives on the work of experienced, inner city high school teachers in the United States. *Teaching and Teacher Education, 22*(7), 812–825. https://doi.org/10.1016/j.tate.2006.04.027.

Buchanan, J., Prescott, A., Schuck, S., Aubusson, P., & Burke, P. (2013). Teacher retention and attrition: Views of early career teachers. *Australian Journal of Teacher Education, 38*(3), 112–129. https://doi.org/10.14221/ajte.2013v38n3.9.

Caires, S., Almeida, L. S., & Martins, C. (2009). The socioemotional experiences of student teachers during practicum: A case of reality shock? *The Journal of Educational Research, 103*(1), 17–27. https://doi.org/10.1080/00220670903228611.

Cameron, M., & Lovett, S. (2015). Sustaining the commitment and realising the potential of highly promising teachers. *Teachers and Teaching: Theory and Practice, 21*(2), 150–163. https://doi.org/10.1080/13540602.2014.928132.

CASEL. (2015). *CASEL guide: Effective social and emotional learning programs*. Chicago: Collaborative for Academic, Social, and Emotional Learning. Retrieved from www.casel.org/guide/

Castro, A. J., Kelly, J., & Shih, M. (2010). Resilience strategies for new teachers in high-needs areas. *Teaching and Teacher Education, 26*, 622–629. https://doi.org/10.1016/j.tate.2009.09.010.

Chan, D. W. (2008). Emotional intelligence, self-efficacy, and coping among Chinese prospective and in-service teachers in Hong Kong. *Educational Psychology, 28*(4), 397–408. https://doi.org/10.1080/01443410701668372.

Chan, D. W. (2011). Burnout and life satisfaction: Does gratitude intervention make a difference among Chinese school teachers in Hong Kong? *Educational Psychology, 31*(7), 809–823. https://doi.org/10.1080/01443410.2011.608525.

Chong, S., & Low, E.-L. (2009). Why I want to teach and how I feel about teaching – Formation of teacher identity from pre-service to the beginning teacher phase. *Educational Research Policy and Practice, 8*, 59–72. https://doi.org/10.1007/s10671-008-9056-z.

Curry, J. R., & O'Brien, E. R. (2012). Shifting to a wellness paradigm in teacher education: A promising practice for fostering teacher stress reduction, burnout resilience, and promoting retention. *Ethical Human Psychology and Psychiatry, 14*(3), 178–191. https://doi.org/10.1891/1559-4343.14.3.178.

Day, C. (2008). Committed for life? Variations in teachers' work, lives and effectiveness. *Journal of Educational Change, 9*(3), 243–260. https://doi.org/10.1007/s10833-007-9054-6.

Day, C., & Gu, Q. (2010). *The new lives of teachers*. London: Routledge Taylor & Francis Group.

Day, C., & Gu, Q. (2014). *Resilient teachers, resilient schools: Building and sustaining quality in testing times*. Oxon: Routledge.

Dicke, T., Elling, J., Schmeck, A., & Leutner, D. (2015). Reducing reality shock: The effects of classroom management skills training on beginning teachers. *Teaching and Teacher Education, 48*(0), 1–12. https://doi.org/10.1016/j.tate.2015.01.013.

Ebersöhn, L. (2014). Teacher resilience: Theorizing resilience and poverty. *Teachers and Teaching, 20*(5), 568–594. https://doi.org/10.1080/13540602.2014.937960.

Ee, J., & Chang, A. (2010). How resilient are our graduate trainee teachers in Singapore? *The Asia-Pacific Education Researcher, 19*(2), 321–331. https://doi.org/10.3860/taper.v19i2.1600.

Gallant, A., & Riley, P. (2014). Early career teacher attrition: New thoughts on an intractable problem. *Teacher Development, 18*(4), 562–580. https://doi.org/10.1080/13664530.2014.945129.

Gardner, S. (2011). Stress among prospective teachers: A review of the literature. *Australian Journal of Teacher Education, 36*(1), 18–28.

Garrison, D. R. (2011). *E-Learning in the 21st century: A framework for research and practice* (2nd ed.). London: Routledge/Falmer.

Goldstein, L. S. (2005). Becoming a teacher as a hero's journey: Using metaphor in preservice teacher education. *Teacher Education Quarterly, 32*(1), 7–24.

Gu, Q., & Day, C. (2013). Challenges to teacher resilience: Conditions count. *British Educational Research Journal, 39*(1), 22–44. https://doi.org/10.1080/01411926.2011.623152.

Gu, Q., & Li, Q. (2013). Sustaining resilience in times of change: Stories from Chinese teachers. *Asia-Pacific Journal of Teacher Education, 41*(3), 288–303. https://doi.org/10.1080/1359866X.2013.809056.

Huisman, S., Singer, N. R., & Catapano, S. (2010). Resiliency to success: Supporting novice urban teachers. *Teacher Development: An International Journal of Teachers' Professional Development, 14*(4), 483–499. https://doi.org/10.1080/13664530.2010.533490.

Jennings, P. A., Frank, J. L., Snowberg, K. E., Coccia, M. A., & Greenberg, M. T. (2013). Improving classroom learning environments by Cultivating Awareness and Resilience in Education (CARE): Results of a randomized controlled trial. *School Psychology Quarterly, 28*(4), 374–390. https://doi.org/10.1037/spq0000035.

Johnson, G., & Broadley, T. (2012). Web-based active learning and frequent feedback: Engaging first-year university students. In A. Herrington, J. Schrape, & K. Singh (Eds.), *Engaging students with learning technologies* (pp. 77–96). Perth: Curtin University.

Kaspereen, D. (2012). Relaxation intervention for stress reduction among teachers and staff. *International Journal of Stress Management, 19*(3), 238–250. https://doi.org/10.1037/a0029195.

Le Cornu, R. (2009). Building resilience in pre-service teachers. *Teaching and Teacher Education, 25*(5), 717–723. https://doi.org/10.1016/j.tate.2008.11.016.

Mansfield, C. F., & Wosnitza, M. (2014). *Teacher resilience scales*. Perth/Aachen: Murdoch University, RWTH Aachen University.

Mansfield, C. F., Beltman, S., Price, A., & McConney, A. (2012). "Don't sweat the small stuff": Understanding teacher resilience at the chalkface. *Teaching and Teacher Education, 28*, 357–367. https://doi.org/10.1016/j.tate.2011.11.001.

Mansfield, C. F., Beltman, S., Broadley, T., & Weatherby-Fell, N. (2016a). Building resilience in teacher education: An evidenced informed framework. *Teaching and Teacher Education, 54*, 77–87. https://doi.org/10.1016/j.tate.2015.11.016.

Mansfield, C. F., Beltman, S., Weatherby-Fell, N., & Broadley, T. (2016b). Classroom ready?: Building resilience in teacher education. In R. Brandenberg, S. McDonough, J. Burke, & S. White (Eds.), *Teacher education – innovation, interventions and impact* (pp. 211–229). Singapore: Springer.

Mayer, D. (2014). Forty years of teacher education in Australia: 1974–2014. *Journal of Education for Teaching, 40*(5), 461–473. https://doi.org/10.1080/02607476.2014.956536.

Meister, D. G., & Ahrens, P. (2011). Resisting plateauing: Four veteran teachers' stories. *Teaching and Teacher Education, 27*, 770–778. https://doi.org/10.1016/j.tate.2011.01.002.

Moore, K. A. (2003). The Deakin coping scale: Strategies for the management of demands. *Australian Journal of Advanced Nursing, 21*(2), 13–19.

Moore, J., Dickson-Deane, C., & Galyen, K. (2011). E-Learning, online learning, and distance learning environments: Are they the same? *Internet and Higher Education, 14*, 129–135. https://doi.org/10.1016/j.iheduc.2010.10.001.

Morgan, M. (2011). Resilience and recurring adverse events: Testing an assets-based model of beginning teachers' experiences. *The Irish Journal of Psychology, 32*(3–4), 92–104. https://doi.org/10.1080/03033910.2011.613189.

Muller, S. M., Gorrow, T. R., & Fiala, K. A. (2011). Considering protective factors as a tool for teacher resiliency. *Education, 131*(3), 545–555.

Naveh, G., Tubin, T., & Pliskin, N. (2010). Student LMS use and satisfaction in academic institutions: The organizational perspective. *The Internet and Higher Education, 13*, 127–133. https://doi.org/10.1016/j.iheduc.2010.02.004.

O'Donnell, E., Lawless, S., Sharp, M., & Wade, V. (2015). A review of personalised e-learning: Towards supporting learner diversity. *International Journal of Distance Education Technologies, 13*(1), 22–47. https://doi.org/10.4018/ijdet.2015010102.

Papatraianou, L. H., & Le Cornu, R. (2014). Problematising the role of personal and professional relationships in early career teacher resilience. *Australian Journal of Teacher Education, 39*(1), 100–116. 10.14221/ajte.2014v39n1.7.

Peters, J., & Pearce, J. (2012). Relationships and early career teacher resilience: A role for school principals. *Teachers and Teaching: Theory and Practice, 18*(2), 249–262. https://doi.org/10.1080/13540602.2012.632266.

Prosser, B. (2008). The role of the personal domain in middle years teachers' work. *Australian Journal of Middle Schooling, 8*(2), 11–16.

Reeves, T. C. (2006). Design research from the technology perspective. In J. V. Akker, K. Gravemeijer, S. McKenney, & N. Nieveen (Eds.), *Educational design research* (pp. 86–109). London: Routledge.

Ryan, M. L., Shochet, I. M., & Stallman, H. M. (2010). Universal online resilience interventions might engage psychologically distressed university students who are unlikely to seek formal help. *Advances in Mental Health, 9*(1), 73–83.

Sammons, P., Day, C., Kington, A., Gu, Q., Stobart, G., & Smees, R. (2007). Exploring variations in teachers' work, lives and their effects on pupils: Key findings and implications from a longitudinal mixed-method study. *British Educational Research Journal, 33*(5), 681–701. https://doi.org/10.1080/01411920701582264.

Schlichte, J., Yssel, N., & Merbler, J. (2005). Pathways to burnout: Case studies in teacher isolation and alienation. *Preventing School Failure, 50*(1), 35–40.

Siu, O. L., Cooper, C. L., & Phillips, D. R. (2014). Intervention studies on enhancing work well-being, reducing burnout, and improving recovery experiences among Hong Kong health care workers and teachers. *International Journal of Stress Management, 21*(1), 69–84. https://doi.org/10.1037/a0033291.

Stallman, H. M. (2011). Embedding resilience within the tertiary curriculum: A feasibility study. *Higher Education Research & Development, 30*(2), 121–133. https://doi.org/10.1080/07294360.2010.509763.

Sullivan, A., & Johnson, B. (2012). Questionable practices? Relying on individual teacher resilience in remote schools. *Australian and International Journal of Rural Education, 22*(3), 101–116.

Tait, M. (2008). Resilience as a contributor to novice teacher success, commitment, and retention. *Teacher Education Quarterly, 35*(4), 57–75.

Wosnitza, M., Delzepich, R., Schwarze, O'Donnel, M., Faust, V., & Camilleri, V. (2018). Enhancing teacher resilience – From self-reflection to professional development. In M. Wosnitza, F. Peixoto, S. Beltman, & C. F. Mansfield (Eds.), *Resilience in education: Concepts, contexts and connections* (pp. 275–288). New York: Springer.

Yonezawa, S., Jones, M., & Singer, N. R. (2011). Teacher resilience in urban schools: The importance of technical knowledge, professional community, and leadership opportunities. *Urban Education, 46*(5), 913–931. https://doi.org/10.1177/0042085911400341.

Zeichner, K. (2010). Rethinking the connections between campus courses and field experiences in college- and university-based teacher education. *Journal of Teacher Education, 61*(1–2), 89–99. https://doi.org/10.1177/0022487109347671.

Chapter 15
Enhancing Teacher Resilience Through Face-to-Face Training: Insights from the ENTREE Project

José Castro Silva, Joana Pipa, Cynthia Renner, Margaret O'Donnell, and Carmel Cefai

Abstract This chapter provides a project overview of the ENhancing Teacher REsilience in Europe (ENTREE) face-to-face training programme aimed to foster teachers' relationships, wellbeing and commitment to education and schooling and, through this, their effectiveness in teaching. Six face-to-face training modules were developed, using the themes of resilience (module 1), relationships in school settings (module 2), emotions and stress management (modules 3 and 4) and pedagogical skills for effective teaching and classroom management (modules 5 and 6). In this chapter, we provide some background to the module development, the theoretical underpinning and structure of each module along with evaluations from the implementation. Implications for further training and development of the programme are discussed.

Teacher resilience has been identified as a significant factor in teachers' ability to cope with the challenges of the teaching profession, in that teachers who possess characteristics of resilience are more likely to persevere in adverse situations, find it easier to adapt to change and ultimately may be less inclined to consider leaving the

---

J. C. Silva (✉) · J. Pipa
ISPA-Instituto Universitário/CIE – ISPA, Lisbon, Portugal
e-mail: jcsilva@ispa.pt; jpipa@ispa.pt

C. Renner
RWTH Aachen University, Aachen, Germany
e-mail: cynthia.breuer@rwth-aachen.de

M. O'Donnell
Dublin City University, Dublin City, Ireland
e-mail: Margaret.Odonnell@spd.dcu.ie

C. Cefai
University of Malta, Msida, Malta
e-mail: carmel.cefai@um.edu.au

M. Wosnitza et al. (eds.), *Resilience in Education*,
https://doi.org/10.1007/978-3-319-76690-4_15

profession (e.g. Beltman et al. 2011). Teacher resilience is neither an individual trait nor a 'state' – rather it refers to the capacity that arises through interactions occurring within educational contexts. Resilience is shaped both by individual and contextual variables that interrelate in dynamic ways to provide risk or protective factors. Resilience can therefore be nurtured through initial training, continuing professional development and supportive networks.

As teacher resilience and wellbeing have become important issues, there has been interest from teachers, employers and educational systems in ways that teacher resilience can be supported. This interest has led to a major international project, ENhancing Teacher REsilience in Europe (ENTREE), involving partners from Germany, Ireland, Malta, Portugal and Australia.

In support of enhancing and developing teacher resilience, a main outcome of the ENTREE project was a face-to-face training programme to be used for professional development of pre-service or in-service teachers to enhance teachers' resilience. The programme consists of six modules and programme training materials and activities intended to help trainers apply and adapt the generic information to their own specific cultural context. Teacher educators may find the theoretical sections particularly useful in informing their own teacher preparation programmes. Those engaged in continuous professional development (CPD) for teachers may choose to focus on the more practical, in-class applications. All professionals using this programme may find it beneficial to adapt the information to suit their particular cultural and educational context.

Development and Implementation of the Training Modules

Six modules were developed to reflect the whole spectrum of 'teacher resilience' as outlined in ENTREE's theoretical framework and explored in the TRSR (Teacher Resilience Self-Reflection) assessment tool. Whilst module 1 (resilience) was mandatory, participants could freely choose from the remaining modules regarding relationships, wellbeing, health, stress and coping and pedagogical skills, according to their personal identified needs.

Workshops and peer group mentoring were implemented in all four European ENTREE partner institutions. Each module description supplied detailed information both about study materials and the approaches that were used. Workshop formats were participant-oriented in that they focused on a combination of theoretical background reading and material such as case studies analysed individually or in small groups. Discussions and debates, simulations and role-playing were an integral part of workshops in order to engage students and early-career teachers and to combine analytic tasks and second-hand experiences for a fuller understanding of resilience-related problems and potential solutions. Workshops and seminars were constituted in groups not exceeding 20–25 participants, and recorded seminars were made available so that participants could have the opportunity to apply for a particular module at any given time.

The next sections give an overview of the modules before discussing the evaluation.

Module 1: Resilience

Theoretical Background

Research evidence suggests that students of highly committed teachers are more likely to perform better academically than their peers whose teachers are not able to sustain their commitment (Day et al. 2007). In recent years, the demands on schools and teachers have increasingly become more complex as teachers, at a national level, are being asked to improve their schools, to respond in a more effective manner to higher social and economic expectations and to transform educational outcomes, often under difficult conditions. In addition, teachers need to deal with a wider diversity of students' needs and keep abreast of innovations in curriculum, pedagogy, assessment and digital learning (Organisation for Economic Co-operation and Development – OECD 2011). This has led to increased stress and burnout within teaching which has been characterised as a profession that is 'emotionally taxing and potentially frustrating' (Lambert et al. 2006, p. 105), resulting in teachers leaving the profession at a significantly higher rate in comparison to other professions (Minarik et al. 2003). The departure rate of newly qualified teachers is even higher with the number of teachers who leave the profession within the first 5 years ranging from one third to one half (Hanushek 2007; Ingersoll and Smith 2003).

Whilst the research focus was formerly on teacher attrition, due to stress and burnout, more recently the focus has moved to examine the attitudes and behaviours of teachers who remain in the profession and maintain their commitment and engagement, despite experiencing challenges (Day and Gu 2007; Gordon and Coscarelli 1996; Howard and Johnson 2004). What makes the difference between the 'stayers' and the 'leavers'? Findings from the study by Hong (2010) revealed that despite similar interest in working as a teacher, when presented with challenging circumstances, 'leavers' showed weaker self-efficacy beliefs than 'stayers'. In addition, 'leavers' held beliefs that imposed heavy burdens on themselves with respect to student achievement which may have created stress and emotional burnout. Unlike 'leavers', 'stayers' often reported effective strategies that they had developed to prevent themselves from being burnt out, such as setting boundaries in their relationships with students. In conclusion, the study points to the fact that the 'stayers' were showing more resilience skills than 'leavers' (Hong 2010).

Overview of the Module

Resilience is the quality that enables teachers to meet the everyday demands of the teaching profession that endeavours to prepare students with the best educational outcomes for lifelong learning. This module aims to enable teachers to reflect on what they already know about resilience, discuss how resilience is currently defined and described in the literature, explore challenges that impact on teachers' lives at different career stages, discuss the importance of building relationships in support of teacher resilience, examine the different scenarios that impact on resilience (risk and protective factors) and explore how and in what manner teachers can be resilient.

Module 2: Relationships in School Settings

Theoretical Background

School climate have an important influence on individuals, including students, parents, school personnel and the whole school community (Cohen et al. 2009). Teachers who work in a collegial environment and perceive a positive school climate are likely to be more motivated and satisfied, more energetic and enthusiastic and more open to personal and professional development (Cefai and Cavioni 2014; Cohen et al. 2009). Literature suggests that when teachers feel supported by both the principal and their peers, they are more committed to their profession (Singh and Billingsley 1998). Conversely, a lack of appropriate support may add to early teachers' sense of incompetence, as well as create feelings of isolation and alienation, which eventually may contribute to the teachers' decision to leave their profession (Peters and Pearce 2012). A positive school climate is also associated with the development of teachers' beliefs that they can positively influence student learning (Hoy and Woolfolk 1993). Furthermore, research has shown that school climate enhances or minimises teacher/staff emotional exhaustion, depersonalisation and feelings of low personal accomplishment (Grayson and Alvarez 2008) as well as attrition (Miller et al. 1999). Teachers' perceptions of resilience are dependent on the organisational conditions of their work and lives (e.g. teachers' trust in school board, colleagues, students and parents) and the nature of relationships created with peers (Gu and Day 2013; Gu and Li 2013). Positive relationships sustain teachers' careers, and consolidate their sense of self-worth, connection and belonging (e.g. Le Cornu 2013; Cefai and Cavioni 2014) and may contribute to the sustainability of resilience (Papatraianou and Le Cornu 2014). Positive relationships also predict positive adaptation, which helps the teacher avoid frustration, distress, burnout, depression, aggression and withdrawal (Ebersöhn 2012).

Overview of the Module

This module comprises three workshops and addressed the following general themes: school climate as a risk and protective factor of teacher resilience, communication flows in the organisation and its impacts on school climate, supportive networks (personal and professional) and community building in school, communication for effective relationships and relationship skills and teacher resilience.

Module 3: Emotions and Stress Management

Theoretical Background

Nurturing teachers' emotional health is a central element of resilience (Day and Gu 2007). Coping skills and emotional regulation are referred as key aspects of a resilient teacher (Mansfield et al. 2012; Sharplin et al. 2011; Tait 2008). Several studies claim that teacher education programmes should address emotional competencies such as self-regulation, empathy, social skills and emotion regulation strategies (e.g. Hagenauer and Volet 2014; Tait 2008), because it has been identified that emotions are at the heart of teaching (Hargreaves 1998). Teachers experience a wide range of emotions from more positive (e.g. joy, humour) to more negative ones (e.g. anger, frustration) (Hargreaves 1998, 2000; Sutton and Wheatley 2003), and these emotions affect and are affected by teaching and learning and by the relationships between students, teachers, colleagues and school leaders (Cross and Hong 2012; Hagenauer and Volet 2014; Hargreaves 2000; Jennings and Greenberg 2009). Teachers often report the importance of emotional regulation (Fried 2011; Gross 1998) in order to accomplish their goals (Sutton 2004), to manage their classrooms and to establish healthy relationships (Jennings and Greenberg 2009). On the other hand, positive emotions play an important role in teacher resilience, motivation and practice (Hagenauer and Volet 2014; Morgan et al. 2010), broadening one's thoughts and actions (e.g. play, explore), helping to build enduring personal resources (Fredrickson 2001) and promoting good teaching practices (Hargreaves 1998, 2000). The dynamic approach proposed by Collaborative for Academic, Social, and Emotional Learning (CASEL) to help teachers to create a safe, satisfying, caring and productive school environment (Brackett and Katulak 2006; CASEL 2014; Jennings and Greenberg 2009) identified key competencies of social and emotional learning (SEL). These included self-awareness, self-management, social awareness, relationship skills and responsible decision-making. SEL also has a critical role in improving children's academic performance and learning (Durlak et al. 2011; Zins et al. 2004).

Maintaining one's health as a teacher is a central prerequisite to achieve resilience in the face of professional challenges (Day and Gu 2007). An overall key element in this process is found in a wholesome work-life balance. There is evidence in the literature of a close link between the psychological and emotional stability of an individual and his or her physical wellbeing (Day 2014). This indicates that aspects of corporeality and mindfulness with regard to one's physical health deserve greater attention within the overall framework of teachers' resilience (Mansfield et al. 2012). Research (e.g. Clauss-Ehlers 2008; Tait 2008) also supports the view that effective time management can contribute significantly towards this goal. A variety of stress management skills specific to the teaching profession should be available and selectively applied depending on contextual factors, thus enabling the teacher to actively control the situation in the classroom (Tables 15.1 and 15.2).

Table 15.1 Overview of the module 'resilience'

Overview of workshop 1: the concept of teacher resilience	
Themes	Importance of resilience in supporting the quality of teaching and learning
	Resilience as a process that needs to be nurtured and developed over time
	Challenges that impact on teachers' lives at different career stages
Aims	Reflect on their current understanding of resilience
	Understand how and in what way resilience is currently understood in the literature
	Understand why resilience is important in dealing with the everyday challenges of the teaching profession
	Understand how resilience contributes to quality teaching and learning and increased outcomes for pupils
	Understand how resilience can be nurtured and developed over a lifetime teaching career
Content	Definition and concept of teacher resilience
	Relation between resilience and quality teaching
	Development of resilience during a teaching career
Training activities	Discussion as to the many uses of the word resilience
	Lecturing about resilience as a multidimensional construct
	Brainstorming about challenges that teachers may experience over different stages of their careers based on two videos ('why is resilience important to teachers' and 'why is teacher resilience important?')
	Case study discussion
Overview of workshop 2: impact factors	
Themes	Dimensions that impact on resilience at a personal level
	Impact of macro-, meso- and micro-factors on teacher resilience
	Risk and protective factors that impact on resilience
Aims	Understand the factors that impact on teachers' resilience at different levels
	Understand the risk and protective factors that contribute to resilience
	Discuss how and in what manner teachers can protect, sustain and develop their resilience in support of quality teaching and learning
	Understand how they will access and engage in the self-directed online learning modules in support of teacher resilience
Content	Examine the different dimensions that impact on resilience at a personal level
	Discuss the impact of macro-, meso- and micro-factors on teacher resilience
	Explore the risk and protective factors that impact on resilience
Training activities	Lecturing on the factors that impact on teacher resilience
	Small group discussion based on worksheets including statements
	Participants explore the risk and protective factors in support of teacher resilience by completing a worksheet on resilience doughnut reflection

Overview of the Module

The module on emotional wellbeing was developed based on the elements of the social and emotional learning model (Brackett and Katulak 2006; CASEL 2014; Jennings and Greenberg 2009). In its three workshops (Table 15.3), the following themes were addressed: emotional self-awareness, emotional regulation, positive

Table 15.2 Overview of the module 'relationships in school setting'

Overview of workshop 1: school climate and teacher resilience	
Themes	School climate and culture
	Organisational climate and commitment
Aims	Appreciate the importance of school climate for teacher resilience
	Identify ways to promote a positive school climate and foster interpersonal effectiveness
Content	Definitions of school climate and culture
	Dimensions of school climate and school climate types
	Measuring and promoting a positive school climate
Training activities	Lecturing about the multidimensionality of school climate
	Brainstorming about school climate types and measuring school climate
	Demonstration of school climate measurement through the manipulation of assessment tools
	Large group discussion on the key factors contributing to a positive school climate
Overview of workshop 2: communication for effective relationships and teacher resilience	
Themes	Communication for effective relationships
	Improving communication and resolving conflict constructively
Aims	Apply effective strategies to communicate with different target groups according to the situational context
	Apply effective strategies to deal with concrete conflict situations
Content	Challenges to communication and effective communication in schools
	Skills for communicating and managing resistance and negativity and problem-solving strategies
Training activities	Lecturing focused on the communication and the role of school principals
	Small group discussion based on worksheets including statements
	Scenarios describing problem-solving strategies
Overview of workshop 3: supportive networks, relationships and teacher resilience	
Themes	Supportive networks and community building in school
	Relationship skills
Aims	To identify existing networks in their professional context
	Develop healthy teacher-parent partnerships
Content	Collaborative teamwork
	Managing interpersonal conflict
	Teacher-parent partnerships
Training activities	Lecturing about the components of a collaborative teamwork
	Scenarios describing the benefits of teacher collaboration and building positive home-school relationships
	Group-based project to plan a guide that could be used by teachers to improve home-school communication and partnerships

emotions, emotional social awareness, empathy, relationship skills, reflective listening and assertiveness. The focus on these competencies is expected to help participants in recognising and understanding their own and others' emotions; being able to regulate their emotions effectively in different situations and understand the relevance of positive emotions in education, perspective taking and empathising with

Table 15.3 Overview of the module 'emotional wellbeing'

Overview of workshop 1: emotions, self-awareness and emotion regulation	
Themes	Self-awareness
	Self-management/emotion regulation
Aims	Identify and understand one's feelings and emotions and strengths and limitations
	Apply different effective emotion management strategies to cope with several situations in the school setting
Content	Teaching as an emotional activity
	Definition of emotions, emotional literacy and emotional process
	Definition of self-awareness, recognising and understanding individual emotions and feelings, being aware of personal strengths and limitations
	Presentation and discussion about different emotion management/regulation strategies
Training activities	Lecturing about the relevance of emotions in education and about the conceptual definition of emotions and the dimensions of SEL
	Identification of most experienced emotions in school setting and the situations related to those emotions
	Producing an individual list of participants' roles and the emotions related to them
	Group discussion on a scenario describing a situation involving emotions in the classroom
	Distribution of a layout for an emotions diary
Overview of workshop 2: self-management/emotion regulation	
Themes	Self-management/emotion regulation
Aims	Apply effective strategies to manage emotions
	Reflect on the applicability of different management strategies
Content	Self-management/emotion regulation
Training activities	Group discussion/reflection about personal emotional situations and the emotion management strategies applied
	Role-play of different scenarios involving teachers', parents' and student's interactions. Final group discussion about the emotions and feelings triggered by each scenario and the emotion regulation strategies used
Overview of workshop 3: positive emotions, empathy and assertiveness	
Themes	The importance of positive emotions as constituents of teacher resilience
	Social awareness: understand and identify others' emotions and be empathetic with others
	Assertiveness
Aims	Understand the importance of positive emotions in teacher resilience and identify some strategies to increase them
	Understand others' emotions and demonstrate empathy towards them
	Assertively communicate one's thoughts and feelings
Content	Positive emotions
	Social awareness
	Assertiveness
Training activities	Case scenario on positive emotions analysing two different strategies to deal to the same setback
	Lecturing about positive emotions, identification of individual positive emotions and strategies to increase them
	Role-play scenarios exploring aggressive, passive and assertive behaviours

Table 15.4 Overview of the module 'stress management'

Overview of workshop 1: stress management	
Themes	Stress theories
	Self-efficacy through mindfulness
	Emotion-oriented coping strategies
	Irrational beliefs vs. professional self-concept
	Resources for dealing with challenges
Aims	Discuss research evidence on stress management skills and coping strategies
	Understanding the interconnection between emotional/psychic and physical wellbeing
	Development of a professional self-concept comprising a healthy work-life balance and time management
	Acquiring coping strategies and autonomously selecting suitable stress management skills in a situational context
	Effective communication with colleagues/students in a simulated context (e.g. role-plays)
Content	Information on stress theories
	Experiment regarding the mind-body relationship
	Ideas and approaches for the prevention or interruption of stress – causing anticipations
	Exercise for the recognition of individual irrational beliefs and support in finding realistic convictions
	Exercise for a conscious perception of positive experiences and occurrences
Training activities	Lecturing about stress theories
	Group discussion on teacher's professional self-concept

others; as well as establishing and maintaining positive relationships and making responsible choices.

The module about stress management (Table 15.4) covered the following themes: stress theories, self-efficacy and emotion-oriented coping strategies, irrational beliefs vs. professional self-concept and resources for coping with the challenges in the teaching profession.

Module 4: Pedagogical Skills

Theoretical Background

A review on risk and protective factors in the resilience literature shows that negative self-beliefs and classroom management issues related to disruptive students were the most common personal and contextual risk factors (Beltman et al. 2011). Results from a recent study indicate a strong relationship between classroom management self-efficacy (CMSE) and the three dimensions of burnout (emotional exhaustion, depersonalisation and personal accomplishment), suggesting that teachers with higher levels of CMSE are less likely to experience burnout (Aloe et al.

2014). Research (Cefai and Cavioni 2014; Hong 2012; Kersaint et al. 2007) suggests that interventions aimed to foster teacher resilience and reduce teacher attrition should employ measures to help teachers address issues and solve problems more effectively. Specifically, programmes should be developed to enhance teachers' classroom management skills both during initial teacher and in-service education programmes.

Teaching effectively and efficiently has often been identified as a keystone for enhancing resilience (Mansfield et al. 2012). As well as motivational, social and emotional aspects, there were also those aspects which are more profession-related such as being reflective, flexible and adaptable. Whilst effectiveness mainly concerns the learning outcomes, efficiency has to do with teachers' preparation. Becoming more efficient helps the teacher to achieve his/her goals with less effort and thus enhances effectiveness. It has been identified that effectiveness and efficiency are strongly connected to the maintenance of motivation and commitment and result in quality teaching (Day and Gu 2007). Resilient teachers are also seen to be effective teachers, namely, being organised and prepared, committed to their students and able to manage their time efficiently.

Overview of the Module

The module covering pedagogical skills for effective teaching includes a series of workshops that focus on some of the key aspects of a resilient teacher, such as participants engaging in reflection about their own and others' teaching practices. Resilient teachers engage in reflection (Johnson et al. 2014; Leroux et al. 2010), and this whole module requires teachers to be reflective. Another example is maintaining a positive work-life balance which can be helped by effective time management strategies which can help reduce teacher stress (Curry and O'Brien 2011; Knight et al. 2010; Thieman et al. 2012). This module explores factors that contribute to quality teaching and learning as identified in the literature. In addition, it gives space for the practical application of resources, materials and strategies for teachers at school and class levels. Workshop 1 gives an overall introduction by giving a first idea on how effective teaching is linked to teacher resilience and presenting all topics mentioned above. Workshops 2 and 3 focus on assisting participants to find ways to become more efficient in their work. Workshop 2 examines ways to reorganise the classroom, so that the teacher has less work preparing the lesson, and may consider reducing the time-consuming and frustrating production of materials and lesson plans through the use of social media (Burden and Byrd 2013). Paperwork such as marking student work is daunting and therefore a potential risk factor for stress. Strategies to restructure and organise paperwork are covered in Workshop 3. Another step towards becoming an efficient teacher and enhancing effectiveness is improving communication. Effective communication is the result of good questioning in combination with a congruency of tone and body language with the content (Walsh and Sattes 2005).

The module on pedagogical skills for classroom management aims to identify classroom management principles and discuss why classroom management influences teacher resilience, to identify the strategies that can be used to successfully manage a learning environment and to discuss how to assess behavioural problems and manage behaviour effectively in the classroom. This module contains three workshops and addresses the general themes of proactive and positive classroom management strategies, affective and social aspects of teacher-student relationships and effective assessment and management of behaviour difficulties (ABCs Model by Hill and Parsons 2012).

Evaluation of the Training Modules

Method

The face-to-face training pilot project was conducted in four countries, namely, Germany, Ireland, Malta and Portugal. In Germany, there were a total of 160 participants specialising in secondary school education. In Ireland, participants included 23 teachers and 1 principal from a school serving an educationally disadvantaged community. In Malta the workshop was organised with 82 third year undergraduate education students at the University of Malta, mostly primary school student-teachers; 65 of these completed the evaluation sheet. The Portuguese participants consisted of 11 postgraduate students studying to become primary school teachers.

In all countries, the training sessions were conducted in workshops focused on the module themes and involving learning activities such as presentations, individual tasks, discussions and small group work. Each workshop lasted between 3 and 4 h and was conducted by qualified teacher educators who were involved in the design of the programme. Participants (undergraduate and postgraduate students and teachers) volunteered to complete an anonymous evaluation form at the end of the training. The evaluation form asked participants to indicate the extent to which they agreed or disagreed with statements about the workshop's structure (e.g. the structure was clear and easy to follow; the materials supported the content addressed; there were opportunities for active participation; the suggested strategies and activities supported the development of more resilience strategies) and content (e.g. the workshop was useful and interesting; the workshop helped to develop skills). Participants also responded to open-ended questions, such as: What were the most helpful aspects of the training session? What were the least helpful aspects? Do you have any suggestions for improvements?

Findings

Structure and Process

Overall, in most countries, the workshop structure was found to be useful, with most participants stating that they were satisfied with the structure, materials, objectives and resources. The majority of participants in all countries stated that the structure of the workshops was clear, the materials were appropriate and supported the content presented and the objectives of the workshops were useful and comprehensive. Half of the participants in Ireland indicated that the theoretical background helped them understand the context for the workshop on resilience, whilst the majority of participants in Malta and Portugal responded positively to the theoretical introduction, with most participants indicating that they agreed or strongly agreed. The German participants commented that the workshop structure presented a good balance between theory and discussion, where the students were invited to share their own experiences. The topics introduced in the workshop were also seen by most participants as specific to the content, with the majority agreeing that there was opportunity for active participation. The suggested strategies were also seen as useful accompanied by valuable activities and resources. In Germany, participants reported that the PowerPoint presentation was well structured and easy to follow, including the diagrams and the videos. However, the students commented that the groups, which were made up of 35–42 students, were too large. The participants also requested more 'real life' examples and case studies to be included in the workshops. The Irish participants commented that the workshop served to enhance their skills through their engagement with other colleagues and through completing the interactive activities. In Malta, the great majority of student-teachers claimed that the activities were interesting and were seen as potential reference points in their future careers. In Portugal, the structure of Module 2 and 3 was unanimously seen as useful and beneficial more than Module 1; some participants disagreed with the clarity of the structure and objectives and the usefulness of strategies and activities to develop resilience presented in the latter module.

Content

The vast majority of participants in the four countries agreed that the workshops' content was important, useful, interesting and helpful to teachers. They also strongly agreed or agreed that they enjoyed the workshops and that through this training they managed to increase their awareness on certain topics that they might not have considered before. The most helpful aspects of the content across countries were:

- The clarification of main concepts and terms such as resilience, school climate and their importance and impact

- The opportunity for discussion and sharing of own experiences within a group, which brought about greater self-awareness and encouraged participants to engage in self-reflection
- The practical side of the workshop content that focused on how to be more resilient as a teacher by suggesting strategies and providing materials with regard to emotional regulation and behaviour/class management

The participants in Ireland specifically mentioned that the content related to how to deal with stress was very useful, whilst participants in Malta appreciated the case studies presented on challenging behaviour. The participants in Portugal highlighted that the demonstrated impact of resilience on students' academic success was also very useful. The common least helpful aspect of the workshop content in all countries was the lack of time for further discussion as participants wanted more time to interact and engage. Participants in Germany and in Malta commented that the groups they worked in were too big. Specifically, some German participants found the workshop had too much theory, and some Portuguese participants commented that they would have preferred if the videos shown were in their native language rather than in English. When the participants were asked what they would suggest to further improve the training modules, most of the participants in all countries mentioned smaller training groups, having more time specially to discuss and interact more actively with each other in order to hear different perspectives on the issues being discussed, to share their experiences and to engage further in particular activities. They also suggested that the modules should present more case studies and real examples and that the training should focus more on the practicality of being resilient. In Ireland, the participants suggested that the workshop gives greater opportunity for self-reflection. The Irish and Maltese participants agreed that there should be more use of videos, whilst the Maltese and Portuguese suggested more use of role-plays and shorter presentations with less text, emphasising more the workshop format rather than lecture format. The participants in Portugal also mentioned that they would have liked more dynamic activities and that a focus on conflict management strategies (for more details about the importance of this internal resource, see Schwarze and Wosnitza 2018, Chap. 3, this volume) and resilience in children should be added to the training.

Practically all participants in the four countries agreed that the workshop content was important, useful, interesting and helpful to teachers. They also strongly agreed or agreed that they enjoyed the workshops and that through this training they managed to increase their awareness on certain topics that they might not have considered before. The most helpful aspects of the content across countries included the clarification of main concepts and terms such as resilience, school climate and their importance and impact; the opportunity for discussion and sharing of own experiences within a group, which encouraged self-reflection and enhanced self-awareness (see Wosnitza et al. 2018, Chap. 16, this volume); and the practical side of the content that focused on how to be more resilient as a teacher by suggesting strategies and providing materials on emotional regulation and behaviour management.

The least helpful aspect of the workshop content mentioned frequently by participants in all countries was the lack of time for further discussion as participants wanted more time to interact and engage. Some participants also commented that the groups they worked in were too big, and that occasionally there was too much theory. When the participants were asked what they would suggest to further improve the training, one of the most common suggestions by the participants in all countries mentioned smaller training groups, having more time to discuss and interact more actively and to share their experiences and to engage further in particular activities. They also suggested that the modules should present more case studies and real examples and role plays and that the training should focus more on the practicality of being resilient.

Conclusions and Recommendations

Overall, the face-to-face training in all four countries was received positively, with participants agreeing about the usefulness of workshop topics, structure, objectives, materials and activities. Participants also commented that they enjoyed the workshop format focused on practical issues, the opportunity to share, discuss and work in groups, and the introduction to concepts and terms.

The recommendations followed a common trend in all the countries, with participants suggesting that whilst they greatly appreciated the training, future training may be improved by having smaller groups, with more case studies and additional opportunities for sharing and discussion, whilst also making use of videos that demonstrate the proposed strategies being implemented within a classroom setting. Participants also recommended that workshops take on a more practical focus, concentrating on real life experiences with more opportunities for active discussions and self-reflection. As a result of these recommendations, future workshops should involve enough qualified instructors to cater for smaller groups with more room for discussion and interaction. Since the participants preferred discussions and practical examples such as case studies, trainers also need to find a balance between using the training material whilst providing ample time for sharing and discussion. Specific topics might be emphasised in different countries as the students or teachers might have different concerns and challenges or might be interested in different aspects of resilience that is dependent on their specific working context. There is also a need to follow up these training sessions, with time for participants to put into practice what they learned, reflect on the process and outcome and then share these experiences again in a group as part of continuing professional learning (Tables 15.5 and 15.6).

Table 15.5 Overview of the module 'pedagogical skills for effective teaching'

Overview of workshop 1: introduction to effective teaching and learning	
Themes	Organising the classroom and materials
	Communication skills for effective teaching
	Managing student work
	Formative assessment
Aims	Good preparation (efficiency) and setting goals and aims enhance effective teaching
	Know that effective teaching and teacher resilience are linked
	Good preparation is less time-consuming than reworking
	Be aware of the dangers of being too flexible or too rigid
	Understand the concepts of efficiency and effectiveness
Content	Planning and conducting effective teaching
	Preparation is the basis of efficient teaching
	Transparency – always knowing where you are heading
	The difficulty of flexibility
	Becoming more efficient means finding ways to achieve goals more quickly without compromising learning
Training activities	Group/class discussions on inefficient teaching
	Case studies on personal experiences of inefficient teaching experiences
	Demonstrations followed by reports of group discussions
	Video as introduction to the module
Overview of workshop 2: organising classroom and producing materials	
Themes	Practical solutions for improving classroom organisation and materials
Aims	Understand how efficiency in work preparation reduces stress
	Have ideas to organise their classroom more efficiently
	Know where to get help developing new materials
	Organise their paperwork
Content	Preparation improves time management and enhances efficiency
	Furnishing and adapting the classroom to the teacher's needs
	Coming up with lesson plans with the help of social media
	Better organisation of a teacher's paper work
Training activities	PowerPoint slides presentation
	Demonstrations followed by reports of group discussions showing their materials
	Materials in form of ideal classrooms and a list of resources teachers can rely on in future
	Video as a time holder
Overview of workshop 3: managing student work	
Themes	Reorganisation of workload, paperwork and classroom procedures to become more efficient by saving timepreparing lessons
Aims	Realistically estimate their workload
	Organise their paperwork more efficiently
	Rethink their classroom organisation

(continued)

Table 15.5 (continued)

Content	Introduction into order-helpers
	Ordering paperwork efficiently
	Reducing workload
Training activities	Group discussions on organisational methods and strategies
	Class discussions followed by reports of group discussions on how trainees keep order in their chaos
	Group or individual projects including the restructuring of old habits
	Trainees-produced materials
	Video as introduction
Overview of workshop 4: communication skills for effective teaching	
Themes	Effective communication as the basis of teaching as trying to convey knowledge and uphold positive teacher-student relations
Aims	Having identified the complexity of communication
	Improving their directions/instructions
	Knowing the basics of body language
	Communicating in an assertive manner
Content	Communication principles
	Listening
	Questioning
	Body language
	Assertive communication
Training activities	Lecturing with the help of a PowerPoint presentation giving theoretical input
	Group discussion on misleading teachers' communication
	Work sheet activities and use of reading material enhancing personal communication skills as group projects
	Demonstrations followed by reports of group discussions
	Observations

Table 15.6 Overview of the module 'pedagogical skills for classroom management'

Overview of workshop 1	
Theme(s)	Proactive and positive classroom management strategies
Aims	Understand the importance of effective classroom management for teacher resilience
	Identify and apply effective proactive classroom management strategies
Content	Skills for effective classroom management
	Characteristics of an effective teacher
	Classroom management profile
	Proactive classroom management strategies
Training activities	Brainstorming about key characteristics or skills for effective classroom management
	Answering the quiz 'what is your classroom management profile'
	Large group discussion on differences between classroom management styles
	Lecturing about the proactive classroom management strategies
	Scenarios describing different classroom management styles

(continued)

Table 15.6 (continued)

Overview of workshop 2	
Theme(s)	Affective and social aspects of teacher-student relationships
Aims	Identify the different needs of different students (different cultural backgrounds, children with special needs, etc.)
	Be aware of the relevance of socio-emotional needs towards children's behaviour and their wellbeing
Content	Antecedents of emotional and behavioural difficulties
	Building a caring teacher-student relationship
Training activities	Lecturing about the 'model of factors influencing emotional and behavioural difficulties'
	'Case study' describing emotional and behavioural difficulties
Overview of workshop 3	
Themes	Effective behaviour assessment (ABC's model) and management
Aims	Assess misbehaviour using ABCs model
	Plan and implement intervention on the basis of ABC assessment
Content	Understanding the nature and causes of behaviour difficulties
	Identifying and assessing pupil behaviour
	Planning and implementing interventions for behaviour difficulties
Training activities	Lecturing on understanding behaviour difficulties
	Filling in questionnaires and forms (behaviour questionnaires, recording misbehaviour, classroom discipline plan)
	Case study describing socio-emotional difficulties
	Small group discussion and work on developing a class discipline plan

References

Aloe, A. M., Amo, L. C., & Shanahan, M. E. (2014). Classroom management self-efficacy and burnout: A multivariate meta-analysis. *Educational Psychology Review, 26*(1), 101–126. https://doi.org/10.1007/s10648-013-9244-0.

Beltman, S., Mansfield, C. F., & Price, A. (2011). Thriving not just surviving: A review of research on teacher resilience. *Educational Research Review, 6*, 185–207. https://doi.org/10.1016/j.edurev.2011.09.001.

Brackett, M., & Katulak, N. (2006). Emotional intelligence in the classroom: Skill-based training for teachers and students. In J. Ciarrochi & J. D. Mayer (Eds.), *Improving emotional intelligence: A practitioner's guide* (pp. 1–27). New York: Psychology Press/Taylor & Francis.

Burden, P. R., & Byrd, D. M. (2013). *Methods for effective teaching: Meeting the needs of all students*. Boston: Pearson.

Cefai, C., & Cavioni, V. (2014). *Social and emotional education in primary school – integrating theory and research into practice*. New York: Springer. https://doi.org/10.1007/978-1-4614-8752-4.

Clauss-Ehlers, C. S. (2008). Sociocultural factors, resilience, and coping: Support for a culturally sensitive measure of resilience. *Journal of Applied Developmental Psychology, 29*(3), 197–212. https://doi.org/10.1016/j.appdev.2008.02.004.

Cohen, J., McCabe, E. M., Michelli, N., & Pickeral, T. (2009). School climate: Research, policy, teacher education and practice. *Teachers College Record, 111*(1), 180–213.

Collaborative for Academic, Social, and Emotional Learning. (2014). *Social and emotional learning core competencies*. Retrieved from http://www.casel.org/social-and-emotional-learning/core-competencies/

Cross, D., & Hong, J. (2012). An ecological examination of teachers' emotions in the school context. *Teaching and Teacher Education, 28*(7), 957–967. https://doi.org/10.1016/j.tate.2012.05.001.

Curry, J. R., & O'Brien, E. R. (2011). Shifting to a wellness paradigm in teacher education: A promising practice for fostering teacher stress reduction, burnout resilience, and promoting retention. *Ethical Human Psychology and Psychiatry, 14*(3), 178–191. https://doi.org/10.1891/1559-4343.14.3.178.

Day, C. (2014). Resilient principals in challenging schools: The courage and costs of conviction. *Teachers and Teaching: Theory and Practice, 20*(5), 638–654. https://doi.org/10.1080/13540602.2014.937959.

Day, C., & Gu, Q. (2007). Variations in the conditions for teachers' professional learning and development: Sustaining commitment and effectiveness over a career. *Oxford Review of Education – Special Issue, 33*(4), 423–443. https://doi.org/10.1080/03054980701450746.

Day, C., Sammons, P., Stobart, G., Kington, A., & Gu, Q. (2007). *Teachers matter: Connecting work, lives and effectiveness*. Buckingham: Open University Press.

Durlak, J. A., Weissberg, R. P., Dymnicki, A. B., Taylor, R. D., & Schellinger, K. B. (2011). The impact of enhancing students' social and emotional learning: A meta-analysis of school-based universal interventions. *Child Development, 82*(1), 405–432.

Ebersöhn, L. (2012). Adding 'flock' to 'fight and flight': A honeycomb of resilience where supply of relationships meets demand for support. *Journal of Psychology in Africa, 27*(2), 29–42. Retrieved from http://repository.up.ac.za/handle/2263/32120?show=full.

Fredrickson, B. L. (2001). The role of positive emotions in positive psychology: The broaden-and-build theory of positive emotions. *American Psychologist, 56*, 218–226.

Fried, L. (2011). Teaching teachers about emotion regulation in the classroom. *Australian Journal of Teacher Education, 36*, 116–127. https://doi.org/10.14221/ajte.2011v36n3.1.

Gordon, K. A., & Coscarelli, W. C. (1996). Recognising and fostering resilience. *Performance Improvement, 35*(9), 14–17.

Grayson, J. L., & Alvarez, H. K. (2008). School climate factors relating to teacher burnout: A mediator model. *Teaching and Teacher Education, 24*(5), 1349–1363. https://doi.org/10.1016/j.tate.2007.06.005.

Gross, J. (1998). The emerging field of emotion regulation: An integrative review. *Review of General Psychology, 2*, 271–299.

Gu, Q., & Day, C. (2013). Challenges to teacher resilience: Conditions count. *British Educational Research Journal, 39*(1), 22–44. https://doi.org/10.1080/01411926.2011.623152.

Gu, Q., & Li, Q. (2013). Sustaining resilience in times of change: Stories from Chinese teachers. *Asia-Pacific Journal of Teacher Education, 41*(3). https://doi.org/10.1080/1359866X.2013.809056.

Hagenauer, G., & Volet, S. (2014). "I don't hide my feelings, even though I try to": Insight into teacher educator emotion display. *Australian Educational Researcher, 41*, 261–281. https://doi.org/10.1007/s13384-013-0129-5.

Hanushek, E. A. (2007). The single salary schedule and other issues of teacher pay. *Peabody Journal of Education, 82*(4), 574–586.

Hargreaves, A. (1998). The emotional practice of teaching. *Teaching and Teacher Education, 14*, 835–854.

Hargreaves, A. (2000). Mixed emotions: Teachers' perceptions of their interactions with students. *Teaching and Teacher Education, 16*, 811–826. https://doi.org/10.1016/S0742-051X(00)00028-7.

Hill, F., & Parsons, L. (2012). *Teamwork in the management of emotional and behavioural difficulties – resource materials for teachers*. London: Routledge.

Hong, J. Y. (2010). Pre-service and beginning teachers' professional identity and its relation to dropping out of the profession. *Teaching and Teacher Education, 26*(8), 1530–1543. https://doi.org/10.1016/j.tate.2010.06.003.

Hong, J. Y. (2012). Why do some beginning teachers leave the school, and others stay? Understanding teacher resilience through psychological lenses. *Teachers and Teaching: Theory and Practice, 18*(4), 417–440. https://doi.org/10.1080/13540602.2012.696044.

Howard, S., & Johnson, B. (2004). Resilient teachers: Resisting stress and burnout. *Social Psychology of Education, 7*(4), 399–420.

Hoy, W. K., & Woolfolk, A. E. (1993). Teachers' sense of efficacy and the organizational health of schools. *The Elementary School Journal, 93*, 355–372.

Ingersoll, R. M., & Smith, T. M. (2003). The wrong solution to the teacher shortage. *Educational Leadership, 60*(8), 30–33.

Jennings, P., & Greenberg, M. (2009). The prosocial classroom: Teacher social and emotional competence in relation to student and classroom outcomes. *Review of Educational Research, 79*, 491–525. https://doi.org/10.3102/0034654308325693.

Johnson, B., Down, B., Le Cornu, R., Peters, J., Sullivan, A. M., Pearce, J., et al. (2014). Promoting early career teacher resilience: A framework for understanding and acting. *Teachers and Teaching, 20*(5), 530–546. https://doi.org/10.1080/13540602.2014.937957.

Kersaint, G., Lewis, J., Potter, R., & Meisels, G. (2007). Why teachers leave: Factors that influence retention and resignation. *Teaching and Teacher Education, 23*(6), 775–794. https://doi.org/10.1016/j.tate.2005.12.004.

Knight, C., Balatti, J., Haase, M., & Henderson, L. (2010). *Preservice teacher stressors and their reactions to those stressors: Resilient responses.* Paper presented at the Australian Teacher Education Association Conference, Townsville, QLD, Australia.

Lambert, R., O'Donnell, M., Kusherman, J., & McCarthy, C. J. (2006). Teacher stress and classroom structural characteristics in preschool settings. In R. Lambert & C. McCarthy (Eds.), *Understanding teacher stress in an age of accountability* (pp. 105–120). Greenwich: Information Age.

Le Cornu, R. (2013). Building early career teacher resilience: The role of relationships. *Australian Journal of Teacher Education, 38*(4), 1–16. https://doi.org/10.14221/ajte.2013v38n4.4.

Leroux, M., Théorêt, M., & Garon, R. (2010). *Exploration of the relations between teacher resilience and teacher reflection in Inner-City schools.* Paper presented at the 2010 AERA Annual Meeting, Denver, Colorado.

Mansfield, C. F., Beltman, S., Price, A., & McConney, A. (2012). "Don't sweat the small stuff:" Understanding teacher resilience at the chalkface. *Teaching and Teacher Education, 28*(3), 357–367. https://doi.org/10.1016/j.tate.2011.11.001.

Miller, M. D., Brownell, M., & Smith, S. W. (1999). Factors that predict teachers staying in, leaving, or transferring from the special education classroom. *Exceptional Children, 65*, 201–221.

Minarik, M. M., Thornton, B., & Perreault, G. (2003). Systems thinking can improve teacher retention. *The Clearing House: A Journal of Educational Strategies, Issues and Ideas, 76*(5), 230–234. https://doi.org/10.1080/00098650309602010.

Morgan, M., Ludlow, L., Kitching, K., O'Leary, M., & Clarke, A. (2010). What makes teachers tick? Sustaining events in new teachers' lives. *British Educational Research Association, 36*(2), 191–208. https://doi.org/10.1080/01411920902780978.

OECD. (2011). *Building a high quality teaching profession: Lessons from around the world.* Paris: OECD Publishing.

Papatraianou, L. H., & Le Cornu, R. (2014). Problematising the role of personal and professional relationships in early career teacher resilience. *Australian Journal of Teacher Education, 39*(1), 100–116. https://doi.org/10.14221/ajte.2014v39n1.7.

Peters, J., & Pearce, J. (2012). Relationships and early career teacher resilience: A role for school principals. *Teachers and Teaching: Theory and Practice, 18*(2), 249–262. https://doi.org/10.1080/13540602.2012.632266.

Schwarze, J., & Wosnitza, M. (2018). How does apprentice resilience work? The conceptualisation of a generic process model of resilience and its application to vocational settings. In M. Wosnitza, F. Peixoto, S. Beltman, & C. F. Mansfield (Eds.), *Resilience in education: Concepts, contexts and connections* (pp. 35–51). New York: Springer.

Sharplin, E., O'Neill, M., & Chapman, A. (2011). Coping strategies for adaptation to new teacher appointments: Intervention for retention. *Teaching and Teacher Education, 27*, 136–146. https://doi.org/10.1016/j.tate.2010.07.010.

Singh, K., & Billingsley, B. (1998). Professional support and its effects on teachers' commitment. *The Journal of Educational Research, 91*, 229–239.

Sutton, R. E. (2004). Emotional regulation goals and strategies of teachers. *Social Psychology of Education, 7*(4), 379–398. https://doi.org/10.1007/s11218-004-4229-y.

Sutton, R. E., & Wheatley, K. F. (2003). Teachers' emotions and teaching: A review of the literature and directions for future research. *Educational Psychological Review, 15*(4), 327–358. https://doi.org/10.1023/A:1026131715856.

Tait, M. (2008). Resilience as a contributor to novice teacher success, commitment, and retention. *Teacher Education Quarterly, 35*(4), 57–75.

Thieman, E. B., Henry, A. L., & Kitchel, T. (2012). Resilient agricultural educators: Taking stress to the next level. *Journal of Agricultural Education, 53*(1), 81–94. https://doi.org/10.5032/jae.2012.01081.

Walsh, J. A., & Sattes, B. D. (2005). *Quality questioning: Research-based practice to engage every learner*. Thousand Oaks: Corwin Press.

Wosnitza, M., Delzepich, R., Schwarze, J., O'Donnell, M., Faust, V., & Camilleri, V. (2018). Enhancing teacher resilience – from self-reflection to professional development. In M. Wosnitza, F. Peixoto, S. Beltman, & C. F. Mansfield (Eds.), *Resilience in education: Concepts, contexts and connections* (pp. 275–288). New York: Springer.

Zins, J. E., Bloodworth, M. R., Weissberg, R. P., & Walberg, H. J. (2004) The scientific base linking social and emotional learning to school success. J. E. Zins, R. P. Weissberg, M. C. Wang & H. J. Walberg, Building academic success on social and emotional learning: What does the research say? (3–22). New York: Teachers College Press.

Chapter 16
Enhancing Teacher Resilience: From Self-Reflection to Professional Development

Marold Wosnitza, Ralph Delzepich, Jennifer Schwarze, Margaret O'Donnell, Vera Faust, and Vanessa Camilleri

Abstract Self-reflection is a crucial element of enhancing personal resilience. The TRSR (Teacher Resilience Self-Reflection) tool is an instrument that can be used by teachers to identify protective and risk factors related to their professional resilience. It is a web-based instrument, with scales adapted, developed and validated for this specific application which reflect the factors that contribute to teacher resilience as outlined in the theoretical framework discussed in this chapter. The TRSR gives users specific individual feedback regarding which aspects of resilience could be enhanced online or in face-to-face workshops. It also gives trainers information regarding their learning group so that they can tailor the workshops to the specific needs of their participants. This chapter gives an overview of the theoretical framework and the TRSR which serves to guide the reflection process. In addition, it details how to use the TRSR and it discusses its educational potential.

M. Wosnitza (✉)
Institute of Education, RWTH Aachen University, Aachen, Germany

School of Education, Murdoch University, Perth, WA, Australia
e-mail: marold.wosnitza@rwth-aachen.de

R. Delzepich · J. Schwarze · V. Faust
Institute of Education, RWTH Aachen University, Aachen, Germany
e-mail: ralph.delzepich@rwth-aachen.de; jennifer.schwarze@rwth-aachen.de; vera.faust@rwth-aachen.de

M. O'Donnell
Dublin City University, Dublin, Ireland
e-mail: margaret.odonnell@dcu.ie

V. Camilleri
University of Malta, Msida, Malta
e-mail: vanessa.camilleri@um.edu.mt

M. Wosnitza et al. (eds.), *Resilience in Education*,
https://doi.org/10.1007/978-3-319-76690-4_16

The project *ENhancing Teacher REsilience in Europe* (ENTREE)[1] is informed by the need to safeguard and promote teachers' resilience and well-being in a profession that has become more complex and potentially more challenging. It is based on the broadly shared understanding that resilience is a key variable that can help teachers to deal with the challenges of a rapidly changing school context and perceived increasing demands, such as pupils' behavioural issues (Gibbs and Miller 2014) or lack of administrative support (Kersaint et al. 2007).

Whilst for decades the focus of resilience research ignored the lives of teachers, in recent times teacher resilience is centre stage (e.g., Ebersöhn 2014; Gu and Day 2007; Mansfield et al. 2016). This change of interest goes along with a move from a reactive perspective on teachers' well-being (e.g., teacher burnout) to a more proactive perspective on how to help teachers to be prepared for their demanding profession. The core of this discussion addresses the question of how teachers handle and experience challenges in their daily life and their profession (e.g., Lohbeck 2018, Chap. 6, this volume; Mansfield et al. 2012).

It is commonly understood that teachers show resilience when they are able to adapt their goals and adjust their beliefs (e.g., teacher efficacy or commitment) (e.g., McInerney et al. 2015; Tait 2008) and behaviours when they encounter challenges and are able to find support in school and in their personal environment. Conversely, teachers who respond in non-resilient ways to challenges may show limited social, emotional, professional and motivational capacity for adaptation and may have counterproductive beliefs like low levels of efficacy, job commitment and limited support at school and in their personal lives which may impact on effectively coping with situations perceived as challenging. In this regard, ENTREE defines teacher resilience as:

> …the process of, capacity for, and outcome of positive adaptation as well as ongoing professional commitment and growth in the face of challenging circumstances. Resilience is shaped by individual, situational and broader contextual characteristics that interrelate in dynamic ways to provide risk (challenging) or protective (supportive) factors. Individuals, drawing on personal, professional and social resources, not only "bounce back" but also are able to thrive professionally and personally, experience job satisfaction, positive self-beliefs, personal wellbeing and an on going [sic] commitment to the profession. (Wosnitza et al. 2014, p. 2)

This proactive perspective of teacher resilience is based on an understanding that resilience needs to be understood as a state and not merely as a trait, suggesting the possibility of enhancing and supporting teacher resilience through professional development to help achieve this goal (e.g., Beltman et al. 2018, Chap. 14, this volume; Castro Silva et al. 2018, Chap. 15, this volume). The overall aim of ENTREE is to provide diverse learning opportunities to empower teachers to thrive despite the everyday challenges in their daily work encounters. Through the use of a specifically designed self-reflection tool (TRSR), participating teachers can personalise

[1] This project has been funded with support from the European Commission (539590-LLP-1-2013-1-DE-COMENIUS-CMP, 2013 – 3324/001 – 001). This publication reflects the views only of the author, and the Commission cannot be held responsible for any use which may be made of the information contained therein.

their learning by engaging in online (see below) and face-to-face activities (see Castro Silva et al. 2018, Chap. 15, this volume) to build their capacity for resilience. This chapter gives an insight into the theoretical framework the TRSR builds on. Furthermore, the development of the TRSR is described as well as the handling of the TRSR. As the participants' feedback is linked to ENTREE's online learning modules, these are briefly presented afterwards. Finally, the handling of the TRSR by teacher trainers, its overall educational potential for teacher trainers and teachers, is discussed.

Theoretical Framework in a Nutshell

ENTREE builds on a theoretical framework (see Fig. 16.1 and Peixoto et al. 2018, Chap. 5, this volume), which assumes that all individual behaviour and actions build on experiences, skills, knowledge and beliefs and develop in interaction with the environment. For early career or beginning teachers, that means entering the profession with a "backpack" of individual beliefs, capacities, skills and strategies that enable effective management of challenges they may encounter as they adapt to a new professional context. It is furthermore assumed that individuals can learn how to respond in resilient ways and that resilience can be enhanced over time by specific support systems and environmental factors (Beltman et al. 2018, Chap. 14, this volume).

Teacher resilience in this framework is understood as a multifaceted phenomenon that results from the process of interaction between individual characteristics and contextual factors. Demonstrating resilience means using existing capacities (emotional, motivational, professional and social) and behaviour dispositions (e.g., strategies) to handle (potentially) stressful situations in a way that the outcome is

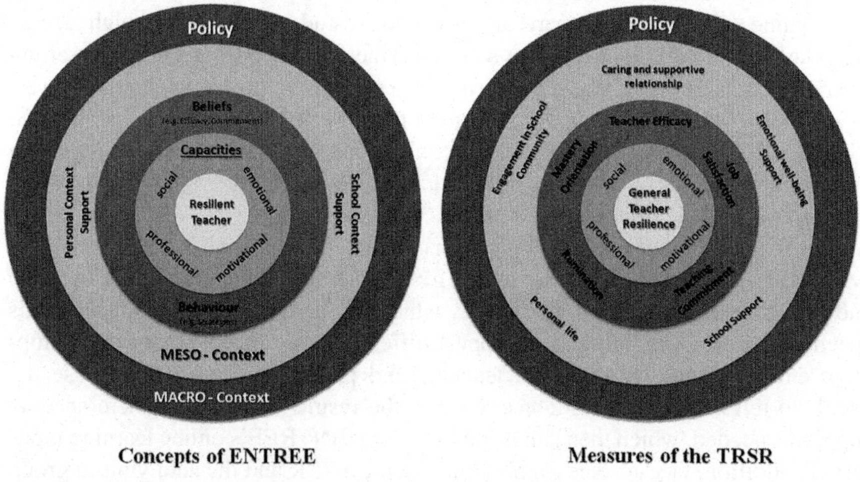

Concepts of ENTREE **Measures of the TRSR**

Fig. 16.1 Concepts of ENTREE and measures of the TRSR

satisfying, acceptable or at least manageable and leads to an experience of well-being and allows thriving professionally and remaining committed to the students and the profession (Mansfield et al. 2012).

In the light of this understanding, ENTREE's aim is to develop a *holistic reflection and learning environment* to enhance teacher resilience. In support of this aim, two different models of interaction were developed – an online platform with modules and materials supporting aspects of teacher resilience and a set of face-to-face workshop materials, which are made available for trainers and university teachers who were willing to engage with their students (Castro Silva et al. 2018, Chap. 15, this volume). These two options in support of developing an individual and differentiated workshop group approach are linked with an online self-reflection platform (TRSR). This platform aims to support teachers in reflecting on their current situation through completing the TRSR, which provides feedback on aspects that are helping or hindering them in becoming more resilient. It also provides face-to-face trainers with information about the groups' resilience-related strengths and challenges. In the next section, the Teacher Resilience Self-Reflection (TRSR) platform is described.

Teacher Resilience Self-Reflection (TRSR) Platform

Online self-assessments are web-based self-tests originally developed for prospective students to self-reflect on their skills, interests and competencies in the light of demands and expectations of a university or a specific programme of study. They aim to support students to make an informed decision through a guided self-reflection (Wosnitza et al. 2015) and are primarily intended to be a self-regulated source of information, which is available on demand and preserves one's anonymity (Kubinger et al. 2012). Studies have shown that data provided by students using such online self-assessments are able to predict study success to a high degree (Hornke et al. 2013). Using online self-assessment to support student counselling offered by universities is a recently growing technique to provide potential university students with the help and information that is actually needed (Wosnitza and Bürger 2015). However, using these technical opportunities to build a reflective instrument to support teachers is new and rarely found in other areas of education and training outside of university settings.

The Teacher Resilience Self-Reflection (TRSR) tool is an online self-assessment system that is grounded in the theoretical framework described above (see Fig. 16.1) and uses scientifically developed scales which are adapted and validated for this specific purpose. The TRSR can support different types of professional development environments, for example, teachers and pre-service teachers can use the TRSR to reflect on their resilience and use the results to identify where specific support is needed, which then can be addressed by ENTREE's online learning modules. In addition, face-to-face trainers can use the TRSR and the anonymised group profile to identify protective and risk factors of the participants, thus allowing them to address priorities in a customised manner as outlined in ENTREE.[2]

Development of Scales

The core of the TRSR comprises a set of 17 validated scales. As a general measure of resilience, the TRSR includes a *general teacher resilience scale* developed by Morgan (2011). The *social, motivational, emotional and professional* capacities of teacher resilience are examined by the four respective teacher resilience scales from Mansfield and Wosnitza (2015). Teacher beliefs are explored in three scales – *teacher efficacy* (Morgan 2011), *teaching commitment* (Morgan 2011) and *job satisfaction* (Castro Silva 2013). With regard to behavioural patterns, the scales *mastery orientation* and *rumination* (both Morgan 2011) are included in the TRSR. The impact of factors at a meso-level of teachers' lives is assessed by three newly developed scales based on Cefai and Cavioni (2014), *caring and supportive relationship, emotional and well-being support* and *engagement in school community*, together with two scales developed by Morgan (2011) – *personal life* and *school support*. The newly developed scale *policy stressors* examines the impact of factors on teachers' lives at a macro-level. The connection and rationale for the use of all scales to the underlying theoretical framework is summarised in Fig. 16.1. Table 16.2 details the numbers of items used (for more information on the scales, see Peixoto et al. 2018, Chap. 5, this volume).

All scales were translated from English to German, Portuguese and Czech. Each scale was evaluated in country-specific studies with teachers and teacher education students. Reliabilities were calculated for each scale and for each country independently. This approach was deliberately chosen so as not to conflict with the theoretically driven differentiated feedback system of the TRSR and the related workshops and online modules offered by ENTREE.[3]

Samples

The overall sample consists of mainly female participants which reflects the gender balance in the teaching profession. The structure of all five samples is presented in Table 16.1. Because of the small sample size, the scale validations for the Czech Republic were not possible, and therefore this sample is not to be found in the next paragraph on the evaluation of scales.

[2] http://entree-project.eu or direct access to TRSR: http://www.global-assess.rwth-aachen.de/entree/

[3] Data were also analysed with regard to its research value (see Peixoto et al. 2018, Chap. 5, this volume).

Table 16.1 Sample sizes for the participating countries

Country	N	Female %	Male %	MD for gender %
Germany	270	70.7	29.3	1.5
Ireland	158	77.8	22.2	1.9
Malta	279	81.4	18.6	6.4
Portugal	232	93.1	6.9	2.1
Czech Republic	25	88.0	12.0	41.6

Results of Evaluation of Scales

Table 16.2 gives an overview of the homogeneity measures (Cronbach's alphas) for each scale for Germany, Ireland, Malta and Portugal. Overall – with some exceptions – the results showed good to very good reliabilities. In the cases of $\alpha < 0.60$, follow-up studies in the respective countries will revalidate the quality of the scale, and depending on the outcome appropriate measures will be taken (e.g., the scale removed or alternative scales implemented).

Development of the Platform

The technical realisation of the TRSR is based on the software testMaker4 developed by the Self-Assessment Team of RWTH Aachen University (Delzepich et al. 2016). testMaker is widely used across Germany and internationally for the development of online self-assessments and self-reflection tools.

As mentioned above, the TRSR includes 17 constructs related to teacher resilience. After logging in, teachers are required to answer 150 Likert scale items. Answering all items is obligatory (Fig. 16.2 shows a typical screen with some of these items to answer).

The TRSR aims to provide trainers and users with information about their profile in regard to the 17 constructs measured in the self-reflection tool.

TRSR for Individuals

The TRSR assessment is the same for all participants; however, there are some differences in relation to the log-in procedures for teachers who want to engage individually with the tool.

Following engagement at an individual level, participants receive individualised feedback showing areas for improvement (Fig. 16.3, screenshot: right) and strengths (Fig. 16.3, screenshot: left). The TRSR furthermore provides suggestions of modules in the online learning platform that the users should engage with first. Analogous

Table 16.2 Scale validations (number of items, Cronbach's alphas, means and standard deviations)

	N of items	Germany	Ireland	Malta	Portugal	All
General teacher resilience	9	0.87	0.92	0.86	0.94	0.90
		(*M* = 18.04 SD = 4.74)	(*M* = 19.08 SD = 5.69)	(*M* = 21.46 SD = 5.12)	(*M* = 19.81 SD = 6.62)	(*M* = 19.66 SD = 5.63)
Professional capacities	6	0.58	0.77	0.50	0.74	0.67
		(*M* = 12.42 SD = 2.69)	(*M* = 11.85 SD = 3.51)	(*M* = 13.57 SD = 2.65)	(*M* = 10.25 SD = 2.66)	(*M* = 12.16 SD = 3.08)
Emotional capacities	6	0.65	0.83	0.72	0.70	0.73
		(*M* = 13.85 SD = 3.18)	(*M* = 11.01 SD = 3.81)	(*M* = 12.01 SD = 3.02)	(*M* = 12.23 SD = 3.30)	(*M* = 12.42 SD = 3.42)
Motivational capacities	10	0.77	0.86	0.75	0.85	0.81
		(*M* = 20.96 SD = 4.69)	(*M* = 17.19 SD = 5.09)	(*M* = 18.63 SD = 4.15)	(*M* = 17.40 SD = 4.79)	(*M* = 18.75 SD = 4.86)
Social capacities	4	0.48	0.79	0.68	0.74	0.68
		(*M* = 7.57 SD = 1.89)	(*M* = 7.22 SD = 2.31)	(*M* = 8.05 SD = 2.17)	(*M* = 7.26 SD = 2.21)	(*M* = 7.58 SD = 2.15)
Teacher efficacy	12	0.86	0.93	0.85	0.93	0.88
		(*M* = 24.78 SD = 6.04)	(*M* = 24.51 SD = 7.32)	(*M* = 27.35 SD = 8.88)	(*M* = 21.54 SD = 7.00)	(*M* = 24.84 SD = 7.74)
Job satisfaction	12	0.83	0.91	0.93	0.94	0.92
		(*M* = 28.42 SD = 6.49)	(*M* = 28.08 SD = 7.57)	(*M* = 32.37 SD = 8.91)	(*M* = 26.05 SD = 9.67)	(*M* = 29.17 SD = 8.60)
General teacher commitment	8	0.84	0.87	0.89	0.89	0.88
		(*M* = 15.18 SD = 5.41)	(*M* = 11.67 SD = 4.24)	(*M* = 15.77 SD = 5.69)	(*M* = 17.28 SD = 6.58)	(*M* = 15.20 SD = 5.87)
Teacher commitment profession	3	0.89	0.93	0.91	0.87	0.91
		(*M* = 12.69 SD = 2.82)	(*M* = 12.67 SD = 3.40)	(*M* = 11.44 SD = 3.43)	(*M* = 10.11 SD = 3.59)	(*M* = 11.69 SD = 3.45)
Mastery orientation	5	0.48	0.52	0.66	0.55	0.55
		(*M* = 11.34 SD = 2.67)	(*M* = 9.68 SD = 2.90)	(*M* = 10.56 SD = 3.12)	(*M* = 11.55 SD = 3.13)	(*M* = 10.85 SD = 3.03)
Rumination	7	0.66	0.77	0.75	0.76	0.74
		(*M* = 16.28 SD = 3.79)	(*M* = 16.66 SD = 4.69)	(*M* = 14.70 SD = 3.84)	(*M* = 13.65 SD = 4.08)	(*M* = 15.31 SD = 4.19)
Caring and supportive relationship	18	0.90	0.93	0.89	0.93	0.91
		(*M* = 40.93 SD = 10.19)	(*M* = 37.52 SD = 10.98)	(*M* = 41.41 SD = 9.50)	(*M* = 44.29 SD = 12.39)	(*M* = 41.22 SD = 10.83)
Engagement in school community	18	0.85	0.92	0.88	0.90	0.88
		(*M* = 45.21 SD = 9.49)	(*M* = 39.34 SD = 10.89)	(*M* = 46.08 SD = 9.45)	(*M* = 45.52 SD = 11.24)	(*M* = 44.82 SD = 10.31)
Emotional and well-being support	18	0.87	0.90	0.84	0.93	0.90
		(*M* = 54.81 SD = 10.23)	(*M* = 40.82 SD = 10.26)	(*M* = 47.90 SD = 10.85)	(*M* = 57.63 SD = 12.94)	(*M* = 50.66 SD = 12.57)

(continued)

Table 16.2 (continued)

	N of items	Germany	Ireland	Malta	Portugal	All
Personal life	4	0.86	0.81	0.80	0.83	0.83
		(*M* = 8.30 SD = 3.69)	(*M* = 6.77 SD = 2.96)	(*M* = 7.66 SD = 2.74)	(*M* = 8.30 SD = 3.18)	(*M* = 7.80 SD = 3.20)
School support	4	0.87	0.91	0.80	0.93	0.89
		(*M* = 7.35 SD = 2.67)	(*M* = 7.17 SD = 2.89)	(*M* = 9,37 SD = 2.68)	(*M* = 10.00 SD = 3.60)	(*M* = 8.55 SD = 3.16)
Policy stressors	6	0.72	0.87	0.83	0.85	0.81
		(*M* = 16.47 SD = 3.81)	(*M* = 15.14 SD = 4.84)	(*M* = 15.39 SD = 4.04)	(*M* = 15.96 SD = 4.59)	(*M* = 15.75 SD = 4.28)

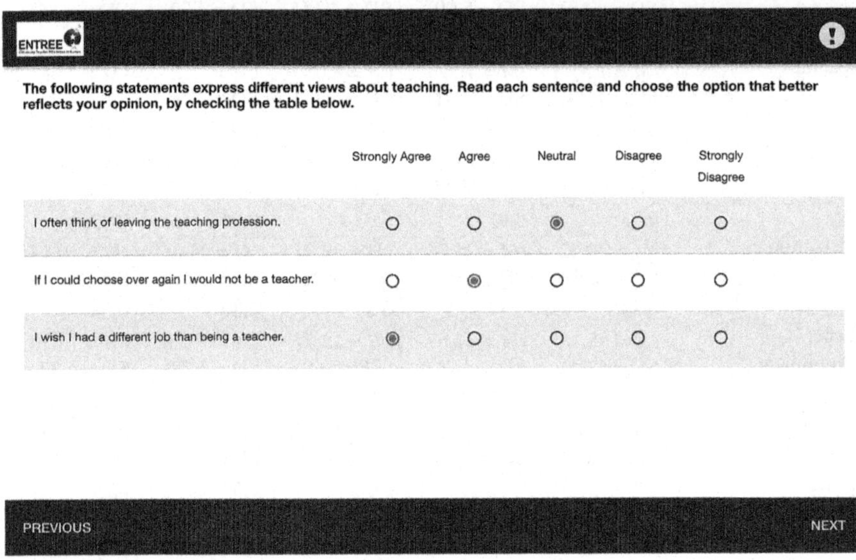

Fig. 16.2 Screenshot TRSR

to the TRSR for trainers, the suggestion is based on the relation between the TRSR scales and the ENTREE modules (see Table 16.3).

Along with the suggested modules, users are provided with a transferable code to be used when registering for the ENTREE online learning platform. This code is used by the platform to transfer the results from the TRSR without exchanging any personal data (Fig. 16.3).

Table 16.3 Allocation of scales to modules

Module	Scales
I. Enhancing Teacher Resilience: An Introduction	General teacher resilience
	Teacher commitment profession
	General teacher commitment
	Professional capacities
II. Building Relationship	Caring and supportive relationship
	School support
	Social capacities
	Engagement in school community
III. Emotional Well-Being	Emotional and well-being support
	Job satisfaction
	Mastery orientation
	Personal life
	Emotional capacities
	Motivational capacities
IV. Health, Stress and Coping	Rumination
	Policy stressors
V. Pedagogical Skills for Effective Teaching	Teacher efficacy
VI. Pedagogical Skills for Effective Classroom Management	

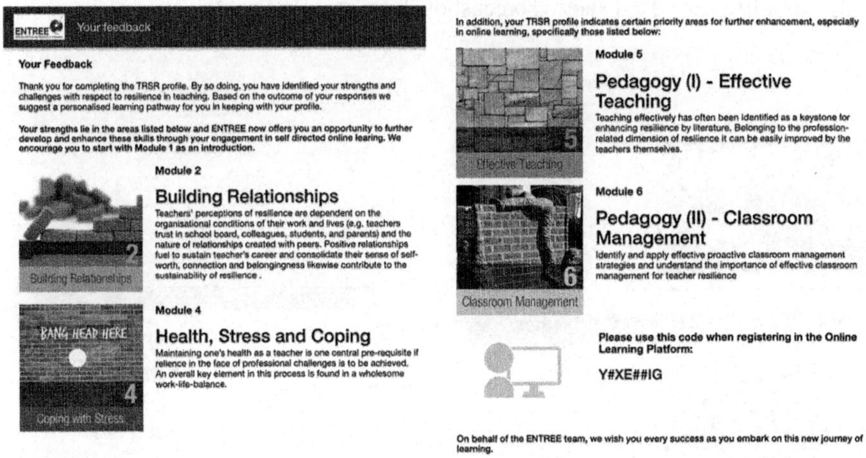

Fig. 16.3 Individualised feedback

The ENTREE Online Learning Platform

ENTREE's online learning platform is designed to give teachers at both, pre-service and in service levels, the opportunity to enhance their resilience in a self-directed and self-reflective way. In support of flexibility, all modules, building on ENTREE's theoretical framework, consist of three to four units. This allows users to choose to work through one unit, save the notes made, and return at a more convenient time, or alternatively to continuously work through the entire module.

In addition, resources, additional readings and recommendations are provided, so users are facilitated in deepening their knowledge on the topics addressed in the modules.

Users of the ENTREE online learning platform are encouraged to use their TRSR feedback to choose modules and thematic topics:

I. Enhancing Teacher Resilience: An Introduction
II. Building Relationships
III. Emotional Well-Being
IV. Health, Stress and Coping
V. Pedagogical Skills for Effective Teaching
VI. Pedagogical Skills for Effective Classroom Management

All six modules, adapted for the online learning environment, are in line with the modules developed for the ENTREE face-to-face workshops, which are described in detail by Castro Silva et al. (2018, Chap. 15, this volume). Therefore, only a short summary of these modules will be given in the following:

The first module *Enhancing Teacher Resilience* is an introductory module that gives an overview of teacher resilience, what it is and why it is so important. Explanatory videos enhance the theoretical knowledge and exercises, such as case studies, and promote self-reflection and the awareness of one's own resources in daily work life (Fig. 16.4 shows screenshots from the platform).

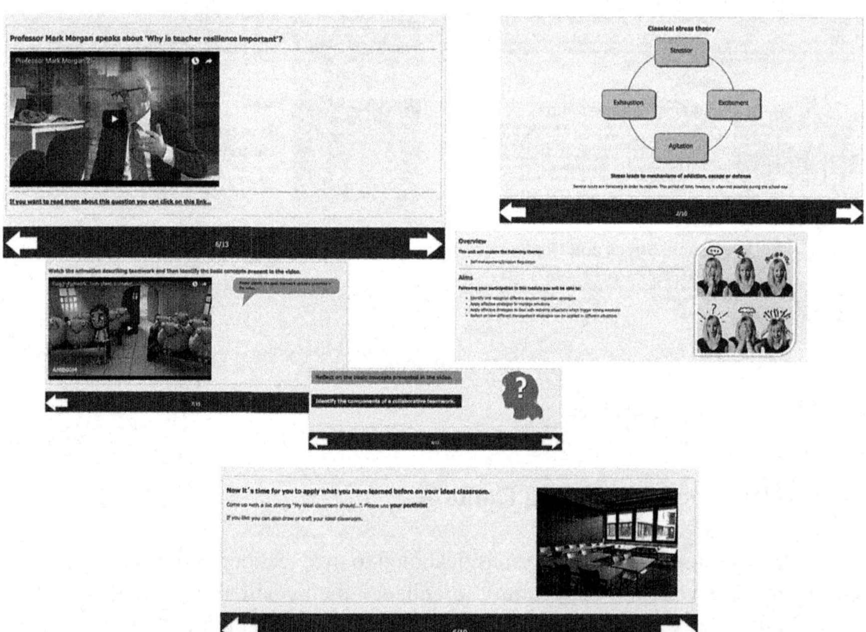

Fig. 16.4 Screenshots from the platform

The second module *Building Relationships* stresses the importance of relationships in working life. By using specific scenarios, this module helps users reflect on their own communication skills and identify communication problems and gives ideas about how to build effective and supportive networks at school with colleagues, school leaders, students and parents.

The module *Emotional Well-Being* gives a theoretical perspective on emotions but also uses exercises to identify others' emotions. The module also focuses on emotional regulation, gives ideas on possible strategies and includes exercises to reflect on one's own strategies.

Health, Stress and Coping focuses on a theoretical view on stress, underlines the importance of body awareness and a good work-life balance and encourages the users to think about their stressful situations and strategies.

The two modules *Pedagogical Skills for Effective Teaching* and *Pedagogical Skills for Effective Classroom Management* focus on the organisation of one's work in school and at home. The user gets information on classroom management strategies and applies this knowledge through the use of scenarios. Users are also encouraged to reflect on their behaviour and their use of strategies, such as the organisation of school materials and of the classroom.

TRSR for Trainers

Having information regarding participants' resilience profiles enables trainers to tailor their professional development workshop to meet the participants' needs. Therefore, trainers should invite their participants to take the TRSR. Each trainer generates a token within the TRSR, which is a unique identifier for their workshop or course and the key to receiving the overall group profile. Trainers then retrieve a list of transaction numbers (TAN) for each participant, which participants then use to log into the TRSR. These individual TANs link the participant to the specific workshop or course the trainer is providing (see Figs. 16.3 and 16.5).

Due to data protection, trainers will never receive an individual profile but can identify the strengths and weaknesses of the whole group and can plan the workshop in the light of this information. Trainers also obtain feedback on suggested ENTREE modules to use in their workshop. This suggestion is based on the relation between the TRSR scales and the ENTREE modules (see Table 16.3).

Trainers can check the group results by entering the specific workshop token and will receive the group profile (see Fig. 16.6). This means that they get the descriptive statistics (group's average (middle of the box), one SD above and below (box), Min and Max (ends of the line)) for the group for each module in form of a boxplot diagram. These results are based on the allocation of scales used in the TRSR to the learning modules (see Table 16.3). The modules are ranked regarding their importance for the group. For the group in the example in Fig. 16.6, this means that the trainer should focus on the content of *health, stress, coping* and *building relationships.*

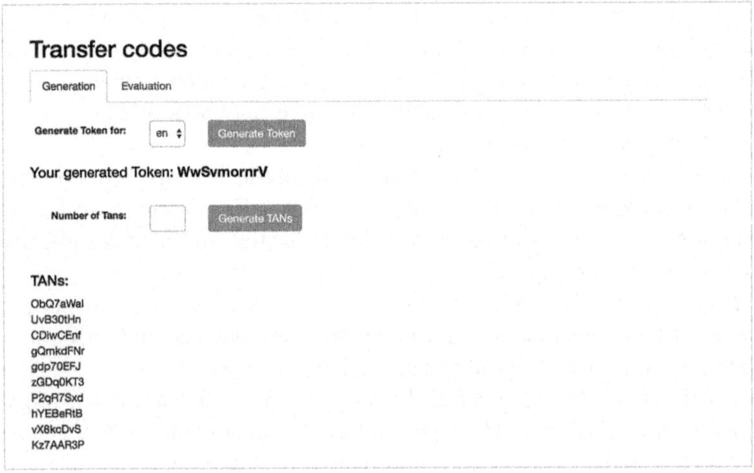

Fig. 16.5 Transfer codes and TAN

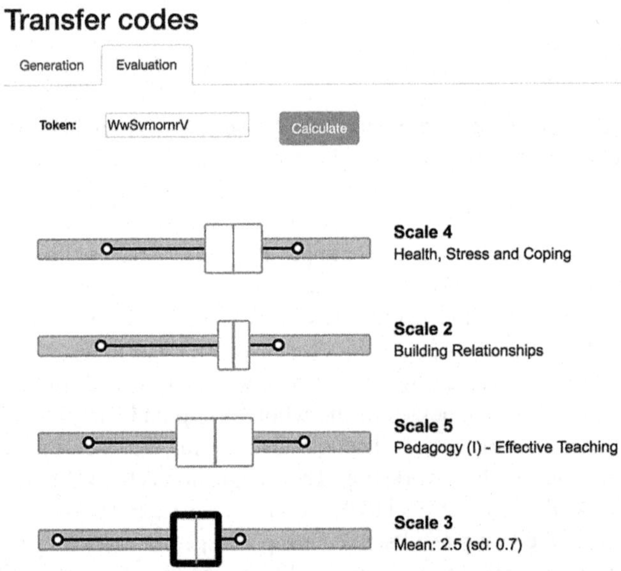

Fig. 16.6 Trainer feedback

Summary

Online self-assessments and online self-reflection tools offer support that allow individuals to reflect on their current situation with regard to a specific area of their life, profession or possible future. These tools are widely used in the area of choice of career or study, to help with decision-making processes; however, there exists a paucity of scientifically sound instruments that allow teachers to reflect on their own professional situation. The Teacher Resilience Self-Reflection (TRSR) tool, developed in the EU-funded project *ENhancing Teacher REsilience in Europe* and available in four languages, is such a tool. It allows teachers to reflect on their resilience based on a broad range of factors that help or hinder teachers being resilient. The TRSR provides teachers with individualised feedback and guides them to areas to be enhanced, with the overall objective of building and strengthening their capacity for professional resilience.

Furthermore, the TRSR allows leaders of resilience workshops and other activities in this area to differentiate and adapt each workshop to meet the needs of their participants based on the outcomes of the TRSR. The potential of such group tailored workshops is that they provide a more efficient and effective model of engagement and as such they serve to sustain teachers' motivation to engage in professional development in support of quality teaching and learning.

Formative evaluation of the TRSR, specifically on the linkage between scales and modules – online as well as face to face – will provide not only information on the usefulness of the TRSR, but also on possible improvements and potential modifications.

In conclusion, the TRSR platform and the supporting materials developed by ENTREE will serve to support teachers to engage in a self-reflective process in examining the *what and how* of teacher resilience in support of achieving quality teaching and learning for all pupils.

References

Beltman, S., Mansfield, C. F., Wosnitza, M., Weatherby-Fell, N., & Broadley, T. (2018). Using online modules to build capacity for teacher resilience. In M. Wosnitza, F. Peixoto, S. Beltman, & C. F. Mansfield (Eds.), *Resilience in education: Concepts, contexts and connections* (pp. 237–253). New York: Springer.

Castro Silva, J. (2013). *Clima escolar, satisfação, stresse profissional e colaboração entre professores: Que relações?* (School climate, job satisfaction, professional stress and collaboration between teachers: What kind of relations?). Unpublished PhD thesis, Universidade Aberta, Lisboa, Portugal.

Castro Silva, J., Pipa, J., Renner, C., O'Donnell, M., & Cefai, C. (2018). Enhancing teacher's resilience through face-to-face training – insights from ENTREE project. In M. Wosnitza, F. Peixoto, S. Beltman, & C. F. Mansfield (Eds.), *Resilience in education: Concepts, contexts and connections* (pp. 255–274). New York: Springer.

Cefai, C., & Cavioni, V. (2014). From neurasthenia to eudaimonia: Teachers' wellbeing and resilience. In C. Cefai & V. Cavioni (Eds.), *Social and emotional education in primary school: Integrating theory and research into practice* (pp. 133–148). New York: Springer.

Delzepich, R., Wosnitza, M., & Schilling, S. (2016). *testMaker4*. Aachen: RWTH Aachen University.
Ebersöhn, L. (2014). Teacher resilience: Theorizing resilience and poverty. *Teachers and Teaching, 20*(5), 568–594. https://doi.org/10.1080/13540602.2014.937960.
Gibbs, S., & Miller, A. (2014). Teachers' resilience and well-being: A role for educational psychology. *Teachers and Teaching: Theory and Practice, 20*(5), 609–621. https://doi.org/10.1080/13540602.2013.844408.
Gu, Q., & Day, C. (2007). Teachers resilience. A necessary condition for effectiveness. *Teaching and Teacher Education, 23*, 1302–1316.
Hornke, L. F., Wosnitza, M., & Bürger, K. (2013). SelfAssessment: Ideen, Hintergründe, Praxis und Evaluation [SelfAssessments: Idea, background, practice and evaluation]. *Wirtschaftspsychologie, 1*, 5–16.
Kersaint, G., Lewis, J., Potter, R., & Meisels, G. (2007). Why teachers leave: Factors that influence retention and resignation. *Teaching and Teacher Education, 23*, 775–794. https://doi.org/10.1016/j.tate.2005.12.004.
Kubinger, K. D., Frebort, M., & Müller, C. (2012). Self-Assessment im Rahmen der Studienberatung: Möglichkeiten und Grenzen [Selfassessment in context of student consultancies: Possibilities and limits]. In K. D. Kubinger, M. Frebort, L. Khorramdel, & L. Weitensfelder (Eds.), *"Wiener Autorenkollektiv Studienberatungstests": Self-Assessment: Theorie und Konzepte* (pp. 9–24). Lengerich: Pabst Science Publishers.
Lohbeck, L. (2018). The interplay between the motivation to teach and resilience of student teachers and trainee teachers. In M. Wosnitza, F. Peixoto, S. Beltman, & C. F. Mansfield (Eds.), *Resilience in education: Concepts, contexts and connections* (pp. 93–106). New York: Springer.
Mansfield, C. F., & Wosnitza, M. (2015). *Teacher resilience questionnaire – version 1.5*. Perth: Murdoch University, RWTH Aachen University.
Mansfield, C. F., Beltman, S., Price, A., & McConney, A. (2012). "Don't sweat the small stuff:" Understanding teacher resilience at the chalkface. *Teaching and Teacher Education, 28*(3), 357–367. https://doi.org/10.1016/j.tate.2011.11.001.
Mansfield, C. F., Beltman, S., Broadley, T., & Weatherby-Fell, N. (2016). Building resilience in teacher education: An evidenced informed framework. *Teaching and Teacher Education, 54*, 77–87. https://doi.org/10.1016/j.tate.2015.11.016.
McInerney, D. M., Ganotice, F. A., King, R. B., Morin, A. J. S., & Marsh, H. W. (2015). Teachers' commitment and psychological well-being: Implications of self-beliefs for teaching in Hong Kong. *Educational Psychology, 35*(8), 926–945. https://doi.org/10.1080/01443410.2014.895801.
Morgan, M. (2011). Resilience and recurring adverse events: Testing an assets-based model of beginning teachers' experiences. *The Irish Journal of Psychology, 32*(3–4), 92–104. https://doi.org/10.1080/03033910.2011.613189.
Peixoto, F., Wosnitza, M., Pipa, J., Morgan, M., & Cefai, C. (2018). A multidimensional view on pre-service teacher resilience in Germany, Ireland Malta and Portugal. In M. Wosnitza, F. Peixoto, S. Beltman, & C. F. Mansfield (Eds.), *Resilience in education: Concepts, contexts and connections* (pp. 73–89). New York: Springer.
Tait, M. (2008). Resilience as a contributor to novice teacher success, commitment, and retention. *Teacher Education Quarterly, 35*(4), 57–75.
Wosnitza, M., & Bürger, K. (Eds.). (2015). Sonderheft: Online-Self-Assessment [Special issue: Online-SelfAssessment]. Das Hochschulwesen, 69(3+4).
Wosnitza, M., O'Donnell, M., Morgan, M., Mansfield, C. F., Beltman, S., et al. (2014). *Teachers resilience in Europe. A theoretical framework.* Aachen: ENTREE. Retrieved from http://entree-project.eu/wp-content/uploads/2014/11/ENTREE1-new-v2_EN-1.pdf.
Wosnitza, M., Bürger, K., & Drouven, S. (2015). Self-assessments: Heterogene Eingangsvoraussetzungen und Prognosen von Studienerfolg [Self-assessments: Heterogeneous entrance requirements and prognosis of study success]. In A. Hanft & O. Zawacki-Richter (Eds.), *Herausforderung Heterogenität beim Übergang in die Hochschule [Challenge heterogeneity in transition to university] (pp. 133–143)*. Münster: Waxmann.

Chapter 17
Making It Real and Making It Last! Sustainability of Teacher Implementation of a Whole-School Resilience Programme

Toni Noble and Helen McGrath

Abstract Life for children and young people in the twenty-first century includes the need to master the usual developmental hurdles along with relatively new challenges such as cyber safety, greater family mobility, higher levels of family breakdown and easier access to addictive drugs and alcohol. These contemporary challenges have prompted widespread interest from governments, policymakers and educators around the world into how educational policy and school practices can help children and young people develop greater resilience. This chapter reviews the importance of resilience for both teachers and students. It then draws on lessons learned from the implementation over 5–12 years of a whole-school resilience programme in ten schools. The research findings demonstrate that a combination of school factors, school system factors and programme-specific factors facilitate all teachers' implementation of a resilience programme. This same combination of factors was also found to be crucial for the capacity of the school to sustain the implementation of the programme over many years and thus achieve positive outcomes for both students and staff.

One of the most important goals for any country is to enable its children and young people to lead happy and fulfilling lives and develop the skills to be resilient in the face of challenges, setbacks and difficult times. Life for children and young people in the twenty-first century not only means mastering the usual developmental hurdles but also managing relatively new challenges. These new challenges include

T. Noble (✉)
Australian Catholic University, Sydney, Australia
e-mail: toni@bounceback.com.au

H. McGrath
RMIT University, Melbourne, Australia

Deakin University, Melbourne, Australia
e-mail: helenmc@deakin.edu.au

M. Wosnitza et al. (eds.), *Resilience in Education*,
https://doi.org/10.1007/978-3-319-76690-4_17

cyber safety, greater family mobility, higher levels of family breakdown and easier access to addictive illicit drugs and alcohol. The unrest in the Middle East has led to recent widespread displacement of families as well as the increased terrorist radicalisation of youth through the Internet. These contemporary challenges have prompted increasing interest from governments, policymakers and educators around the world in how educational policy and school practices can help children and young people develop greater resilience.

This chapter reviews the importance of resilience for children and young people. It then draws on lessons learned from the implementation and sustainability of one specific whole-school resilience programme. Interviews were conducted in ten schools that have been implementing the resilience programme for between 5 and 12 years. The research findings demonstrate that a combination of school factors, school system factors and programme-specific factors can facilitate teachers' implementation of a resilience programme. This same combination of factors was also found to be crucial for the capacity of the school to sustain the implementation of the programme over many years and thus achieve positive outcomes for both students and staff.

Why Does Student Resilience Matter?

The health and wellbeing of a country's young people are at the heart of a country's wellbeing. As Elias has noted 'in every society, children will inherit social roles now occupied by adults. Our education systems have the job of preparing children for this eventual responsibility' (Elias 2003, p. 6). Global figures show that about 10% of young people have a diagnosable mental disorder. Given that approximately one-third of the world's population is under 18 years of age (UNICEF 2014), this represents over 220 million children (WHO 2003; Global Burden of Disease Study 2012). Over half of the children who experience mental illness in childhood will also suffer from a mental illness in their adult lives (Kim-Cohen et al. 2003; Layard and Hagell 2015). In the richest countries, only 25% of children with mental health issues receive specialist help. In the poorest countries, very few have access to any help at all (Layard and Hagell 2015). From a humanitarian perspective, this is a great loss, but it also creates an economic cost. In most countries mental illness is reducing gross domestic product (GDP) by over 5% (OECD 2014). Given that the aim of all countries is to enable their children to be educated within a school context, a core concern for all schools around the world needs to be how they can best develop their students' sense of wellbeing and resilience in order to support both their academic performance and their mental health.

Do Schools Have a Role to Play in Developing Student Resilience?

Schools are important social institutions for helping young people to develop their wellbeing and resilience. Children and adolescents spend much of their waking time in school. For example, in Australia, 5–18-year-olds typically spend 30–35 h per week in school. What children learn at school and the relationships they establish in their day-to-day interactions and experiences with their peers and teachers are integral to their wellbeing. Understanding the conditions and processes that contribute to wellbeing and resilience in individuals, groups and institutions is at the core of the relatively new discipline of positive psychology (Gable and Haidt 2005), and increasingly educators are now looking to the subdiscipline of positive education for direction.

Traditionally a country's prosperity has been equated with a country's wealth. Martin Seligman, one of the founders of positive psychology, has stated that the time has come for a new prosperity 'that combines well-being with wealth. Learning to value and to attain this new prosperity must start early—in the formative years of schooling— and it is this new prosperity, kindled by Positive Education, that the world can now choose' (Seligman 2011, p. 97).

Positive education is defined by Seligman et al. (2009) as education for both traditional skills and for happiness. We define positive education as:

> The integration of the core principles of Positive Psychology with the evidence-informed structures, practices and programs that enhance both wellbeing and academic achievement. The aim of positive education is to enable all members of a school community to succeed and prosper (Noble and McGrath 2015, p. 4; Noble and McGrath 2016, p. 19)

What Is Resilience?

All students face some kind of adversity at one time or another. The development of resilience in the face of adversity involves a developmental progression in which new challenges, vulnerabilities and opportunities emerge with changing circumstances at different times in one's life. Typically the challenges that children face are related to changes or losses associated with family or friendship, concerns in relation to academic performance as well as setbacks and disappointments when things don't go their way in other areas of their lives. Some students have more serious adversity to deal with such as ongoing poverty and disadvantage, abuse or serious illness. Luthar (2006) has warned that children can sometimes seem resilient in terms of their behaviours but might still struggle with inner distress in the form of mental health problems such as depression and anxiety. It is important to recognise that resilience is a multi-faceted developmental process that is not fixed or immutable (Cicchetti 2010, p. 146) and is influenced by a range of different factors.

We define resilience as:

> The ability to persist, cope adaptively and bounce back after encountering change, challenges, setback, disappointments, difficult situations or adversity and to return to a reasonable level of wellbeing. It is also the capacity to respond adaptively to difficult circumstances and still thrive (Noble and McGrath 2015, p. 13).

Our model of resilience includes the environmental protective factors that contribute to a child's resilience as well as the personal skills of resilience that can be taught and strengthened. Protective factors are considered to be those that may reduce or mitigate the negative impact of risk factors (Kim-Cohen 2007). One of the strongest protective environmental factors that help children to become more resilient is feeling connected to their family, school and community.

There is a wealth of research that highlights the important role that schools can play in helping to provide the type of safe, protective and supportive environment which is especially important for those children who may be more at risk. Being connected to school includes feeling connected to both teachers and peers. School connectedness is linked to increased student engagement and participation in school (O'Shaughnessy et al. 2003; Osterman 2000), higher levels of academic achievement (e.g. Catalano et al. 2003; Severson and Walker 2002; Zins et al. 2004), completing school (Bond et al. 2007; Zins et al. 2004) and exhibiting less disruptive or antisocial behaviour (Lonczak et al. 2002; Zins et al. 2004). School connectedness is also linked to lower rates of health-risking behaviour and mental health problems (Bond et al. 2007; Catalano et al. 2003; Lonczak et al. 2002; Zins et al. 2004). The personal skills and attitudes that have the potential to contribute to wellbeing and academic success include helpful and positive thinking skills and attitudes, skills and beliefs related to being resourceful and being self-regulated and adaptive, social-emotional learning skills and having a sense of personal competence (McGrath and Noble 2003, 2011). Skills for being resilient can be seen as essential for both academic and personal success in school and in life.

Evaluating Resilience-Based Programs for Schools

Well-developed and well-implemented, school-based resilience programs have been shown to produce a range of positive effects on children's academic, behavioural and social-emotional functioning. The findings of a large-scale meta-analysis of social and emotional learning (SEL) programs (Durlak et al. 2011) confirmed the positive impact of school-based social and emotional learning programs on learning and achievement. This meta-analysis focused on 213 school-based, universal social-emotional learning programs and involved over 270,000 students from primary school entry to year 12. Compared to controls, students who had participated in social-emotional learning programs demonstrated, on average, an 11-percentile-point gain in academic achievement as well as demonstrating significant improvements in their social and emotional skills, attitudes and behaviour within the school context.

Similarly Diekstra and Gravesteijn (2008) conducted a large worldwide meta-analysis of 19 meta-analyses (published between 1997 and 2008) evaluating the effectiveness of student wellbeing programs that focused on teaching social and emotional skills. The studies had focused on either primary or secondary schools and comprised many hundreds of thousands of students. Their conclusions were similar to those of Durlak et al. (2011), namely, that such programs significantly enhanced students' social and emotional competence and their connection to the school reduced or prevented behaviour and mental health problems or disorders and significantly enhanced academic achievement. Students from low socio-economic status and different ethnic backgrounds benefited at least as much as other students (and often more).

More recently the World Health Organization commissioned a review of mental health promotion interventions in low- and middle-income countries (Barry et al. 2013, including Gaza/Palestine, South Africa, Uganda, India, Chile, Mauritius, Nepal and Lebanon. The majority of the studies (>60%) were published between 2010 and 2012. Findings from the 14 school-based interventions indicated reasonably robust evidence that school-based programs implemented in these diverse countries can have significant positive effects on students' emotional and behavioural wellbeing, including reduced depression and anxiety and improved coping skills.

All these meta-analyses of studies from around the world demonstrate the great potential of school-based social-emotional learning programs for making a significant impact on the wellbeing and resilience of young people. They are based on the premise that when children have the opportunity to learn the skills of resilience in the early years of schooling, they have a greater chance of lifelong wellbeing.

However a number of researchers in this area have also identified some key concerns. Most programs target only one age cohort in a school and are implemented for only a short time. They may produce good results in the short term, but these results are often not sustained over time. This is not surprising given that the programs typically average 20 h duration (Durlak et al. 2011; Barry et al. 2013). Barry et al. (2013) also expressed concern that the programs were generally limited in their scope in terms of the program's focus, the short-term nature of the intervention and the small number of students who had access to the intervention. Even if prior research demonstrates a strong evidence base for a particular programme, there is no guarantee the programme will be effective when implemented in a different setting or different social or cultural context. Barry's review recommended that the interventions be expanded to regional and national levels and inform a country's national educational and health policies (Barry et al. 2013).

In their evaluation of school-based resilience programs, Hart and Heaver (2013), based in the UK, were particularly critical of what happens when the funded resilience research project is completed and external resources supporting the resilience program's intervention are withdrawn. They found that most interventions in their review were researcher-led and that 7 of the 12 interventions in the research implementation phase did not even include the teachers who would be the people working with the students at the end of the research period. They concluded that most interventions were of no practical use to any educators wishing to replicate and implement the programme in a normal educational context. From the perspective of educational practitioners, such as teachers and classroom assistants, reviews of research under these conditions can be 'frustrating, difficult to digest and hard to learn from' and thus 'present serious challenges' to practitioners in terms of continuing implementation (Hart and Heaver 2013).

Similar criticisms have been voiced in the USA (e.g. Han and Weiss 2005; Elias 2003). Most of the programs in large-scale meta-analyses conducted by Durlak et al. (2011) were American-based research projects, financially supported by US government research grants or other sources of funding external to the school system. Durlak (2015), one of the leaders in the science of the implementation of social-emotional learning programs, has written about the complexity of this type of research. He stated: 'the 8 components of implementation, the over 20 contextual factors potentially affecting implementation, and the 14 steps necessary to achieving effective implementation leave a staggering array of possible permutations that could affect any attempt at implementation' (p. 1124). He added 'Unfortunately, we do not know the most effective implementation threshold for different evidence-based interventions or whether this threshold varies over time' (p. 1125).

Contemporary educational research constantly affirms that what happens inside the regular classroom is what will have the greatest impact on student's learning and indeed on school and system improvement (Hattie 2012; Marzano 2007; Munby and Fullan 2016). Academic improvement as well as social and emotional improvement is more likely when teachers (rather than external consultants or professionals) implement a social-emotional learning programme (Durlak et al. 2011; Weissberg and O'Brien 2004). Hence there is a significant need for research that looks at the 'real-world' school and programme factors that are most likely to contribute to classroom teachers' implementation of social-emotional/resilience programs and what factors facilitate the ongoing implementation of such programs over many years. This type of research also acknowledges that the typical process of 'real-world' programme implementation in schools is not always linear and often recycles through adoption, training, implementation, integration and maintenance (Scheirer 2012).

The Focus of This Research

The research outlined in this section sought to identify the features of the school, the school system and the programme itself that had contributed to the implementation and the sustainability of one specific resilience programme in the 'real world'. None of the ten primary schools in this study were involved in a funded research project nor received any other kind of specific funding support. The ten primary schools that were selected as the focus of this research had all been implementing the Bounce Back Wellbeing and Resilience Programme (McGrath and Noble 2003, 2011) for between 5 and 12 years. Nine of the schools were implementing the programme as a whole-school initiative taught to all students from the foundation year (first year of primary) through to year 6 (final year of primary). One K–12 school did not include students in year 6. Four of the schools were state government primary schools, three were Catholic primary schools, and three were independent private schools.

A research assistant funded by the program's publisher contacted the ten schools which had been identified as successful long-term users of the programme and who were willing to be interviewed. She initially contacted the schools in order to identify the teacher in charge of each school's implementation of the programme. These ten coordinators (including one who was also the principal) were then contacted to confirm their interest in participating in the study. Two additional classroom teachers also participated, at their request, in the interview conducted with one of the schools. A semi-structured interview protocol was developed, and university ethics clearance was obtained. Information sheets and consent forms were then mailed to each of the 12 participants.

The research assistant then conducted a 20–30 min phone interview with the 12 teachers. The focus of the interviews was the identification of the factors that were perceived by the schools to have contributed to their school's successful implementation and ongoing sustainability of the Bounce Back classroom resiliency programme.

Overview of the Bounce Back Classroom Resiliency Programme

The first edition of the Bounce Back! programme, which was published in 2003, was the world's first comprehensive, whole-school positive education programme. It aimed to build protective, supportive and respectful school communities as well as teach students the social and emotional skills that underpin both resilience and wellbeing. The programme integrates a combination of the core principles of CBT (cognitive behaviour therapy; Beck 1979) and REBT (rational emotive behaviour; Ellis and Dryden 2007) with the specific skills that underpin resilience and wellbeing and the evidence-based foundations of positive education. It was developed as a multi-faceted early prevention resilience programme for children from kindergarten (5 years old) to early adolescence (14 years old) and includes three volumes of age-appropriate curriculum lessons, activities, games and other resources across three levels i.e. years K–2, years 3–4 and years 5–8. It is a whole-school universal programme that aims to assist teachers to embed the teaching of resilience within the academic curriculum. It incorporates:

- Evidence-based pedagogy, especially relationship-focused teaching strategies such as cooperative learning (e.g. Roseth et al. 2008).
- The teaching of critical and creative thinking skills.
- The use of an extensive collection of (mostly) award-winning children's literature.

All three levels of the programme include the following nine curriculum units:

1. The *Core Values* unit encourages children to be honest, fair, kind, cooperative and respectful of self and others and be inclusive and accepting of individual differences.
2. The *People Bouncing Back* outlines and details the Bounce Back acronym which consists of ten coping statements based mainly on the principles of cognitive behaviour therapy. The focus is on teaching children to think realistically, positively and flexibly about problems and challenges.
3. The *Looking on the Bright Side* unit focuses on the teaching of optimistic thinking skills and the importance of gratitude (as highlighted in positive psychology).
4. The *Courage* unit teaches 'everyday' courage of having a go at something that is challenging despite experiencing fear or anxiety. It includes activities that highlight that everyday courage is different to heroism, thrill-seeking and foolhardy behaviour.
5. The *Emotions* unit encourages children to have empathy for others and teaches skills for managing uncomfortable emotions (such as anxiety and anger) and for amplifying positive emotions.
6. The *Relationships* unit teaches skills for making and keeping friends as well as managing conflict.
7. The *Humour* unit incorporates ideas for building class connectedness and positive emotions through humour using 'a giggle gym' and other activities. The unit also focuses on the appropriate use of humour as a coping strategy and highlights the difference between humour that is helpful and humour that is hurtful or trivialises a difficult situation.
8. The *No Bullying* unit helps children to identify and safely manage face-to-face and cyberbullying behaviour and teaches skills for acting confidently and assertively and skills for supporting others who are being bullied.
9. The *Success* unit provides activities that enable children to identify their character and ability strengths and also teaches skills and strategies for goal setting, persistence, effort and overcoming obstacles. It also encourages students to gain a sense of meaning and purpose through contributing to class and community activities.

Findings and Discussion

The names of the schools were removed from the transcripts and each of the ten schools was allocated a number from one to ten by the research assistant. Three researchers independently coded the data and then together agreed on the main themes based on the commonality of keywords and categories. The themes that emerged were then organised and categorised as either school-based factors, school system factors or programme-specific factors.

School-Based Factors

The strongest school-based factors that were perceived by schools as supporting the effective implementation and long-term sustainability of the programme are summarised in Table 17.1.

Table 17.1 shows that the wellbeing coordinators in all the participating schools placed a high priority on student wellbeing and social-emotional learning. All school leaders in the ten schools provided leadership support for the programme, and the schools kept parents informed about the programme. Nine of the coordinators perceived that student wellbeing and students' social-emotional skills underpinned effective academic learning, nine of the schools had provided opportunities for teachers' professional learning that supported their teaching of the programme, and nine of the schools advocated a weekly designated Bounce Back lesson. Eight of the coordinators gave examples of how they facilitated the teachers' implementation of the programme, and seven spoke about how the programme linked to other school initiatives.

Table 17.1 School-based factors identified by participating schools as contributing to their success in implementing and sustaining the programme

School-based factors	Number of schools endorsing it
1. Prioritising student wellbeing and social-emotional learning	10
2. The importance of full leadership support for the programme	10
3. Adopting a whole-school approach	10
4. Keeping parents informed about the programme and its contents through newsletter and meetings	10
5. A belief by school leaders and teachers that social and emotional learning and student wellbeing underpin effective academic learning	9
6. Opportunities for staff to undertake professional learning that supported their teaching of the programme	9
7. Having a weekly designated lesson (once per week or more often) for teaching the programme	9
8. The supporting role of key people within the school who undertook actions that facilitated implementation and maintained its profile within the school over time	8
9. Linking the programme to other components of the school e.g. school values, behaviour management policy, school improvement plan, assembly awards	7

Prioritising Student Wellbeing and Social and Emotional Learning

A school's vision predicts its priorities and is anchored in the values and ethics of the whole school community. According to Leithwood et al. (2004), an effective school leader builds a shared vision for the direction their school should take, identifies effective ways to develop staff and redesigns the organisation of their school to align with the school vision. The wellbeing coordinators in all ten schools perceived that student wellbeing was a school priority: 'it is our number one priority', 'student wellbeing is at the forefront of our school priorities', and 'it is our school's highest priority'.

Four of the schools explicitly stated how the focus on student wellbeing underpinned their schools' values. Nine of the schools also saw that the social-emotional learning skills that facilitate student wellbeing were also essential for academic learning: 'If you can't get social-emotional stability and wellbeing, our students won't learn'. Brackett et al. (2012) have suggested that, since teachers' beliefs about SEL have been shown to significantly influence programme implementation and outcomes, school leaders should assess the 'readiness' of their school and its teachers to implement and support a selected SEL programme. They have suggested some ideas that could be used in written survey questions (Brackett et al. 2012). However it could be argued that in some cases such an assessment could be carried out more informally as has occurred in these schools.

Adopting a Whole-School Approach

School-based programs that adopt a whole-school approach have been found to more likely be effective, especially when they focus on the promotion of mental health rather than the prevention of mental illness (Wells et al. 2002). The teaching of the Bounce Back programme to all students at every year level in the primary school was identified by all ten schools in this study as a major factor in the successful implementation and sustainability of the programme. For nine schools this was for all grades from kindergarten to year 6; for one school it was from pre-school to year 5. The wellbeing coordinators believed that this whole-school commitment enabled them to provide a consistent message and more effectively embed the language of resilience across their whole school community.

The whole-school approach also provided the opportunity for five of the schools to allocate the same curriculum topic (e.g. People Bouncing Back) for a designated few weeks. These wellbeing coordinators saw that this designated topic provided school-wide opportunities to provide consistent messages about resilience across the whole school community. Some examples include the wellbeing coordinator sending out a reminder to staff in the staff newsletter, developing a scope and sequence of lessons from K to 6; notifying parents in the parent newsletters and including weekly assembly items on the topic (mentioned by three or the ten schools: 'each class presents a snippet at assembly depending on the topic').

Another coordinator talked about how their school's whole-school approach was supported by the introduction of a Bounce Back Award to students across all year levels. The award was seen as a way to maintain the profile of the programme across the school:

> We regularly at assembly present children with the Bounce Back Award, where they're given a certificate – and it might be something that we've seen in the schoolyard, in the classrooms. Teachers might nominate a particular student because they've seen them 'bounce back' after a bit of a challenge... And so the children can see then that, hey that's something that's important.

Leadership support for a whole-school approach was also illustrated by the school's organisational structures and, in particular, the school timetable. Nine of the ten schools allocated a designated time once a week for Bounce Back lessons (and in some cases more often) in the school timetable:

- 'Everyone has one lesson a week. It's expected that it's taught explicitly once a week, but then that it's successfully woven throughout the rest of the curriculum'.
- 'Bounce Back lessons are compulsory, not negotiable'.
- 'One hour a week is essential and then we also address key concepts in other curriculum areas or playground as required'.
- 'Bounce Back lessons are just as important as Maths and Reading blocks'.

Leadership Support for Implementation and Maintenance

In their role as leaders of their school, principals serve as both the 'gatekeepers' and 'promoters' of new programs (Hallinger and Heck 1996). The principal's support for a programme can significantly affect the quality of the teachers' implementation of that programme (Gottfredson and Gottfredson 2002; Han and Weiss 2005). All ten schools in this study perceived that the ongoing support for Bounce Back by their leadership team was an essential component of the successful implementation and sustainability of the programme in their school.

The school leaders offered a variety of practical support across the ten schools in order to facilitate their teachers' implementation of the programme. In all but one of the schools, the principal had assigned a key person who was a member of their school executive or leadership team to be responsible for overseeing all the teachers' implementation of the programme: For example, one wellbeing coordinator explained that 'The assistant principal has a major commitment to the programme and has a team of four pivotal people maintaining it'.

All coordinators articulated the importance of facilitating teachers' implementation of the programme. Five coordinators explicitly spoke about the importance of making it as easy as possible for the teachers to implement the programme. For example, one coordinator provided support by mapping the Bounce Back units to curriculum outcomes and compiled a glossary of key terms so that all teachers were using the same definition (e.g. of courage). Several described how they printed off handouts for student workshops and provided staff with key resources that they needed.

Several coordinators outlined how they used structured staff meetings to maintain the program's profile, conduct professional learning about aspects of the programme, encourage staff to share innovative ideas for teaching the programme and introduce teachers to new picture books. As one coordinator said, you need to 'present it, resource it, and package it for teachers so it is easy to go'. The key message from all these comments is that making it as easy as possible for their staff to teach the programme produced more effective implementation.

Taking a whole-school approach also facilitated the school leadership's capacity to link the programme to other school components such as the academic curriculum, (especially language and literature) and the school's positive behaviour management policy and the school's values programme. Eight of the coordinators explicitly stated that assisting teachers to make those links had contributed to their successful implementation of the programme. Leadership commitment was also demonstrated by ensuring that all teachers in the ten schools were given their own individual copies of the relevant *Bounce Back! Teacher Resource Book.*

Opportunities for Professional Learning and Induction of New Staff

Professional development for teachers in regard to the programme has been widely recognised as a significant determinant of success in school programme implementation (Han and Weiss 2005; McCormick et al. 1995). Six of the ten schools referred to receiving some training in the Bounce Back programme, two schools had received some training in social-emotional learning, and one school had received intensive training in positive education but not in the programme itself. However no school had received more than 1 day of training on the programme, and there were no schools in which all teachers currently at their school had received formal training in the programme. This is significantly different to what occurs in many well-funded research projects (Durlak et al. 2011).

Two challenges identified by the school coordinators were the need for induction of new staff and strategies for maintaining the whole school momentum for implementing the programme. Example:

> We do have a stable staff but there are a couple of new teachers who come in and out every year, so it's been really important to make sure that they learn about Bounce Back in their induction and to get their mentor teacher to come and give them that practical help and explain how it would be implemented over time.

The implication from this research is that if other factors such as leadership support for implementation and the program's attributes are strong, then these school and programme factors may compensate for the minimal teacher training.

Monitoring and Communication

Monitoring the implementation of any new programme has been found to produce much better outcomes (Dubois et al. 2002). One way of monitoring implementation is to provide in-classroom performance feedback, and this has also been shown to significantly impact on teachers' success in implementing a programme (Leach and Conto 1999; Han and Weiss 2005). Half of the coordinators highlighted the importance of monitoring the teachers' performance and progress in a supportive way. For example, one coordinator talked about observing different teachers' Bounce Back lessons and then engaging in follow-up discussion, and five of the coordinators talked about checking the teachers' work programme to ensure that it included reference to their Bounce Back lesson plans. One coordinator described how sometimes he and individual teachers taught selected lessons from the programme together:

> Every time there's a Positive Education lesson through Bounce Back, I'm in the room with the class. I'll go in and I'll spend 15 minutes with each of the classes, so the teachers can then use me as a resource while I'm there, or they can watch me – we can put the classes together. I can teach the programme. I can introduce it. I can work with them.

Another coordinator explained:

- 'The teachers have been using it for a long time. We need to maintain showing them how they can get the most out of it and making sure that they keep that up. That's been something we've really had to look at'.
- As one coordinator said: 'It's essential that the executive value the programme and we have a committee to keep its profile up'.

Another component of communication was keeping parents informed about the programme. All ten schools consistently keep parents informed about the programme and its contents through school newsletters, classroom meetings and/or parent evenings. Most coordinators also spoke about the fact that many parents also gave feedback to teachers about their observation of the positive behaviour changes they were seeing in their children within the family context.

School System Factors

A school's implementation of a programme does not occur within a vacuum but rather reflects and is strongly influenced by the policies and priorities of the school system they belong to. An important factor in the sustainability of any social-emotional/resilience programme is how well the programme aligns with their school system's educational policy and priorities at either the regional, state or national level (Noble and McGrath 2015; Han and Weiss 2005; Adelman and Taylor 2003; Elias 2003; Coburn 2003).

Three of the ten schools were participating in 'KidsMatter', a national Australian government mental health initiative which aims to help schools to develop safe and supportive school communities and to teach the social and emotional skills that children and young people require to meet life's challenges and be resilient. As part of their role, KidsMatter makes available an online directory of programmes from which schools can select. These three KidsMatter schools had chosen Bounce Back because they perceived that the programme aligned well with the policy guidelines, recommendations and important research outcomes as outlined on the KidsMatter site. The KidsMatter research evaluation (Dix et al. 2009) on the benefits of social-emotional learning showed statistically and practically significant improvements in students' measured mental health in terms of both reduced mental health difficulties and increased mental health strengths. The impact of KidsMatter was especially apparent for students who were rated as having higher levels of mental health difficulties at the start of the trial (Dix et al. 2009). Two schools indicated that the Kidsmatter's evaluation of Bounce Back influenced their choice of the programme.

Three of the schools also had system support from their regional Catholic Education Office, which had made student wellbeing and social-emotional learning a very clear school system priority. This was reflected in this school system's strategic plan and explicit support for schools. For example, the system support included funding for each school's student wellbeing coordinator to complete a master's degree in student wellbeing and to attend a student wellbeing cluster group meeting that met once every school term for professional learning. These three schools perceived that Bounce Back fulfilled their school system's expectations for a whole-school focus on student wellbeing.

Programme-Specific Factors

As indicated in Table 17.2, all ten wellbeing coordinators expressed in different ways how the programme was user-friendly and easy to teach. The programme factors identified as important by all the coordinators were the structure of the programme and the program's use of high-quality children's literature that allowed the teachers to embed the teaching in the primary curriculum. The flexibility as well as the multifactored nature of the programme was also seen by nine of the coordinators as the programme features that contributed to their long-term implementation of the programme.

Table 17.2 Programme features identified by participating schools as contributing to their success in implementing and sustaining the programme

Programme features	Number of schools endorsing this factor
User-friendly and easy to teach	10
Importance of the high quality children's picture books junior novels and follow-up literature and language activities	9
The structure of the programme and the consistency of key messages	9
Multi-faceted approach in each unit and links to a range of curriculum areas (e.g. maths, science, music, art)	9
Flexible, adaptable and can be customised to fit with other aspects of the school and classroom	9

Discussions of these programme attributes are organised under four broad programme factors that have been identified in the research literature as characterising sustainable teacher-implemented classroom prevention and intervention programmes in mental health (Han and Weiss 2005). Teachers are more motivated to implement and continue teaching a programme when:

- It is acceptable to their school and to themselves as practitioners and doesn't require too much time or effort.
- It is effective in making a difference.
- It is feasible and can be implemented on an ongoing basis with 'minimal but sufficient' resources.
- It is flexible and adaptable.

Acceptability of the Programme to the Schools and Their Teachers

Teachers' evaluation of the acceptability of a programme significantly influences not only their preparedness to implement a new programme but also the extent to which they implement it accurately (Durlak et al. 2011; Han and Weiss 1995; Reimers et al. 1987). The widespread acceptability of Bounce Back by the teachers in this study appears to be one of the most significant factors in its sustained implementation in these ten schools. A number of key features of this programme appear to have contributed to this teacher acceptability. Firstly teachers perceived that it was important to teach resilience to their students. Examples of the coordinators' comments include:

- 'I think resilience is a really important concept. I think that's why Bounce Back has stayed as a programme in our school'.
- 'It makes sense and it's really relevant to how to teach resilience to students'.
- 'We've all seen how resilience impacts on their learning'.

As one coordinator said, 'the programme has everyone's whole-hearted support'. The importance of whole-school acceptability of the programme is illustrated in the following quote from one of the coordinators who was the school principal:

> It's one of the few programs that the whole school is keen to work with and that's not really a common thing. Programs come in through schools all the time, we know that, but on a regular basis you find that it's not being used and so you put it on the shelf and you think, well, that was a waste of money. You might have some programs where a couple of teachers will use it and they swear by it but the rest of the school doesn't. Bounce Back is one programme where there's not one teacher at this school who does not use it.

A combination of programme-specific features appears to have contributed to high teacher acceptability of the programme. All ten schools perceived the programme to be teacher-friendly and easy to teach. For example:

> It has great lessons that are easy to implement;
>
> It's easy to teach because you get all that background information and worksheets that go with the lessons and Its use of child-friendly resources was important to us.

Another coordinator commented that 'The psychological and educational rigour that underpins the program' was also very important to their school.

The program's structure was identified as one of the most important factors that contributed to the resource being teacher-friendly, as illustrated by the following comments:

- 'The organisation of the units is really, really helpful, especially for teachers who have never really taught most of these skills before and its developmental sequence of units (across all three Teacher resource books) is really helpful'.
- 'The book's layout and the access to the research base behind is really easy to understand'.
- 'It has well-structured, thorough lessons'.
- 'The best thing is the structure of the programme and the lessons that develop competency and social and emotional skills'.
- 'The structure provides a consistency of key messages across year levels'.

The use of children's literature to teach the program's key messages was also identified by nine of the schools as another key factor that contributed to making the programme easy to teach e.g.:

- 'The literature element appeals to a lot of us'.
- 'I do think it's easy to teach. I choose a really enjoyable fabulous literature piece and I will teach ideas through that'.
- 'The children's picture books are the absolute stand out in the programme for me. They are all so relevant and the kids can relate to them so well'.
- 'Our teachers love its use of good children's literature'.
- 'The use of high quality children's picture books and follow-up literature and language activities is great'.

The use of children's literature to teach the resilience concepts was also seen as an essential factor for developing teacher confidence in using the programme.

> If you're not 100% sure you can start with the books (recommended children's literature) and then you can have your resource manual next to you. Then as you start going with the flow, you will start to learn the prompting questions that help to generate discussions, and you start getting ideas of your own.

Teacher confidence in teaching a programme has been shown to impact on the effort they are willing to give to planning and implementing a programme and persisting with teaching it despite setbacks (Tschannen-Moran et al. 1998). Teachers' investment in putting effort into the implementation of a programme is, in turn, more likely to lead to successful experiences with new strategies (Han and Weiss 2005). This is reflected in the following comment:

> I am more comfortable with Bounce Back now and I now take it to the next level …When you first start you're sort of dancing around as to how much you'll get out of the kids… I definitely now ask more challenging questions and provoke more detailed discussions because I now know what you can get from the children.

Programme Effectiveness

One of the most significant factors that has been shown to contribute to a program's acceptability from the teachers' perspective is that they perceive that the behaviour of their students has changed as a result of their implementation of the programme (Han and Weiss 2005; Datnow and Castellano 2000). Five of the teachers explicitly mentioned that the programme had helped their students learn the language of resilience as illustrated in the following comments:

- 'Giving the students the licence to use the language of resilience, and giving them the vocabulary through the range of activities, puts their wellbeing at the forefront of everything we do'.
- 'Helping children to learn the language of resilience so they learn to self-manage their own behaviour'.
- 'It's really clear terminology for even teaching kindergarten students. They like the idea of 'bouncing back' and the vocabulary is appropriate'.

Teachers also spoke about how they observed the children acting more resiliently:

- 'The children are now able to talk about Bounce Back quite clearly. And we've really can see it in their behaviour. … it's embedded in them and they talk about it, and they also put it into action as well'.
- 'The older kids now realise that what they think affects how they feel and affects those choices they make. For example looking on the bright side, using their thinking caps, learning from their mistakes and all those sort of things are really embedded in all the kids, so that's good. They almost do it automatically now and they don't put their heads down and sulk if something goes wrong. They are definitely more resilient'.

One of the participating school communities had been adversely affected by very severe bushfires which involved a significant loss of life. The coordinator spoke about how the programme helped the children build relationships, support each other and be more resilient:

> One of the first years I taught Bounce Back I had Grade six boys, and I had some of the grade six boys crying in the room, and it was just phenomenal because one boy was one of the kids, who was one of the hierarchy if you know what I mean, and all the other kids turned around and said 'my goodness, we didn't realise that he actually had issues as well'. That sort of changed the class dynamics around and really helped the children be more resilient.

Another coordinator expressed how teaching the programme helped her connect more with her students: 'I just reckon I've become a lot closer to my kids'. A Scottish study (Axford et al. 2011) which conducted an evaluation of the impact of Bounce Back in 16 primary schools that had been implementing Bounce Back for 18 months concluded that one of the main effects of the programme was enhanced student-student relationships, enhanced teacher-student relationships and increased classroom connectedness. Positive student-teacher relationships have been found to be a key aspect of not only teachers' job satisfaction but also increased learning outcomes (Hagelskamp et al. 2013; Sutton and Wheatley 2003). Additionally, this Scottish study not only found an increase in student resilience and social skills but also identified a highly significant increase in teacher resilience and wellbeing as a result of their teaching the programme.

One of the ten coordinators in this current study spoke about how the teachers' belief in the effectiveness of the programme also had an impact on the children's response to the programme:

> I think the important thing is that our teachers really believe in it as well. And so when they're conducting their lesson, the children can see that too.

Eight of the ten schools reported observations by staff of more resilient student behaviours in class and in the playground and also noted that they had received feedback from many parents about their observations of their children behaving more resiliently at home. All ten schools perceived that the relationship-building pedagogy of cooperative learning strategies and circle time that underpinned the programme had also contributed to the effectiveness of the programme.

Feasibility: It Can Be Implemented on an Ongoing Basis with Minimal But Sufficient Resources

As well as being acceptable to the teachers and demonstrably effective, the Bounce Back programme was seen as practical and feasible for the teachers to implement in their classrooms. This was important given that none of the schools involved in this research received designated ongoing funding to specifically run the Bounce Back programme. One coordinator referred to 'being creative' in accessing current infrastructure funding to provide some money to purchase an individual copy of the Bounce Back handbook for each classroom teacher. Another coordinator spoke about the benefits of only having to purchase one resource book for each teacher and not needing to purchase student workbooks that would be a recurring cost.

Flexibility and Adaptability

Each new school year brings a new cohort of students with diverse abilities, family situations, backgrounds and personal and educational needs. Classrooms and students may also change across a school year as students progress, deal with challenges or encounter difficulties. A dramatic example, as mentioned above, was that one of the schools interviewed had experienced severe bushfires in their area that had led to a significant loss of lives and properties. Hence, according to Han and Weiss (2005), a programme must be:

- Developed and structured in such a way that it can be flexible and readily adaptable for changing circumstances.
- Well enough understood by teachers so that they are able to adapt it without losing its core principles and key messages.

Adaptability can refer to either the provision of a range of options for teaching specific content or the addition or integration of content or teaching approaches that may depart from those outlined in the original programme. Nine of the schools perceived the flexibility and adaptability of the Bounce Back programme was one of its great strengths.

- 'It's a flexible programme that can be customised for your school and for specific students'.
- 'It (Bounce Back) has got room for creativity and it's open to your own individual way of teaching it slightly differently'.
- 'I've gone from grade six to grade three now and all of a sudden I had different problems. So now I've got a whole group of bossy girls in the grade three room. So of course I go to the Bounce Back programme and start looking up resources. We used the suggested children's literature that dealt with bossing each other and we've done things about how does it make you feel, how does it make other people feel, all that sort of stuff'.
- 'Teachers have become quite savvy about how to use Bounce Back for their particular areas of learning. They dip in and out of it. So when they observe behaviours of concern in a group of kids, they go 'okay I know that what's happening is about Success (a Bounce Back unit of work) so I'm going to access the list of resources and we're going to do some bits and pieces around that'. So I think that is really positive as a long-term issue. The teachers have been upskilled in a way that enables them to pinpoint what's available in Bounce Back and they can use it in a range of different settings or situations'.

In contrast to Bounce Back, one coordinator described a different social-emotional learning programme that was highly prescriptive: 'I remember looking at the (Named) programme and it was just horrendous. It was so prescriptive– you've got to do this at this time, and you've got to read this, and you've got to do that. It was so "staged" and so – it was just awful. With Bounce Back you start a talk and it creates so many incredible conversations amongst the kids, it's just incredible'.

The flexibility of the programme was also seen as an asset in that it enabled teachers to more easily integrate the programme with other curriculum areas and other school components and initiatives. One could argue that the more teachers adapt the programme, the more the essential principles of the programme may be diluted. Early implementation science advocated that teachers adhered rigorously to a programme with no adaptations (Durlak 2015). Now adaptations are seen as the rule in school-based research rather than the exception (Dusenbury et al. 2005; Ringwalt et al. 2003). This research indicated that as teachers developed confidence in teaching a programme, they made adaptations that then contributed to their greater commitment and sustainability in continuing to teach the programme. Perhaps the risk to dilution is less important than the benefits of teachers' ongoing commitment to teaching the programme.

Conclusions

A school-based focus on supporting children and young people to develop resilience is a central component of effective education for their future, their country's future and for the future of our world. Increasingly schools and teachers are being expected to deliver social-emotional learning programs that can enhance students' wellbeing, resilience and academic achievement. Hence it is critical that research identifies the school-based factors, school system factors and the programme-specific factors that contribute to the effective implementation and sustainability of such programs. The focus must be on what works in the real world of schools where there is no access to research funding.

This chapter has reviewed the key factors that contributed to the successful implementation and sustainability of one specific social and emotional learning programme (Bounce Back) in ten primary schools. Although it is a small qualitative study, it is the only study to our knowledge that reviews both the school and programme factors that has sustained the 'real-world' implementation of a social-emotional learning programme for up to 12 years without any research funding.

In summary, three categories of factors were identified as important in contributing to the implementation and sustainability of the programme. These three categories were school-based factors, school system factors and programme-specific factors. The school-based factors included the school leadership prioritising student wellbeing and social and emotional learning, adopting a whole-school approach to the implementation of the programme, providing leadership support for teachers' implementation and maintenance of the programme, monitoring the teachers' implementation of the programme, communicating with parents about the programme and linking the programme with other school initiatives. The school system factors were varied and included support for three of the schools from the regional educational authority (Catholic schools) and three of the schools accessing support through a government mental health school-based initiative (KidsMatter).

However ultimately the success of a programme is not only dependent on leadership support for implementation but also on whether individual teachers effectively teach the programme in their classroom. Four programme attributes were identified as critical to promoting different teachers' sustained efforts to implement the programme effectively: the programme was acceptable to them because it was teacher-friendly and easy to implement; it was perceived to be effective in terms of enhancing their students' resilience, behaviour and engagement in their lessons; it was feasible to implement without significant extra funding or resourcing; and it was flexible in the different ways as it enabled teachers to adapt the lessons to meet the needs of their own students and the schools. In conclusion schools should consider incorporating the factors identified in this qualitative study when planning for effective implementation and sustainability.

References

Adelman, H. S., & Taylor, L. (2003). On sustainability of project innovations as systemic change. *Journal of Educational and Psychological Consultation, 14*, 1–25.

Axford, S., Schepens, R., & Blyth, K. (2011). Did introducing the Bounce Back Programme have an impact on resilience, connectedness and wellbeing of children and teachers in 16 primary schools in Perth and Kinross, Scotland? *Educational Psychology, 12*(1), 2–5.

Barry, M. A., Clarke, A. M., Jenkins, R., & Patel, V. (2013). A systematic review of the effectiveness of mental health promotion interventions for young people in low and middle income countries. *BMC Public Health, 13*, 835. http://www.biomedcentral.com/1471-2458/13/835.

Beck, A. T. (1979). *Cognitive therapy and the emotional disorders*. New York: Penguin Books.

Bond, L., Butler, H., Thomas, L., Carlin, J., Glover, S., Bowes, G., & Patton, G. C. (2007). Social and school connectedness in early secondary school as predictors of late teenage substance use, mental health, and academic outcomes. *Journal of Adolescent Health, 40*(357), 9–18.

Brackett, M. A., Reyes, M. R., Rivers, S. E., Elbertson, N. A., & Salovey, P. (2012). Assessing teachers' beliefs about social and emotional learning. *Journal of Psychoeducational Assessment, 30*, 219–236.

Catalano, R. F., Mazzab, J. J., Harachia, T. W., Abbott, R. D., Haggerty, K. P., & Fleminga, C. B. (2003). Raising healthy children through enhancing social development in elementary school: Results after 1.5 years. *Journal of School Psychology, 41*(2), 143–164.

Cicchetti, D. (2010). Resilience under conditions of extreme stress: A multilevel perspective. *World Psychiatry, 9*(3), 145–154.

Coburn, C. (2003). Rethinking scale: Moving beyond numbers to deep and lasting change. *Educational Researcher, 32*(6), 3–12.

Datnow, A., & Castellano, M. (2000). Teachers' responses to success for all: How beliefs, experiences, and adaptations shape implementation. *American Educational Research Journal, 37*, 775–799.

Diekstra, R. F. W & Gravesteijn, C. (2008). *Effectiveness of school-based social and emotional education programmes worldwide.* http://www.lions-quest.org/pdfs/EvaluationBotinEnglish.pdf

Dix, K.L., Owens, L., Skrzypiec, G., & Spears, B. (2009). *KidsMatter evaluation executive summary.* Beyond Blue. www.kidsmatter.edu.au

Dubois, D. L., Holloway, B., Valentine, J. C., & Cooper, H. (2002). Effectiveness of mentoring programs for youth: A meta-analytic review. *American Journal of Community Psychology, 30*(2), 157–197.

Durlak, J. A. (2015). Studying program implementation is not easy but it is essential. *Prevention Science, 16*(8), 1123–1127.

Durlak, J. A., Weissberg, R. P., Dymnicki, A. B., Taylor, R. D., & Schellinger, K. B. (2011). The impact of enhancing students' social and emotional learning: A meta-analysis of school-based universal interventions. *Child Development, 82*(1), 405–432.

Dusenbury, L., Brannigan, R., Hansen, W. B., Walsh, J., & Falco, M. (2005). Quality of implementation: Developing measures crucial to understanding the diffusion of preventive interventions. *Health Education Research, 20*, 308–313.

Elias, M. (2003). Academic and social-emotional learning. *International Academy of Education, 11*, 5–31.

Ellis, A., & Dryden, W. (2007). *The practice of rational emotive behaviour therapy* (2nd ed.). New York: Springer Publishing Co..

Gable, S. J., & Haidt, J. (2005). What (and why) is positive psychology? *Review of General Psychology, 9*(2), 103–110.

Global Burden of Disease Study 2010. (2012). *Global burden of diseases, injuries, and risk factors study 2010.* Seattle: Institute for Health, Metrics and Evaluation.

Gottfredson, D. C., & Gottfredson, G. D. (2002). Quality of school-based prevention programs. Results from a national survey. *Journal of Research on Crime and Delinquency, 39*(1), 3–35.

Hagelskamp, C., Brackett, M. A., Rivers, S. E., & Salovey, P. (2013). Improving classroom quality with the RULER approach to social and emotional learning: Proximal and distal outcomes. *American Journal of Community Psychology, 51*(3–4), 530–543.

Hallinger, P., & Heck, R. H. (1996). Reassessing the principal's role in school effectiveness: A review of empirical research, 1980–1995. *Educational Administration Quarterly, 32*, 5–44.

Han, S. S., & Weiss, B. (2005). Sustainability of teacher implementation of school based mental health programs. *Journal of Abnormal Child Psychology, 33*(6), 665–679.

Hart, A., & Heaver, B. (2013). Evaluating resilience-based programs for schools using a systematic consultative review. *Journal of Child and Youth Development, 1*(1), 27–53.

Hattie, J. (2012). *Visible learning for teachers: Maximizing impact on learning.* New York: Routledge.

Kim-Cohen, J. (2007). Resilience and developmental psychopathology. *Child and Adolescent Psychiatric Clinics of North America, 16*, 271–283.

Kim-Cohen, J., Caspi, A., Moffitt, T. E., et al. (2003). Prior juvenile diagnoses in adults with mental disorder. *Archives of General Psychiatry, 60*, 709–717.

Layard, R., & Hagell, A. (2015). Healthy young minds: Transforming the mental health of children. In J. H. Helliwell, R. Layard, & J. Sachs (Eds.), *World happiness report 2015.* New York: Sustainable Development Solutions Network. www.unsdsn.org/happiness.

Leach, D. J., & Conto, H. (1999). The additional effects of process and outcome feedback following brief in-service teacher training. *Educational Psychology, 19*, 441–462.

Leithwood, K., Seashore, L. K., Anderson, S., & Wahlstrom, K. (2004). *How leadership influences student learning.* New York: Wallace Foundation.

Lonczak, H. S., Abbott, R. D., Hawkins, J. D., Kosterman, R., & Catalano, R. (2002). The effects of the Seattle social development project: Behavior, pregnancy, birth, and sexually transmitted disease outcomes by age 21. *Archives of Pediatrics and Adolescent Health, 156*(5), 438–447.

Luthar, S. S. (2006). Resilience in development: A synthesis of research across five decades. In D. Cicchetti & D. Cohen (Eds.), *Developmental psychopathology: Risk, disorder and adaptation* (pp. 739–795). New York: Wiley.

Marzano, R. (2007). *Art & Science of teaching: A comprehensive framework for effective instruction*. Alexandria: Association for Supervision & Curriculum Development.

McCormick, L. K., Steckler, A. B., & McLeroy, K. R. (1995). Diffusion of innovations in schools: A study of adoption and implementation of school-based tobacco prevention curricula. *American Journal of Health Promotion, 9*, 210–219.

McGrath, H., & Noble, T. (2003). *Bounce back! A classroom resiliency programme. Teacher's handbook*. Sydney: Pearson Education.

McGrath, H., & Noble, T. (2011). *Bounce back! A wellbeing & resilience program* (Lower primary K-2; middle primary: Years 3–4; upper primary/junior secondary: Years 5–8). Melbourne: Pearson Education.

Munby, S, & Fullan, M. (2016). *Inside-out and downside-up. How leading from the middle has the power to transform education systems*. Education Development Trust. http://michaelfullan.ca/wp-content/uploads/2016/02/Global-Dialogue-Thinkpiece

Noble, T., & McGrath, H. (2015). PROSPER: A new framework for positive education. *Psychology of Well-Being Theory, Research and Practice, 5*, 2.

Noble, T., & McGrath, H. (2016). *PROSPER for student wellbeing: Pathways and policy*. The Netherlands: Springer Brief.

O'Shaughnessy, T. E., Lane, K. E., Gresham, F. E., & Beebe-Frankenberg, M. E. (2003). Children placed at risk for learning and behavioural difficulties. Implementing a school-wide system of early identification and intervention. *Remedial & Special Education, 24*(1), 27–35.

OECD. (2014). *Making mental health count: The social and economic costs of neglecting mental health care, OECD health policy studies*. Paris: OECD Publishing.

Osterman, K. (2000). Students' need for belonging in the school community. *Review of Educational Research, 70*(3), 323–367.

Reimers, T. M., Wacker, D. P., & Koeppl, G. (1987). Acceptability of behavioral interventions: A review of the literature. *School Psychology Review, 16*(2), 212–227.

Ringwalt, C. L., Ennett, S., Johnson, R., Rohrbach, L. A., Simons-Rudolph, A., Vincus, A., & Thorne, J. (2003). Factors associated with fidelity to substance use prevention curriculum guides in the nation's middle schools. *Health Education & Behavior, 30*, 375–391.

Roseth, C. J., Johnson, D. W., & Johnson, R. T. (2008). Promoting early adolescents' achievement and peer relationships: The effects of cooperative, competitive and individualistic goal structures. *Psychological Bulletin, 134*(2), 223–246.

Scheirer, M. A. (2012). Planning evaluation through the program lifecycle. *American Journal of Evaluation, 33*, 263–294.

Seligman, M. E. P. (2011). *Flourish: A visionary new understanding of happiness and wellbeing*. New York: Simon and Schuster.

Seligman, M. E. P., Ernst, R. M., Gillham, J., Reivich, K., & Linkins, M. (2009). Positive education: Positive psychology and classroom interventions. *Oxford Review of Education, 35*(3), 293–311.

Severson, H. H., & Walker, H. M. (2002). Proactive approaches for identifying children at risk for sociobehavioral problems. In K. L. Lane, F. M. Gresham, & T. E. O'Shaughnessy (Eds.), *Interventions for children with or at risk for emotional and behavioural disorders* (pp. 33–53). Boston: Allyn & Bacon.

Sutton, R. E., & Wheatley, K. F. (2003). Teachers' emotions and teaching: A review of the literature and directions for future research. *Educational Psychology Review, 15*(4), 327–358.

Tschannen-Moran, M., Hoy, A. W., & Hoy, W. K. (1998). Teacher efficacy: Its meaning and measure. *Review of Educational Research, 68*, 202–248.

UNICEF. (2014). *The state of the world's children 2014 in numbers*. Available from www.unicef.org/sowc2014/numbers/

Weissberg, R. P., & O'Brien, M. U. (2004). What works in school-based social and emotional learning programs for positive youth development. *The Annals of the American Academy of Political and Social Science, 591*, 86–97.

Wells, J., Barlow, J., & Stewart-Brown, S. (2002). A systematic review of universal approaches to mental health promotion in schools. *Health Education, 103*(4), 197–220. https://doi.org/10.1108/09654280310485546.

World Health Organisation (WHO). (2003). *Caring for children and adolescent with mental disorders: Setting WHO directions*. Geneva: World Health Organisation.

Zins, J. E., Weissberg, R. P., Wang, M. C., & Walberg, H. J. (Eds.). (2004). *Building academic success on social and emotional learning: What does the research say?* New York: Teachers College Press.

Chapter 18
Promoting Resilience: A European Curriculum for Students, Teachers and Families

Valeria Cavioni, Maria Assunta Zanetti, Giusy Beddia, and Mara Lupica Spagnolo

Abstract This chapter presents the development of an early years and primary school curriculum for the promotion of resilience in schools in Europe called RESCUR. The curriculum is developed on the basis of the current social, economic and technological needs and challenges and seeks to develop in learners the requisite competences needed to overcome such challenges in their lives to achieve academic success and social and emotional wellbeing as young citizens. It takes a developmental, inclusive and culturally-responsive perspective, with activities reflecting the diversity of learners, particularly vulnerable children coming from disadvantaged backgrounds. The first part of the chapter discusses the conceptual framework underpinning the curriculum and the content areas of the activities. The second part describes the findings of the pilot implementation carried out in Italy that involved 84 teachers from kindergarten up to secondary school with a total of 738 students.

The Commission Communication "Early Childhood Education and Care" underlines the need of quality and effective early education systems across the European Union (EU) as a key foundation for fruitful lifelong learning, social inclusion, personal development and later employability (European Commission 2011). Access to good-quality early childhood education includes building resilience skills as core outcome indicators for quality education which promotes social inclusion and educational success and prevents school failure and early school leaving. Therefore, it is essential to develop supportive educational contexts to help children, from an

V. Cavioni (✉)
University of Milano-Bicocca, Milan, Italy
e-mail: valeria.cavioni@unimib.it

M. A. Zanetti · G. Beddia · M. Lupica Spagnolo
University of Pavia, Pavia, Italy
e-mail: zanetti@unipv.it; giusy.beddia01@gmail.com; mara.lupicaspagnolo@gmail.com

M. Wosnitza et al. (eds.), *Resilience in Education*,
https://doi.org/10.1007/978-3-319-76690-4_18

early age, face the challenges in their lives, overcome difficulties, and develop healthily and successfully. Developing resilience in early childhood is a foundation for healthy development and educational success and a sound preparation for the challenges of adult life.

Promoting Resilience at Schools

Although the conceptualisation of resilience may vary, and the skills and qualities embedded in the definition are broad (Shaikh and Kauppi 2010), resilience can be defined as successful adaptation and growth in the face of adversity and environmental stressors, including life transitions, socio-economic disadvantage, or times of personal or family cumulative stress (Masten 2011). Mental health problems may occur in children due to stressful events, and these difficulties can have negative outcomes both during childhood and adulthood (Kim-Cohen et al. 2003).

Resilience represents a strong protective factor to support positive mental health, especially in children (Dray et al. 2015; Hazel 2018, Chap. 13, this volume; Hjemdal et al. 2011; Kessler et al. 2008).

A large body of existing research identified factors linked with resilience on three levels, namely, personal, family and community, with each level contributing to an individual's overall ability to adapt to, or manage, significant sources of stress or trauma (Werner and Smith 1992; Resnick et al. 1997). The personal resilience level is associated with the individual's psychological, cognitive and emotional processes as internal resources, whilst family- and community-level (e.g. schools) protective factors are the main external resources in the healthy development of children and young people. Researchers have emphasised children who have higher levels of these protective factors showed lower levels of mental health problems such as depression and anxiety disorders (Hjemdal et al. 2007, 2011).

Although educational settings, such as schools, play a critical role in promoting the resilience (Lohbeck 2018, Chap. 6; Theron 2018, Chap. 12 – both this volume), wellbeing and health of children facing or experiencing risks in their development, and research has increasingly underlined this role in the past decades (Benard 2004; Rutter 1993, 2015; Ungar 2005), there is still a limited number of school-based programmes focused on resilience. Healthy school contexts with close relationships with caring adults, meaningful engagement as well as opportunity to learn and practise social and emotional skills, help young children facing adversity to cope and thrive academically, socially and emotionally (Castro Silva et al. 2018, Chap. 15; Noble and McGrath 2018 Chap. 17 – both this volume; Doll et al. 2004; Rutter 2006).

Aim of the Study

The aim of this study is to describe findings of a pilot resilience programme named *RESCUR Surfing the Waves*.

RESCUR Surfing the Waves is a school-based programme for early years and primary schools, which has been developed to help young children facing adversity, disadvantage and significant challenges in their lives, to grow, thrive and develop healthily and successfully. The following section describes the conceptual framework underpinning the programme, the content areas and the activities. The second section describes the findings of a pilot implementation of the programme carried out in Italian schools.

RESCUR Surfing the Waves Curriculum

RESCUR Surfing the Waves is a multi-year, universal prevention programme for the promotion of resilience as well as social and emotional competence in students 4–11 years of age. It is a universal programme, and it contains activities targeted to promote inclusion of vulnerable children such as children coming from ethnic minorities, for example, Roma, immigrant and refugee children, other children coming from socially disadvantaged families and communities and children with special educational needs. These children may be more vulnerable to challenges including poverty, mobility, unemployment, family stress, discrimination, bullying, violence, social exclusion, early school leaving, absenteeism, school failure and mental health problems amongst others. The programme seeks to provide these children with the key tools to overcome the disadvantages and obstacles in their development whilst making use of their strengths. It aims to enhance children's social and emotional skills as well as resilience, promote their positive mental health and wellbeing, and improve their academic learning and engagement.

Framework

RESCUR Surfing the Waves consists of a resilience curriculum for early and primary education in Europe, developed through the intercultural and transnational collaboration amongst six European universities, tapping into the resources and expertise of the various partners involved.[1] The curriculum has been built on the following key principles (see Fig. 18.1):

[1] RESCUR was a Comenius Lifelong Learning Programme project (2012–2015).

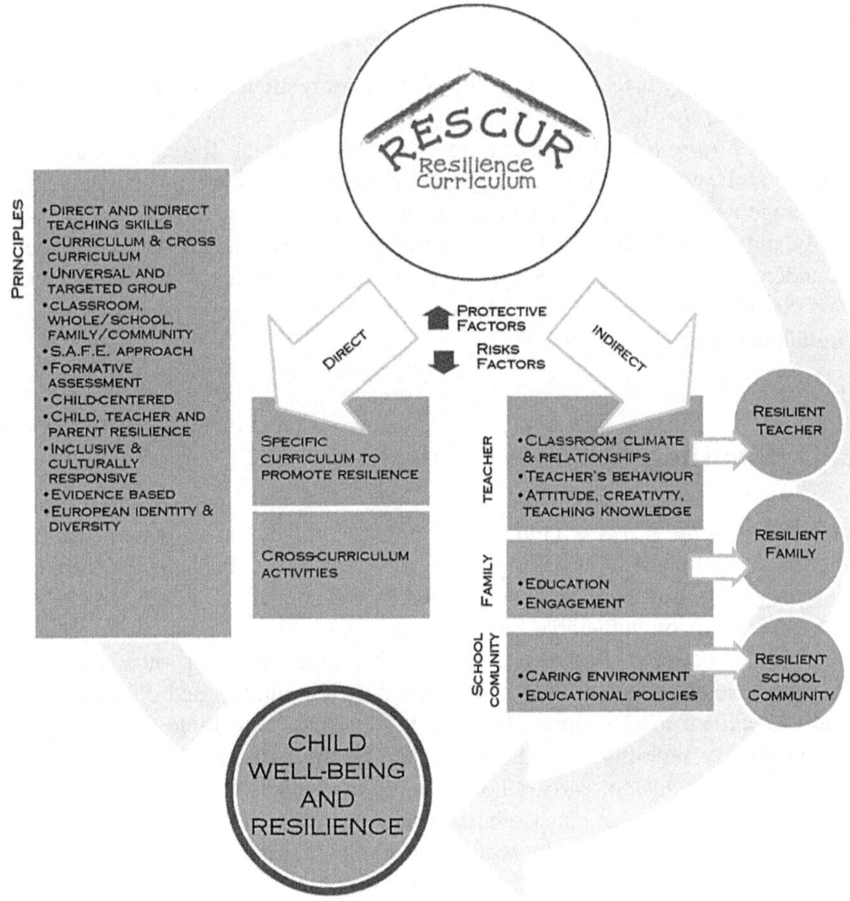

Fig. 18.1 Framework underpinning RESCUR Surfing the Waves. (Adapted from Cefai et al. 2016)

- The curriculum will be embedded within the mainstream curriculum taught by the classroom teachers, who will be trained, mentored and provided with the necessary resources.
- It is developmental and inclusive, being flexible and responsive to the needs of individual learning differences. The curriculum underlines the right of all learners for a quality resilience education, including a commitment towards social justice with an awareness of the risk for discriminatory practices due to individual educational needs, minority statuses and poverty amongst others.
- It adopts a spiral approach, with six major themes stretching across the early and primary school years at higher levels of complexity.
- It will be infused in the other content areas of the curriculum as well as in pedagogy, relationships and classroom management.

- It is based on the existing evidence of good practice in promoting resilience in school children.
- Assessment of learning outcomes is formative rather than summative, undertaken by both the classroom teacher and the students themselves.
- It is built on the reality and needs of the European context whilst appreciating the diversity of it at the same time.

Structure and Activities

RESCUR Surfing the Waves consists of six themes and 16 subthemes. Table 18.1 summarises the six themes and subthemes that are featured across the three age stages: early years (4–5 years), early primary (6–8 years) and late primary (9–11 years). Each theme consists of two subthemes which include three topics each, and the topics contain three activities at increasing levels of complexity (basic, intermediate and advanced levels). Theme 6, *Turning Challenges into Opportunities*, consists of six subthemes.

The classroom activities are designed to be used and applied by the classroom teachers in the standard mainstream curriculum. Each activity includes a mindfulness exercise, storytelling, discussion and processing of the story, practical activi-

Table 18.1 RESCUR themes and subthemes

Themes	Subthemes
Developing communication skills	Effective communication
	Assertiveness
Establishing and maintaining healthy relationships	Healthy relationships
	Cooperative skills, empathy and moral reasoning
Developing a growth mindset	Positive and optimistic thinking
	Positive emotions
Developing self determination	Problem-solving
	Empowerment and autonomy
Building on strengths	Positive self-concept and self-esteem
	Using strengths in academic and social engagement
Turning challenges into opportunities	Dealing with adversity and setbacks
	Dealing with rejection
	Dealing with family conflict
	Dealing with loss
	Dealing with bullying
	Dealing with change and transition

Fig. 18.2 Sample of the mascots by Italian primary school students

ties (such as puppetry, singing, drawing, colouring, role play and drama) and take-home activities. A Parents' Guide with information and practical activities is also included for use with the parents (see Cefai et al. 2016). The activities are designed to be implemented regularly by the teacher in class, one or more times per week, with each session lasting around 30–45 min. The activity (with clearly set learning goals and learning outcomes) starts with a brief mindfulness exercise, followed by a story. In the early years and early primary years, the stories are built around two specially created mascots, Sherlock the purple, bespectacled squirrel and Zelda the hedgehog with the broken spikes. In the late primary years, the stories make use of legends and real-life stories related to resilience (see Fig. 18.2). The story is then followed with a discussion, bringing out the successful resolution of the challenge or difficulty faced in the story. Students then engage in a practical activity on the topic, making use of drawing, role play, drama, crafts, singing and others. A take-home activity worksheet will then be completed by the student and his or her parents at home to reinforce the skill learnt at school. During the week, the classroom teacher will also refer to the topic in the other activities of the classroom to give the students the opportunity to transfer the resilience skills to the other content areas of the curriculum as well as during play. At the end of each theme, both teachers and students complete an individual checklist, assessing the level of competence achieved by the students in the various learning goals and learning outcomes within that theme.[2]

[2]The programme consists of five manuals as follows: A Teachers' Guide, A Parents' Guide, Early Years Manual of Activities (4–5 years), Early Primary School Years Manual of Activities (6–8 years) and Late Primary School Years Manual of Activities (9–11 years).

Establishing and Maintaining Healthy Relationships: A Pilot Study in Italian Schools

Theme

The Italian theme was the theme 2 titled "Building healthy relationships". It seeks to enable learners to develop healthy relationships and deal successfully with the challenges they face in building and maintaining such relationships. Various studies have underlined the relationship between resilience and positive, healthy social relationships with adults and peers (Benard 2004; Masten 2011; Rutter 1990). Children who do not have a functional social support system are more vulnerable to stress and difficulties and less likely to cope effectively with adversity (Doll et al. 2004). High-quality social relationships offer opportunities for children to feel socially accepted and loved; conversely, when the quality of the social relationships is poor, it might foster a sense of vulnerability and obstruct healthy social and emotional development (Ruzek et al. 2016). This theme seeks to enable vulnerable children to develop high-quality/healthy relationships with both peers and adults such as teachers and to overcome and resolve difficulties in these relationships. Table 18.2 provides an overview of the subthemes, topics and learning goals of the theme, according to the programme's age stages.

The activities of the first subtheme, *Healthy relationships*, are designed to support the development of the skills required to create a strong network of positive relationships. They focus on key areas such as making and sustaining friendships, prosocial behaviour, nurturing relationships and a supportive and inclusive school climate.

The activities in the first topic help children to reflect on the value of friendship and allow them to develop strategies to build, maintain and protect positive relationships with friends and deal successfully with situations which put friendship at risk.

The second set of activities focuses on the development of skills to seek and provide support to others facing difficulties. Researchers have linked resilience to active prosocial strategies that include positive social interactions and support (Hobfoll et al. 2009). Social support leads a person to believe that he or she is cared for and loved, esteemed and valued, and/or that he or she belongs to a network of communication and mutual obligation (Hupcey 1998). An important aspect of this social support system is the ability to ask for help from others in an appropriate manner. This is an important communication skill which enables the child to recruit physical, social and emotional support from others that protect the child from the impact of negative events. Nurturing relationships are a crucial foundation for both academic and socio-emotional development.

The third topic focuses on the creation of a classroom and school climate built on trust and sense of belonging. School climate is considered as a product of the beliefs, values and attitudes in the social interactions amongst students and with teachers, defining the parameters of acceptable behaviours within the school's context (Koth et al. 2008).

Table 18.2 Subthemes, topics and learning goals in the theme "Establishing and maintaining healthy relationships"

Subthemes	Topics	Learning goals Early years	Early primary	Late primary
Healthy relationships	Making and having friends	Share experiences of being with friends	Identify strategies to maintain positive relationships with peers	Increase trust in one another
				Recognise the importance of trust in friendship
		Understand the experience of missing a friend		Identify ways of coping with betrayal, *including forgiving* others
			List strategies to get along with others	
		Understand and overcome the difficulties that can arise in making new friends who may be different	Identify situations where friendship is put at risk	
	Prosocial behaviour	Identify their needs to feel safe and happy with friends	Identify friends from whom they can seek support	Describe how to help someone in difficulty
		Experience ways to thank people	Listen carefully to what other people say to recognise their needs	Identify strategies to help others who are discriminated
		Understand the importance of asking for support from an adult		Identify ways how to support friends
			Pay attention to the needs of others	
	Nurturing relationships and school climate	Feel confident in trusting adults	Understand and respect individual differences	Identify ways to show care and concern for others
				Identify the positive qualities of the classroom climate
		Be able to say what makes them feel safe and protected	Identify behaviours that reflect one's prejudices	Express caring behaviours towards classroom peers
		Understand that they can get warmth and security from relationships with adults	Identify and value cultural differences in friendship	

Cooperative skills, empathy and moral reasoning	Sharing, cooperation and teamwork	Take turns during play activities	Work with another peer on a common task	Make collective decisions with everyone participating
				Work collaboratively towards a common purpose, identifying individual tasks and roles
			Work together with others towards a common goal	
		Describe the importance of sharing	Recognise the importance of working in collaborative group work	Encourage and support each other during play
		Participate collaboratively in a group artwork that involves playing and working with others		
	Empathy	Consider others' point of view	Understand how others feel	Recognise the emotional needs of others
		Enquire how another person is feeling	Recognise how others' emotions can affect their own emotions and behaviours	
				Recognise that empathy is a key quality for building and maintaining friendship
		Be open to change perspective and opinions		
				Identify ways to empathise with, and offer support to others in difficulty
			Identify the feelings and needs of learners who were forced to emigrate and/or became refugees	
	Ethical, responsible and moral behaviour	Engage in positive behaviours towards animals	Identify the reasons why it is important to obey rules	Identify alternative solutions to a moral problem
			Describe why it is important to forgive others for their mistakes	Identify ways of looking after other people
		Engage positive and responsible actions that benefit others		
				Evaluate ethical behaviours
			Apologise for mistakes and take responsibility for one's own actions	
		Engage in responsible and positive actions towards peers who are disadvantaged or with a disability		

The second subtheme, *Cooperative skills, empathy and moral reasoning*, is composed of activities to enhance cooperative skills, empathy and moral reasoning. Activities are organised for children to work together and cooperate to achieve the same goal, discussing the best way to undertake a task and ensuring that everyone actively participates. With the help of these activities, students will also learn how to take others' perspectives into consideration through social interactions with peers and critically reflect on their own moral arguments and ethics.

The first set of activities provides materials to strengthen skills, ranging from the ability to take turns and share, to cooperation and teambuilding activities, such as making artwork, making collective decisions or playing games in teams. Collaboration amongst peers fosters children's social and emotional development (Slavin 1980), including positive attitudes towards others. Furthermore, working with peers, both in academic and leisure activities, helps children be more cooperative and respectful and exhibit higher self-esteem (Gensemer 2000). Activities are organised for children to work together collaboratively to achieve the same goal, discussing the best way to undertake a task and ensuring that everyone actively participates.

The second set illustrates activities to support the ability to recognise and appreciate the motives, behaviours, desires and feelings of others. Empathy is an essential building block for successful interpersonal relationships (Reid et al. 2013). The term refers to having an affective response that corresponds with the emotional state of another person as well as the ability to mentally understand another person's perspective (Davis 1983). Considered a necessary prerequisite for social and prosocial behaviour, empathy also influences the individual's acceptance by peers and contributes to the development of morality (Belacchi and Farina 2012; Coplan 2011; Eisenberg 2000).

The third set of activities helps students, with the teacher's guidance, to critically reflect on, discuss and elaborate co-constructed solutions to moral and ethical dilemmas (Gasser and Malti 2012). Children learn how to take others' perspectives into consideration through social interactions with peers and critically reflect on their own moral arguments and ethics. Practising ethical and responsible behaviours requires children to focus beyond self and develop intellectual and emotional honesty and a willingness to confront and articulate their vulnerabilities in order to make necessary changes in their personal lives (Staub and Vollhardt 2008).

Method

Study Design and Sample

The implementation of the pilot project started with 10 h of teacher training sessions within a 1-month period with 84 teachers from 17 kindergarten, primary and secondary schools from the areas of Milan and Pavia in the Northern part of Italy. Teachers' training focused on enhancing teachers' knowledge and skills on helping students to establish and maintain healthy relationships and adopting a skill-based workshop approach (using puppets, videotapes, role plays and discussions). The topics covered included developing friendship and positive relationships at school, both with peers and adults, sharing, cooperation, empathy, teamwork and prosocial and ethical behaviours. Teachers were encouraged to discuss challenges and difficulties they faced in their professional life to give them the opportunity to discuss resilience building from their own practical experiences. They were also trained in storytelling and use of puppets, using mindfulness exercises with the students and in completing the assessment checklists and the implementation index. Each teacher was provided with a set of materials to implement the theme, including the activities' manual, take-home worksheets for parents, assessment checklists, visual aids (e.g. pictures to describe the main character of the stories), original music – to introduce the sessions – and additional resources, such as mindfulness activities and theme posters. The teachers implemented the programme theme over a 6-week period as part of their classroom activities. A monthly classroom supervision session was conducted by the researchers with the assistance of two trained psychologists with each group of teachers coming from the same school.

Figure 18.3 shows an example of an activity taken from the early years manual for children aged 6–8 years.

Instruments

Evaluation of the effectiveness of the programme theme was conducted at the end of the implementation in 35 classes from kindergarten through secondary schools (first level), involving a total of 738 pupils (348 males and 390 females). The following instruments were used:

1. *Classroom behaviour questionnaire.* Teachers completed a whole classroom checklist on students' improvement in the areas covered by the six topics (Making and having friends; Prosocial behaviour; Nurturing relationships and school climate; Sharing, cooperation and teamwork; Empathy; Ethical, responsible and moral behaviour).
2. *Focus group.* Discussions were led in classes to explore students' own experiences of the activities, including what they liked, did not like and found useful. Data were collected by two methods: notes were taken by the facilitator and later transcribed and drawings of mascots or significant stories were made by the children. The average time for discussion and drawings was between 40 and 90 min for each group. The discussion was set to encourage conversation on main topics of the theme; students were asked their opinions and reflections on activities, materials and home activities. Photos of posters and students' worksheets were also taken at the end of the focus groups.
3. *Reflective diary.* Teachers were required to keep a narrative diary which they completed weekly during the implementation period. At the end of each of the

ACTIVITY 4: Friends are precious

Learning goal

- Identify strategies to keep positive relationships with peers.

Learning outcome

By the end of this activity, I will be able to:

- Identify ways hot to keep positive relationships with my friends.

Level: Basic

Materials needed: Hand or finger puppets, sheets of papers, posters, activity sheet 'Special friends of mum & dad'.

Activity steps

1. Start with a mindfulness activity
2. Read the following story "An old friend"

That day was a special day for Sherlock as his family was organizing a big surprise party for his grandfather's birthday. There were lots of decorations in the house and Sherlock's mother prepared many cakes and sweets for everybody. When Sherlock's grandfather came back home he found all the family singing "Happy birthday to you, happy birthday to you!!!".

Grandfather was really moved by this unexpected party, partly because he met some of his old childhood friends again. He was happy at the beginning but then suddenly he got upset when he noticed that his best friend when he was a child was not at the party.

"How are you? Do you feel ok, grandpa? You look sad," Sherlock said. "I wanted to see my old friend Robert," whispered the grandfather, "but I am afraid he forgot about me because some years ago we argued and he did not want to be my friend anymore."

"What happened with Robert?" asked Sherlock. "You know, my dear, friends are really precious but I didn't realize that until I was missing him. We were very close friends when we were children, but one day we had an argument. He was not very tall and I made fun of him in front of the children because of this. He was very hurt, he did not want to speak to me anymore and I had no opportunity to apologize for it. I would really like to meet him again. I'm so sorry for what I did. I made a very big mistake!". As soon as he finished this story, Robert came out from behind a door, he had heard everything. He hugged the grandfather and he said he was happy to have rediscovered an old friend.

3. First help the learners to process the story by asking the following questions
- What do you think about the story? How did the grandfather feel at the party?
- What happened between the grandfather and Robert?
- In your opinion, why did the grandfather want to see Robert again?
4. Ask learners to first reflect individually on following questions:
- Who are your friends? What do you like about them? What things do you do with your friends?
5. Let them write their own answers on sheets of papers.
6. Divide learners in small groups, let the learners discuss the following questions :
- What are friends? Why are friends important? What characteristics do you think friends should have?
7. After the discussion, ask each group to make a list of behaviours of how they can value friends and keep positive relationships with them.
8. At the end, collect all raised ideas on a poster.

Take home activity

The learners can ask their parents to talk about a special friend they have and explain why this person is special. They can fill the "Special friends of mum/dad" activity sheet and/or make a drawing of a nice event that parents shared with him/her.

Fig. 18.3 Example of an activity for primary school students

six sessions with the students, teachers wrote their own reflections based on the statement "Looking back on today's session, think about one aspect/incident that you think was very successful and engaging for students or unsuccessful and uninteresting for students. Describe it and reflect on why it was or was not successful and possibly what you would change about it".

4. *Individual interview*. In-depth interviews were conducted to ask teachers about their experiences of implementing the programme, including strengths, weaknesses and usefulness.

Ethics

Ethical approval was given by the Department of Brain and Behavioural Sciences Committee of the University of Pavia. Written informed consent was obtained from all teachers. As students' evaluation involved observations of the whole class rather than individual children, the ethics committee did not require parental consent. Parental consent was obtained for the students taking part in the focus groups.

Results

Classroom Behaviour Questionnaire

Thirty-three classroom behaviour questionnaires were collected from 23 schools for a total of 693 children (see Table 18.3).

The vast majority of the 33 classroom teachers, who completed the questionnaires, reported that the piloting of the activities had positive effects on the students' positive behaviours. Improvements in all the areas covered by the six topics were observed. Figure 18.4 shows the frequencies of the students' behaviour change expressed by the classroom teachers in the six areas explored in the behaviour questionnaires. Substantial improvements were noticed in sharing, cooperation and teamwork in 31 classes out of 33 (93.9%).

Focus Groups

Focus groups were conducted in all classes ($N = 33$) involved in the implementation. When analysing the data by age groups, the early years children liked the opportunity to play new games in the classroom most, the adventure stories of Sherlock and Zelda as well as role plays and story dramatisation. Furthermore, they liked their parents' involvement and the opportunity to express their thoughts and emotions with their parents. The early primary years students said that they learned to follow

Table 18.3 Total number of students by class, age and gender represented in the classroom behaviour questionnaire

Grade	Age (years)	Total	Male	Female
Kindergarten	4 and 5	64	22	20
1st Grade primary school	6	74	33	37
2nd Grade primary school	7	215	87	118
3rd Grade primary school	8	158	80	70
4th Grade primary school	9	96	36	51
5th Grade primary school	10	86	44	40
1st Grade secondary school 1st level	11	64	22	20
Total		693	324	356

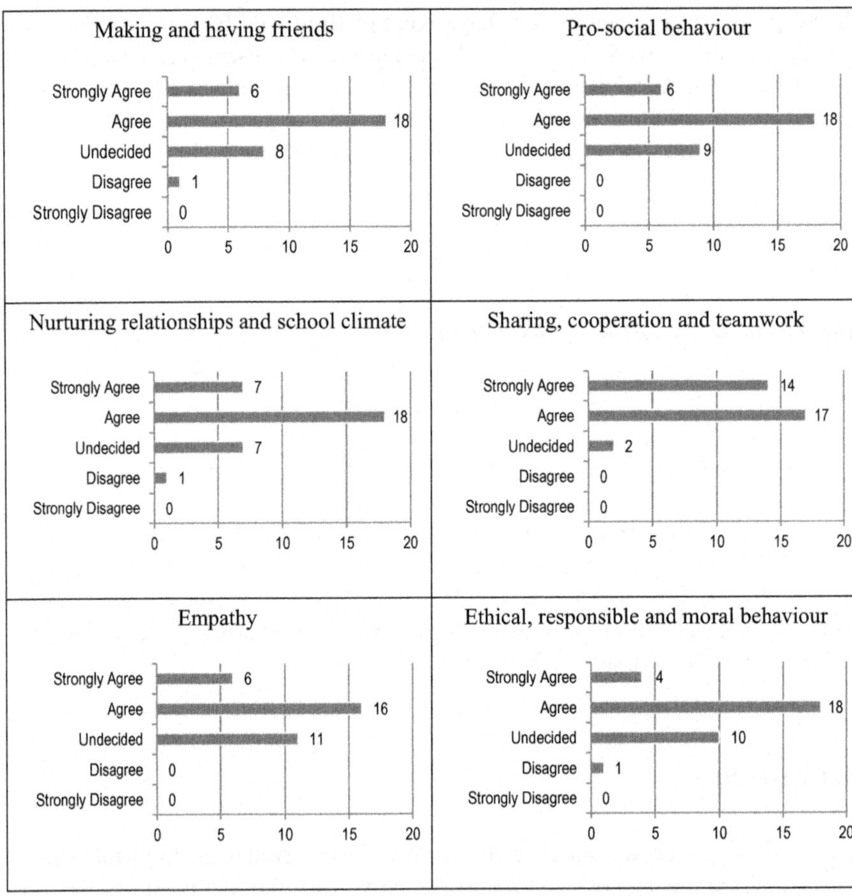

Fig. 18.4 Results of the classroom behaviour questionnaires over the 6 weeks' intervention period

rules and help each other because everything becomes "easier and nicer", which indicates the benefits of collaboration and friendship. The older students (late primary school) mentioned empathy and helping others as the most beneficial aspect of the activities. They said they learned to trust their peers, to use these skills in their everyday life, to share emotions with others and to find support and encouragement from their group and the teachers. They also underlined their satisfaction in working in teams which is not usually practised in their everyday classroom life. They suggested that the take-home tasks could be less personal (e.g. reflecting with parents) and more fun.

Reflective Diaries

All participating teachers completed their reflective diary for each activity they did over the 6-week period. Some of the most common comments by the teachers were that students appreciated the stories and practical activities and that the activities helped them to build a sort of "pact of cooperation" with the students. They mentioned that the students were especially excited about working in groups and the take-home activities with their parents. The take-home worksheets gave them the opportunity to work closely with their parents and discuss personal issues, concerns and stories with them. One issue mentioned by the teachers was the time required for the activities: the allotted time of 30–45 min was insufficient most of the time, and they suggested more time for the completion of the activity. All teachers recommended the programme for the future.

A selection of teachers' quotes on the impact of the programme on children, as well as on their own personal and professional development, is provided in Fig. 18.5.

Teacher's Interview

An individual interview was held with a primary school teacher. The teacher explained that the whole project, specifically the teachers' training and the implementation, was a valuable tool used to get to know her students better and address their educational and emotional needs. She found the activities useful to give students the opportunity to "give a name to their feelings" and, in general, to talk about themselves. She reported that it was not common to use school time to listen to children's relational and emotional needs and concerns, and this project provided the time for it. She also mentioned it was a great idea to present the two main characters for all stories; they became a sort of friend for the students, and they were able to create connections between Sherlock and Zelda's adventures and their own life events. The teacher stated the parents liked the homework, because they enjoyed doing something of the sort together with their children, and they were disappointed when the project was over. The teacher said she planned to make use of this programme in the future.

Teachers' training and the implementation was a precious tool to know more about my students. I also completed, through the activities, the annual formative unit on "The self and the others", according to the Italian guideline for kindergarten teachers.

Kindergarten school teacher

RESCUR activities represent a real and useful source of personal and professional enrichment to develop resilience not only for children and teachers, but also for families and the whole school community.

Primary school teacher

It's not common to use school time to listen to children's relational and emotional needs and worries. This project provided the time for it. It was a great idea to present the 2 main characters (Sherlock and Zelda) for all stories. They became sort of friends for pupils and children were able to create connections between Sherlock and Zelda's adventures and their own life's events.

Primary school teacher

Parents liked home tasks. They said it was really nice to do something together with their children and they were really disappointed when the project was over. I'm going to keep this method also in the future.

Secondary school teacher

Fig. 18.5 Teachers' quotes from the reflective journals

Conclusion

This study represents the first pilot project exploring the effects of a resilience programme aimed both at universal and target level in Italian schools.

The overall results from the focus groups with students, teachers' reflective diaries and the teacher's interview all showed that both teachers and students greatly appreciated the activities of the Italian theme and found them useful, relevant as well as enjoyable. According to teachers' feedback, findings showed the Italian pilot programme helped students to increase sharing, cooperation and teamwork skills over the intervention period.

Building healthy relationships provides safety and protection; it's an important foundation for both academic and socio-emotional development and represents a source of wellbeing and resilience for children (Doll et al. 2004).

Although these results are encouraging and promising, the study design had several methodological limitations. No control group was used as a pre- and post-design was not possible due to the limited time to complete the project. Furthermore, the project piloted only one of the six themes of the programme, and the intervention was limited to 6 weeks with one lesson per week. Finally, another limitation may be teachers' bias, because teachers that implemented RESCUR were the same that assessed the programme itself.

Therefore, a more long-term, comprehensive intervention is needed in order to evaluate the effectiveness of *RESCUR Surfing the Waves* in bringing about a positive change in behaviour, particularly amongst vulnerable students.

A particular strength of *RESCUR Surfing the Waves* is the attention to contextual and cultural diversity as the activities were designed by partners coming from several European countries. The RESCUR programme is currently the only European programme on the promotion of resilience in schools, and the indications so far are that this is a promising tool for early years and primary schools to protect vulnerable children from the risks of school failure and social exclusion whilst promoting their health and wellbeing. Researchers in Italy and other partner countries are currently implementing the programme with a larger sample of students using pre-post design and control groups.

Although various national initiatives to promote student wellbeing in schools have been organised in Europe and across the world, Italy does not yet have a national curriculum to support mental health in educational contexts (Cavioni and Zanetti 2015). With this study and other studies on the programme, we intend to increase the awareness of policymakers in Italy on the importance of promoting social and emotional skills as well as resilience in education, taking a holistic approach that encompasses students, teachers and families (Cavioni et al. 2015; Cefai et al. 2015).

Acknowledgement The authors would like to thank the coordinator of the project Carmel Cefai (University of Malta, Malta) and the other partners and authors of *RESCUR Surfing the Waves*, namely, Renata Miljević-Riđički, Dejana Bouillet, Tea Pavin Ivanec, Mirjana Milanović (University of Zagreb, Croatia), Anastassios Matsopoulos, Mariza Gavogiannaki (University of Crete, Greece), Paul Bartolo, Katya Galea (University of Malta, Malta), Celeste Simões, Paula Lebre, Anabela Caetano Santos (University of Lisbon, Portugal), Birgitta Kimber and Charli Eriksson (Orebro University, Sweden).

References

Belacchi, C., & Farina, E. (2012). Feeling and thinking of others: Affective and cognitive empathy and emotion comprehension in prosocial/hostile preschoolers. *Aggressive Behavior, 38*, 150–165.

Benard, B. (2004). *Resiliency: What we have learned.* San Francisco: WestEd.

Castro Silva, J., Pipa, J., Renner, C., O'Donnell, M., & Cefai, C. (2018). Enhancing teacher resilience through face-to-face training – Insights from ENTREE project. In M. Wosnitza, F. Peixoto, S. Beltman, & C. F. Mansfield (Eds.), *Resilience in education: Concepts, contexts and connections* (pp.). New York: Springer.

Cavioni, V., & Zanetti, M. A. (2015). Social-Emotional Learning and Students' Transition from Kindergarten to Primary School in Italy. In H. Askell-Williams (Ed.), *Transforming the Future of Learning with educational research* (pp. 241–258). Hershey: IGI Global. ISBN 978-1-4666-7495-0. https://doi.org/10.4018/978-1-4666-7495-0.ch013.

Cavioni, V., Lupica Spagnolo, M., Beddia, G., & Zanetti, M. A. (2015). Promuovere la resilienza a scuola: Un curricolo europeo per docenti e studenti. Strumenti e metodologie per l'identificazione e l'intervento. *Psicologia e scuola*, 42–49.

Cefai, C., Cavioni, V., Bartolo, B., Celeste Simões, C., Ridicki Miljevic, R., Bouillet, D., Pavin Ivanec, T., Matsopoulos, A., Gavogiannaki, M., Zanetti, M. A., Galea, K., Lebre, P., Kimber, B., & Eriksson, C. (2015). Social inclusion and social justice: A resilience curriculum for early years and elementary schools in Europe. *Journal of Multicultural Education, 9*(3.) ISSN: 2053-535X. https://doi.org/10.1108/JME-01-2015-0002.

Cefai, C., Miljević-Riđički, R., Bouillet, D., Pavin Ivanec, T., Milanovic, M, Matsopoulos, A. ..., Eriksson, C. (2016). RESCUR Il Curriculum per promuovere la Resilienza a scuola. Guida per il docente. In V. Cavioni, & M. A. Zanetti (Eds.). Pavia: Department of Brain and Behavioral Sciences, University of Pavia.

Coplan, A. (2011). Will the real empathy please stand up? A case for a narrow conceptualization. *The Southern Journal of Philosophy, 49*(Suppl), 40–65.

Davis, M. (1983). Measuring individual differences in empathy: Evidence for a multidimensional approach. *Journal of Personality and Social Psychology, 44*, 113–126.

Doll, B., Brehm, K., & Zucker, S. (2004). *Resilient classrooms: Creating healthy environments for learning*. New York: Guilford Press.

Dray, J., Bowman, J., Wolfenden, L., Campbell, E., & Freund, M. (2015). Systematic review of universal resilience interventions targeting child and adolescent mental health in the school setting: Review protocol. *Systematic Reviews, 4*(186), 1–8.

Eisenberg, N. (2000). Emotion, regulation and moral development. *Annual Review of Psychology, 51*, 665–697.

European Commission. (2011, February 17). *Communication from the commission. Early Childhood Education and Care: Providing all our children with the best start for the world of tomorrow*. Retrieved June 16, 2016, from http://eur-lex.europa.eu/LexUriServ/LexUriServ.do?uri=COM:2011:0066:FIN:EN:PDF

Gasser, L., & Malti, T. (2012). Children's and their friends' moral reasoning: Relations with aggressive behavior. *International Journal of Behavioral Development, 36*(5), 358–366.

Gensemer, P. (2000). Effectiveness of cross-age and peer mentoring programs. *Information Analysis, 30*, 1–15.

Hazel, G. (2018). Finding a place for resilience in teacher preparation. In M. Wosnitza, F. Peixoto, S. Beltman, & C. F. Mansfield (Eds.), *Resilience in education: Concepts, contexts and connections* (pp. 221–235). New York: Springer.

Hjemdal, O., Aune, T., Reinfjell, T., & Stiles, T. C. (2007). Resilience as a predictor of depressive symptoms: A correlational study with young adolescents. *Clinical Child Psychology and Psychiatry, 12*(1), 91–104.

Hjemdal, O., Vogel, P. A., Solem, S., Hagen, K., & Stiles, T. C. (2011). The relationship between resilience and levels of anxiety, depression, and obsessive–compulsive symptoms in adolescents. *Clinical Psychology and Psychotherapy, 18*(4), 214–321.

Hobfoll, S. E., Palmieri, P. A., Johnson, R. J., Canetti-Nisim, D., Hall, B. J., & Galea, S. (2009). Trajectories of resilience, resistance and distress during ongoing terrorism: The case of Jews and Arabs in Israel. *Journal of Consulting and Clinical Psychology, 77*(1), 138–148.

Hupcey, J. E. (1998). Clarifying the social support theory-research linkage. *Journal of Advanced Nursing, 27*, 1231–1241.

Kessler, R., Angermeyer, M., Anthony, J. C., Graaf, R. D., Demyttenaere, K., Gasquet, I., …, Tsang, C. A. (2008). Lifetime prevalence and age-of-onset distributions of mental disorders in the World Health Organization's world mental health survey initiative. In R. C. Kessler, & T. B. Ustan (Eds.), *The WHO world mental health surveys: Global perspectives on the epidemiology of mental disorders*. Cambridge: Cambridge University Press Published in collaboration with the World Health Organization.

Kim-Cohen, J., Caspi, A., Moffitt, T. E., Harrington, H., Milne, B. J., & Poulton, R. (2003). Prior juvenile diagnoses in adults with mental disorder: Developmental follow-back of a prospective-longitudinal cohort. *Archives of General Psychiatry, 60*(7), 709–717.

Koth, C. W., Bradshaw, C. P., & Leaf, P. J. (2008). A multilevel study of predictors of student perceptions of school climate: The effect of classroom-level factors. *Journal of Educational Psychology, 100*, 96–104.

Lohbeck, L. (2018). The interplay between the motivation to teach and resilience of student teachers and trainee teachers. In M. Wosnitza, F. Peixoto, S. Beltman, & C. F. Mansfield (Eds.), *Resilience in education: Concepts, contexts and connections* (pp. 93–106). New York: Springer.

Masten, A. (2011). Resilience in children threatened by extreme adversity: Frameworks for research, practice, and translational synergy. *Development and Psychopathology, 23*(2), 493–506.

Noble, T., & McGrath, H. (2018). Making it real and making it last! Sustainability of teacher implementation of a whole school resilience program. In M. Wosnitza, F. Peixoto, S. Beltman, & C. F. Mansfield (Eds.), *Resilience in education: Concepts, contexts and connections* (pp. 289–312). New York: Springer.

Reid, C., Davis, H., Horlin, C., Anderson, M., Baughman, N., & Campbell, C. (2013). The Kids' Empathic Development Scale (KEDS): A multi-dimensional measure of empathy in primary school-aged children. *British Journal of Developmental Psychology, 31*, 231–256.

Resnick, M., Bearman, P. S., Blum, R. W., Bauman, K. E., Harris, K. M., Jones, J., …, Udry, J. R. (1997). Protecting adolescents from harm. Findings from the National Longitudinal Study on adolescent health. *Amazoniana, 278*(10), 823–832.

Rutter, M. (1990). Psychosocial resilience and protective mechanisms. In J. Rolf, A. S. Masten, D. Cicchetti, K. H. Nuechterlein, & S. Weintraub (Eds.), *Risk and protective factors in the development of psychopathology* (pp. 181–214). Cambridge: Cambridge University Press.

Rutter, M. (1993). Resilience: Some conceptual considerations. *Journal of Adolescent Health, 14*(8), 626–631.

Rutter, M. (2006). Implications of resilience concepts for scientific understanding. *Annals of the New York Academy of Sciences*, 1–12.

Rutter, M. (2015). Resilience: Concepts, findings, and clinical implications. In A. Thapar, D. S. Pine, J. F. Leckman, S. Scott, M. J. Snowling, & E. A. Taylor (Eds.), *Rutter's child and adolescent psychiatry* (pp. 341–351). Oxford: Wiley-Blackwell.

Ruzek, E., Hafen, C. A., Allen, J. P., Gregory, A., Yee Mikami, A., & Pianta, R. C. (2016). How teacher emotional support motivates students: The mediating roles of perceived peer relatedness, autonomy support, and competence. *Learning and Instruction, 42*, 95–103.

Shaikh, A., & Kauppi, C. (2010). Deconstructing resilience: Myriad conceptualizations and interpretations. *International Journal of Arts and Sciences, 3*(15), 155–176.

Slavin, R. E. (1980). Cooperative learning. *Review of Educational Research, 50*(2), 315–342.

Staub, E., & Vollhardt, J. (2008). Altruism born of suffering: The roots of caring and helping after victimization and other trauma. *American Journal of Orthopsychiatry, 78*(3), 267–280.

Theron, L. C. (2018). Teacher championship of resilience: Lessons from the pathways to resilience study, South Africa. In M. Wosnitza, F. Peixoto, S. Beltman, & C. F. Mansfield (Eds.), *Resilience in education: Concepts, contexts and connections* (pp. 203–217). New York: Springer.

Ungar, M. (2005). Studying resilience across cultures. *Journal of Ethnic and Cultural Diversity in Social Work, 14*(3–4), 1–19.

Werner, E., & Smith, R. (1992). *Overcoming the odds: High-risk children from birth to adulthood.* New York: Cornell University Press.

Part V
Conclusion

Chapter 19
Resilience in Education: Emerging Trends in Recent Research

Marold Wosnitza and Francisco Peixoto

What Makes Me Resilient?

There is an agreement in all chapters of this volume that resilience is not given. Resilience should not be understood as something someone has or does not have but as a toolbox an individual brings to a specific situation, more specifically, a box of tools and resources that helps a person to solve a problem. Being resilient means having the necessary tools or resources to handle a specific challenging situation. What are these tools in the box? The research in this volume shows that such tools and resources can be *personal* or based on *external* resources (Gu, Chap. 2).

With regard to personal resources, most authors discussing them in their chapter focus on social, professional, and affective capacities of a person or their beliefs (e.g. Helker et al., Chap. 11; Leroux, Chap. 7; Lohbeck, Chap. 6; Peixoto et al., Chap. 5; Wosnitza et al., Chap. 16). Schwarze et al. (Chap. 3) and Lohbeck (Chap. 6) make a case for also considering more stable personal resources like intelligence, or optimism. From a conceptual perspective, these two different views speak for a further distinction rarely discussed in the literature, namely, the distinction between personal state and trait resources that can influence the individual resilience process in different ways. The understanding of the nature of these potential different influences is still not fully understood and has to be a subject of future research.

Looking at the external resources, Mansfield et al. (Chap. 4) as well as Schwarze et al. (Chap. 3) show that external resources potentially utilised by the individual

M. Wosnitza (✉)
Institute of Education, RWTH Aachen University, Aachen, Germany

School of Education, Murdoch University, Perth, WA, Australia
e-mail: marold.wosnitza@rwth-aachen.de

F. Peixoto
ISPA-Instituto Universitário/CIE – ISPA, Lisbon, Portugal
e-mail: fpeixoto@ispa.pt

M. Wosnitza et al. (eds.), *Resilience in Education*,
https://doi.org/10.1007/978-3-319-76690-4_19

can conceptually be structured according to their proximity to the person. They categorise these external resources into micro-, meso-, exo-, and macro-resources. Peixoto et al. (Chap. 5), Helker et al. (Chap. 11), and Wosnitza et al. (Chap. 16) follow the same idea but use only three levels (micro, meso, and macro). Digging deeper into the nature of these external resources, Theron (Chap. 12) and Mansfield et al. (Chap. 4) find another dimension – not explicitly thematised but nonetheless interesting for the understanding of external resources – namely, that such resources can have a social nature (i.e. relationships), a material nature (i.e. teaching resources), or a formal nature (i.e. rules and regulations).

The environment can (and should) therefore provide the resources that nurture and enable the development of resilience by means of facilitating the construction of positive relationships, the construction of identity (personal and/or professional), and the development of a sense of competence (e.g. self-efficacy, self-concept, competence self-beliefs) (e.g. Beltman et al., Chap. 14; Cavioni et al., Chap. 18; Flores, Chap. 10; Helker et al., Chap. 11; Noble et al., Chap. 17; Peixoto et al., Chap. 5). Resilience can be seen as a result of the interplay between personal and contextual resources. This interplay impacts both the process and outcome of resilience. Beltman et al. (Chap. 14, p. 2) emphasise this aspect referring to the "dynamic nature of resilience where personal and contextual resources are harnessed through the use of various strategies which then enable resilience outcomes" (see also Crosswell, Chap. 8). Flores (Chap. 10, p. 26) also refers to the contribution of "positive atmosphere at school, encouraging leadership and supportive colleagues" for teachers' resilience. Similarly, Leroux (Chap. 7) calls attention to the need of development of cooperative and collaboration skills in the pre-service teachers training as well as the importance of being supported by colleagues and school administration. Related to the construction of resilience in children, Theron (Chap. 12, p. 11), speaking about vulnerable young people, stresses that beyond the role of teachers, "whole school and education system response" is needed in a way that young people "understand that they form part of the school system and need to be involved in resilience-enabling initiatives". Elaborating on the role of context or environment for resilience, and going a little further, Gu (Chap. 2, p. 16) talks about resilient organisations as places where people are "aspired to their own learning and development", and where the "system functions as a whole to create a supportive environment for individuals' professional learning and development". Also, Hazel et al. (Chap. 13) and Noble et al. (Chap. 17) emphasise the importance of the organisational dimension calling attention to the "whole-school" approach that is needed in order to have effective interventions for the promotion of students' resilience.

When Am I Resilient?

Over time, the content of this toolbox changes. New and more efficient tools are added, existing tools are updated, and useless tools are replaced or discarded. But what are these tools for? They are used by an individual to cope with stressful or potentially stressful situations. Furthermore, the knowledge of having these tools available if needed has an influence on the evaluation of a situation in regard to its potential stressfulness. The theoretical challenge is that a situation is not stressful or not not stressful per se. What may be stressful for one person may not be stressful for another. But why is that the case? Schwarze et al. (Chap. 3), following Lazarus and Folkman (1984), stated that a significant factor in the resilience process is how a situation is appraised in the light of relevance and potential harmfulness. It was shown that the resources available to a person are of great significance whilst appraising a situation at hand. If a situation is familiar and the supposed necessary resources are available, the situation will potentially be appraised as less stressful or not stressful at all, and routines will be activated. If, on the other hand, the situation is of relevance to the person, but the necessary resources are not available, the situation will potentially be appraised as stressful by the person. People who can resort to routines or are able to activate necessary resources to manage stressful situations can be described as resilient. Crosswell et al. (Chap. 8) and Galea (Chap. 9) show intriguing examples of resilient teachers having resources and routines at hand to cope with professional stressors or risks. The study of Flores (Chap. 10) stresses the importance of these resources in retaining teachers in the profession and them being resilient. Whilst available resources – as discussed above – can be personal or external, the same can be said for stressors or risks. Mansfield et al.'s (Chap. 4) or Theron's (Chap. 12) research, for example, show a broad range of such personal risks or stressors (e.g. serious illness, loneliness). On the other hand, context can similarly be a significant, sometimes even more significant stressor. This is the case when it threatens positive functioning, like extreme adversity in the case of children (e.g. Cavioni et al., Chap. 18; Gu, Chap. 2; Theron, Chap. 12) or the problematic work conditions of teachers arising from a heavy workload, the lack of resources, or the challenges set by the phases of professional life (e.g. Flores, Chap. 10; Gu, Chap. 2; Helker et al., Chap. 11).

Let us move away from the tool box metaphor and picture a person as a Jenga tower. Each block of the tower symbolises one capacity, skill, or available resource – personal or external – of a person. All blocks are linked, and every block missing in the structure is destabilising the tower, but not all blocks are necessarily needed to keep the tower from collapsing. Just like in a Jenga tower, not all supporting resources have to be constantly present or available to a person to make them resilient. Some of them are not of relevance in a specific situation, others are supportive, and some of them are potential cornerstones for being resilient. If you pull out a cornerstone block, the tower will most likely collapse. If these cornerstone resources truly exist, what exactly they are will be one of the leading questions for future research. It is to be expected that one of these potential cornerstones is *having* or *building personal relationships*, as it was identified by several authors in this volume (e.g. Mansfield et al., Chap. 4; Galea, Chap. 9; Flores, Chap. 10; Helker et al.; Chap. 11; Castro Silva et al.; Chap. 15). Most of the research presented here gives a clear indication that relationship is one of the significant resources for being a resilient person. Besides the question about the existence of such cornerstone resources, another question has to be discussed in future research: How far can such resources compensate missing other resources – e.g. can having supportive relationships compensate for missing coping strategies?

How Do I Develop Resilience?

If one follows the rules of Jenga, one cannot add new blocks to stabilise the tower. But adding blocks to help strengthen the tower's stability is the essence of the discussion regarding developing or enhancing a person's resilience. There are different approaches discussed in this volume.

Grounded in the idea of resilience as something that can be learned and developed, several intervention programmes are presented. Despite the differences between them, similarities can be observed. Based on the idea that supportive relationships have an important impact on resilience, modules addressing the construction and development of relationships are common in all the programmes. Also, all the programmes include modules intending to strengthen positive self-beliefs, such as self-concept or self-efficacy (e.g. Beltman et al., Chap. 14; Castro Silva et al., Chap. 15; Hazel et al., Chap. 13; Noble et al., Chap. 17). The key element of all active change is self-reflection and a better understanding of who you are and what you want to be. If you understand where or what you want to be, you can purposefully seek support and actively enhance your resilience profile. With regard to this, some of the intervention programmes presented in this volume provide more or less elaborated self-reflection tools aiming to provide the user of the programme with help in identifying his or her individual strengths and areas to be improved regarding his or her resilience profile (e.g. Beltman et al., Chap. 14; Wosnitza et al., Chap. 16).

Whilst these programmes aim to directly enhance resilience with interventions and training, other authors explain, on a more conceptual level, that resilience develops by getting through a potentially stressful situation (e.g. Crosswell et al., Chap. 8; Leroux, Chap. 7; Schwarze, et al., Chap. 3). Getting through this stressful situation can be understood as an individual learning process, in which the actual experience will change the understanding of stressful situations as well as the use of available but also missing strategies and resources. This experience can lead to the identification of missing resources and an understanding of ways to strengthen them and to an individual being better equipped for future stressful situations.

Am I Resilient or Do I Just Cope?

What becomes more obvious when reading this volume is the conceptual difference between resilience and coping. All definitions and conceptual frameworks describing resilience as a process – even if not specifically mentioned – and specify two main dimensions:

First, what we want to call a *declarative dimension of the resilience process*: It describes a specific status of being resilient at a specific point in time and in a specific context. For example, Paul is a resilient student and has the capacities and resources to overcome problems and potentially stressful situations at school. The declarative dimension of a resilience process also includes the understanding that resilience might depend on context – Paul can be resilient in school, and at the same time, he can be not resilient in critical situation with his family. Furthermore, it has to be noticed that this dimension changes over time with experience, learning, and support from others. This emphasises the argument that resilience is not absolute (e.g. Lohbeck, Chap. 6; Peixoto et al., Chap. 5; Cavioni et al., Chap. 18).

Second, there is the *procedural dimension of the resilience process*: It focuses on *how* a stressful situation is handled – how Paul coped in this situation and which strategies he used. This procedural dimension is accompanied by a *conditional dimension*, which describes the conscious or unconscious knowledge of *when* to use *which* of the resources available to handle a stressful situation at hand. When Paul experiences a stressful situation, he knows or does not know which of his available resources to choose to solve the problem at hand (e.g. Galea, Chap. 9; Beltman et al., Chap. 14; Theron, Chap. 12).

This distinction between a *declarative dimension* and a *procedural dimension* has the conceptual potential to describe the difference between being *resilient* and *coping*. If resilience is defined as a process, coping is the link that transforms the potential (declarative) into action (procedural). It is the difference between being resilient and doing something that helps handle a stressful situation. Hence, coping is an integral dynamic part of the resilience process. Future research and conceptual work will show how fruitful this distinction is.

What's Next?

A large amount of current resilience research – not only in this volume – focuses on how to cope with stressful situations and how to make sure that one can handle such situations (e.g. Crosswell et al., Chap. 8; Galea, Chap. 9; Leroux, Chap. 7). Another large body of research focuses on the description of what makes a person potentially resilient and what resources are necessary to be resilient (e.g. Gu, Chap. 2; Mansfield et al., Chap. 4; Lohbeck, Chap. 6). The intervention studies presented in this volume show the potential for enhancing resilience (e.g. Beltman et al., Chap. 14; Castro Silva, et al., Chap. 15; Hazel, et al., Chap. 13; Noble et al., Chap. 17). The research approach applied is mainly qualitative and follows a constructivist paradigm. Three chapters report research using a quantitative approach with large samples (Flores, Chap. 10; Lohbeck, Chap. 6; Peixoto et al., Chap. 5) focusing on structural relations and contextual differences. The understanding and description of the concept of resilience as well as the development, respectively, the modification of theories and theoretical frameworks stand in the centre of most research. Rigorous validations and evaluations of the developed models are still scarce, which is understandable in light of the complexity of the concept and its dynamic nature (Gu, Chap. 2). The research of resilience in educational contexts is still in its infancy. Future research has to focus on the effectiveness of the "tools in the toolbox", the identification of potential cornerstone resources, and whether or not some resources can substitute for others. Furthermore, the effectiveness of training and self-reflections in regard to enhancing resilience in educational contexts has to be determined.

Hence, future research needs to focus on longitudinal studies (e.g. Beltman et al., Chap. 14; Leroux, Chap. 7) to identify how resilience changes over time and a person's biography and what leads to these changes or absence of changes. It has to focus on dynamic measures, exploring the situation without interference, such as experience sampling measures which allow the collection of micro data and reduce the impact of a retrospective description of the situation. It has to focus – specifically concerning the intervention studies – on control group designs, which need a distinct identification of resilient individuals (e.g. Galea, Chap. 9).

The interventions presented in this book each include some kind of evaluation. Despite the encouraging results of the evaluations, showing positive progress due to the participation in the programme, the reported studies used a single-group design, some of them with pre- and posttest evaluations. Only a control group design can give robustness to the evidence found. The distinct identification of resilient and non-resilient individuals will allow for a better understanding of the interplay of personal as well as external resources and their influence on being resilient.

In conclusion, this volume makes a significant contribution in the still relatively new and under-researched field of resilience in educational contexts. It gives an elaborated overview of the *conceptualisation*, *context*, and *practice* of *resilience in education*. The 17 chapters represent the current state of research in this field and show clear perspectives for future research. This book shows the need for a pragmatic research paradigm that consequently leads to a mixed method approach and the need for fundamental and applied research.

Reference

Lazarus, R. S., & Folkman, S. (1984). *Stress, appraisal, and coping*. New York: Springer.

Printed by Printforce, the Netherlands